116806

DEVOTIONAL COMMENTARY ON EXODUS

by
F.B. Meyer

DEVOTIONAL COMMENTARY ON EXODUS

by
F.B. Meyer

KREGEL PUBLICATIONS
Grand Rapids, Michigan 49501

Devotional Commentary on Exodus by F.B. Meyer
Copyright © 1978 by Kregel Publications
a division of Kregel, Inc. All rights reserved.

Library of Congress Cataloging in Publication Data

Meyer, Frederick Brotherton, 1847-1929.
  Exodus.

  Reprint of the ed. published by Purnell, London.

  1. Bible. O.T. Exodus—Commentaries. I. Title.
[BS1245.3.M48   1978]   222'.12'07   78-9530
ISBN 0-8254-3225-1

Printed in the United States of America

CONTENTS

5

INTRODUCTION

As a new king arose over Egypt who did not know Joseph, so a new generation has come who does not know saintly F.B. Meyer. This dedicated and highly successful English pastor, teacher, and evangelist has written some of the finest devotional books. His biographical devotional books are par excellent. Maybe it was his keen insight, which he so frequently displays in his writings, that caused Meyer to become a lifelong friend to D.L. Moody. It was F.B. Meyer who introduced Mr. Moody to the British churches.

As you study this commentary, the warm sunshine of God's revelation will energize your life with practical concepts. You will find it to be DESCRIPTIVE. You will sense the awesomeness of Sinai. You'll almost feel the sand in your shoes as the trudging becomes a teacher. Meyer paints a word landscape allowing the mind's eye to scan the panorama of rich red sandstone mingled with granite, limestone, and porphyry.

You will find this book to be DIRECTIVE. Meyer was and is God's teacher. From Egypt to Caanan he directs our minds to God's purpose, plan, and person. He points out that the wilderness wanderings will teach self-knowledge, self-reverence, and self-control. This book bears reading and re-reading to get, to grasp, and to garner the eternal truth. This commentary, although not exhaustive nor critical, will be an extra special help to the hungry soul, the busy pastor, the pressured evangelist, the weighted missionary, and the searching scholar.

You'll find Meyer to be above all, DEVOTIONAL. Here is a

volume which can easily be used as a devotional guide for a family or in the Christian school class-room. The scholarly saintly author dips his pen into founts of plain practical blessing and writes with guidance from the Lord. The writing breathes forth the odor of the sweetness of His Presence.

May the enlightenment, enrichment, and enjoyment of the blessed Holy Spirit fill your life as you study this volume with much profit.

J. Arnold Fair

Greenville, Michigan

THE BOOK AND ITS MESSAGE

The Purpose of the Book. For our present purpose it is not material to consider how this Book came into existence. That is too wide a subject to be discussed in a treatise which is primarily intended for purposes of personal devotion. Let those whose training and taste incline them to such studies be permitted to pursue them without prejudice. Already the great and varied intellects that have wrought in this quarry have vastly enriched our stores of Bible-knowledge. But, after all, though the processes through which corn becomes bread are of themselves deserving of careful inquiry, the main question for those who need strength for daily living is, Whether the bread served on their tables is nutritious?—an inquiry which is best solved by experience.

How to Study the Book. As we open the Book of the Exodus, we are face to face with words that have been wrought into the life of successive generations of saints. The circumstances of their composition may be legitimate inquiry for the archaeologist and linguist, but for us there is a more absorbing question, How can we so consider these pages and paragraphs as to extract the greatest amount of spiritual nutriment? The geologist will delve into the earth, and show the successive strata of which it has been built up for the habitation of man, but when his investigations are completed, the main point for practical life is to discover whether the soil presents a healthy and solid foundation on which to build the homes of life. And the fact that from the days of our Lord and before, this Book has been prized and assimilated by the noblest of our race, is enough to whet our appetite and stir our souls in anticipation of its yield.

The Story of God's Love and Care. It is the story of Jehovah's espousals with the Hebrew race. When they were cast out in the open field, to the abhorring of their persons, the Almighty passed by and looked upon them. It was a time of love, when He spread

His skirts upon them and sware unto them and entered into covenant with them, and they became His.[1] He at least could never forget the kindness of their youth, or the love of those early days, when they went after Him even into the wilderness, a land that was not sown,[2] nor how He had borne them on eagles' wings and brought them to Himself, that they might be a peculiar treasure above all peoples.[3] The hymn beside the Red Sea was the nuptial ode, celebrating the union between God and His people, which was intended to last for ever; and would have lasted, had they not turned aside after many lovers.

The History of a Nation. This book recites also how, for the first time, the chosen people commenced to have a history. From being a tribe under patriarchal government, they suddenly leapt into a kingdom of priests, a holy nation and peculiar people beneath the theocratic rule of Jehovah Himself. Bunsen said that history dates from the night of the Exodus. Whether that affirmation would stand in the light of recent discoveries, as, for instance, of the existence and might of the Hittite empire, is open to question; but this at least is true, that amid the anguish of a common suffering and the triumph of a common deliverance, in the brick-kilns of Egyptian bondage and the passes of the Sinaitic peninsula, the undisciplined shepherds of Joseph's day became a disciplined nation of more than two million souls, who went up harnessed, i.e. in battle array, to the conquest of Canaan.. Who hath heard such a thing? Who hath seen such things? A land was born in a day, and a nation brought forth at once.[4]

A Lasting Covenant. The anguish was acute, but its results were lasting. Tribulation lasted for 230 years, but its effect has become the permanent possession of all the subsequent centuries. Scattered in every country, driven in turn from every great city, derided, persecuted, pillaged, and massacred, this people still subsists. "Considerest thou not what this people have spoken, saying, The two families which the Lord did choose, He hath cast them off? thus do they despise My people, that they should be no more a nation before them. Thus saith the Lord: If My covenant of day and night stand not, if I have not appointed the ordinances of heaven and earth; then will I also cast away the seed of Jacob, and of David

---

[1] Compare Ezek. xvi. 1–9.
[2] Jer. ii. 2.
[3] Exod. xix. 4.
[4] Compare Isa. lxvi. 8.

The Book and Its Message / 11

My servant, so that I will not take of his seed to be rulers: . . . for I will cause their captivity to return, and will have mercy on them."[1]

Plan of the Book. This book is divisible into three principal divisions:

REDEMPTION	Chapters 1-15
CONSECRATION	„ 16-24
WORSHIP	„ 25-40

And in each of these there is a climax towards which the subject-matter of each division culminates.

The *first* part culminates in the Passage of the Red Sea, when Israel went through the Flood on foot, amid the rattle of the storm; the *second*, in the giving of the Law amid the thunders of Sinai; and the *third*, in the erection of the Tabernacle according to the pattern shown on the Mount.

A Great Story. It is a great story. Through the centuries the gaze of myriads has been turned to that supreme hour when a nation of slaves went forth from cruel bondage and grinding tyranny into the broad spaces and exhilarating air of the wilderness—itself the vestibule of a national existence, which has affected the history of mankind more deeply and permanently than of Greece or Rome or Britain. The principles, also, by which nations thrive and become virile are embedded in the subsequent pages. The statutes and distinctions of the Mosaic legislation lie at the basis of our own, and have powerfully influenced modern civilisation.

Transition from Tabernacle to Church. From the Tabernacle the transition to the Temple and the Church was natural and easy; and the Levitical Priesthood and institutions are strongly quoted by influential bodies within the precincts of Christendom. No intelligent person can afford to ignore this Book, which is only second in importance to that of Genesis in the Old Testament and the Gospel of Matthew in the New.

Conspicuousness of Moses. Throughout this Book the prominent figure is Moses, "the servant of the Lord," whose song is sung around the sea of glass before the throne. His portraiture, as pre-eminently "the servant, faithful in all God's House," is the heritage of all who have sought to do the will of God on earth as it is done in Heaven. His unshaken fidelity, meekness, selflessness,

[1] Jer. xxxiii. 24–26.

and faith stand out as conspicuously as the outlines of mountains that front the Western Sun. But for us the most salient characteristic in his commanding personality, and the one on which we desire to lay the principal stress, is his partnership with God.

Exodus a Human Book. But the story of the Exodus is repeated in every soul that seeks deliverance from the enmeshing and enervating influence of the World. From this point of view the Book is human from the first verse to the last. The things that happened were by way of figure, and they were written for our admonition, upon whom the ends of the ages are come.[1]

There are very few of us who have not gone down into Egypt; very few that have not tasted of the leeks, melons, onion, and garlic; very few that have not eaten of the flesh-pots; very few that have not been tempted to sell our birthright for a life of selfish and even swinish pleasure. The fact that the infant Jesus was taken down into Egypt is, in this sense, profoundly significant.

A Significant Parallel. There is, therefore, an extraordinary depth of meaning in the Evangelist's quotation of Hosea,[2] in his allusion to the flight of the Holy Family from Herod's destructive sword. Why should he say that "Joseph took the young child and His mother by night and departed into Egypt; and was there until the death of Herod: that it might be fulfilled which was spoken by the Lord through the prophet, saying, Out of Egypt did I call my Son"?

—And Divine Appeal. Is it not because the life of the Son of Man is the epitome of the experiences of the sons of men—sin excepted? Is not God always calling His sons out of Egypt? Is He not always summoning the souls of men to forsake the brick-kilns and flesh-pots, and become part of the elect race, the chosen generation, the royal priesthood? Life is one long appeal to arise and depart, since this world can never be our rest. Go forth, O Christian soul! Be not content with speaking of the Exodus that should be accomplished—arise to accomplish it![3] Do not linger behind at the sounding of the trumpet! Depart ye, depart ye, go ye out from hence, touch no unclean thing, be ye clean, that bear the vessels of the Lord!

[1] 1 Cor. x. 11. [2] Hos. xi. 1; Matt. ii. 15. [3] Luke ix. 31 (*Greek*).

THE BITTERNESS OF LIFE

Exodus 1:1-22

1. Now these *are* the names of the children of Israel, which came into Egypt; every man and his household came with Jacob.

2. Reuben, Simeon, Levi, and Judah.

3. Issachar, Zebulun, and Benjamin,

4. Dan, and Naphtali, Gad, and Asher.

5. And all the souls that came out of the loins of Jacob were seventy souls: for Joseph was in Egypt *already*.

6. And Joseph died, and all his brethren, and all that generation.

7. And the children of Israel were fruitful, and increased abundantly, and multiplied, and waxed exceedingly mighty; and the land was filled with them.

8. Now there arose up a new king over Egypt, which knew not Joseph.

9. And he said unto his people, Behold, the people of the children of Israel *are* more and mightier than we:

10. Come on, let us deal wisely with them; lest they multiply, and it come to pass, that, when there falleth out any war, they join also unto our enemies, and fight against us, and *so* get them up out of the land.

11. Therefore they did set over them taskmasters to afflict them with their burdens. And they built for Pharaoh treasure cities, Pithom and Raamses.

12. But the more they afflicted them, the more they multiplied and grew. And they were grieved because of the children of Israel.

13. And the Egyptians made the children of Israel to serve with rigour:

14. And they made their lives bitter with hard bondage, in mortar, and in brick, and in all manner of service in the field: all their service, wherein they made them serve, *was* with rigour.

15. And the king of Egypt spake to the Hebrew midwives, of which the name of the one *was* Shiphrah, and the name of the other Puah:

16. And he said, When ye do the office of a midwife to the Hebrew women, and see *them* upon the stools; if it *be* a son, then ye shall kill him: but if it *be* a daughter, then she shall live.

17. But the midwives feared God, and did not as the king of Egypt commanded them, but saved the men-children alive.

18. And the king of Egypt called for the midwives, and said unto them, Why have ye done this thing, and have saved the men-children alive?

19. And the midwives said unto Pharaoh, Because the Hebrew women *are* not as the Egyptian women; for they *are* lively, and are delivered ere the midwives come in unto them.

20. Therefore God dealt well with the midwives: and the people multiplied, and waxed very mighty.

21. And it came to pass, because the midwives feared God, that he made them houses.

22. And Pharaoh charged all his people, saying, Every son that is born ye shall cast into the river, and every daughter ye shall save alive.

THE BITTERNESS OF LIFE

Exodus 1:1-22

Egypt the Strangest Country on Earth. Rightly enough, Egypt
has been described as the strangest country on earth. Strictly speaking, it consists of a long, narrow strip of green vegetation, stretching
from south to north on an outspread carpet of bright yellow sand.
This strip of fertile soil is about seven miles broad by five hundred
miles in length, and is maintained against the incursion of drought
and sand by the presence of the river, which annually overflows the
lands on either bank, and holds dominion over them for one hundred
days during which its waters amply enrich the soil.

The Reason Why. This marvellous phenomenon is due to rains
and melting snows on the highlands of Central Africa, the waters
of which flood the upper reaches of the river and enload its current
with rich silt, to be spread over the waiting fields that eagerly anticipate its advent. So delicate and unerring are the balances of Nature,
that for uncounted millenniums the Nile has continued to rise and
fall, to enrich and fructify, as with the rhythm of the human heart.

A Land of Ease and Civil Progress. *Life, therefore, in Egypt has
always been comparatively easy.* From the earliest dawn of history
the valley of the Nile, like those of the Euphrates, the Ganges, and
the Yang-tse, has been the home of a large and prolific family of the
human race. The soil is most productive. The plough is hardly
required. In the sculptures the ploughshare is a slight instrument that
can be managed by a single hand. Though not manured by artificial
means, the soil is as fruitful to-day as in the days of the Pharaohs.
It is easy, therefore, to understand the ease and rapidity with which,
under such circumstances, the apparatus of a complex and enduring
society, highly organised, with its arts and sciences, its political and
religious systems, came into existence. "While the Hebrew patriarchs were still feeding their flocks on the wolds of Canaan and
struggling with the landowners for wells, Egypt had a settled and

complicated polity, castes of priests, soldiers, and labourers, a court of intricate ceremonialism, and relations with the most distant nations of the world, so far as it was then known."

But for this very reason, and because the means of obtaining a livelihood were so cheap, *life in Egypt was apt to become self-indulgent and stagnant.*

Egypt not the Land to Produce Sturdiness of Character. Wherever Nature smiles continuously upon her children, and scatters her gifts with lavish hands, man misses the highest incentives to action, and suffers from lack of that propitious environment in which the nobler qualities of the soul mature. For these the colder air and stormier aspect of the temperate and colder zones are needed. Not where the balmy breezes blow soft o'er Ceylon's isle, but where the north-easter sweeps through the forest with icy blast, lashes the waves to foam, and searches the house of life for the ill-clad and weakly, will you encounter the highest ideals and sturdiest heroism. Not where the rich soil laughs with plenty, though only tickled by the plough, but where the ground is sterile, where the tree-roots have to be extracted, and the wrestle with thorn and thistle seems endless, will you meet with the noblest examples of courage, patience, faith, endurance, and care for others.

A Contrast and a Lesson. Contrast, for instance, Naples and Helsingfors. In the sweep of that noble bay, lying always under the caress of the sun, vast numbers will be content, if you guarantee them a daily dole of bread, a slice of melon, and a drink of sour wine. Granted these, and they will be content to doze in indolence through the long and lazy days. During successive centuries the Neapolitans produced no hero, but lay under the heel of the tyrant. In an earlier age she harboured sins for which Sodom was destroyed. But under the sombre skies of the North, Finland had produced a race of strong men and women, who love liberty, and have elaborated a noble constitution, in which a virile people has grown to maturity. Not for nothing have they wrung their bread from the unwilling hand of Nature. The wrestle has strengthened their moral muscles and elicited the noblest attributes of the human soul.

Egypt a Favoured Child. But Egypt has been the favoured child of the family of nations gathered around the Mediterranean seaboard. It literally teemed with life. The waters of the Nile abounded with fish and its banks with fowl. The soil was prolific with various kinds of vegetables as well as with great harvests of corn. In after-years the children of Israel wept, and said, "We remember the fish, which we did eat in Egypt for nought; the cucumbers, and the melons, and the leeks, and the onions, and the garlic." There was every inducement, therefore, to say to the soul, "Eat, drink, and be merry." Under the spell of the enchanted air and the enchanted soil, the song of the Lotos-eaters might have come naturally to the lip:

> " All things have rest: why should we toil alone?
> We only toil, who are the first of things,
> And make perpetual moan,
> Still from one sorrow to another thrown."

Egypt the Emblem of the Evils of Worldly Prosperity. There was a distinction in this respect between Egypt and Babylon. Babylon stood on the great highway of the world. For the traffic of the old generation the valley of the Euphrates was the natural highway between east and west; but Egypt lay as it were in a nook, a corner by herself, hemmed in by mighty deserts. She could live and die to herself. She could pamper and caress her children till their nobler qualities became enervated and dwarfed; and therefore she has always stood as the symbol of the enervating influence of worldly prosperity. There were the seed-germs of noble things in Egypt, as in the rest of the human family; but they were diverted from the service of God and man to the gratification of sense; and, as we know, the prostitution of the best is always worst. The soil that would be ideal for cereals is prolific in the poppy. So that the total contribution of Egypt to the world is a race of slaves, the poor ryots, who for two thousand years at least have been the drudges of their rulers and the helots of the human family.

Enervating Effect on the Israelites' Morality. *Into this land, as we learn from the opening verses of this chapter, Israel came.* At first they met with great favour. The reigning family counted them as valuable allies. *"In the best of the land,"* said the Pharaoh of that time to Joseph, "make thy father and brethren to dwell." But evidently beneath the seductive influences of the Egyptian climate, to which we have referred, their character became greatly relaxed. The ideals of Abraham's monotheistic faith and strenuous hardihood grew dim and faint. On this point an interesting light is thrown by the prophet Ezekiel. He tells us that Jehovah pleaded with His people, as the time of their emancipation drew near, to cast away the abominations of their eyes, and forsake the idols of Egypt;

but they would not hearken; so much so that it became a question whether He would not pour out His anger upon them and consume them in the midst of the land of Egypt.[1] The worship of the calf, the lusting of Kibroth-Hataavah, the outbreak of iniquity on the frontiers of Moab, all proved how deeply the taint of Egyptian idolatry and impurity had wrought. The Lord God brought a vine out of Egypt, but during the four hundred years of its sojourn there, it had undeniably become inveterately degenerate and wild. If the process had been allowed to run to its full course, obliteration must have ensued.

A Peril Escaped. The Hebrew race would have become intermingled with the Egyptians. Intermarriage seems already to have commenced, and it would have become more and more usual till that absolute coalescence would have taken place which the Pilgrim Fathers dreaded for their children in Holland, and which is absolutely and surely obliterating the old spirit of antagonism between Boer and British in South Africa.

Moses Typical of the Hebrew Race. *But such a close to God's dealings with the fathers was impossible.* Let us recall that ancient word of Hosea: "When Israel was a child, then I loved him, and called *My son* out of Egypt." In a special sense the Hebrew race had been called to a Divine Sonship. They were an elect race, elect in the sense of having capacity within them to become the Light-bringers, Prophets, Priests, and Psalmists of the world. The possibilities that were latent in the Hebrew people are apparent in the character and work of Moses, the Man of God. What he was actually, they were possibly. He was the flower of the race, revealing its rare quality. You must look to the great Lawgiver and Leader if you would see what it was that Jehovah espied in the chosen race and led Him to redeem it. The Divine purpose of revealing God to man through men would have been frustrated unless there had been an exodus from Egypt, with its idolatry, sensuality, and enervating luxury, to the free air of the desert and the highlands of Canaan.

Are You in Egypt? *Is this not always true?* God has His sons to-day who are capable of becoming the leaders of the coming time. Some of them may read these words! You are becoming enervated by success; your position is assured; your income is increasing; your prospects of a prosperous career are brightening; but your soul fibre is relaxing; you are becoming less strenuous in the quest of your

[1] Ezek. xviii. 6-8.

olden ideals; your heart is suffering from fatty degeneration! It will never do! You were not made for this. A world's redemption needs you! The sins and sorrows of men may be relieved only through your agency! You are capable of playing a redemptive part in the great arena of the world! Arise ye, and depart, for this is not your rest!

God Calls You Out. In Matthew, as we have seen, we find that verse, "Out of Egypt have I called My Son," applied to our Lord. His going down into Egypt proves that this history is significant for all human life and for the race. If to you, therefore, there has already come the descent into Egypt; to you also comes the Divine Call.

But when the Divine Call comes to the sons of God, it is for the most part accompanied by sufferings which make the earthly life bitter. Whilst Joseph lived, for perhaps seventy years, the Hebrews received remarkable consideration. Then for some 260 years they were treated with quiet contempt by the Egyptian Court, Priesthood, and Aristocracy, much as Hindoos of the lower castes are treated by the Europeans in India to-day. Finally, when a new King arose, who had not known Joseph, their position became intolerable. This new King was probably Seti I, whose predecessors had driven Joseph's friend and patron from the throne. Nations soon forget benefits received. Within fourteen years of Salamis the Athenians banished Themistocles; and within seventeen years of Waterloo the Duke of Wellington was compelled to protect the windows of Apsley House with iron shutters.

Beginning of the Oppression. A Reason for It. At the time this Book opens, the Hittites were threatening the invasion of Egypt, and it was a grave question what might happen if the Hebrews, now probably 1,000,000 strong, joined Egypt's enemies. They occupied that part of the land which the hostile forces must first enter; and if, as an alien race, they allied with them, it would give the invaders a very important strategical advantage. It was deemed urgently necessary, therefore, that their power and numbers should be greatly diminished and crushed.

Tasks—Brickmaking. The methods for effecting this readily suggested themselves. The Pharaoh was a builder of cities, especially of store-cities, and needed immense quantities of bricks. The brick was the staple of Egyptian architecture, as only the temples and palaces were constructed of stone. The Hebrews were therefore taken from tending their flocks and herds in the pasture-lands, and pressed into what to them was a particularly irksome service. They were compelled to dig the stiff clay, knead it with hands and feet, shape it in moulds, and produce a specified "tale of bricks," which had to pass under the sharp eyes of the taskmasters.

All the males not absolutely incapacitated were probably reduced to this hard and distasteful service. They were "afflicted" by these taskmasters, as ruthless as Turks to Armenians. Think of them labouring from morning to night, beneath a scorching sun, in constant dread of the lash, which the officers were encouraged to use freely, as the quickest method by which their lives might be worried out of them. Often, without doubt, the helpless serfs would be beaten to death.

Field-service. Another task is described as "service in the field." Probably, as Dean Stanley suggests, it was such as we still see along the banks of the Nile, where the peasants, naked under the burning heat, are engaged, as beasts of burden, drawing buckets of water from the river-level for field-irrigation. Here again every endeavour was made to add to the hardness of the service, with the object of breaking down their energy. "All their service, wherein they made them serve, was with rigour."

Infanticide as a Means of Lessening the Israelitish Peril. A further method of reducing the hated race is mentioned in verses 15–22. Infanticide was commonly practised by the nations of antiquity. Pharaoh, therefore, had no qualms in applying it as a swift expedient for diminishing the Hebrew race, first through Shiphrah and Puah! and, when they failed him, by open proclamation that all male children should be cast into the Nile. Perhaps he deemed, also, that in this way the River-god would be still further propitiated.

The Measures Ineffectual. It was expected that all these methods would soon bring the people under; but their persecutors were greatly deceived. "The more they afflicted them, the more they multiplied and grew." God's promise to Abraham that his seed should be as the stars of heaven, and as the sand upon the seashore, could not be set aside by the will of a cruel and heathen despot. Jehovah had promised, and would perform. Tyrants like Pharaoh and Herod have set themselves against Jehovah and against His Christ, But He that sits in the Heavens laughs!

God's Reasons for the Sufferings of the Israelites. Nevertheless, without question, the Hebrew people were at this time suffering great bitterness of spirit, with the object of stirring up their nest, of making Egypt distasteful, and of preparing them to obey the supreme call to arise and follow God, even into a land that was not sown. These stern measures were needed to quicken that love of their espousals, of which their Almighty Lover speaks so touchingly in after days.

The Clue to a Difficulty. *Is not this a clue to the bitterness of our human lot, both of the whole and of the individual.* Life is bitter in many of its aspects. To the man accounted too old at forty, and doomed to inactivity, when his life is yet strong in him! To the woman who is condemned to spend her life yoked to a man for whom she has neither love nor respect! To the child who is cruelly repressed until all childlaughter dies from its pinched features! It would be impossible to give an adequate conception of the bitterness of human life, as myriads experience it, because so much is heroically concealed. Apart from the teachings of Scripture, the problem is inexplicable, but the line of argument suggested by the scope of the present chapter seems to point the direction in which an answer may be found.

Love Behind It All—To Bring Out Hidden Possibilities. When, for instance, we are told that the ground was cursed for man's sake, and that woman was called to suffering, does it not mean that the lot of man was purposely made bitter, that he might not settle down to the pursuit of animal enjoyment, but might become the pilgrim of the unseen? Does not the primeval sentence suggest that the cultivation of a garden could never be an adequate occupation for the sons of God? Was not the Angel who drove them forth, and kept them out, an Angel of Love? Is it not better to create a garden out of a wilderness; and to become pilgrims who seek a city, nay, who build a city? The long sad history of man bears witness that he has God-given qualities, that he is a son, not a brute, that there are possibilities within him, waiting to be evoked, which will never obey a summons unless accompanied by the embittering of most of the cups that Earth puts to his lips.

—And also Hidden Beauties. We do not realise the value of the human soul. Its greatness, its sub-conscious depths, its God-like and God-given qualities. We do not understand the transcience and hollowness of the supports around which our weak heart clings, nor the worth and permanence of the unseen and eternal. All around us are things which eye hath not seen, nor the ear heard, nor the heart of man conceived. Living waters bursting from the everlasting hills; amaranthine flowers that were grown on the soil of Paradise. But we heed them not; and some of us never will heed them, till our lives have become bitter with hard bondage.

Man Craves Something Better than the Fleshpots. This is the meaning of your life. Oh, sons of God, you cannot be permanently satisfied with the loveless kiss, and the contents of the swine-trough! You were not made for these! Your appetite may be arrested for the time, but it cannot be permanently satisfied. Not the flesh-pots but the manna: not the sweet waters of the Nile, but the water from the Rock: not the leeks, onions, and garlics, but grapes of Eshcol: not the land of the Sphinx with its open-eyed wonder, nor the Pyramids with their mystery are for you, but a land that is the glory of all lands! Oh, do not be surprised, if God has made the sense-world bitter, that you may arise to realise your sonship, and to start on an everlasting pilgrimage.

God Offers Deliverance from Slavery. You have groaned in the service of sin; you have hated and cursed yourself; you have longed to be free with a desire that God has implanted! You have awoke to know yourself a slave, and to long unappeasably for deliverance! Then the bitterness has done its work! The acid has gnawed your fetters, and you are able to hear and follow the call of God! Choose then! Arise! Is not the breath of a new era on your cheeks? Christ has come down to deliver you! He stands beside you at this hour! Rise and follow Him! What though the Red Sea lies between you and the Land of Promise, He will bear you on eagle-wings and bring you to Himself! See the Christ stand!

"The Morning Cometh, and also the Night"

Exodus 2:1-22

1. And there went a man of the house of Levi, and took *to wife* a daughter of Levi.

2. And the woman conceived, and bare a son: and when she saw him that he *was a* goodly *child*, she hid him three months.

3. And when she could not longer hide him, she took for him an ark of bulrushes, and daubed it with slime and with pitch, and put the child therein; and she laid *it* in the flags by the river's brink.

4. And his sister stood afar off, to wit what would be done to him.

5. And the daughter of Pharaoh came down to wash *herself* at the river; and her maidens walked along by the river's side; and when she saw the ark among the flags, she sent her maid to fetch it.

6. And when she had opened *it*, she saw the child: and, behold, the babe wept. And she had compassion on him, and said, This *is one* of the Hebrews' children.

7. Then said his sister to Pharaoh's daughter, Shall I go and call to thee a nurse of the Hebrew women, that she may nurse the child for thee?

8. And Pharaoh's daughter said to her, Go. And the maid went and called the child's mother.

9. And Pharaoh's daughter said unto her, Take this child away, and nurse it for me, and I will give *thee* thy wages. And the woman took the child, and nursed it.

10. And the child grew, and she brought him unto Pharaoh's daughter, and he became her son. And she called his name Moses: and she said, Because I drew him out of the water.

11. And it came to pass in those days, when Moses was grown, that he went out unto his brethren, and looked on their burdens: and he spied an Egyptian smiting an Hebrew, one of his brethren.

12. And he looked this way and that way, and when he saw that *there was* no man, he slew the Egyptian, and hid him in the sand.

13. And when he went out the second day, behold, two men of the Hebrews strove together: and he said to him that did the wrong, Wherefore smitest thou thy fellow?

14. And he said, Who made thee a prince and a judge over us? intendest thou to kill me, as thou killedst the Egyptian? And Moses feared, and said, Surely this thing is known.

15. Now when Pharaoh heard this thing, he sought to slay Moses. But Moses fled from the face of Pharaoh, and dwelt in the land of Midian: and he sat down by a well.

16. Now the priest of Midian had seven daughters: and they came and drew *water*, and filled the troughs to water their father's flock.

17. And the shepherds came and drove them away: but Moses stood up and helped them, and watered their flock.

18. And when they came to Reuel their father, he said, How *is it that* ye are come so soon to-day?

19. And they said, An Egyptian delivered us out of the hand of the shepherds, and also drew *water* enough for us, and watered the flock.

20. And he said unto his daughters, And where *is* he? why *is* it *that* ye have left the man? call him, that he may eat bread.

21. And Moses was content to dwell with the man: and he gave Moses Zipporah his daughter.

22. And she bare *him* a son, and he called his name Gershom: for he said, I have been a stranger in a strange land.

"THE MORNING COMETH, AND ALSO THE NIGHT"

Exodus 2:1-22

Opposing Forces. "*By faith Moses . . .*" There is a moment in the dawn when the coming Day and the lingering Night appear to struggle for mastery. It is not for long, for the reign of darkness is doomed, so soon as the first glimmer of light trembles in the chambers of the East. Thus, in this chapter, we notice the conflict between hope and despair, between faith and doubt, between the heroism of the mother who hid her baby boy, and the pessimism of the nation, which sighed unto heart-break.

The Birth of Moses. THE RIVER'S BRINK. Already two children— Miriam, a daughter, and Aaron, a son, born twelve years later, had been given to Amram and his kinswoman, Jochebed.[1] These enlivened the humble cottage with those sweet child-voices that chime through all national and individual sorrow, as church-bells through clinging mists. Three years passed: a third child was given— a boy, "a goodly child," "fair to God."[2] But there was no other indication that the founder of the Hebrew nation, and one of the greatest of the sons of men, had stepped down into the arena of human history.

A Brave Mother Who Reckoned on God. Something in the babe's lovely countenance appeared to the mother's eye as the halo of special Divine affection. A voice whispered to her heart that her child was specially dear to God. Was not its smile the result of the Divine embrace? And did not those limpid eyes look into the face of the Angel of the Covenant? She was, therefore, encouraged to brave the royal edicts, and screen the little taper from the gale of destruction that was sweeping through the land. She probably hid him for three months in the female apartments, reserved for women. Each

---

[1] vi. 20.   [2] Acts vii. 20; Heb. xi. 23.

day his lungs were stronger and his infant-cries more likely to attract attention; but her faith was stedfast and immovable. She reckoned on God. Greater was He who was for her than all they who were against her. By faith Moses was hid by his parents, and "they were not afraid." This act of theirs secured their admission to that long sacred corridor, where the busts of the great cloud of witnesses to the power of faith stand chiselled by immortal strokes.

The Ark of Bulrushes, an Expression of Mother Love. Finally, acting beneath a divine impulse, she made "a paper-boat," i.e. an ark or chest with a cover, by weaving together rushes of papyrus. Its slight texture was made strong and waterproof by repeated coats of vegetable-pitch; but her love and faith lined it with the softest down, and built up the strongest safeguards that ever sheltered a tiny babe. With a devouring kiss, she placed the babe within its novel cradle, bore it to the river-side, and laid it in a thicket of reeds, lest it might float out on a voyage to distant and unwelcoming banks. "His sister stood afar off, to know what would be done to him."

Waiting for God to Act. That something would be done they had no doubt. They knew that God always prepared good things for those who love Him, which pass human thought; but what they might be, was a matter of reverent interest, not of fear or mistrust.

Turning Evil to Good Account. Pharaoh's cruel edict was turned to good account. There is always a soul of good in things evil. The glory of God's providence is to carry out His eternal purposes, in spite of human opposition, and often by His reversal of human plans. Had it not been for those extreme measures of repression, the child would never have been exposed; and if it had never been launched in its slight skiff on the waters of the Nile, Moses would have missed the education "in all the wisdom of Egypt," which became so important a factor in his after history.

But it was a remarkable reversing of the situation, when Pharaoh's designs were neutralised by the action of his own daughter, and when the emancipation of the hated Hebrews was nurtured in his own court. God maketh the wrath of man to praise Him, and the remainder of it He restrains.

A Warrant for Other Parents. There is abundant warrant, afforded by this narrative, for Christian parents to cast their children upon God. The mother whose child goes to earn her living among strangers; the father whose son must leave the quiet homestead for the mighty city; the parents who, as missionaries, are unable to nurture their children on the mission-field, because of the pernicious moral climate, more harmful than the heat of the plains of India; or those who on their death-beds must part with their babes to the care of comparative strangers, may all learn a lesson from the faith that cast the young child on the providence of God, even more absolutely than on the buoyancy of the Nile. God lives, and loves, and cares. More quick and tender than Miriam's, His eye neither slumbers nor sleeps.

The Princess Finds Moses. The providence of God, ever working through means, brought the princess to the river-brink at the critical moment, accompanied by the high-born maidens who constituted her personal attendants. It was His hand that guided her eye to the ark half concealed by the rushes; and it was at His prompting that her maid was sent to fetch it. All this came forth from the Lord of hosts, who is wonderful in counsel and excellent in effectual working.[1]

With her own hands the princess opened the lid of the little basket. It is not impossible that she guessed what its contents were. In any case, she was not surprised when she saw the babe, who had just awoke from its sleep and was crying for its mother. Was it the Hebrew physiognomy, as marked then as now, or a swift intuition, that made her exclaim, "This is one of the Hebrews' children"? But however it was, she was more than willing to fall in with the shrewd suggestion of Miriam that a nurse of the Hebrew race would be the more fitting to rear it.

Till Three Years Old He is Called "Moses." So it befell that Moses' life was saved, that he was nourished from the breasts of his own mother, and received as his earliest impressions those sacred teachings which had come down as a rich heritage from the tents of Abraham. Till he had grown, probably to the age of three years, he remained under the protection of the princess, though in his parents' home, and Jochebed's wages were duly paid till she brought him to the palace, and he became her son. "And she called his name Moses" ("Drawn forth").

Amram's Faith. We generally ascribe the faith that saved Moses to his mother: but his father also must have been characterised by it to no ordinary degree. That he married in face of the strong current flowing against family-life; that he dared risk the punishment of death, by sheltering his helpless child; that he encouraged his wife

[1] Isa. xxviii. 29.

in her project of casting him on the care of the Almighty, *all* testify to Amram's faith. "Faith wrought with his works, and by works was faith made perfect."[1]

The Childhood of Moses. THE TRAINING OF MOSES. The sapling grew as other saplings grow in the deep forest. His own mother's training must have been an important factor in it. The knowledge of God, the God of his fathers; the certainty that the God of Abraham would be true to the ancient Covenant; the love of liberty; devotion to the national ideals—these and such-like must have formed part of the curriculum by which Jochebed prepared her son, being a proper child, i.e. a marvellously quick and intelligent lad, for his life-work.

In addition to this, he was sent to the great city and university of Heliopolis, by the banks of the Nile, to be instructed in all the learning of that time. It was with considerable emotion that, on one memorable afternoon, I stood on the ruins of that ancient city, and tried to imagine Moses as a young man, one of 10,000 students, drawn from the whole known world.

The Youth of Moses. Of the result of this training, Stephen says, "Moses was instructed in all the wisdom of the Egyptians; and he was mighty in his words and works."[2] As to his *words*, it is remarkable that he afterwards excused himself from the great task to which he was summoned, because he was not eloquent, but of a slow tongue —showing how profound an effect the desert silence had had upon him. As to his *works*, Josephus tells us that he became an illustrious soldier, and led the Egyptian troops against the Ethiopian city of Meroë, which he took.

Moses and "His Brethren." But in the hours of greatest success, so far as this world was concerned, he never forgot his brethren, the children of Israel. His *brethren*! Note that word. We shall never get society right, until that word, brotherhood, becomes its keynote. That Moses and the Hebrew slaves were brothers was no more a truth than that the millionaire of Park Lane and the docker, fighting for his place at the big gates to earn bread for wife and bairns, are brothers, sprung from the same father, and sent forth to share together the heritage of the earth. Well is it that there is an increasing willingness on the part of the upper classes to visit their brethren and share their burdens!

The Example of Moses. The conditions of poverty, misery, and

---

[1] James ii. 22.   [2] Acts vii. 22.

temptation, in which large numbers spend their lives, are admittedly bitter in the extreme, and would never be tolerated, if the principles of Christ's kingdom were universally practised. It may be long before His ideals are the actual code of personal and collective existence; but in the meanwhile we can at least manifest sympathy both in word and act, and may win the welcome which the King shall utter to those on His right hand, "I was an hungered, and ye gave Me meat: thirsty, and ye gave Me drink: I was a stranger, and ye took Me in: I was naked, and ye clothed Me: I was sick, and ye visited Me: I was in prison, and ye came unto Me."[1]

The Vision of Duty. THE IMPOTENCE OF MERE HUMAN FORCE. "When he was well-nigh forty years old," so Stephen told the Sanhedrim, "it came into his heart to visit his brethren the children of Israel."[2]

It may be that that visit transformed the career of the future law-giver of Sinai. He may have gone merely out of curiosity, or at the passing impulse of pity; but the scenes he witnessed changed his life-current, and diverted it into an entirely new channel. Vows were made for him, that he should become, else sinning greatly, "a dedicated spirit."

A Noble Resolve. Gradually the sentiment of casual interest and pity strengthened into a noble resolve that he would descend from the steps of Pharaoh's throne, refuse to be called the son of Pharaoh's daughter, and choose rather to suffer affliction with the people of God than enjoy the pleasures of sin for a season.

Already some dreams of a deliverer—"the Christ"—had floated before the minds of his suffering compatriots, though they were the subject of ridicule and reproach among their Egyptian oppressors. What deliverance could that suffering race count on? But he reckoned that dim hope to be greater riches than all the treasures of Egypt; for he looked unto the recompense of reward, of which his mother had spoken, years before, as the undoubted heritage of Abraham's race.[3]

A Deed that was a Turning-point. Among other heart-rending scenes in the slave-camp was that of an Egyptian smiting a Hebrew. Probably the Hebrew was doing his best; but either because of imperfect nutrition, or old age, or fever, was unable to supply the prescribed tale of bricks, much as the Congolese the required amount

---

[1] Matt. xxv. 35, 36.   [2] Acts vii. 23.
[3] Heb. xi. 24–26.

of rubber. In any case, Moses felt that he was suffering a grievous wrong, and defended him, and avenged him that was oppressed.[1] The arm that was wielding the scourge was suddenly arrested. With one blow of that powerful fist the Egyptian official was felled to the ground, and lay dead. It was not entirely an act of reckless passion, because we are told that "he looked this way and that" before delivering the death-dealing blow. But, after making all allowances, we can hardly admit that he was authorised to interfere, either by God or man.

Motive of the Act. Certainly the punishment was disproportionate to the offence. It was the act of a warm, sympathetic, masterful nature, apart from the guidance and control of the Spirit of the Highest.

Some consciousness of this appears to have occurred to Moses himself so soon as the deed was done, for we are told that he hid the body in the sand. The man whom he had delivered was apparently too exhausted, or too terrified, to lend a hand in the interment, and crept away home. Moses also went from the scene, not altogether easy in his mind, but comforting himself with the thought that the rescued would surely, for his own sake, not scatter the intelligence of what had transpired. He little realised that by that one act he had disqualified himself for the service he longed to render, or that long years must pass before by his hand God could give deliverance.

An Unexpected Result. On the second day, it was no longer the case of Egyptian against Hebrew, but of Hebrew against Hebrew. It was not a question of the foreigner demanding enforced labour, but of hot blood between brethren of the same race. The memory of yesterday withheld Moses from using force. He did not smite the wrong-doer; perhaps because his conscience was slightly uneasy. He was content to remonstrate with the wrong-doer, who—having no sufficient answer to give to his inquiry, "Why smitest thou thy fellow?"—turned on Moses as a meddler, and cast in his teeth the memory of the high-handed act, which had already got wind: "Who made thee a prince and a judge over us? thinkest thou to kill me, as thou killedst the Egyptian?"

The Symbol of Degradation. Did not that sharp repartee reveal the besotted degradation of the Hebrew soul and temper? What but a slave's tongue could have reproached a Hebrew for slaying an

[1] Acts vii. 24.

Egyptian? Surely, if this were the depth to which the Hebrew race had sunk, they required long years of stern, strong discipline before becoming the teachers and inspirers of mankind.

The Swiss still acclaim the assassination of a Gessler, and had the Hebrews not sunk to a low degree of demoralisation, they would have gloried in the consciousness that at last one of their race would face and floor an oppressor. By their silence, they would have become accomplices in his act. None would have reproached him with what would have seemed a generous and splendid act.

The Fruits of Oppression. This pusillanimity is the invariable result of centuries of oppression. The oppressed not only lose all hope, and resign themselves to their fate, but they imitate the vices of their oppressors. If an Egyptian smites a Hebrew to-day, a Hebrew will smite his fellow-Hebrew to-morrow; and even if a deliverer appears, his intrusion will be resented as an impertinence.

National Perils. Read again the story of the French Revolution. The long pent-up passion of the people at last burst all bounds, destroyed the ancient barriers of law and order, brought Louis and his Queen to the guillotine, and sought to inaugurate an era of liberty, equality, and fraternity. But in fact they installed a more hideous tyranny than that which they superseded.

You may change the constitution of the state by some summary act of revolution, but unless the moral and religious elements have been consulted and conserved, unless your new state expresses, not passionate revenge, but a regard and veneration for higher ideals than those of the system you destroy, you only erect one despotism on the ruins of another,—the smiting of the Hebrew by the Hebrew, instead of by the Egyptian.

—And Mixed Motives. Through the long centuries of our island story, Britain has escaped the sanguinary scenes of revolution, witnessed in other European capitals, by the religious spirit of her people, which has pervaded them, and prepared the way for each upward step in the great process of historical evolution. For instance, the accession of William and Mary was brought about, less by a passion of resentment to James II, than by that devotion to the highest ideals of patriotism and freedom which religion inspires.

Reform v. Revival. Political movement must follow and express the high and noble sentiments by which the community is animated. The emancipation of the slaves, the amelioration of the condition of the working-classes, the vast advance in prison-reform, which marked the nineteenth century, were only possible, because the great Methodist revival, followed by the revival in the Church of England, had moved and moulded the religious conditions of the entire nation.

Moses has Still Much to Learn. It was clear that Moses had acted unadvisedly. His impulse was in the right direction, but it was hot, raw, and ill-considered; and the wrath of man worketh not the righteousness of God. You can never redress a nation's wrongs by offering brute force to brute force, or by a number of rash, violent acts. More haste makes worse speed. What would have been the end for Moses or for Israel, if he had gone on day after day smiting this man and that? Even if his strong hand had enforced a temporary cessation of wrong-doing, it would have reasserted itself so soon as he had turned his back! He had much to learn before he became the meekest of men.

His Efforts Vain Because not God-directed. How often the young reformer, the student fresh from college, the brilliant dreamer of noble dreams, supposes that he has only to wield axe or sword with a few swift, strong strokes, and at once a way will be cleft through the jungle to the canopy of the over-arching sky; but at forty or sixty he still finds himself labouring to disentwine the entangling branches, or tear up the resisting roots. We can effect nothing effectual or lasting apart from God. It is not by might, nor by power, but by His Spirit that the world will be saved. Not what we do for Him, but only what He does through us, will be wholly beneficent and permanent in result. But our hands must be very clean, if God is to use them; and our tongue must have become empty of its own speech, if God is to put His Word there.

The Flight of Moses. Why He Chose Midian. THE LAND OF MIDIAN. There was a special clause in the treaty between Rameses II and the contemporary Hittite King to the effect that fugitives along the northern route to Syria should be arrested and extradited. The knowledge of this fact probably led Moses to turn his steps to the S.E. "Moses fled from the face of Pharaoh"—who sought to slay him—"and dwelt in the land of Midian." Egypt had possessions, especially mines, in the Sinaitic peninsula, but it was quite easy to avoid them; and before Sinai was reached the fugitive would be in complete safety, for the Egyptians seem never to have penetrated to the southern or eastern portions of the great triangle. He was probably further attracted by the knowledge that the Midianites on the further side of the peninsula were monotheists, and cherished the knowledge and workship of God Almighty.

Moses and the Priest's Daughters. No sooner had he reached that distant spot than Moses found himself face to face with the same high-handed wrong that had aroused his soul in Egypt. Here it was not the tyranny of man over man, but of man over woman. There a weaker race had been oppressed, here the weaker sex. In Egypt woman held a high place, and therefore he was the more incensed, when the unmannerly sons of the desert not only would not wait their turn, but actually used the water which the priest's daughters had drawn. The following verse, with the exclamation of their father's surprise, shows that this had become a matter of daily occurrence, and that these lazy shepherds made it a practice to evade the trouble of drawing water for themselves. Though one against many, Moses would not brook this act of oppression. He sprang up from the well, beside which he was seated, helped the girls, and saw that their flocks were watered.

He Marries Zipporah. The temporary residence in Reuel's encampment led to a permanent relationship. "Moses was content" to dwell with him, and he gave Moses Zipporah, his daughter, to wife.

Oppressed by Loneliness, Yet Trusted in God. But the name given to his first-born—Gershom, "a stranger here"—suggests that a sense of depression still clung around him. In those great desert spaces, far removed from the life and stir of Egypt, the isolation and exile of his lot bore down upon him, with the weight of an overwhelming incubus. The confession of his fathers was often on his lips. He had no abiding-city under those silent stars, or beneath that majestic canopy of intense blue. He was a stranger and pilgrim on the earth.

Probably by the time his second son was born the depression had somewhat lightened, and faith had asserted itself. He named him Eliezer, "my God is my help." But these alternations between the depths of despair and the heights of courageous faith were destined to give place to the settled resolve of the servant in God's House, who would merge his private concerns in uncompromising fidelity to the vast responsibilities with which he became charged.

THE DARKEST HOUR BEFORE THE DAWN

Exodus 2:23-25

23. And it came to pass in process of time, that the king of Egypt died: and the children of Israel sighed by reason of the bondage, and they cried, and their cry came up unto God by reason of the bondage.

24. And God heard their groaning, and God remembered his covenant with Abraham, with Isaac, and with Jacob.

25. And God looked upon the children of Israel, and God had respect unto *them.*

THE DARKEST HOUR BEFORE THE DAWN

Exodus 2:23-25

The King—Rameses II. Who this King of Egypt was is not of great importance, from the standpoint of these chapters. On the whole, it seems probable that the Pharaoh "who knew not Joseph"[1] was Rameses I, or his son Seti, the great conqueror, renowned for having carried his victorious arms as far as Mesopotamia. The flight of Moses to Midian would then have taken place under Rameses II, under whom Egyptian civilisation reached its highest point; and it is he who is referred to here as having died.

After eighty years of life and sixty-seven of regal power this illustrious ruler was gathered to his fathers, having built up the national magnificence at the cost of myriads of lives, partly in war and specially in his colossal works. A modern writer says that every stone in the edifices which he reared was cemented by the blood of a human victim. Thousands of miserable slaves wrought incessantly to add to his glory and cover his land with obelisks, temples, and cities. For years the toiling masses had longed for his death, as likely to bring a relaxation of their miseries, but when at last it befell and he passed, and when his successor, Menepthah, instead of relaxing the inexorable cruelty of his father, maintained and enforced his measures, it seemed as though their heart-strings, long stretched to breaking-point, could endure the strain no longer.

The Oppression Becomes More Intense. "It came to pass in the course of those many days, that the King of Egypt died: and the children of Israel sighed by reason of the bondage."

The Sigh of Oppressed Nations. It is terrible to hear a sigh—a child's, a woman's, a man's! But how much more a nation's! The sigh of the Congo! The sighs of oppressed nations, doomed to see their liberties suppressed and their free-speech forbidden! The sigh of the enslaved everywhere! "The children of Israel sighed."

[1] i. 8.

It is an inexplicable problem why the good God should permit it all. Surely the goal for which He has destined our race must be one of transcendent glory, or He would never conduct it thither at such an awful cost. Tennyson's *In Memoriam*, the noblest Epic ever penned to human love, proves surely that thoughtful men at the close of the last century not only recognised the sorrow of the world, but felt that, in the last resort, it must be traced back to God.

The World's Sorrow Traced Back to God. He cannot have been surprised by the entrance of sin, with its attendant pain and anguish. It must have been included in His original scheme. Though in no sense the Author of evil, He anticipated it, for the Lamb was slain from before the foundation of the world. Apparently there was no other way by which the highest happiness of the greatest number could be secured than by the endowment of freewill, with its evident and awful liabilities of abuse.

Why God Permitted Sin. But the Heavenly Father accepted these, as a small price to pay for the far more exceeding and eternal weight of glory; and when the whole plan has been worked out to its completion, and He shall have put down all rule and authority and power, and shall have gathered all things together in Christ, the whole universe of intelligent moral beings will acknowledge that He has done all things well, saying, "Who shall not fear, O Lord, and glorify Thy name? for Thou only art holy; for all the nations shall come and worship before Thee; for Thy righteous acts have been made manifest."[1]

This only is our solace amid all the awful perplexity of the world's anguish; that God is not indifferent, that He is infinitely the greatest Sufferer of all, that in bringing His many sons unto glory He has made the Captain of their Salvation perfect through suffering.

The Sighs of the Saviour. We turn from the sighs of the world to those of our Lord. When they brought the deaf-mute to Him, He looked up to Heaven and sighed; and when the Pharisees tempted Him, He sighed deeply in His spirit.[2] These are the two causes of His sighing, not then alone, but always. Human suffering and human unbelief! Undoubtedly He knew that ultimately He would succeed in banishing all sorrow and sighing from the world, but so long as it lasted it lay heavily—and lies heavily—on His holy and tender heart. In those two single instances He saw specimens of the whole weltering sea of pain and sin that rolls round the world.

[1] Rev. xv. 4.　　　　[2] Mark vii. 34; viii. 12.

Can we wonder that in the midst of the throne He is beheld as a Lamb that was slain? He knows what man might have been.

The Burden of Sin and Suffering Rests on the Saviour's Heart. He comprehends the entire aggregation of sin and sorrow. The burden of it all rests on His heart—a burden that He alone can sustain. When we bear one another's burdens, we fulfil the law of His life, to which He is perpetually subject.

The unbeliever taunts us with believing in a God of Love, and we might feel the justice of the taunt, had our Lord passed through this world with dry eyes and unmoved heart, or if He had only taught with dry logic and elegant phrase, or if He had never wept with the sisters or groaned at the gates of the grave. But how triumphant is our reply to the taunting cynicism of unbelief, when the ancient words have had such ample verification in His life: "Surely He hath borne our griefs, and carried our sorrows."[1] "It behoved Him in all things to be made like unto His brethren, that He might be a merciful and faithful High Priest."[2]

What is Meant by the "Angel of His Presence." Isaiah's allusion to the Divine sympathy with Israel is full of pathos, when He says: "In all their affliction He was afflicted, and the Angel of His Presence saved them." Exactly what is meant by the Angel of His Presence is difficult to define; but this surely implied that He was at hand, walking beside them in the iron-furnace, passing with them through the rivers of sorrow, and seeing to it that they did not absolutely despair.

Four Statements. Four statements are made here: God heard; God remembered; God saw; God knew.

God Heard. "Their cry came up unto God." Probably it did not articulate itself in petition. It was just a cry of misery, in which the deeper voice of manhood blended with the anguish of the bereaved mother and the wail of the babe. But God understood it, and was able to trace each formative element to its source. In the graphic language of the chroniclers, it "came up unto God."

There are times when we cannot speak, and our minds, bewildered with grief and pain, refuse to formulate specific petitions. We can only lie at the foot of the throne, and cry, as startled babes might. But our cries enter unto the ears of the Lord God of Sabaoth. Each is registered, and kept, as a letter may be, to which you have not yet returned an answer. God hears the voice of our groaning;

[1] Isa. liii. 4; Matt. viii. 17.   [2] Heb. ii. 17.

and listens to the language of the tears, which we brush away almost before they form.

Tears have a voice: and God interprets it.

The Seeming Silence of God. Silent as God seems through the long hours and years, He is not indifferent. He is only waiting that He may be gracious. The hour has not yet struck for emancipation, though the hands on Heaven's Great Clock are moving inevitably towards it. Presently He will rend the Heavens, and come down; but in the meanwhile there is not a groan in all this travailing Creation which is undetected. Each drop which exhales from the ocean of pain is conserved somewhere. It is transfigured in the rainbow, and shall return in showers of blessing.

God Remembered. "They were rebellious in their counsel, and were brought low in their iniquity. Nevertheless He regarded their distress, when He heard their cry." "He remembered His holy word, and Abraham His servant."[1]

We are carried back to that solemn watch of two nights and a day that Abram kept, and when, conforming to the wont of the sons of the desert, God gave visible confirmation of the validity of His Covenant. "And He said unto Abram, Know of a surety that thy seed shall be a stranger in a land that is not theirs, and shall serve them; and they shall afflict them four hundred years; and also that nation, whom they serve, will I judge: and afterward shall they come out with great substance."[2]

The Covenant that was Ratified with Additions. That Covenant was afterwards solemnly ratified with additions, and is described as an everlasting or eternal Covenant.[3] In some respects it still lies at the basis of all God's dealings with those who, by faith, are the children of faithful Abraham. Though four long centuries had passed, that covenant was as fresh as at its inauguration in the heart of Jehovah, and not because of the worthiness of the people, but because of the two immutable things that made it impossible for Him to lie, when the time of the promise drew nigh, He began to carry its provisions into execution.

The Covenant is Ratified in Christ. With us also God has entered into an eternal Covenant, and has ratified it with the Blood of His Son, who on the night when He was betrayed took the cup and gave thanks, and gave it to the disciples, saying, "Drink ye all of it;

---

[1] Ps. cvi. 43; cv. 42.   [2] Gen. xv. 13, 14.
[3] Gen. xvii. 7.

for this is My blood of the Covenant." It was through the blood of that Eternal Covenant that He approved Himself worthy to become the Great Shepherd of the sheep.[1] When, therefore, we place that cup to our lips at the Holy Supper, we remind God of that Covenant, on the sanctions of which we venture all that we are and hope for, in time and eternity.

The All-embracing Provisions of the Covenant. On His part, also, He comes near to us, and says, "I remember: Not one jot or tittle shall pass, until all be fulfilled: Heaven and earth shall pass away, but My words shall not pass away." Recount to yourself the seven-fold provisions of that Covenant, as they are set forth in Hebrews viii. There is no circumstance that can befall you that may not be brought in under one or other of those gracious provisions. Though there be no answering voice, you may be absolutely certain that your appeal is acknowledged and responded to. As you draw nigh to God, He draws nigh to you.

God Saw. "The eyes of the Lord are toward the righteous, and His ears are open unto their cry"; and though Israel was not righteous for their own sake, they were beloved for their father's sake. "And the Lord said, I have surely seen the affliction of My people which are in Egypt."[2]

There is a remarkable succession of affirmations made of the Father by our Lord in the Sermon on the Mount:[3]

God Sees and Knows.

> *Your Father which is in Heaven:*
> *Thy Father which is in secret:*
> *Thy Father which seeth in secret:*
> *Your Father knoweth:*
> *Your Heavenly Father will forgive you:*
> *Your Heavenly Father feedeth:*
> *Your Father which is in Heaven shall give good things.*

To realise that He sees and knows, that nothing which concerns us is hidden from Him, that the darkness shines as the day, and the lowest part of the earth conceals nothing from His omniscience—this carries with it all the rest: for He cannot see without coming down in pitying help. When in after days the children of Israel were assured that Jehovah had seen their affliction, "then they

[1] Matt. xxvi. 27; Heb. xiii. 20.   [2] Psa. xxxiv. 15; Exod. iii. 7; Matt. vi. vii.
[3] Matt. vi. 7.

bowed their heads and worshipped," as though they had nothing more to ask[1]; and the result justified their act.

Every blow of the hand that buffets you, every cut of the scourge, every scorching hour under the noontide sun, every lonely hour when lovers and friends stand aloof, every step into the valley of shadow, every moment of sleep beneath the juniper-tree, is watched by the eyes that never slumber nor sleep.

A Holy Watcher. "I saw in the visions of my head upon my bed, and, behold, a watcher and an holy one came down from Heaven."[2]

"When even was come, the boat was in the midst of the sea, and He alone on the land. And seeing them distressed in rowing, for the wind was contrary unto them, about the fourth watch of the night He cometh unto them, walking on the sea."[3]

"I have surely visited you, and seen that which is done to you in Egypt: and I have said, I will bring you out of the affliction of Egypt.[4]

God Took Knowledge. "*God took knowledge of them.*" Literally, "And God knew." He notes all things in His book, puts every tear into His bottle, counts the hairs as they fall from the head or turn white with anguish. "I have surely seen the affliction of My people. . . . I know their sorrows."

We are Individuals to God. God knows with a *personal* knowledge. It has been truly said that the word "masses" does not occur in God's vocabulary. We are not masses, but units; not a forest, but trees; not a race, but individuals. It is as though there was but one child in the Father's house, and each of us is that child.

He Feels with Each One. God knows with a *sympathetic* knowledge. He is touched with the feeling of our infirmities, and whatever is done to us is accepted as done to Him. "I was in prison, . . . and ye visited Me not." "He that rejecteth you rejecteth Me; and he that rejecteth Me rejecteth Him that sent Me."[5] Just as the head suffers with each throb of pain in any of its members, so does Christ suffer through the centuries each slight or wrong meted out to one of His own. God knows with a *knowledge, bathed in love*.

His Love Transcends His Knowledge. It is much to know that God knows, but infinitely better that God loves us better than He knows. He is not primarily Knowledge but Love, and His love is different from human love only in its intensity and profundity. It has heights

---

[1] Exod. iv. 31.   [2] Dan. iv. 13.   [3] Mark vi. 47, 48.
[4] Exod. iii. 16, 17.   [5] Luke x. 16.

and depths, lengths and breadths, that pass our discovery, but it is essentially the same as inspires the love of mother, father, husband and friend. These are bars in its oratorio, notes in its organ, flashes of its radiance, syllables in its majestic speech. We could not bear to think that He knew all, unless we were assured of this perfect, all-understanding, enduring, and patient love, which beareth all things, believeth all things, hopeth all things, and never fails, until it has brought us into perfect unity with itself.

And Waits to Perfect Us. That love waits to perfect whatever concerns us. Through all the dark maze of life, it will accompany; by every fiery furnace it will act as a refiner of silver. It will wipe all tears from our eyes, it will comfort us as a mother comforts her firstborn, it will explain in the peace of eternity the *wherefore* of life's sad discipline. Therefore the redeemed of the Lord shall return and come with singing into Zion. They shall obtain gladness and joy, and sorrows and sighings shall flee away. Weeping can endure only for the night, but Joy shall usher in the Eternal Dawn.

The Preparation of the Messenger

Exodus 3:1-12

1. Now Moses kept the flock of Jethro his father-in-law, the priest of Midian: and he led the flock to the backside of the desert, and came to the mountain of God, *even* to Horeb.

2. And the angel of the Lord appeared unto him in a flame of fire out of the midst of a bush: and he looked, and, behold, the bush burned with fire, and the bush *was* not consumed.

3. And Moses said, I will now turn aside, and see this great sight, why the bush is not burnt.

4. And when the Lord saw that he turned aside to see, God called unto him out of the midst of the bush, and said, Moses, Moses. And he said, Here *am* I.

5. And he said, Draw not nigh hither: put off thy shoes from off thy feet, for the place whereon thou standest *is* holy ground.

6. Moreover he said, I *am* the God of thy father, the God of Abraham, the God of Isaac, and the God of Jacob. And Moses hid his face; for he was afraid to look upon God.

7. And the Lord said, I have surely seen the affliction of my people which *are* in Egypt, and have heard their cry by reason of their taskmasters; for I know their sorrows;

8. And I am come down to deliver them out of the hand of the Egyptians, and to bring them up out of that land unto a good land and a large, unto a land flowing with milk and honey; unto the place of the Canaanites, and the Hittites, and the Amorites, and the Perizzites, and the Hivites, and the Jebusites.

9. Now therefore, behold, the cry of the children of Israel is come unto me: and I have also seen the oppression wherewith the Egyptians oppress them.

10. Come now therefore, and I will send thee unto Pharaoh, that thou mayest bring forth my people the children of Israel out of Egypt.

11. And Moses said unto God, Who *am* I, that I should go unto Pharaoh, and that I should bring forth the children of Israel out of Egypt?

12. And he said, Certainly I will be with thee; and this *shall be* a token unto thee, that I have sent thee: When thou hast brought forth the people out of Egypt, ye shall serve God upon this mountain.

THE PREPARATION OF THE MESSENGER
Exodus 3:1-12

"I am come down . . ."
"Come now, I will send thee . . ."

God Works Through Human Instrumentality. Is there no discrepancy between these two announcements? If God has Himself come down to do the work of redemption, what need of Moses? Would not a word from those Almighty lips be enough? Why summon a shepherd, a lonely and unbefriended man, a man who has already failed once, and from whom the passing years have stolen his manhood's prime, to work out with painful elaboration, and through a series of bewildering disappointments, the purposed emancipation? But this is not an isolated case. Throughout the entire scheme of Divine government, we meet with the principle of mediation. God ever speaks to men, and works for them, through the instrumentality of men. Chosen agents are called into the inner circle, to catch the Divine thought and mirror the Divine character, and then sent back to their fellows, to cause them to partake. God never works from the many to the individual, but from the individual to the many. "He made known His ways unto Moses," but only His acts unto the children of Israel.

What is My Part? Each of us should therefore put to himself the questions: What is my destiny? What am I here for? What part am I to play in the Redemption of this world? How can I best help Christ in His mighty programme of putting down all rule and authority and power, so that God may be All in all?

Quite certainly a project vast as this may involve long and stern education; but more than half the bitterness of human sorrow disappears, if we understand that we are being trained for some high purpose, which shall react, not only on ourselves, but on others in ever-widening circles.

NOTICE THREE OF THE FACTORS THAT WERE EMPLOYED TO FIT MOSES FOR THE STUPENDOUS TASK THAT AWAITED HIM:

Three Kinds of Preparations: In the Home. (1) THE TRAINING OF THE HOME. In after-life he described himself as a nursing-father, carrying the whole congregation in his bosom—a metaphor surely borrowed from his experiences with his two infant-boys. We can hardly imagine Elijah being qualified to lead a great mixed host of men, women, and children! He lacked some of that humanness which characterised the great lawgiver, who was probably less stern that Michael Angelo's noble statue suggests. Even the greatest mountains have foothills covered with gardens and vineyards. The letters of Martin Luther to his little daughter reveal the tender warmth of his strong and virile nature. Gershom and Eliezer probably awoke emotions of pity and patience, which stood Moses in good stead in after days, when the petulance and murmuring of the people threatened to become unbearable.

In the Desert. (2) THE SILENCE AND SOLITUDE OF THE DESERT. For the most part, so travellers say, the Sinaitic region is one of unvarying calm and stillness. The sun rises out of a dull haze in the East, and moves through the heavens in unclouded majesty, bathing the earth in a perfect flood of light. The great gaunt mountains cast broad shadows, morning and afternoon, over the plains and valleys at their base; whilst at noon they are scorched by an almost vertical heat. In the evening, the orb of day sets in a purple haze. The stars come out immediately in the purple sky, till all their hosts are assembled. "No song of birds enlivens the solitude. No hum of insect life breaks the stillness." The bleat of a goat by day may be heard at a distance of half-a-mile; and by night the occasional cry of a jackal makes the environing silence only more absolute.

The Value of the Solitudes. When the shepherd has led his flock from the rude sheepfold where they have spent the night, to the pastures where they are to browse—he has little else to do, but watch that they do not stray far away. What an opportunity is thus afforded, and was afforded to Moses, for recalling the past, anticipating the future, or meditating on those great mysteries of life and death, of God and the future life, which have always wielded so great an influence over the Oriental. Solitude like this is of priceless value in the nurture of strong and noble souls, and has given the wilderness, the hermitage, and the monastic cell a singular power in the formation of the religious leaders of the world.

Heart Hunger. (3) THE HUNGER OF AN EXILE'S HEART. There are clear evidences of an Egyptian occupation of the Sinaitic peninsula, in those portions at least, adjacent on the Red Sea. Mines were worked there, in the workings of which, long deserted, inscriptions have been discovered that throw a flood of light on the early inhabitants of this region. It is more than probable, therefore, that though the secret was rigorously withheld from Pharaoh, Moses' resort was well known among his kinsfolk. He would be kept informed of the increasing anguish of his people. Suffering as a mother suffers when watching her sick child, he was quite powerless to assist, and this sense of impotence wrought powerfully in tempering the impetuosity of his nature.

The Service of Waiting. A Christian minister, invalided from active service, whilst his life was yet young in him, once told the writer that he felt as the prisoner in some embattled fortress may, who from the beetling crag on which his prison is perched looks down on the former scenes of his activity, compelled to watch others engaged in prosecuting and achieving the very objects to which he was once devoted. Some such heart-sickness must often have eaten like acid into the eager nature of Moses. It seemed as though he were a lover doomed to stand by and see his betrothed perish at his side, whilst he was unable to give succour, or even warning. All that he could do was to pray with strong cryings and tears.

The Influence of This Training. The effect of all this revealed itself in his response to the first intimation of the Divine intention for him to become the chosen messenger and instrument of Redemption —"Who am I, that I should go unto Pharaoh, and that I should bring forth the children of Israel out of Egypt?"

Modesty of Moses Accompanies Competence. The idea staggered him. The light shone too strongly for eyes long accustomed to obscurity. He could mind a flock of sheep, but never emancipate a nation. But in speaking thus he showed how perfectly the discipline of the forty years in the wilderness had wrought his fitness for the stupendous task. As long as a man holds that he is easily able to do some great deed of heroism and faith, he is probably incompetent for it, but when he protests his inability, and puts away the earliest proposals, though made by the Almighty Himself, he gives the first unmistakable sign that he has been rightly designated.

God's Noblest Servants Similarly Humble. This sense of unfitness has been characteristic of God's noblest servants. When Israel was brought very low because of Midian, and the Angel-Jehovah bade Gideon go and save his country, he replied, "Oh Lord, wherewith shall I save Israel? behold, my family is the poorest in Manasseh, and I am the least in my father's house." And when the word of Jehovah came to Jeremiah with the assurance that he was to be a prophet unto the nations, the young scion of a family of priests answered, "Ah, Lord God! behold, I cannot speak: for I am a child." It was only after Peter had confessed that he was a sinful man, and had asked Christ to depart from him, that the Lord told him he should henceforth catch men.

The Evidence of Later Centuries. All through the subsequent centuries, the men who have felt that they were not worthy or able, have been God's chosen instruments, it being always granted that with their sense of incompetence there have been present also a willingness to yield themselves to the will of God, and a strong faith in His almightiness. I cannot, but He can; I am but a brittle shaft, but He can wing me to the heart of His foes; I am but a broken pitcher, yet if I can only hold a cup of water, He will use me! The jawbone of an ass, an ox-goad, a sling and stones, five barley-loaves and two small fish, a quill dropped from the wing of the bird—such are the instruments by which the Master wins His greatest victories!

The Burning Acacia Bush. THERE MUST BE ADDED THE SYMBOL OF THE BURNING BUSH. The tree most characteristic of that locality is the wild acacia, a shaggy thorn-bush. On one occasion—perhaps at night, else it had been less easy to discern the gleam of sacred fire—when the sheep were folded in some rude pen, or resting on a green oasis, Moses suddenly found himself confronted by a thorn-bush wrapt in flame. Such a spectacle was not absolutely novel. The ashes of an Arab fire, or the flash of the forked-lightning, will sometimes kindle the dry gorse or grass of the wilderness. The flame suddenly darts upwards and lightens the whole sky, but as suddenly dies down.

The remarkable fact in the present instance was, that though the bush burned with fire, it did not crackle or diminish, no leaf curled and no branch charred. It burned, but was not consumed.

Its Import. It has been generally supposed that this was intended as an emblem of Israel in Egypt, existing undiminished amid their fiery trials. The fathers of the Presbyterian Church took it to be a symbol of the words: "Persecuted, but not forsaken: cast down, but not destroyed." Undoubtedly it is a great truth, that we may be enwrapt in the flame of acute suffering, and the fire will only consume the cankerworms and caterpillars that preyed upon the verdure of our spiritual life, without scorching the tiniest twig, or consuming the most fragile blossom. The burning fiery furnace will not singe a hair of your head, though it will free you from your fettering bonds. But this can hardly be the truth which the Divine Spirit designed to teach, for it would not have been needful to bid Moses unsandal his feet, if the fire had simply stood for pain. Great as is our respect for suffering, and for those who are called to suffer, we could not feel that so it demanded a homage which is befitting for God alone.

Fire an Emblem of Deity. Throughout Scripture, Fire is the emblem of Deity. Even the rites of heathendom were based on the belief that the swift power and ruddy tongues of fire were symbols of Divine attributes. When God entered into covenant with Abram, His Presence was denoted by the lamp of fire that passed between the pieces. The pledge of God's leadership of Israel was the pillar which in the daylight seemed only a column of wavering smoke, but when darkness fell was shown to be composed of flame—a veritable fire-cloud. "Who among us," exclaims Isaiah, referring evidently to the environing Presence of Jehovah, "shall dwell in the everlasting burnings?" The mission of our Lord was a Baptism of Fire; and on the Day of Pentecost the Holy Spirit's chosen symbol was the fire that sat on each meekly bowed head. In the Apocalyptic Vision seven lamps of fire are seen burning perpetually before the Throne.

The Burning Bush the Symbol of God's Presence. Therefore when this bush is said to have burned with fire, which evidently differed from all other fire in not requiring fuel, and in the presence of which Moses must needs take the lowliest posture of reverence, we are constrained to conclude that it was the symbol of Jehovah's Presence, and that in its undiminishing yet unreplenished energy, this unfuelled fire was another expression of the Divine announcement, I AM.

God does not Despise the Humble Bush. It is not said that the bush was in the fire, but that the fire was in the bush; clearly, therefore, we have here a picture of God's Presence in the midst of His despised and suffering people. Note that the selected emblem for them was not the oak in its strength, the cedar with its fragrance, the fir-tree for its elegance or height, but just a common thorn. The same Hebrew word is used here as in Judges ix. 14, where it is rendered "bramble"; and yet God condescended to make this lowly common shrub His Throne. It is the old old story: "The base things of the world, and the things that are despised, did God choose, yea, and the things that are not, that He might bring to nought the things that are: that no flesh should glory before God. But of Him are ye in Christ Jesus."[1]

He Dwelt 'Midst a Nation of Slaves. IT WAS TRUE OF THE HEBREW PEOPLE. Amid all their degradation and misery they were dear to God. Though to the proud Egyptians they seemed as the common bramble, God was in the midst of them, and God would help them right early. Let us not forget this, when we look out upon the masses of mankind, and especially the savage-races, and the child-races. Wordsworth taught us the value of lives which were apparently commonplace and uninteresting. Here are the titles of some of his poems: *The Little Cottage Girl, Alice Fell, Lucy Grey, The Old Waggoner, The Sailor's Mother, The Old Leech Gatherer.* In the meanest flower that blows, and in the humblest life embosomed in our great cities, lie thoughts too deep for tears. This, however, is the greatest glory of all, that there is no stratum of the world's population, no classes in the national life, no circles or sects which God contemns. He who broods over the waste places of the wilderness, and clothes the grass of the field, cares as much for the gipsy encampment on the common as for the occupants of an imperial palace.

God With Man. Though He is the High and Holy One, "inhabiting Eternity," a stable is His chosen birthplace, and a borrowed grave His only resting-place after the sore travail of the Cross. Emmanuel is His rightful name—"God with man."

In the glow of that celestial fire, Moses caught sight of the light of heaven shining above the lot of his enslaved brethren; his faith beheld their dearness to God, their safety under His care, their glorious destiny, and the recompense of their reward; and he felt more than ever ready to suffer in their affliction, to share their present nearness to God, and their ultimate recompense of reward.

Moses' Humility Brings Him Renewed Hope for His People. IT WAS ALSO TRUE OF HIMSELF. Before that bush burned at his feet, Moses had probably felt his limitations so acutely that he had seemed to himself a sherd of broken pottery, forgotten as a dead man out-of-mind, forsaken and forlorn. But when he beheld the emblem of the Almighty burning steadily in a common bush, a new conception

[1] 1 Cor. i. 28–30.

leapt up in his heart. His life-work might yet be accomplished by the union of his worthless nature with the Eternal Being of God. He was required to become, not an agent, but an instrument; not a promoter, but a conveyer; not a source, but a channel.

This transformed him. The question was no longer, What can I do for God? but, What may not God do through me? He had simply to walk with God, and do His bidding; nay, to yield himself to God, that the Almighty might work in and through him for His own good pleasure.

On one occasion, when a crowded audience had assembled to hear Paganini play, the great violinist, to the dismay of those who had paid great prices for their seats, deliberately broke all the strings of his instrument save one; and then triumphantly holding up the violin before the people cried, "One string and Paganini!" Ah, what cannot God do, when He obtains entire possession and control of one nature, wholly yielded to Him? There are no limits, except those imposed by our Unbelief.

The Fire of God's Presence Needs no Fuel. Yield yourself to Him; and if you should ever be tempted to fear that you cannot retain His mighty indwelling by your vows, prayers, or tears, remember that this Fire needs no Fuel, that it is not by our works of Righteousness, but by His grace that He comes to dwell with us and in us. You need supply nothing, but a humble, lowly, penitent, and obedient heart.

"When I am weak, then am I strong."
"I live, yet not I, but Christ liveth in me."
"I can do all things in Christ that strengtheneth me."
"His strength is made perfect in weakness."
"And the Lord clothed Himself with Gideon."

THE NAME OF NAMES!

Exodus 3:13-22

13. And Moses said unto God, Behold, *when* I come unto the children of Israel, and shall say unto them, The God of your fathers hath sent me unto you; and they shall say to me, What *is* his name? what shall I say unto them?

14. And God said unto Moses, I AM THAT I AM: and he said, Thus shalt thou say unto the children of Israel, I AM hath sent me unto you.

15. And God said moreover unto Moses, Thus shalt thou say unto the children of Israel, The Lord God of your fathers, the God of Abraham, the God of Isaac, and the God of Jacob, hath sent me unto you: this *is* my name for ever, and this *is* my memorial unto all generations.

16. Go, and gather the elders of Israel together, and say unto them, The Lord God of your fathers, the God of Abraham, of Isaac, and of Jacob, appeared unto me, saying, I have surely visited you, and *seen* that which is done to you in Egypt:

17. And I have said, I will bring you up out of the affliction of Egypt unto the land of the Canaanites, and the Hittites, and the Amorites, and the Perizzites, and the Hivites, and the Jebusites, unto a land flowing with milk and honey.

18. And they shall hearken to thy voice: and thou shalt come, thou and the elders of Israel, unto the king of Egypt, and ye shall say unto him, The Lord God of the Hebrews hath met with us; and now let us go, we beseech thee, three days' journey into the wilderness, that we may sacrifice to the Lord our God.

19. And I am sure that the king of Egypt will not let you go, no, not by a mighty hand.

20. And I will stretch out my hand, and smite Egypt with all my wonders which I will do in the midst thereof: and after that he will let you go.

21. And I will give this people favour in the sight of the Egyptians: and it shall come to pass, that, when ye go, ye shall not go empty:

22. But every woman shall borrow of her neighbour, and of her that sojourneth in her house, jewels of silver, and jewels of gold, and raiment: and ye shall put *them* upon your sons, and upon your daughters; and ye shall spoil the Egyptians.

THE NAME OF NAMES!

Exodus 3:13-22

Jehovah or Jahveh. "I AM THAT I AM." The capital letters here indicate that "the Lord" stands for the four Hebrew consonants which represent the personal name of the God of Israel. For centuries they have been pronounced *Jehovah*, but probably that pronunciation is a mistake. Scholars tell us that the sacred Name should be pronounced *Jahveh*. It is impossible, however, to be sure that even this is the correct pronunciation, because the Jews have always refused to utter that mysterious and awful word. They shrink from taking it on mortal and polluted lips. Whenever they meet it in reading the Scriptures aloud they substitute the word *Adonai*.

It is strange that for some reason this name of God is obscured to the English reader. For the most part it is rendered by the word "Lord." And though the printers have tried to remedy the mistake by printing *Lord* in capitals, whenever it stands for the sacred name, yet the English Version misses its majestic repetition. In this the American Revised Version is to be preferred to our own; for there the Name is printed as Jehovah, whenever these four consonants occur in the original. Whilst admitting that *Jehovah* is probably not the original pronunciation of the word, it has so many hallowed associations, that, in face of the difficulty of knowing what the original pronunciation was, common use and wont justify us in retaining it.

The Divine Name. I. THE DIVINE NAME. When Moses anticipated that the Hebrew people would almost certainly ask for the Name of the God Who had commissioned him, he did not mean that they had no knowledge of the God of their fathers, but that they would be anxious to be assured as to His essential quality and nature. In the ancient world a name stood for some special trait or characteristic; and men gave names to their gods, to specialise some attribute of their nature that seemed predominant. The Egyptians, for instance, set much store by the names of their gods, which in every case had a significance. Ammon was "the concealed"; Phthah, "the revealer"; Ra, "the swift." Hitherto the God of Israel had borne no name which could be called His proper name. He had been described as El "the High"; or Shaddai, "the Mighty"; or Jehovah, "the Existent"; but none of these had been distinctly His proper name. What was done at this time was to select from among these titles one that should be distinctly His own, and to impart to it a new connotation.

The Name Becomes Fixed. Henceforth this Name, which had previously been little used, and perhaps less understood, predominated over every other, was cherished by the Hebrew race as a sacred treasure, and recognised by those around them as the proper appellation of the one and only God whom they worshipped. In this sense it is inscribed on the famous Moabite Stone.

Its Significance: Personality. The significance of this word is so deep, that, as the margin indicates, no one rendering can convey all its connotation. The first element in it is *the Personality of God.* Mark that sublime egoism, "I am." We may not be able to define what personality is; but we know what we mean when we speak of ourselves or of others as persons; and whatever we mean to convey, when we use the term in these limited senses, is obviously what we mean when we speak of the personality of God. There cannot be less in the Creator than we discover in the creature. God could not be less a personality than Moses, whom He addressed and called into fellowship with Himself. Over the veiled statue of the Egyptian Isis was the famous inscription, "I am the thing that is, and was, and shall be": but henceforth Israel was not to bear witness to a mere characterless substance underlying the universe, but to a living Personality, distinct from all other beings and things, and transcendent above them—not It, but He. "There is one God and Father of all, Who is over all, and through all, and in all";[1] and John, writing to the seven Churches, is equally emphatic in his benediction: "Grace to you, and Peace, from Him which is and which was and which is to come . . . the Almighty."[2]

We must beware against losing the Personality of God in a formless mist of being. He is in all, but He is distinct from all; and if we are humble pupils of our Lord He will reveal to us the Father, "for no

[1] Eph. iv. 6.   [2] Rev. i. 4, 8.

one knoweth the Son, save the Father; neither doth any know the Father, save the Son, and to whomsoever the Son willeth to reveal Him."

Not an Egyptian "It" but a Living He. We should be unwilling to receive anything less. As the Spirit reveals the Son, so does the Son reveal the Father. In our daily prayer we should linger before the Infinite Holy, until we become aware of the personal contact of our nature with His. It is a supreme moment in the experience, when what had been a cloud of nebulous luminosity suddenly yields to the lens of faith, and the Sun of the Divine Nature becomes apparent. Such was the experience which befell Moses at the burning bush, when his spirit was confronted by the Spirit of the Eternal God, and when that Voice broke the silence of the ages, saying, I AM. The words of another of God's ancient saints must have been suggested by just such an ecstatic hour: "I had heard of Thee by the hearing of the ear; but now mine eye seeth Thee."[1]

The Eternity of God. The next element in this sublime name is THE ETERNITY OR UNCHANGEABLENESS OF GOD. "I AM." The Eternal is not primarily the ever-enduring or everlasting; but that which is independent of time, which is not measured by the flight of years, which is unregistered by the revolutions of the earth, or unaffected by the sweep of systems through vast cycles around some central sun. Strictly speaking, there is no past or future tense in the Divine Vocabulary. When God appears to employ them, it is by way of accommodation to our limited horizons. There is no *was* or *will be* with Him, but always the present tense. All that He was to the fathers, He is to-day; and all that He will be to their children, He is now. Nothing to learn: nothing to acquire: nothing to become. He alone is Reality, as contrasted with the vanities of heathen deities. "The gods of the heathen are idols, but He made the Heavens."

The Reality of God. He alone exists in the majesty of unchanging Being, and abides unaltered amid the ceaseless flux and mutation of His creations. "Thou, Lord, in the beginning hast laid the foundation of the earth, and the Heavens are the works of Thy hands: they shall perish; but Thou continuest: and they all shall wax old as doth a garment; and as a mantle shalt Thou roll them up . . . and they shall be changed: but Thou art the same, and Thy years shall not fail."[2]

[1] Job xlii. 5.   [2] Heb. i. 10–12.

The Unapproachable Glory of God. There is a further suggestion in this Name—THE UNAPPROACHABLE GLORY OF THE DIVINE BEING. "I am *that* I am." There is no equivalent for God but God. If you place God on the one side of your symbol of equation (=), there is nothing to put on the other but Himself. The whole creation, from the loftiest seraphim to the lowest zoophyte, would not balance the scale of His Ineffable Personality. When we speak of Him, we have no comparison with which to describe Him. God is God. "To whom then will ye liken God? or what likeness will ye compare unto Him?" "To whom then will ye liken Me, that I should be equal to Him? saith the Holy One."[1] "I am God, and there is none else; I am God, and there is none like Me." "I am *that* I am."

The Redemptive Purpose of God. In addition, this further thought may be added, as suggested by the tense in the Hebrew, OF THE DIVINE GOINGS FORTH OF GOD IN REDEMPTION. It would take too long to prove the identification of the name of God with Redemption. It is one of the commonplaces of biblical knowledge and interpretation. But the superlative glory of God's redemptive purpose cannot be realised in any one age or act. It is progressive, ever-widening in scope, ever-increasing in volume. The deliverance of the chosen people from the bondage of Egypt was but one of the earliest chapters in the great volume of redemption, which is being studied in successive chapters by other orders of being, as they are struck off from the types of our human story. When, therefore, the margin suggests, as one rendering of Jehovah, "I will be that I will be," we are not to infer that God was capable of becoming what He was not already; but that He was going to unfold before the eyes of men thoughts and purposes which from the beginning had been latent within His nature, but waited to be unfolded in acts of grace and salvation, that in turn were destined to live for ever in the memory of man.

These then are the contents of this great Name, which is God's "memorial to all generations." The name by which He would be recognised; His signature written across nature, history, and religion; the keep-sake and forget-me-not in the hearts of those who love Him. There is an especial tenderness and beauty, therefore, when we utter reverently and humbly that great name in our devotions, never forgetting that our Father which is in Heaven is Jehovah.

[1] Isa. xl. 18, 25.

God's Immanence. II. THE UNITY AND SIGNIFICANCE OF NATURE. That Jehovah should make Himself known in the bush teaches us His Immanence in the commonplaces. As we have already seen, Israel, in comparison with the mighty nations around, was only as a thorn-bush. Those might be compared with oak, cedar, or elm, but the chosen people with the bramble. One obvious lesson of the extraordinary phenomenon that arrested Moses must therefore have been, that God, whose presence is ever symbolised by flame, was in the midst of His people.

The Symbolism of the Burning Bush. But is not the symbol capable of further applications? *May not that bush stand for Nature generally?* The ordinary man sees in the world around only what a brute sees, but the saint detects a divine beauty there. The Poet-priest of nature, Wordsworth, was on one occasion rambling through his beloved Lake District, and came on a single primrose growing upon a rock. He began to think about it, and all that lay behind and beyond its fragile beauty, until it opened as a door into the infinite. His mystical reverie finally expressed itself thus: "Thou hast become to me court of Deity." Did not the fire burn in that primrose! The poet Blake has given utterance to the same thought in his own gorgeous phrasing: "When the morning sun ascends the Eastern sky, you may behold a yellow disc, whereas I shall see and hear the infinite multitude of the heavenly host, crying Holy, Holy, Holy."

The Christian Doctrine not Pantheism. These moods and expressions must not be confounded with pantheism. Pantheism says, All is God, and God is the All. But to us God is more than the totality of His works. He is in all, but He is above all. The Bible affirms that everything which our senses and minds are aware of is part of a universal order, and the manifestation of the Will, the Thought, and Being of God: but that God is as distinct as the artist from the picture. In a book recently published there are some interesting reminiscences of a very brilliant woman, Susan Ferrier. She was once asked to write her name in a birthday-book, and in addition her deepest wish. She wrote, "My deepest wish is, that life to me may never lose its halo." That was a noble wish. That there should always be a mystical light on life, a mysterious significance, a divine fire; that from everything there might be a path leading out to the infinite; that on common objects might tremble the gleam of that light which is the light of all our seeing, and which never shone on sea or shore. This, however, is not given to every one. Mrs. Barrett Browning spoke truly when she sang:

> "Every common bush aglow with God,
> But only he who sees takes off his shoes."

May we, like Moses, ever have the seeing eye which is begotten by Purity of Heart. "Blessed are the pure in heart, for they shall see God."

Jehovah the God of the Past. III. THE UNITY OF THE GENERATIONS OF MANKIND. Twice over Jehovah spoke of Himself as the God of the great past. "I am the God of thy fathers, the God of Abraham, the God of Isaac, and the God of Jacob." And again: "And God said moreover unto Moses, Thus shalt thou say unto the children of Israel, Jehovah, the God of your fathers, the God of Abraham, the God of Isaac, the God of Jacob, hath sent me unto you." How tender was that assurance! As the people reviewed the past, together with their reverence for the patriarchs, they must have been aware of phases of character and incidents of experience which were far from creditable. Did not Abraham go down into Egypt, and deny Sarah? Did not Isaac do the same? Did not Jacob merit the name which was afterwards altered to Israel? Yet God bore with, forgave, and saved them! Would He do less for their children?

He had Saved Their Fathers of Old. Did not His past mercies and promises to their fathers prove Him to be the God of their succeeding race? Need they fear One who for so many centuries had shown Himself to be long-suffering and gracious, full of mercy, and abounding in loving kindness and truth!

IV. Our Lord discovered yet more in these words than all this. THEY SPOKE TO HIM OF THE UNITY BETWEEN THE TWO WORLDS.

The Testimony of Jesus. The Sadducees came to Him one day. Their main position was that there could be neither resurrection, angel, nor spirit. They challenged therefore the teaching of Jesus as to the eternal world and life beyond death. The only authority that they would acknowledge was that of Moses, and our Lord had to rebut their theories from the Pentateuch. This He did with amazing and crushing power, by referring to this passage. "What," said He in effect, "did God mean, when He described Himself as the God of men who had died long before? Did He not infer that they were still alive? He is not the God of dead people, but of living.

When therefore He said, I *am* the God of your fathers, He must have meant that they were all existing somewhere, within His ken, and beneath His care."

Jehovah not the God of the Dead, but of the Living. In other words, you cannot predicate non-existence of souls that He describes as living unto Him! The dead are only the living who have passed through the experience of dying, which is as definite and specific as birth. Death is an act, not a state; a transition, not a condition; a passage across a bridge, like that which links palace and prison above the still lagoons at Venice. Some one has said that death is no more than if in an express train a man were suddenly to stand up, take off his coat, wrap it together, and cast it through the window on the metals—he would go on with his journey without it.

Death but a Passage Across a Bridge. What a thought is this! All the myriads that have fallen on the battlefield or gone down to the depths of ocean, or have been overwhelmed in the snow or sand, the myriads upon myriads of the human family who have died, are all living somewhere, in the full possession of their faculty, in the buoyant exercise of their energy, revelling in a life not less but more intense, than that which was theirs in the days of their flesh.

The Meeting at the Bush in the Presence of Witnesses. May we not combine with the idea of their continued existence the further thought, which seems implied in the Divine reference to the fathers, that they were watching the evolution of the Divine ideal? It was as though God felt (speaking in human terms) that with their expectant eyes fixed on Him, he could not do otherwise than redeem the chosen people and perform the promises, on which He had caused them to hope. It was in the presence of a great cloud of witnesses that God met Moses at the bush, pledged Himself to deliver His people, and ultimately led them forth.

It is in the presence of our fathers that God still deals with *us*! He remembers the prayers which they poured out for our welfare and salvation, and can never disappoint them. We are compassed about with a great cloud of witnesses, who are not only watching us, but watching the steps by which God is working out His perfect plan with regard to us.

The Active Invisible. In a subsequent interview God is represented as saying: "I am Jehovah. I also established my covenant with

Abraham, with Isaac, and with Jacob . . . and I have remembered My covenant, and I will bring you out." This again corroborates what we have just said. With the wistful, expectant gaze of "the fathers" upon Him, it was as though God had no alternative but to act as He did.

—the Cause of God's Covenant. He would have been ashamed to be called their God, if He had not led their children forth to the City which He had prepared.[1] He cannot deny Himself: He must needs work for His own name sake. "Hath He said, and shall He not do it? Hath He spoken, and shall He not make it good?"

Covenant Ties. Let us look often into the Covenant with which our God has bound Himself with Christ and His Seed. Let us claim its provisions: let us expect Him to do as He has said: let us push the fences of our appropriation further and further back, until they reach the furthest limits of His engagement with past generations and our own. He owes much to them as well as to ourselves!

Men "Die" but Are Alive with God. There is a sense, therefore, in which our fathers and we are one. We are come to the spirits of the just made perfect. Those who have passed the flood, and those who are passing it, compose one great congregation, one mighty host. The Jerusalem which is above is the mother of us all. In sympathy and love the sainted dead are still with us. We touch them in our loftiest experiences, and commune with them when nearest to our Lord. Though in man's common talk they are said to be dead, it is not so. They have died, that is all. They are yet with us in sympathy and love, because without us they cannot be made perfect.

> " Secure from change in their high-hearted ways,
> Beautiful evermore, and with the rays
> Of morn on them, white shields of Expectation.
> I with uncovered head
> Salute the sacred dead;
> They come transfigured back.

New Testament Testimony in Christ's Words. IV. THE FULFILMENT OF THIS NAME IN CHRIST. We recall Christ's own words: "I am come in My Father's Name." On three separate occasions He used the great and awful Name which was spoken at the bush. Once it was in the murky night, when He came to His disciples through the

---

[1] Heb. xi. 16.

storm, and quieted their outcry, saying, "Be of good cheer, *I am*."[1]
Another time it was uttered, not to the teachers of Israel, or to the
listening multitudes, or even to His disciples, but to one sinful woman,
an outcast and an alien, and He said, "*I am*, I that speak to you."[2]
The third time was when the Jews were insisting that He could not
have seen Abraham, and He replied, "Before Abraham was, *I am*."[3]

Indeed, throughout His earthly ministry, He was filling in the
meaning of the great words, I AM. "I am the Bread of Life"; "I
am the Light of the World"; "I am the Door of the Sheep"; "I am
the Good Shepherd"; "I am the Resurrection and the Life"; "I am
the true Vine." Age-long is the cry of the human heart, "What is
His Name?" "Show us the Father." There is but one answer: "He
that hath seen Me hath seen the Father"; "God was in Christ,
reconciling the world unto Himself." "He was manifested in the
flesh, justified in the spirit, seen of angels, preached among the
nations, believed on in the world, received up in glory." "The Word
was made Flesh, and tabernacled among us, and we beheld His
Glory, as of the Only Begotten of the Father."

> " And so the Word had breath, and wrought
> With human hands the Creed of Creeds,
> In loveliness of perfect deeds,
> More strong than all poetic thought."

[1] John vi. 20.   [2] John iv. 26.   [3] John viii. 58.

THE CREDENTIALS OF THE MESSENGER

Exodus 4:1-9

1. And Moses answered and said, But, behold, they will not believe me, nor hearken unto my voice: for they will say, The Lord hath not appeared unto thee.

2. And the Lord said unto him, What *is* that in thine hand? And he said, A rod.

3. And he said, Cast it on the ground. And he cast it on the ground, and it became a serpent; and Moses fled from before it.

4. And the Lord said unto Moses, Put forth thine hand, and take it by the tail. And he put forth his hand, and caught it, and it became a rod in his hand:

5. That they may believe that the Lord God of their fathers, the God of Abraham, the God of Isaac, and the God of Jacob, hath appeared unto thee.

6. And the Lord said furthermore unto him, Put now thine hand into thy bosom. And he put his hand into his bosom: and when he took it out, behold, his hand *was* leprous as snow.

7. And he said, Put thine hand into thy bosom again. And he put his hand into his bosom again; and plucked it out of his bosom, and, behold, it was turned again as his *other* flesh.

8. And it shall come to pass, if they will not believe thee, neither hearken to the voice of the first sign, that they will believe the voice of the latter sign.

9. And it shall come to pass, if they will not believe also these two signs, neither hearken unto thy voice, that thou shalt take of the water of the river, and pour *it* upon the dry *land*: and the water which thou takest out of the river shall become blood upon the dry *land*.

THE CREDENTIALS OF THE MESSENGER
Exodus 4:1-9

"Wonder" and "Sign", how they Differ. "THE VOICE OF THE SIGN." The word *sign* should be noticed. The Hebrew word thus translated is entirely different from that rendered *wonder*. A *"wonder"* is marvellous and terrific. It represents the startling and awful. It is used in Exodus xxxiv. 10 to give prominence to the terribleness of the wonders by which Jehovah would compel the attention of the heathen. But *"a sign"* is rather the revelation in our ordinary life of some characteristic of the Divine nature or work. It is a symbol of the Unseen. In the *wonder* there is a predominance of the Divine Power and Majesty; in the *sign*, of the Divine Truth and Grace. The one is terrible, the other tender.

Christ's Miracles Were Signs. It is interesting to find that our Lord's miracles, especially in the fourth Gospel, are repeatedly described as *signs*; i.e. they were revelations in view of men of the benevolence of His heart, the beneficence of His will. The three signs described in this chapter were symbolic revelations, therefore, to Moses and the Hebrew race, of the methods which the Almighty Jehovah was about to adopt in the redemption of His people.

Egyptian Magic. It should be remembered that Egypt, whence we derive our word "Gypsy," was steeped in belief in supernaturalism apart from God. The Egyptians, to use the common speech of our time, were adepts in spiritualistic beliefs and practices. They practised necromancy and magic. On one of the monuments "a planchette" is depicted in bas-relief. Whether the phenomena generally designated spiritualism are due to disembodied spirits, or to other spirits not human, or to an unknown power of the human mind, it was absolutely necessary to prove that they were easily within the province of the God of Israel, and that His servants could be empowered by His aid to perform equal and greater marvels.

Three Signs. Therefore these three signs were communicated to Moses, to accredit him for the work on which he was about to engage, and compel the attention of Egypt.

The First Sign. THE SIGN OF THE ROD. What is that in thine hand? It was just a simple shepherd's crook or club; but it was destined to play a notable part in the history of the Exodus. In verse 20, and afterwards, it is described as "the rod of God"; and it was used as an essential feature in many startling miracles that followed, notably at the Red Sea and at the smitten rock. What could more suitably symbolise Moses, in all his limitations and helplessness, than that rod, cut from its root, dry and sapless, without vitality or power of its own?

Moses Cites His Seven Disqualifications. Seven distinct objections were raised by Moses as reasons why he should not undertake the arduous task to which he was called. They have been thus epitomised: Lack of fitness, "who am I, that I should go?" (iii. 11); lack of words, "what shall I say?" (iii. 13); lack of authority, "they will not believe me" (iv. 1); lack of power of speech, "I am not eloquent" (iv. 10); lack of special adaptation, "Send by whom Thou wilt send" (iv. 13); lack of success at his first attempt, "neither hast Thou delivered Thy people at all" (v. 23); lack of acceptance, "the children of Israel have not hearkened unto me" (vi. 12). There never was a completer list! Yet if only he would yield to God, as the rod did to him, if only he were content to be whatever God would have him be, if he would but let God work His will in and through him, there was simply no limit to the service that his individuality might render to God and man.

Steps to the Higher Life. There are three steps which every individual must take in order to fulfil the highest life. Obviously, the first step is *the consciousness of our individual and personal existence.* To some this awakening comes with startling suddenness. In rare biographical records cases are cited of a supreme moment, in which the soul suddenly awoke, and knew that it was distinct from all other beings and things, as an individualised personality. But for most of us self-consciousness comes gradually, as of a sleeper stirring, and starting, and awakening. In one way or another it comes to us all. It is sometimes associated with a revelation of God. We hear Him say, as to Moses, I AM; and we answer forthwith, "Here am I."

Consciousness of Special Gifts. The second step is to self-consciousness, when we become conscious of *capacity*; *with its special* *gifts and endowments.* God says to us, "What is that in thine hand?" These are very various. The gift of *speech*, the eloquence of a Robert Hall or a Dale, of Burke or Sheridan. The gift of *song*, as of a Jenny Lind or a Clara Butt. The gift of *musical composition*, as of a Handel, a Mendelssohn, or a Mozart. The gift of *discovery of natural laws*, as of a Humphry Davy, a Newton, or a David Brewster. The gift of *scholarship*, as Dr. Johnson; or of *healing*, as Sir Frederick Trèves. The gift of *leadership*, as of a Gordon or Havelock; of *teaching*, as Arnold of Rugby; of *statesmanship*, as of a Gladstone or Disraeli; of *mechanical construction*, as of a Brunel; or of *quiet plodding work*, the inestimable gift and capacity for taking pains.

There is always Something in Our Hand. Every life has some capacity. God says to each of us, "What is that in thine hand?" He takes it for granted that there is something there. Do not envy each other, or despise one another. For if you do, you will paralyse your personal capacity and threaten your life with failure. To every one of us is given grace, according to the measure of the gift of God; and perhaps the hardest lesson that any one can learn, is to believe that every gift from heaven is of equal intrinsic worth. Our success is to be measured, not by the character of the capacity, but its realisation and full use.

God Uses what We Have. God always begins by using what we have in hand. Page after page of God's Word reveals that there is a chance for true usefulness, in the consecrated employment of whatever we have already in possession. In the Book of Judges, left-handed Ehud had a single dagger in his hand, and Shamgar an ox-goad: Gideon's three hundred had only pitchers and lamps, and Samson the jawbone of an ass. When David went to smite Goliath, he had a sling in his hand. When the widow appealed to Elisha for help, he said, "What hast thou in the house?" and though there was only a pot of oil, it was sufficient. Six waterpots full of water were all that was needed for our Lord's first sign at Cana; and five barley-loaves with two small fishes were sufficient for the great miracle of hospitality.

But the Capacity must be Trained. This capacity must, of course, be trained by use. We need to be industrious; quick to take the suggestions of friends, and learn from failure; willing to discover many mistakes, but careful never to make the same mistake twice. Many pages of MSS. will be cast into the waste-basket; many a canvas will be spoiled; many a piece of wood or metal will be rendered useless! No preacher and no poet is born. A Robert Hall breaks down in his first sermon, a Tennyson fails to mount at once to fame. The vocalist who is one day to move vast audiences to passionate tears, will have to practise for hours daily and for years. The little girl whose work will one day be the admiration of a wide circle begins with large rude stitches. Dare to begin: dare to fail: dare still to persevere. The muscle grows by use. The hand becomes defter by each fresh operation.

And All must be Consecrated to God. All faculty must be consecrated to God. He gave it. It is the offspring and bears the image of Heaven. The Hallmark of the Creator is upon it. And as we surrender all to His use, we simply give Him back His own. In Him we live, and move, and have our being. In His hand are life and breath and all things. How many of us have really placed our all at His disposal? How many are ready to hold their position, not for the red gold it earns, but as a means of glorifying Christ? Every morning we should kneel down before our Redeemer, and say, "Thou hast made me a physician or a surgeon, a merchant or a salesman, an architect or contractor, a mechanic or a domestic servant, and now I consecrate this calling for to-day, and the opportunities it may bring, to be used by Thee for Thy blessed service." Trust in the Lord with all thine heart, and lean not unto thine own understanding. . . . He shall direct thy path.

Capacity and Opportunity. God unlocks the door of opportunity. It stands open. "Behold, I have set before thee an open door." But it needs pushing and entering. God gives me the chance, but I am responsible to Him for stepping out to use it. It is here that so many lives have failed. Men and women have been conscious of possessing faculty, and have allowed the years to drift past whilst they have been expecting the advent of a supreme crisis. Finally, as they look back, they see that the opportunity did come in some insignificant and commonplace appeal, which they overlooked; and once forfeited, it is never allowed to return.

The Call not Recognised Except by the Few. It was because Dr. Barnardo recognised the appeal of one little street arab, that his noble work for waifs and strays was inaugurated; and because General Booth spoke to a few outcasts in Whitechapel, that the Salvation Army sprang into existence. How apt are those words that Shakespeare puts into the lips of Brutus:

> " There is a tide in the affairs of men
> Which taken at the flood leads on to fortune;
> Omitted, all the voyage of their life
> Is bound in shallows and miseries."

Tennyson puts it in another way, when he says:

> " But well I know
> That unto him who works, and feels he works,
> This same grand year is ever at the doors."

Of course the fact that the opportunity is a lonely and solitary one, of which no one knows but we, or the fact that the exercise we made of it holds us in a secluded and unvisited spot, matters nothing. It is glorious when a human soul is content to work for the eye of God alone, in the spirit of the old monks, who carved the unseen stonework of the minster-roof with as much care as the screen-work of the chancel. Those often quoted words of Gray are not quite accurate:

> " Full many a flower is born to blush unseen,
> And waste its sweetness on the desert air."

Sweetness is never wasted, and there are no deserts. The Lord peoples every solitude with His Presence, and accepts the incense of each sweet floweret. He rejoices in His works. The door of opportunity is there, just where you are, only ask for wisdom to see, and grace to use it aright.

What Opportunity Is. May we not say that opportunity is Christ moving on with set and earnest face towards Jerusalem, and calling on us to accompany Him; or Christ feeling for the multitude thronging Him and asking us to discover who touched Him; or Christ, seeing the crowds gathering, and asking for our loaves and fish, and using our poor service to distribute the fragments from His hands!

It may be that your long years of preparation may eventuate in but one brief hour of triumph, but you will have lived. It may be that after one great act, you will be, like Florence Nightingale, doomed to years of patient suffering, but all those years will be radiant with the after-glow.

It may be that none will understand, none appreciate, none thank you, but you will hear heavenly voices, like chimes of golden bells, hailing you as a companion of their high order.

Heed the Call of God. Be heedful to the call of God; His voice is very small and still. Submit without complaint, not answering again. Obey promptly and courageously the call of duty, which is the call of God. Trust that He will bear the responsibility and ensure success. Be faithful in God's house, as a servant. Thus you will be led in the paths of useful service. God will be glorified and His name hallowed; and you will realise that as you draw upon Him, you can draw; as you give, you can give; as you work, you can work. Whatsoever they did there, He was the doer of it, for of Him, and through Him, and to Him are all things, to Him be the glory for ever!

The Second Sign. THE SECOND SIGN WAS THE CLEANSING OF THE LEPROUS HAND. We may not be able to understand all that the sign meant for Moses; but it means for us, and it may have meant for him, that the terrible taint of pride and uncleanness which besets all God's people, and especially threatens those who are engaged in Christ's work, needs to be cleansed away. It is so easy to become contaminated by the corruption which is in the world through lust. We may be taught a profound lesson by the care with which the instruments required for a surgical operation are rendered aseptic.

God's Instruments must be Clean. The life that is to be a mission from God to the world must be a clean, pure, and holy one. There is the animal in us all, and the man or woman who is anxious to help others must first take that animal by the throat, and choke it, and beat it, until the life is pounded out of it. But this goeth not forth, save by prayer and fasting.

Dr. Labaree was a notable Presbyterian missionary in Persia. After forty years of service he died on the Atlantic, on his way home to the United States. At his funeral, a Persian who had lived from boyhood in the city where Dr. Labaree laboured, said that the two traits which most impressed the natives of that city were, first, his carefulness—he was so faithful and punctilious in the little veracities of life—and second, his unsullied innocence. He had lived for seventy-two years, and went back in cleanness and honour to the great God from whom he came.

"A Message for All." The last address of Bishop Philips Brooks to young men was delivered at the Convention of St. Andrew in his own church at Boston. He came down out of the pulpit, and spoke to them out of his own pure heart from the words, "Be ye clean, that bear the vessels of the Lord." It is a message for us all.

The holy chalice of God's grace may not be carried by a leprous hand. And if any are conscious of the defilement of flesh or spirit, from which the apostle bids us cleanse ourselves, let us now repair to Him Who of old said to the leper "I will: be thou clean." Thrust your hand into your own bosom, and it becomes leprous: thrust it into the wound pierced by the soldier in the side of the Redeemer, and it will become clean as the flesh of a little child.

The Third Sign. THE THIRD SIGN WAS THE WATER TURNED TO BLOOD. We will not stay on it now, because we shall have further opportunities of doing so. It is enough to say that when men are unclean and evil, Nature herself seems to be affected. The whole creation groans and travails until now for the reason of human sin that has subjected it. Indeed, sometimes she seems sentient, and suffers after her fashion. We need not wonder that the rocks were rent when Jesus died; and may be quite willing to believe that even water ran red. There are houses to-day where enormous crimes have been committed, which are uninhabitable, because of the impression which those scenes of blood have left behind on the sentient atmosphere, together with the accompaniment of awful sounds.

Moses is Punished for Holding Back. But though these three signs were given, Moses still held back, and a terrible thing befell. As he declined the sole leadership, he was deprived of its honour and happiness. Aaron was summoned to meet him, and appointed to share the honour of the office, and when speech was needed he must be the chief speaker. "In all outward appearances," as Dean Stanley observes, "Aaron, and not Moses, must have been, in the eyes of the Egyptians, the representative and leader of Israel." Moreover, by his persistent refusal, Moses lost the chance of the high gifts that God would doubtless have conferred.

Let us all beware. If you refuse to use your powers, they will atrophy. If you will not step up to the opportunity which God offers, you will not only miss it, but will live to see it filled by an inferior man to yourself, through whom you may have to suffer many sorrows:

> " Children of yesterday; heirs of to-morrow,
>   What are you weaving—labour or sorrow?
> Look to your looms again; faster and faster
> Fly the great shuttles, prepared by the Master,
>   Life's in the loom; Room for Him—room."

From Servant to Friend

Exodus 4:10-17

10. And Moses said unto the Lord, O my Lord, I *am* not eloquent, neither heretofore, nor since thou hast spoken unto thy servant: but I *am* slow of speech, and of a slow tongue.

11. And the Lord said unto him, Who hath made man's mouth? or who maketh the dumb, or deaf, or the seeing, or the blind? have not I the Lord?

12. Now therefore go, and I will be with thy mouth, and teach thee what thou shalt say.

13. And he said, O my Lord, send, I pray thee, by the hand *of him whom* thou wilt send.

14. And the anger of the Lord was kindled against Moses, and he said, *Is* not Aaron the Levite thy brother? I know that he can speak well. And also, behold, he cometh forth to meet thee: and when he seeth thee, he will be glad in his heart.

15. And thou shalt speak unto him, and put words in his mouth: and I will be with thy mouth, and with his mouth, and will teach you what ye shall do.

16. And he shall be thy spokesman unto the people: and he shall be, *even* he shall be to thee instead of a mouth, and thou shalt be to him instead of God.

17. And thou shalt take this rod in thine hand, wherewith thou shalt do signs.

FROM SERVANT TO FRIEND

Exodus 4:10-17

The Struggle between Moses and the Angel. It was a long struggle between the Angel of the Covenant and Moses, which the division into chapters somewhat obscures, for it is almost certain that this wonderful dialogue continued unbroken from the first arrest of the shepherd before the burning bush till his ultimate decision to go and return to Jethro.

His Excuses. When Isaiah was charted with his great commission, he did hesitate for a moment, but cried, "Here am I, send me." Not so, Moses. Again and again he sought to excuse himself; but as often as he alleged excuses, the Divine Spirit met his objections with infinite patience and tenderness.

And Moses said unto God, Who am I, that I should go unto Pharaoh, and that I should bring forth the children of Israel out of Egypt?
And He said, Certainly I will be with thee.
And Moses said unto God, Behold, when I come unto the children of Israel, and shall say unto them, The God of your fathers hath sent me unto you; and they shall say to me, What is His name? what shall I say unto them?
And God said unto Moses, I AM THAT I AM.
And Moses answered and said, But, behold, they will not believe me, nor hearken unto my voice: for they will say, The Lord hath not appeared unto thee.
And the Lord said unto him, What is that in thine hand?
And Moses said unto the Lord, Oh, Lord, I am not eloquent, neither heretofore, nor since Thou hast spoken unto Thy servant: for I am slow of speech, and of a slow tongue.
And the Lord said unto him, Who hath made man's mouth . . . is it not I, the Lord? Now therefore go, and I will be with thy mouth, and teach thee what thou shalt speak.
And he said, Oh Lord, send, I pray Thee, by the hand of him whom Thou wilt send.
And the anger of the Lord was kindled against Moses, and He said . . .

A Wonderful Colloquy. This was a most remarkable colloquy, and showed with convincing cogency that this diffident and modest man was the predestined instrument for the stupendous work of Redemption. It must be borne in mind that God Himself had come down to redeem. His own right hand and His holy arm were to get Him the victory. He needed no assistance from man, but only an instrument or agent, through whom He might pour forth His saving might.

The Pride and Self-will of Moses. At first, as we have seen, there was much proud self-will in Moses, which needed to be eliminated from his resourceful nature, and therefore he was sent into the wilderness to tend the sheep for forty years, on such pastures as were afforded by the scanty grass or the aromatic shrubs which grew on the rocky ledges of the hill-sides and by the margin of the still mountain lakes. On every side he would be environed by mighty wastes of sand, and red sandstone peaks resembling pyramids of solid flame; whilst over all reigned the silence of an intense solitude, broken only by the occasional bleating of sheep or the musical rush of sand in a tiny glissade—the hour-glass of the desert.

The Advantages of Solitude. It is well for all God's servants to get to the back parts of the desert. There the world and its prizes seem to be child's baubles. The din and noise, the strife and rivalry of human life fail to reach the ear; the crash of an empire, the rumours of war, the plaudits and curses of the crowd are but whispers. No sigh of ambition is heaved there, no fading laurels tempt, no thirst for gold parches the lip. All is hushed, that the soul may sink to its true proportions before the great Glory of God.

Moses had Learned. Moses had learnt his lesson well. Indeed, there was now the danger of exaggeration on the other side. Henceforth he would be as an emptied channel, along which the saving strength of the Most High would pass forth to save Israel from the extremity of suffering in which they sighed, and from which their cry came up unto God. His long sojourn amid the silences of the wilderness, the rusticity of a shepherd's lot, his estrangement from the ways of courts, the slow movement of his speech, the shy diffidence of a man who had become content to be forgotten—these were the reasons why he would have gladly evaded the Divine commission, and dropped back into his lonely and uneventful life.

The Losses of Moses. In his last reply, however, Moses had clearly yielded a pace or two backwards. When he said, "Send, I pray Thee, by the hand of him whom Thou wilt send," he had practically surrendered his resistance. It meant that God must have His way, even though the Divine choice involved his own mission. It was as though he said, "I go because I must: I have no hope of success: I greatly question Thy choice: but if there is no alternative, be it so." "Then was the anger of Jehovah kindled against him." Only on one other occasion did this befall—at the waters of Meribah. In that case he lost Canaan, and in this, as we have seen, he forfeited the sole leadership, which henceforth he shared with his brother, and he missed the endowment of forcible and persuasive speech which seemed to be within his reach, for had not God said, "I will be with thy mouth, and teach thee what thou shalt say?"

Danger of Being too Humbleminded. Well indeed is it when the soul cries with the great Apostle, "We are not sufficient of ourselves to think anything as of ourselves." It is good to go further and, like him, even rejoice in our infirmities, as supplying a better opportunity for the exercise of that Divine Power, which is only perfected in weakness. But we must beware, for there is a hidden line over which self-distrust may not pass, lest it become unbelief. Cherish the lowliest thought you choose of yourself, but unite it with the loftiest conception of God's All-Sufficiency. Self-depreciation may lead to the marring of a useful life. We must think soberly of ourselves, not too lowly, as not too extravagantly. The one talent must not be buried in the earth. Jacob may be only a worm in his own thought, but God can make him a new sharp threshing instrument having teeth, before which the mountains shall become as chaff.

The Result in the Hour of Hesitation. Many of the greatest in the history of the Church have shrunk back abashed and afraid before the call of their age, which has been the call of God. But they have been driven back on Him Who shepherds the starry hosts as flocks in the plains of heaven, gives power to the faint, increases might to them that have no strength.

Moses Yields, and is Rewarded. While there was much in Moses' attitude that grieved the Holy Spirit of God, it is clear, as we have seen, that there was finally the yielded though reluctant will, and the desire to fulfil God's behest. "Send me, if there is no alternative" —that was the utterance of one in whom the Spirit of God had prevailed, and it constituted this the crucial hour in Moses' career. For forty years Moses had acted as a servant, performing his Master's will, so far as he knew it. He had been faithful in the great Household of God as a servant. He had no far horizon, and knew not what his Lord was doing. But from this solemn interview the Lord began to speak with him "face to face," as a man speaketh with his friend.

God's Agents are Helped by Him. The Lord can do much with us as servants, because He knows exactly where to place and how to direct us; but when we have served our apprenticeship on the lower level He summons us, as Moses, to the higher, saying, "No longer do I call you servants; for the servant knoweth not what his lord doeth: but I have called you friends; for all things that I heard from My Father I have made known unto you."[1]

The Experience of Moses may be Ours. Such a transition from the attitude of the servant to the happy fellowship of a friend is within the reach of us all. It is the peculiar glory of Christianity that it annihilates the gulf of the centuries, and admits its adherents to become the trusted Friends of its Founder. Of course it is impossible that we should ever cease to be His loyal and obedient servants. Redeemed at so great a cost, we can never have anything but the most profound reverence for our Redeemer. The surrender with which our real life began will always deepen. Paul, the great apostle, commences his most important Epistle by inscribing himself as "the bondservant of Jesus Christ." Even in the blessed future, we are told that His servants shall serve Him.

Passing from Servant to Friend. But as time goes on, a subtle, but most real, change takes place. We still serve, but as friends, with the most exact and careful service that love inspires. For the wife and mother will do what paid service would never do.

> The bondservant has no option:
> *but the friend serves by choice.*
> The bondservant has his work entrusted to him in pieces:
> *but the friend is initiated into the programme.*
> The bondservant is not at liberty to discuss:
> *but the friend's suggestions are welcomed.*
> The bondservant counts on a reward:
> *but the friend's reward is in the fellowship.*
> The bondservant is jealous of his fellows:
> *but the friend is only too glad of any help that may hasten the conclusion on which his friend is set.*

[1] John xv. 15.

The Confidences of Friendship. It is part of friendship to trust your friend with your ideals and plans. When two of the three mysterious guests who had come to the patriarch's tent went on their way down the descending pathway to the plains of Sodom, and Abraham stood yet before the Lord, the Lord said, "Shall I hide from Abraham that which I do . . . for I have known him." Surely the Lord God will do nothing without first revealing His secret counsel to His friends! "The secret of the Lord is with them that fear Him, and He will show them His covenant."

This gives us the precise view-point of this great interview with Moses, when the entire landscape of the future was divested of clouds and exposed to his view. Read again iii. 16–22, where the programme of the Exodus is recorded with the precision of history. God set before His servant the line of procedure which He was about to adopt, that he might become an intelligent participant.

A Parallel. May we not compare this experience with the relations between a Michel angelo and a Raphael? At first the young student would be bidden to perform the elementary service of the studio; but as he showed himself attentive and careful in cleansing the brushes or preparing the palette, he would be promoted to higher and more delicate duties, until the master would unfold to him the glorious fancies that filled his own heart, and confide to him the execution of certain portions of the canvas which was to live for ever.

There was a sense in which God was alone responsible for the redemption of His people and their creation into a nation; but it was also certain that He could not do it apart from Moses. Browning says, "If any two hearts shall grow into one, they will do more than the world has done." If this is true as between man and man, how much more between man and God; and how truly the might of that union was manifested in the Life-work of "the man of God!"

The Description of Time. To such a Fellowship we are called. It may be that at the beginning of our life we made some egregious blunder, which has cast its shadow on our whole after-career. We also slew our Egyptian and hid him in the sand, but the slow-moving years which have succeeded have altered a great many things in us. We are less confident and boastful, more humble and dependent. The tongue is less arrogant and the bearing less masterful. You have quieted yourself as a wearied child, as a child weaned from its mother. The desert solitudes and silences have wrought their last effect on your character. Reluctant you may be, but you are not rebellious, neither do you turn yourself backward. You have stood the ordeal of perfect obedience and submission. Faithful in a few things, you are now to rule over many, and to enter into the joy of your Lord, which is surely found in the inner secrets of Fellowship.

MEET FOR THE MASTER'S USE

Exodus 4:18-26

18. And Moses went and returned to Jethro his father-in-law, and said unto him, Let me go, I pray thee, and return unto my brethren which *are* in Egypt, and see whether they be yet alive. And Jethro said to Moses, Go in peace.

19. And the Lord said unto Moses in Midian, Go, return into Egypt: for all the men are dead which sought thy life.

20. And Moses took his wife and his sons, and set them upon an ass, and he returned to the land of Egypt: and Moses took the rod of God in his hand.

21. And the Lord said unto Moses, When thou goest to return into Egypt, see that thou do all those wonders before Pharaoh, which I have put in thine hand; but I will harden his heart, that he shall not let the people go.

22. And thou shalt say unto Pharaoh, Thus saith the Lord, Israel *is* my son, *even* my firstborn:

23. And I say unto thee, Let my son go, that he may serve me: and if thou refuse to let him go, behold, I will slay thy son, *even* thy firstborn.

24. And it came to pass by the way in the inn, that the Lord met him, and sough to kill him.

25. Then Zipporah took a sharp stone, and cut off the foreskin of her son and cast *it* at his feet, and said, Surely a bloody husband *art* thou to me.

26. So he let him go: then she said, A bloody husband *thou art*, because of the circumcision.

MEET FOR THE MASTER'S USE

Exodus 4:18-26

Moses Sets Out. Every objection that Moses could advance being answered, he set out on his return journey from the central uplands of the Sinaitic Peninsula. It was, of course, necessary that he should hand over the flock to the head of the clan, and receive his permission to return to Egypt on the proposed visit to his people.

A Tedious Journey and Many Reflections. Long and slow would be the progress of that return journey. The flocks must not be overdriven; and thus ample time was given him for reflection on the revolution in his thoughts and plans which the vision of the burning bush had caused. Did he ever question the reliableness of his senses, and wonder whether he might not have been the victim of delusion? Did the objections and arguments which he had already advanced return in all their apparent cogency? How strange it appeared that he, an old man, from whom the world seemed to have receded for ever, and who had absolutely no ambition but to die quietly in a shepherd's tent, should be suddenly summoned to lead to freedom a nation of slaves! The children of the promises had already surrendered many of the noblest traditions of their race, and lay as an abandoned child, weltering in blood.[1] Was it possible to resuscitate a nation?

The Pharaoh of the Exodus. The power and pride of the Pharaohs showed no symptom of waning. Indeed, Menephthah had inherited so much of the arrogance and cruelty of his father that the task was as formidable as if the great Rameses were still alive. He claimed to be equal with the gods! For him the Nile flowed, and the heavenly bodies cast their horoscope. To him the unseen world, as well as the seen, yielded tribute; and if a nation of slaves perished in adding one sand-weight to his magnificence, it was no more than his due! Son of a union between the Hittite and Egyptian empires, no

[1] Ezek. xx. 7–9; xvi. 4–6.

obstacle that man could raise seemed likely to arrest or dim his glory. It was against this man that Moses was sent with the summons, "Thus saith the Lord, Israel is my son, my firstborn: and I have said unto thee, Let my son go, that he may serve Me."

Stephen's Reference to Moses. There is a ring of exultation in Stephen's reference to the setting forth of Moses on this great programme: "This Moses whom they refused, saying, Who made thee a ruler and a judge? him hath God sent to be both a ruler and a redeemer."[1] The contrast between the last word in each sentence is very remarkable. The people resented his coming as a judge, but were quite willing to accept him as a redeemer. Men are always afraid of the advent of Divine help, because they suppose it is certain to condemn; they do not realise that God comes forth not to judge, but to save; not to condemn, but to redeem. Moses returned to Egypt as a redeemer and saviour.

The Angel of the Presence. Stephen also lays stress on the Divine Companion who went beside Moses on that return journey. "God sent him to be a ruler and a redeemer *with the hand of the angel which appeared to him in the bush.*" More than once in subsequent Scriptures we are reminded of the co-operation of that gentle and strong hand. The Psalmist prays: "*Let Thy hand be upon the man of Thy right hand,* upon the son of man whom Thou madest strong for Thyself."[2] We are told of the simple evangelists, who founded the Church at Antioch: "*The hand of the Lord was with them*: and a great number believed."[3] Stephen goes on to say that Moses was in the congregation in the wilderness "together with," or in partnership with, the angel that had spoken to him on Mount Sinai. Was not this what the great lawgiver referred to when he cried: "Except Thy presence go with me, carry us not up hence?" Did not Isaiah have the same thought in his mind when he spoke of "the Angel of His presence," as having saved them, bearing and carrying them all the days of old?[4]

All Illustrated. The most perfect illustration of this hand of the accompanying Angel is presented by the statue of the great bishop, Philips Brooks, in the precincts of the churchyard in Boston, U.S.A., where he ministered during so many brilliant years. No one who has seen it can forget it. In the busy streets of the great city, it is a perpetual reminder of things not visible to the eye, but which the

---

[1] Acts vii. 35.
[2] Ps. lxxx. 17.
[3] Acts xi. 21.
[4] Isa. lxiii. 9.

heart-instinct recognises as true. The bishop stands in a characteristic attitude, with uplifted right hand. His left hand is on the open Bible, and in the background stands the Cross. Just behind him on the left is the figure of Christ, which is evidently intended to represent Him as ascended and glorified. His right hand rests on His servant's left shoulder, as though empowering and strengthening him. Would that every servant of Christ could claim the same endorsement; and that every congregation might be conscious of that two-fold ministry!

Man Allied with Nature Capable of Great Deeds. I. THE ALLIANCE OF THE DIVINE WITH THE HUMAN SPIRIT. We are living through a silent revolution. In the last hundred years vaster changes have taken place than in all the thousand years that lie behind us. Our fathers were content with the stage-coach and the sailing-vessel; but to-day the aviator navigates the air, the automobile flashes along the country road, and the express train covers sixty miles an hour. Nothing seems too great to attempt, or too impossible to conquer. The reason for all this lies in the fact that man, by patient observation, has mastered the laws and conditions on which the vast forces of Nature, unknown before, operate, and has suited his machinery to entrap and compel them. What neither Caesar nor Napoleon could do is easily possible to a child who presses a button or turns a switch, because she puts herself in alliance with stupendous natural forces, working strictly on ascertained and unchanging condition.

It is an overwhelming moment in a man's life when, for the first time, he awakes to see what co-operation with a newly discovered force may effect; and in the spiritual realm some such discovery broke on the mind of Moses, when God called to him out of the infinite, and said, "Certainly I will be with thee." What mattered it though he was reduced to the lowest and least, if he was included in a divine partnership and allied with Him Who spoke worlds into being at His word! Under such circumstances, all things would be possible.

Alliance with the Creator of Nature Possible. This should be the attitude of Christian people still. We have been called into partnership with the Son of God.[1] Our mission to the world, touching as it does the most stupendous spiritual issues, is only possible when we recognise and use the union of the human and the divine, of the spirit of man and the Spirit of God, which is the special gift of the

[1] 1 Cor. i. 9.

Incarnation and Work of Christ. To know this union makes us strong and confident in the face of difficulties which would otherwise prove insurmountable. Still God says: "I will be with thy mouth, and with this mouth, and will teach you what ye shall do."

Conditions of Partnership. II. THE CONDITIONS ON OBEDIENCE TO WHICH THIS PARTNERSHIP CAN BE REALISED. We have already seen that the human partner must be reduced to a sense of his own nothingness and helplessness. So long as Moses was confident in the prowess of his own courage, and the might of his own right hand, there could be no effective co-operation.

Moses Prepared for Union with God. God will not give His glory to another. Not for nothing is it written that He hath chosen things that are not to bring to nought things that are, that no flesh should glory in His presence. It may be that the long weary disappointments through which many of God's children pass are intended to reduce them to this emptiness and helplessness, that God may be all in all.

The only fear is lest they should become so hopeless of effecting aught in their lives, that they become hopeless of God effecting anything through them. God's discipline is intended to reduce their self-sufficiency, but to enhance their faith in His all-sufficiency. It was therefore when Moses confessed that he was not able to fulfil the Divine commission, that he had clearly attained to that precise level of death to his own resources, at which the soul is best suited to become the vehicle for God.

Jethro Gives Moses His Blessing. But there is another condition to be fulfilled—absolute obedience, and at all costs. Apparently Moses had no great difficulty in obtaining Jethro's leave to revisit Egypt. There was no need for him to rehearse the incident that had given a new direction and incentive to his life, or tell of that wonderful vision of the possibilities of God in and through man, that had been vouchsafed to him. These were secrets locked in his own heart, even from his wife. It was enough to obtain permission to see if his kinsfolk were yet living. The "Go-in-peace" of the head of the clan was sufficient carrying as it did the implicit promise that God would prosper his journey, and speed him in every step.

Moses Halts in Midian. It seems as though Moses lingered longer than was necessary, as years before Abraham did at the fords of the Euphrates; for a further enforcement of the Divine call was required. "The Lord said unto Moses *in Midian*, Go, return into Egypt." So he departed. One ass, on which were mounted his wife and children, served for his modest requirements. His rod was his only equipment; the Divine promise his guiding-star and stay.

So fared forth the man who was to meet Pharaoh in the greatest duel that ever shook the world, wrest Israel from his hand, and return thither, having spoiled the Egyptians.

Renewal of the Rite of Circumcision. It is clear that either in deference to the wishes of Zipporah, or for some other reason, he had failed to comply with the initial rite which had been enjoined on Abraham as the sign and seal of the covenant. However insignificant this omission may have appeared in itself, it could not be tolerated in one who was to stand out as God's chosen and honoured servant. If God remembered the covenant, it was surely necessary that His servant should; and if the covenant was the basis of His interposition, it was imperative that the whole congregation should stand true to its obligations as well as its privileges. A sharp illness that smote Moses in the Khan seems to have reminded his wife as well as himself of this neglected rite; and Zipporah with an ill-gace yielded beneath the stern pressure of the hour. Probably she had been the stumbling-block, and now only gave way because she must. So her husband's life was spared.

Zipporah Sent Back to Jethro. It was clear that Zipporah would be of no real help to him in the difficult and perilous enterprise on which he was engaging; and Moses appears to have renounced his intention of taking her. Probably he sent wife and children back from this point, under the care of some attendant whom he could trust. They were not destined to meet again until the Exodus was complete.[1]

Conditions of Service Fulfilled. Thus, without having heard them formally enunciated, Moses fulfilled two New Testament injunctions, compliance with which is absolutely necessary, if God's work is to be wrought through the human instrument. The first of these bids us lay aside every weight and the sin that so easily besets us; and the second insists that if a man is not prepared to hold as second to his life-call, father and mother, wife and children, brethren, sisters, and his own life, he cannot be a disciple. In fulfilling the omitted rite, Moses laid aside a weight, if not a sin; and in overriding the reluctance of his wife, and finally sending her back to Midian, he showed that he was prepared to count all things but loss, if only he might fulfil the high commission on which he had been sent.

[1] Ex. xviii. 2–4.

To Serve God the Whole Will must be Surrendered. The scientific man, intent on unravelling the secrets of Nature and utilising her powers, knows by experience the necessity of minute obedience and absolute devotion to her least demands; and it is equally imperative for all who would serve God. You must live up to the furthest limit of your light. There must be no conscious defalcation from the standard of your high calling. Any secret rift will make the music mute. Any speck of decay will spread rottenness in the fairest promise of fruit. The great God whom we serve is particular of the jots and tittles of commandment. The finest machinery may stand absolutely useless if there is the smallest failure to obey. Only as the soul yields itself utterly and absolutely to God, will He give Himself utterly and absolutely to the soul. We must not confer with flesh and blood; and we must not be disobedient to the heavenly vision. This story of Moses shows that God would rather have us die than take up His work with unconsecrated hearts and unsurrendered wills.

THE FIRST CHALLENGE TO PHARAOH

Exodus 4:27-31;5:1-23;6:1

27. And the Lord said to Aaron, Go into the wilderness to meet Moses. And he went, and met him in the mount of God, and kissed him.

28. And Moses told Aaron all the words of the Lord who had sent him, and all the signs which he had commanded him.

29. And Moses and Aaron went and gathered together all the elders of the children of Israel:

30. And Aaron spake all the words which the Lord had spoken unto Moses, and did the signs in the sight of the people.

31. And the people believed: and when they heard that the Lord had visited the children of Israel, and that he had looked upon their affliction, then they bowed their heads and worshipped.

1. And afterwards Moses and Aaron went in, and told Pharaoh, Thus saith the Lord God of Israel, Let my people go, that they may hold a feast unto me in the wilderness.

2. And Pharaoh said, Who *is* the Lord, that I should obey his voice to let Israel go? I know not the Lord, neither will I let Israel go.

3. And they said, The God of the Hebrews hath met with us; let us go, we pray thee, three days' journey into the desert, and sacrifice unto the Lord our God; lest he fall upon us with pestilence, or with the sword.

4. And the king of Egypt said unto them, Wherefore do ye, Moses and Aaron, let the people from their works? get you unto your burdens.

5. And Pharaoh said, Behold, the people of the land now *are* many, and ye make them rest from their burdens.

6. And Pharaoh commanded the same day the taskmasters of the people, and their officers, saying,

7. Ye shall no more give the people straw to make brick, as heretofore: let them go and gather straw for themselves.

8. And the tale of the bricks, which they did make heretofore, ye shall lay upon them; ye shall not diminish *ought* thereof: for they *be* idle; therefore they cry, saying, Let us go *and* sacrifice to our God.

9. Let there more work be laid upon the men, that they may labour therein; and let them not regard vain words.

10. And the taskmasters of the people went out, and their officers, and they spake to the people, saying, Thus saith Pharaoh, I will not give you straw.

11. Go ye, get you straw where ye can find it: yet not ought of your work shall be diminished.

12. So the people were scattered abroad throughout all the land of Egypt to gather stubble instead of straw.

13. And the taskmasters hasted *them*, saying, Fulfil your works, *your* daily tasks, as when there was straw.

14. And the officers of the children of Israel, which Pharaoh's taskmasters had set over them, were beaten, *and* demanded, Wherefore have ye not fulfilled your task in making brick both yesterday and to-day, as heretofore?

15. Then the officers of the children of Israel came and cried unto Pharaoh, saying, Wherefore dealest thou thus with thy servants?

16. There is no straw given unto thy servants, and they say to us, Make brick: and, behold, thy servants *are* beaten; but the fault *is* in thine own people.

17. But he said, Ye *are* idle: therefore ye say, Let us go *and* do sacrifice to the Lord.

18. Go therefore now, *and* work; for there shall no straw be given you, yet shall ye deliver the tale of bricks.

19. And the officers of the children of Israel did see *that* they *were* in evil *case*, after it was said, Ye shall not minish *ought* from your bricks of your daily task.

20. And they met Moses and Aaron, who stood in the way, as they came forth from Pharaoh:

21. And they said unto them, The Lord look upon you, and judge; because ye have made our savour to be abhorred in the eyes of Pharaoh, and in the eyes of his servants, to put a sword in their hand to slay us.

22. And Moses returned unto the Lord, and said, Lord, wherefore hast thou *so* evil entreated this people? why *is* it *that* thou hast sent me?

23. For since I came to Pharaoh to speak in thy name, he hath done evil to this people; neither hast thou delivered thy people at all.

1. Then the Lord said unto Moses, Now shalt thou see what I will do to Pharaoh; for with a strong hand shall he let them go, and with a strong hand shall he drive them out of his land.

THE FIRST CHALLENGE TO PHARAOH

Exodus 4:27-31;5:1-23;6:1

God's Call to Us. MOSES AND AARON. There are divine promptings which come to us all, and to which we do well to take heed. The nearer we live to God, the more sensitive we become to His presence, and the quicker we are to detect His voice. It is only in the beginning of our spiritual experience that we think that Eli has called us, when in fact the voice is God's. As we become more filled with the spirit of wisdom and understanding, we become more quick of scent and swift of hearing. By reason of use our senses are exercised to discern good and evil, and to detect the Shepherd's voice.

God's Adjustments for Us. It is perfectly wonderful, as we live near God, how many adjustments He makes for us. It seems as though there is an invisible power always at work in our lives, planning for us, arranging meetings with persons we need to meet, introducing us to those whom we are to address. He besets us behind and before.

Aaron Goes to his Brother. It is not surprising therefore that "the Lord said to Aaron, Go into the wilderness to meet Moses." For forty years he had not felt that movement or heard that summons: but now the predestined hour had struck, and the divine voice sang as an alarum in his heart. Here were two old men, separated for half a life-time, set in motion to each other. Moses knew that Aaron was on his way, and Aaron knew that Moses was coming towards him. Each step they took diminished the space between them; and each quickened his pace, in the anticipation of that greeting and reunion. An unerring hand was conducting them from opposing points of the compass, and could not make a mistake. The next jutting corner of sandstone rock might hide the long looked-for figure of a brother. Each sun rising at early dawn from the blood-red hues of the Eastern heavens might witness the embrace of long-severed lives.

The Meeting. Presently, in the solemn recesses of Sinai, they caught sight of each other, hastened forward, and became locked in each other's embrace. "He met him in the Mount of God, and kissed him." How much there was to talk of! On his part, Aaron would tell of the old home, of the passing away of the generation to which they belonged, of Miriam, of his own marriage and children, and specially of the gathering shadows and deepening anguish of their people.

Moses has News for Aaron. Moses, on the other hand, had news of an even more thrilling nature. Of Zipporah and his two boys, of course, there was much to tell; but he soon passed from matters of personal interest to tell Aaron "all the words of the Lord wherewith He had sent him, and all the signs wherewith He had charged him." The extent of the Divine commission; the assurance that God would be with them, and that the emancipated hosts would worship on that very mountain-range, the lower slopes of which they were skirting; God's remembrance of the ancient covenant and determination to fulfil it; the certainty that Pharaoh would not let Israel go until Egypt had been smitten with all God's wonders—all these things were carefully detailed, as he had himself received them from the voice that spoke to him at the bush. The signs of the burning-bush, of the rod transformed and retransformed, of the cleansing of the leprous hand, and of the water changed to blood, would be minutely detailed.

The Need of a Colleague. Finally, this humblest of men, on whose lips the solitude of the desert seems to have imposed a great silence, confessed to Aaron his distrust of himself, and told him of the provision which Jehovah had made to meet his felt deficiency. "You, dear brother," he would say, "are to be the spokesman. The God of our fathers has promised to be with my mouth and thy mouth, and teach us what we shall do. I shall wait for the words of God, and pass them on to you, that you may speak them in the ears of the people and Pharaoh."

The Support of God's Power. In such loving converse the two brothers journeyed forward, not knowing all that awaited them, but knowing enough to make them pause, were they not conscious that He who was with them was greater than all that could be against them. He was their Rock, His way was perfect, a God of faithfulness, and without shadow of turning. As the eagles that had their nests in those towering splintered peaks, and rose like black specks into the blue heavens, would flutter beneath and around their fledglings teaching them to fly, and bearing them on their mighty pinions, in order that no hurt should befall them, so the Lord was leading them, and would make them ride on the high places of the earth.

Divinely Appointed Companionships. He Who sent forth His disciples two by two, and knows well how our human nature craves for sympathy and support, thus helped His servants by pairing them for their mighty task, and through the two wrought out His eternal purpose. Yet one questions whether Aaron's weaker nature did not introduce an element of anxiety into Moses' career, which added to his already heavy burdens.[1] From this, Elijah, the man of God, was saved; yet Paul needed Timothy and Luke; and Luther Melanchthon. Be it so; only let us see to it that our companions are tried by long spans of fellowship, before we finally adopt them; and only when we are absolutely sure of our affinity and comradeship should we enter into an inseparable alliance. In some respects it is best to stand alone, with no ear but God's for our secrets, and no hand but His for our help.

The Summoning of the Elders. MOSES, AARON, AND THE ELDERS. The marching-orders had been definite and precise. At the bush, Moses was bidden to go and gather the elders of Israel, his very address to them had been outlined.[2] Without delay, therefore, a summons was issued for a consultative gathering, to which all the elders of the children of Israel came. It is clear that the nation, through all its trials, had retained its tribal and patriarchal organisation.

The Elders' View of Moses. What a gathering that must have been! It was probably held under shadow of night, and at some secluded spot in the heart of Goshen. Stealthily, and by ones and twos, the grey-beards of the oppressed race gathered for conference with one of whom they had probably heard, but whom they had never seen. The strange story of his rescue from the Nile, of his adoption by the Egyptian princess, of his renunciation of the proud position to which she had raised him, was still passed from lip to lip. But he had vanished into the wilderness; nothing had been heard of him for decades of years. His own family were ignorant of what had become of him. That he had fled from the wrath of the King was well-known, but the veil of the desert-solitudes shrouded all else. It

[1] Exod. xxxii. 1–25; Num. xii. 1–10.
[2] Exod. iii. 16.

was almost weird to look on the face of one of whom they had heard so much. They saw his face, but apparently he maintained his shy reticence. "Aaron spake all the words which the Lord had spoken unto Moses, and did the signs in the sight of the people."

Objections Met. Whether they asked for the name of the God of their fathers, i.e. the special characteristic or quality of His Being by which He was about to help them, or whether they professed themselves incredulous, we are not told. Moses expected that he would be met by these two objections.[1] But, in any case, he was forearmed with the fitting answer, and the representatives of his people were satisfied. "The people believed." Probably they were predisposed to believe, because, according to their calculation, the prescribed period, of which the Almighty Covenant-keeper had spoken to Abram, was on the point of running out. "Know of a surety," He had said, "that thy seed shall be a stranger in a land that is not theirs, and shall serve them; and they shall afflict them four hundred years; and also that nation, whom they shall serve, will I judge; and afterward they shall come out with great substance. . . . In the fourth generation they shall come hither again."[2] To borrow Stephen's words, "the time of the promise drew nigh."[3]

Prayer and Patience. Probably this consciousness had led them to pour out their souls in prayer. We are told that their cry came up unto God.[4] In after years, when Daniel understood by books the number of the years whereof the word of the Lord came to Jeremiah the prophet, for the accomplishing of the desolations of Jerusalem, he set his face to seek the fulfilment of the promise by prayer and supplication, with fasting, and sackcloth, and ashes; and the pious Hebrews may have acted on the same principle. A later voice put into immortal words the petitions that must have emanated from their lips:

> "*Remember this, that the enemy hath reproached, O Lord,*
> *And that a foolish people have blasphemed Thy name.*
> *O deliver not the soul of Thy turtle-dove unto the wild beast:*
> *Forget not the life of Thy poor for ever.*
> *Have respect unto the Covenant:*
> *For the dark places of the earth are full of the habitations of*
> *violence.*"[5]

[1] Exod. iii. 13; iv. 1.
[2] Gen. xv. 13, 14, 16.
[3] Acts vii. 17.
[4] Exod. ii. 23.
[5] Ps. lxxiv. 18–20.

The Israelites Recognise their God-sent Leader. It was not difficult therefore, for them to believe that the Lord had visited the children of Israel, and that He had seen their affliction. It was enough! They bowed their heads in solemn worship and assent. Recognising that God had taken their cause into His own hands, there was nothing more to do, except to follow the leaders whom He had so clearly designated, and await the unfolding of the Divine plan.

We Rest on God's Promises. It is not enough for us to have the promises which are Yea and Amen in Christ, or the covenant ordered in all things and sure. It is our part to claim their fulfilment, not with a prayer that doubts the Divine willingness or ability, but with an assured faith that knows that God can be reckoned on. There is no need, by vehement and importunate entreaties, to urge God to keep His word. It is enough to place our finger upon the letter of His Covenant, and say reverently and humbly, "Do as Thou hast said." The mountains may depart and the hills be removed, before God can be unfaithful to His promise. He will not dishonour the drafts that bear His autograph. Wait, child of God, His time! He will not be a moment before the appointed hour, not a moment behind.

King and King's Messenger. MOSES, AARON, AND PHARAOH. The Pharaohs still look forth from their statues and inscriptions, with the air of imperial and arrogant strength, their lip curled with scorn, their haughty pose betokening centuries of unbroken pride. It required no ordinary daring to confront the representative of a long line of kings who had been taught to consider themselves as the representatives and equals of the gods. They were accustomed to receive Divine titles and honours, and to act as irresponsible despots. Their will was indisputable, and all the world seemed to exist for no other reason than minister to their state. It was before such a man, seated in the inner court of some sumptuous palace, decorated with the hieroglyphed writing of his ancestors, and thronged with courtiers, statesmen, soldiers and priests, that the two aged Hebrew brethren appeared. How little he realised in that hour that his one claim on the attention of coming generations would be in his behaviour to that deputation!

It was not unnatural, then, when he heard Moses and Aaron challenge him in the name of Jehovah to let the people of Israel go, that he should reply, "I know not Jehovah."

Akhnaton. More than a century before this reign, the throne of the Pharaohs had been occupied by Akhnaton,[1] whose view of God had more nearly approximated to that of the Bible than that of anyone of whom we have record in those far-away days.   For him God was the tender Father of all creation, and ever present in all the beauties of Nature, and in the sanctities of human life. No graven image was to be made of Him. The sun's disc was His symbol, from which numerous rays extended, each ray ending in a hand; but this symbol was not to be worshipped. Not a sigh from the lips of a babe that He did not hear; no lamb bleated for its mother, but He hastened to soothe it. He was the Loving Father and Mother of all creatures that He had made, compassionate and merciful, knowing no anger, and without wrath. His love included men, women, and children, the beasts of the field, the flowers, and the birds.

The Pharaoh with a Tender Heart. God's unspeakable goodness and love were as clearly interpreted by Akhnaton as ever they have been by mortal man. But he was born before his time, and was unable to cope with the opposition of the traditional religion. When war and bloodshed broke out, and he refused to offer armed resistance because his deity was too tender of heart to permit it, he was overwhelmed in darkness and death at an early age, though still trusting in Aton—the name he gave to God. The priests of Amon, the chief deity of Thebes, triumphed, and they took care that all traces of these religious novelties should be obliterated. The Pharaoh of Moses' time, therefore, knew nothing of them, and certainly did not associate them with Jehovah of Israel, in whose name Moses spoke.

The First Refusal. "I know not Jehovah." The reply was neither unnatural nor unreasonable, and the plagues, as they are called— plague meaning stroke—were enacted in the realm of Nature, which he well understood and appreciated, that he might be without excuse. If the first, which involved no loss of life or property, and was only the source of much inconvenience, had been properly apprehended and appreciated by him; if he had been willing to admit the lesson of the Divine Superiority which it taught; if he had acted on the summons of Jehovah and conceded Israel's demand for liberty, there would have been no need for the other nine plagues, and we should never have heard of the death of the firstborn or the overthrow in the Red Sea.

[1] *The Life and Times of Aknaton.* Blackwood & Sons.

The Hardened Heart. But beneath his plea of ignorance there was another reason for refusal. Not only did he say, "I know not Jehovah," but he added, "Neither will I let Israel go." That was the stronger argument, which hid beneath the other, and made him secretly glad that he did not know Jehovah, and unwilling to know Him, that under the excuse of ignorance he might still have his way.

Pride Leading on to Wilful Resistance. It is impossible to find a more exact illustration of the truth of Rom. i. than that presented in this story of Pharaoh's conflict with Jehovah. His invisible perfections—i.e. His eternal power and Divine nature—were rendered intelligible and clearly visible by His works, so that Pharaoh was without excuse; but when he came to know God he did not give Him glory as God, nor render Him thanks, but yielded himself to his own self-will, so that his senseless heart became darkened; and as he refused to have the perfect knowledge which the Divine Spirit endeavoured to impart, God, after nine proofs of His power and grace—power towards Egypt and grace towards His shielded people—gave him up to learn in the terror of the Red Sea the lesson which he had refused to learn in an easier school. This pride of heart flamed forth in the vehement outburst of angry utterance with which he fell on the two brethren. He upbraided them for raising false hopes and hindering their people in their toils. They were sedition-mongers, dangerous firebrands, mob-orators, and the like. Instead of dictating to him, let them get back to their own burdens among the brick-kilns! What were they but insolent bondmen, who thought to conceal their indolence beneath the plea of religion!

But the Refusal not Surprising. The royal refusal could not have been a great surprise. When furnishing Moses with his earliest commission, Jehovah had made it clear that at the first he must expect it. "I know that the King of Egypt will not give you leave to go, no, not by a mighty hand." It was, moreover, only what he had told Aaron to expect, when they found the door angrily slammed in their faces. Probably they had not expected the aggravation of the situation which was meted out on that same afternoon, at Pharaoh's own initiative.

The Harsh Resultant Sentence. At a meeting of the taskmasters, who were probably Egyptians, and of the Hebrew officials and representatives, Pharaoh announced that from that time onward no straw would be given for the binding of the clay in the brickyards, and yet the daily tasks must be maintained.

The Anguish of the Oppressed. As these orders were passed on to the miserable people, already strained to the utmost, they must have seemed weighted with the sentence of doom. What hope had they of rendering their tale of bricks under that new and heavy addition to their tasks! A sob of bitter anguish must have broken forth in each squalid hut, as the news was discussed that night in whispered tones. Their lot had become more unbearable! The Hebrew gangers were beaten with the terrible knout! Their appeal to Pharaoh was received with heartless disdain! And their bitter retaliation on Moses and Aaron, who awaited them on their way back from the royal audience-room, must have stung the latter to the quick. "The Lord look upon you, and judge."

The Helplessness of Man. MOSES AND JEHOVAH. Moses could not take Aaron with him on this errand. As Jehovah had sent him, he must deal with Jehovah alone. He must enter his closet, and shut the door, and pray to his Father in secret. Ah, there are moments in the lives of all God's servants when they must have matters out with God—they and He alone—in the bitterness of their soul. When they have been true to truth; when they have done what they thought was His will; when they have wrought their utmost, and all has ended in failure; when they seem to have done harm rather than good, and to have marred what they longed to adjust—what resort is there save that of prayer? "Lord, why is it that Thou hast sent me? and where is Thy promised aid? Since I came to Pharaoh to speak in Thy name, he hath evil entreated this people; neither hast Thou delivered Thy people at all!"

But all these things were working together for good!

The Salvation of the Lord. Listen to God's reply. It was not for that moment only, but for all time; not for Moses alone, but for thee! "*Now*"—when thou art reduced to the very dust of despair, when all hope is abandoned, when Aaron and you are at the end of yourselves—"*now* shalt thou see what I will do to Pharaoh." It was thus that Moses first learnt those memorable words which rang out over the Red Sea, "Fear ye not, stand still, and see the salvation of the Lord!"

ON EAGLES' WINGS

Exodus 6:2-9

2. And God spake unto Moses, and said unto him, I *am* the Lord:

3. And I appeared unto Abraham, unto Isaac, and unto Jacob, by *the name of* God Almighty, but by my name JEHOVAH was I not known to them.

4. And I have also established my covenant with them, to give them the land of Canaan, the land of their pilgrimage, wherein they were strangers.

5. And I have also heard the groaning of the children of Israel, whom the Egyptians keep in bondage; and I have remembered my covenant.

6. Wherefore say unto the children of Israel, I *am* the Lord, and I will bring you out from under the burdens of the Egyptians, and I will rid you out of their bondage, and I will redeem you with a stretched-out arm, and with great judgments:

7. And I will take you to me for a people, and I will be to you a God: and ye shall know that I *am* the Lord your God, which bringeth you out from under the burdens of the Egyptians.

8. And I will bring you in unto the land, concerning the which I did swear to give it to Abraham, to Isaac, and to Jacob; and I will give it you for an heritage: I *am* the Lord.

9. And Moses spake so unto the children of Israel: but they hearkened not unto Moses for anguish of spirit, and for cruel bondage.

ON EAGLES' WINGS
Exodus 6:2-9

Chapter VI a Repetition of III and IV. The longer this paragraph is studied the more clear does it become that it is a retelling of the contents of III and IV. It seems to be another version of the same wonderful incidents of the call of Moses and the Divine commission with which he was entrusted. There is no mention of the burning bush, of the special signs given him as credentials, because there was obviously no need to repeat these; but there are several sentences and phrases included in this narrative which are peculiar to itself, and abundantly justify its inclusion. Just as Matthew and Mark give in their Gospels fragments of our Lord's sayings which had escaped the evangelist Luke, which either he never heard or which were not pertinent to his object, so here are gold-shavings and diamond-filings, carefully gathered from the floor, and collected and passed on from hand to hand, to confirm and illustrate the main statement already made.

For this we must thank the Spirit of Inspiration, who has set His seal on these sacred reminiscences, transmitted at first orally, but finally set down in writing for the nourishment of all generations.

The Sacred Name. I. JEHOVAH'S FRESH REVELATION OF HIMSELF. Three times over we meet the remarkable phrase, "I am Jehovah." In the Hebrew, "Jehovah I" (see vv. 2, 6, 8). This mysterious and sacred name was not absolutely unknown among the Hebrews. For instance, it was incorporated in Jochebed, the name of Moses' mother; but it was not in common use, and the truth which it contained was not generally recognised or appreciated. There is all the difference between our hearsay knowledge of a word, and our appreciation of its meaning, when associated with the personality of a beloved friend. A word which has passed the lips a hundred times may suddenly become almost too sacred, for love's sake, to mention, except in circles where the beloved one is known and appreciated.

Knowledge of God and Names of God. The upward march of the generations has been determined and marked by successive names for God, indicative by an ever-increasing knowledge of the Divine nature. Each new development of religious experience has dated from a better understanding of God. It was when Abram's faith was strained to breaking-point by the delay in the gift of the promised heir, that God revealed Himself as El-Shaddai. From that name sprang the promise that he should become Abraham, the father of many nations, and from that hour the river of his life issued into further reaches of deep and hallowed experience.

Jehovah-Sabaoth, First Use of the Name. It was when Israel came into collision with the marshalled hosts of the heathen that Jehovah became known as Jehovah–Sabaoth, the Lord of Hosts, as though to hearten them in conflict by the knowledge that unseen squadrons were riding through the Heavens to their help.

Later Names of "Father" and "Redeemer." It was when the world lay crushed under the iron empire of Rome; when, throughout the break-up of the old mythologies, men were becoming disillusioned and hopeless, that Jesus made God known as the Father in Heaven. Throughout the Christian centuries the Divine Teacher has been unfolding new and unexpected qualities in the Word that was made flesh. Each Council of the Church, called to deal with a fresh heresy, has affirmed some fresh aspect of the Redeemer, as the antidote and corrective of the error.

The Saviour's Supply of Our Needs. In Christian experience, also, we find that each fresh temptation or trial serves as the background against which some unexpected jewel of our Saviour's character will be exhibited. The precious stones of His breastplate lie, so to speak, in a deep chest or coffer, from which, as the need arises, the Spirit takes and holds up to view the appropriate stone which will befit our need. It was therefore in harmony with the experience of the Church and of the individual, when the great name Jehovah became the formative conception of the Exodus. The sorrows of Israel were the foil on which it flashed to fullest advantage. We recall the words, "To him that overcometh, to him will I give of the hidden manna, and I will give him a white stone, and upon the stone a new name written, which no man knoweth but he that receiveth it."

"For His Holy Name's Sake." JEHOVAH'S OBLIGATION TO HIM-
SELF. In a very illuminating chapter,[1] Ezekiel unveils a principle
of Divine providence, which had characterised the successive epochs
of Hebrew history. Four times over, we are told, He wrought for
His holy Name's sake, that it should not be profaned among the
nations.[2] Often and again He must have cast the chosen people
aside, if His action had been simply determined by their merits;
but other considerations prevailed. His name and character were
so intimately wrapt up in the fortunes of His people that He could
not abandon them to the full consequences of their sins, without
endangering the cause of religion in the world.

This also was a potent argument with the noblest of His servants,
who stood in the breach and pleaded it, when there was no other
excuse to be made for the people. "If," argued Moses on one
occasion, "Thou shalt kill this people as one man, then the nations
which have heard the fame of Thee will speak, saying, Because the
Lord was not able to bring this people into the land which He sware
unto them, therefore He hath slain them in the wilderness."[3] And
when Joshua was lying in the dust, after the defeat at Ai, he cried,
"Oh Lord, what shall I say, after that Israel hath turned their backs
before their enemies! For the Canaanites and all the inhabitants of
the land shall hear of it, and shall compass us round, and cut off
our name from the earth: and *what wilt Thou do for Thy great
name?*"[4]

That thought underlies the remarkable references of Ezekiel xx.
5-9, to Israel's sojourn in Egypt:

A Later Reference to the Bondage of the Israelites.

" Thus saith the Lord God: In the day when I chose Israel, and lifted
up mine hand unto the seed of the house of Jacob, and made myself
known unto them in the land of Egypt, when I lifted up mine hand unto
them, saying, I am Jehovah your God; in that day I lifted up mine
hand unto them, to bring them forth out of the land of Egypt into a
land that I had espied for them, flowing with milk and honey, which
is the glory of all lands: and I said unto them, Cast ye away every man
the abominations of his eyes, and defile not yourselves with the idols
of Egypt; I am Jehovah your God. But they rebelled against me, and
would not hearken unto me; they did not every man cast away the
abominations of their eyes, neither did they forsake the idols of Egypt:
then I said I would pour out my fury upon them, to accomplish my

---

[1] Ezek. xx.
[2] vv. 9, 14, 22, 44.
[3] Num. xiv. 15, 16.
[4] Joshua vii. 8, 9.

anger against them in the midst of the land of Egypt. *But I wrought for my name's sake, that it should not be profaned in the sight of the nations, among whom they were*, in whose sight I made myself known unto them, in bringing them forth out of the land of Egypt."

God's Dealings with the Israelites an Object Lesson for Mankind. This paragraph is one of the most illuminating and touching references to the facts of the Egyptian bondage on the page of Scripture. We learn from it, what we infer from the inveteracy of their love for the calf-god and its lascivious worship—that the chosen people became deeply infected with Egyptian idolatry; that the God of their fathers was constantly pleading for a fuller consecration; and that their ultimate deliverance was due, not to any outstanding merit, but to those plans for the education of mankind on which God was set. It was necessary for the world's redemption that the Hebrew race should be disintegrated from Egypt as ore from its matrix; and lodged in Canaan, that it might provide the Psalms, the Prophecies, the moulds for Apostolic thought, and, above all, the proper setting for the white flower of the race—the human nature of Jesus. Poor as the material was, the Divine Potter had no alternative but to make it again and yet again. "I do not this," He said frankly, "for your sake, O house of Israel, but for mine holy name, which ye have profaned among the nations, and I will sanctify my great name".[1]

Our Unworthiness and His Covenant. This also is in harmony with experiences with which most of us are familiar. Are there not times when we feel more deeply than ever that we have forfeited all claim on God? We cannot base our plea for help in our dire extremity upon our victories or services. Indeed, our faith lies stifled under the weight of our shortcomings. We cannot believe that God can help us, until we recall the covenant. Placing our finger on its provisions, we falter: "Remember the Covenant by which Thou hast bound Thyself: have respect unto it for Thine own sake. Interpose, and work for Thine own great name after which we are called; we cannot believe, but do Thou remain faithful, for Thou canst not deny Thyself." "Help us, O God of our salvation, *for the glory of Thy name*: and deliver us, and purge away our sins, for Thy name's sake. Wherefore should the heathen say, Where is their God?"[2] When we have begun to plead thus, the clouds seem to part and the

[1] Ezek. xxxvi. 23.   [2] Ps. lxxix. 9, 10.

blue sky gathers overhead. We know that God cannot put us away. He may have to chasten us for our sins, but He cannot abandon, or allow us to be desolate. You have no plea of your own? Be it so; then ask Him to work "for His Name's sake."

The Seven "I Wills." II. THE POSSIBILITY OF THE IMPOSSIBLE. As we glance down the seven "I wills" of this paragraph, they become very remarkable, as contrasted with the condition of Israel at that time:

"I will bring you out,"
"I will rid you out of their bondage,"
"I will redeem you,"
"I will take you to me for a people,"
"I will be to you a God,"
"I will bring you in unto the land,"
"I will give it you for an heritage."

The Impossible Suggested. Nothing could have seemed more unlikely. The nation had descended into the valley of Death-shadow. The dread sentence of gradual destruction and extinction seemed brooding over them. Strange to be told that they would soon be transported to the broad wolds of the wilderness, with the rights and opportunities of free men! It seemed absolutely incredible that they could arise from that low level of degradation to those fair tablelands, on which as they lifted their heavy eyes they could see the sun was shining!

But God Brought It to Pass. But so it befell. Within a twelvemonth of this time the transition had been made, and Jehovah, addressing them through Moses, said, "Ye have seen how I bare you on eagles' wings, and brought you unto Myself."[1]

The imagery is sublime. We catch sight of some parent-bird, bearing on its mighty wings the young fledglings of its nest, and carrying them through the dizzy steeps of air to the crested summits of the mighty Sinaitic range, 10,000 feet above the sea-level. How magnificent, how effortless, how incomparable, that flight! So God spread abroad His wings, took His people, and bare them on His pinions, and made them ride upon the high places of the earth; they ate the increase of the field, sucked honey out of the rock, and drank wine of the blood of the grape.[2]

[1] Exod. xix. 4.   [2] Deut. xxxii. 11–14.

The Christian Path. Christian living often resembles the climb of a mountain range. You pass easily through the cornfields at the base, and over the foot-hills, with their woodlands and lawns. The walk through the firs and pines is comparatively easy; but when all these are left behind, and the steep mountain cliffs spring perpendicularly upwards, opposing themselves to your further advance, your resolution is challenged, and your ambition threatened with defeat. So in the early stages of Christian experience, it is not impossible to cut off the right hand or foot and pluck out the right eye, and to deal with obvious inconsistencies and faults. But when these stages are passed, the soul is repeatedly brought up face to face with unscalable cliffs. Amongst them we may cite these: To love your neighbour better than yourself; to pray for the success of another as you would for yourself; to be glad for the Master to obtain more glory from the labours of others than your own; to love perfectly, not with an effort, but naturally and gladly! Those peaks of unconscious humility, of unstudied meekness, of genuine child-likeness, how hard they are to climb! It is not so difficult to seem good; but to be really good, here is the work, here the labour. It is not so hard to frame the lips in pious prayer for others; but to intercede for them as though for our own life, this needs Divine grace. To hear a rival receive his just mead of praise, and to be really glad! To make a sacrifice which costs blood, and to delight in it for the love of God!

Difficulties Only to be Conquered by God's Grace. Are not these steep and beetling cliffs? Thank God that they face us! We would not have a soft and easy life! Yet as we come back to them again and again, they defy us. The young ruler came to their foot, and turned back foiled; though probably he came again, and surmounted them, having learnt what the Master meant when He said, "With men it is impossible, but not with God, for with God all things are possible." Saul of Tarsus, whose early life might have been described in the same terms as his, said that he was easily able to scale those cliffs, because he did all things in the strengthening grace of Christ. By no other talisman can we conquer; by no other clue extricate ourselves from the meshes of selfishness. But God's grace is sufficient for us, and is made more evident and abundant in our weakness. Our Lord spoke of some poor labourers who had only wrought for one hour in the vineyard, but the difference between their legitimate wage and the full day's wage, which was paid them, was compensated by the generosity of their employer; and He surely means us to infer that those who by reason of their natural inabilities seem least able to scale inaccessible heights, shall find more grace than others, grace adequate to their need, grace that shall laugh at the impossible.

Jehovah the Strength of His People. Is not this what God meant when He told Moses that He had borne the people whom He loved on eagles' wings, and brought them to Himself? Will not He do as much for each of us? Whilst you stand at the foot of the cliffs, overwhelmed with the magnitude of the task to be accomplished, and whilst you steadfastly look away from yourself to God, you will find yourself transported by strong and steady wings upward. As the aviator cannot rise into the air by his unaided powers, but must skilfully utilise the laws and forces of Nature, so the soul that must fail, if left to its unaided efforts, succeeds when it unites itself by faith to the power of God. What we cannot do of ourselves, we can do in union with Him! When we are weakest, we are strongest! He gives power to the faint, and to those that have no might He increases strength. The youths shall faint and be weary, and the young men shall utterly fall, but they that wait on the Lord shall change their strength, they shall mount up with wings as eagles.[1] "Jehovah, the Lord, is my strength, and He maketh my feet like hinds' feet, and will make me to walk upon mine high places."[2]

[1] Isa. xl. 29–31.   [2] Hab. iii. 19.

THE SECOND CHALLENGE TO PHARAOH

Exodus 6:10-30;7:1-13

10. And the Lord spake unto Moses, saying,

11. Go in, speak unto Pharaoh king of Egypt, that he let the children of Israel go out of his land.

12. And Moses spake before the Lord, saying, Behold, the children of Israel have not hearkened unto me; how then shall Pharaoh hear me, who *am* of uncircumcised lips?

13. And the Lord spake unto Moses and unto Aaron, and gave them a charge unto the children of Israel, and unto Pharaoh king of Egypt, to bring the children of Israel out of the land of Egypt.

14. These *be* the heads of their fathers' houses: The sons of Reuben the firstborn of Israel; Hanoch, and Pallu, Hezron, and Carmi: these *be* the families of Reuben.

15. And the sons of Simeon; Jemuel, and Jamin, and Ohad, and Jachin, and Zohar, and Shaul the son of a Canaanitish woman: these *are* the families of Simeon.

16. And these are the names of the sons of Levi according to their generations; Gershon, and Kohath, and Merari: and the years of the life of Levi *were* an hundred thirty and seven years.

17. The sons of Gershon; Libni, and Shimi, according to their families.

18. And the sons of Kohath; Amram, and Izhar, and Hebron, and Uzziel: and the years of the life of Kohath *were* an hundred thirty and three years.

19. And the sons of Merari; Mahali and Mushi: these *are* the families of Levi according to their generations.

20. And Amram took him Jochebed his father's sister to wife; and she bare him Aaron and Moses: and the years of the life of Amram *were* an hundred and thirty and seven years.

21. And the sons of Izhar; Korah, and Nepheg, and Zichri.

22. And the sons of Uzziel; Mishael, and Elzaphan, and Zithri.

23. And Aaron took him Elisheba, daughter of Amminadab, sister of Naashon, to wife; and she bare him Nadab, and Abihu, Eleazar, and Ithamar.

24. And the sons of Korah; Assir, and Elkanah, and Abiasaph: these *are* the families of the Korhites.

25. And Eleazar Aaron's son took him *one* of the daughters of Putiel to wife; and she bare him Phinehas: these *are* the heads of the fathers of the Levites according to their families.

26. These *are* that Aaron and Moses, to whom the Lord said, Bring out the children of Israel from the land of Egypt according to their armies.

27. These *are* they which spake to Pharaoh king of Egypt, to bring out the children of Israel from Egypt: these *are* that Moses and Aaron.

28. And it came to pass on the day *when* the Lord spake unto Moses in the land of Egypt,

29. That the Lord spake unto Moses, saying, I *am* the Lord: speak thou unto Pharaoh king of Egypt all that I say unto thee.

30. And Moses said before the Lord, Behold, I *am* of uncircumcised lips, and how shall Pharaoh hearken unto me?

1. And the Lord said unto Moses, See, I have made thee a god to Pharaoh: and Aaron thy brother shall be thy prophet.

2. Thou shalt speak all that I command thee: and Aaron thy brother shall speak unto Pharaoh, that he send the children of Israel out of his land.

3. And I will harden Pharaoh's heart, and multiply my signs and my wonders in the land of Egypt.

4. But Pharaoh shall not hearken unto you, that I may lay my hand upon Egypt, and bring forth mine armies, *and* my people the children of Israel, out of the land of Egypt by great judgments.

5. And the Egyptians shall know that I *am* the Lord, when I stretch forth mine hand upon Egypt, and bring out the children of Israel from among them.

6. And Moses and Aaron did as the Lord commanded them, so did they.

7. And Moses *was* fourscore years old, and Aaron fourscore and three years old, when they spake unto Pharaoh.

8. And the Lord spake unto Moses and unto Aaron, saying,

9. When Pharaoh shall speak unto you, saying, Shew a miracle for you: then thou shalt say unto Aaron, Take thy rod, and cast *it* before Pharaoh, *and* it shall become a serpent.

10. And Moses and Aaron went in unto Pharaoh, and they did so as the Lord had commanded: and Aaron cast down his rod before Pharaoh, and before his servants, and it became a serpent.

11. Then Pharaoh also called the wise men and the sorcerers: now the magicians of Egypt, they also did in like manner with their enchantments.

12. For they cast down every man his rod, and they became serpents: but Aaron's rod swallowed up their rods.

13. And he hardened Pharaoh's heart, that he hearkened not unto them: as the Lord had said.

Psalm cv. 23–26.

23. Israel also came into Egypt;
And Jacob sojourned in the land of Ham.
24. And he increased his people greatly;
And made them stronger than their enemies.
25. He turned their heart to hate his people,
To deal subtilly with his servants,
26. He sent Moses his servant;
And Aaron whom he had chosen.

THE SECOND CHALLENGE TO PHARAOH

Exodus 6:10-30;7:1-13

Moses and Aaron are Commanded to again Approach Pharaoh.
Once more, because God, in His loving-kindness and justice, always
repeats His demands, to prevent the possibility of mistake, the
brothers were commissioned to demand from Pharaoh that he should
grant the request of the children of Israel for liberty. It seemed to
Moses a useless and futile errand. His old haunting self-distrust
awoke. At the bush, he had repeatedly insisted on his incompetence.
His lack of eloquence, through the disuse of public speech for forty
years, clung to him, like saturated clothes around the spent swimmer.
He was not eloquent, but slow of speech, and of a slow tongue. To
increase his self-distrust, when he had addressed words of encouragement to his people, they had turned from him, sick of heart, "for
anguish of spirit and cruel bondage." How then could he expect
better success with the proud tyrant, who had already dismissed
him from his presence with arrogant contumely!

The Discipline of Failure. I. THE DISCIPLINE OF FAILURE. "How
then shall Pharaoh hear me, who am of uncircumcised lips?" That
qualifying adjective seems to mean more than that he was uneloquent;
it carries with it the suggestion of uncleanness and unworthiness.
We recall the words of another, in the same great line of prophets,
who cried beneath the vision of the seraphim, "Woe is me! for I
am undone; because I am a man of unclean lips, and I dwell in the
midst of a people of unclean lips: for mine eyes have seen the King,
the Lord of Hosts."[1]

—Hard to Bear. Probably there is no pain more acute and crushing, with the exception perhaps of jealousy, which is more terrible
to a sensitive spirit, than the sense of failure. In proportion to the
greatness of the ideal, and the precision of previous preparation,
will be the poignancy of the regret, when the kite has failed to rise,

---

[1] Isa. vi. 5.

and the arrow has become a spent force before it reached the mark. You shrink from speaking of your failure, you hide your chagrin from your closest friends, you affect an outward interest in the achievements of your rival, when your heart is being drained of life-blood. You secretly vow that you will never make another effort; you wonder where you can hide; you are reminded of your failure in the expression of every face, in the considerateness of every voice, and in the kindness which invents apologies.

—But a Divine Revelation. If your sense of failure arises from mortified pride, it is well to let the acid eat out the proud flesh, and to permit the fire to search for the dross. Dare to regard the process as a permission of the Great Refiner to reveal what you are, and as a prelude to the operation of His more tender and compassionate grace.

Some Causes of Failure. The sense of failure often arises from an overtaxed nervous system, which has been strung almost to breaking-point, and has suddenly collapsed. It was so with Elijah, when he lay beneath the juniper tree, and asked for death. But He who knows our frame knew better than to send the Angel of Death, and commissioned another to provide him with food and sleep. Often, after some great deliverance, the late Dr. Maclaren would be over-whelmed with the sense of failure. "I must not speak again on such an occasion," would be his exclamation, whilst the whole audience, as they dispersed, went away inspired and blessed. We must always allow for the depression which comes from the rebound of the overstrung bow.

Failure sometimes arises from the nature of the soil which we are sent to cultivate. Suppose that the husbandman has only the stony-ground or the light sandy-soil in his fields! Suppose, as in Moses' case, the people are so engrossed in their bitter struggle for bread that they have no thought or care for anything beyond! Suppose, as in Isaiah's case, hearts are fat and ears are heavy!

Times when Failure is no Failure. Failure under such circum-stances is not really failure, so far as the workman is concerned. His Master has no fault to find with him. In the words of the great Servant, he may say,

> "I have laboured in vain, I have spent my strength for nought, and in vain: yet surely my judgment is with the Lord, and my work with my God . . . Though Israel be not gathered, yet shall I be glorious in the eyes of the Lord, and my God shall be my strength."[1]

[1] Isa. xlix. 4, 5.

At such times, God will even grant a wider commission to His servant.

> " Thus saith the Lord . . . to him whom man despiseth, to him whom the nation abhorreth, to a servant of rulers, Kings shall see and arise, princes also shall worship, because of the Lord that is faithful, and the Holy One of Israel, and He shall choose thee."[1]

In such cases, when the son of peace is not within the house, peace comes back again to the heart from which it issued forth.

Where the Blame Should Lie. At the same time, we should be more willing to blame ourselves than the people; and more anxious, like Moses, to find the cause of failure in our uncircumcised lips, than in the obtuseness and hardness of their hearts. Perhaps there has not been enough of the wooing-note in our voice! Perchance our manner disinclined them to receive our matter! What if they discerned the coldness and indifference of our stony hearts! Better that we should accuse ourselves wrongfully, than that we excuse ourselves wholly!

Always go into your own uncircumcised heart, to learn the reason why the people are gainsaying and rebellious, until God comforts you by saying,

> " I will call that my people, which was not my people; and her beloved, which was not beloved. And it shall be that in the place where it was said unto then, Ye are not my people, there shall they be calle d sons of the living God."[2]

Our Source of Help. In the meanwhile, if our lips are uncircumcised, let us ask that a live coal may be brought from the altar of God and laid on them, that our iniquity may be cleansed, and that we may become the fitting spokesmen for God.

A High Calling needs High Living and Thinking. Let us specially remember and act upon the Apostle's injunction, that fornication, and all uncleanness, and foolish talking, and jesting, must be put away, as becometh saints.[3] No speech of such things may defile with its muddy foot-prints the lips which belong to God, for the utterance of His messages to men. Only high-born thoughts, clothed in white vesture pure and clean, may tread on thresholds where the feet of the King are wont to go to and fro. It is too sad, sometimes, to hear men, who, an hour before, had been apparently the vehicles and mediums of the oracles of God, stooping to silly and foolish

---

[1] Isa. xlix. 7.   [2] Rom. ix. 25, 26.   [3] Eph. v. 3, 4.

stories, utterly unworthy of their high vocation. It would seem as though they made haste to prove that they were even as others, whereas the fact that God has condescended to use them as His messengers should for ever impose a careful reserve. The wearer of royal livery, carrying royal letters, is expected to bear with him the manners and speech of the court.

The Family of Moses and Aaron. II. AN OLD-WORLD CEMETERY. Tread gently here! This is a private burying-ground, the last resting-place of the founders of a family to which the world is deeply indebted for priceless service. The reference to the sons of Reuben and Simeon is only casual and introductory. The main object of this genealogical table is to trace the roots of the family out of which Moses and Aaron sprang. Not far from London, near Chalfont where Milton first conceived the plan of "Paradise Regained", is the quiet Friends' meeting-house of Jordans, and in front a few little mounds of earth that mark the sacred spot where lie the remains of William and Gulielma Penn, and of others of their family. One bares one's head, and hushes one's voice, as the presence of the mighty dead seems to enwrap one. With similar emotions, we may thread our way through these names. Amram and Jochebed are already familiar.

Their Ancestors. We shall hear again of Phinehas, Eleazar, and Korah. Prophets, Priests, Judges, singers, statesmen will come from this family, whose words and acts shall light the march of generations, when the proud Pharaohs shall be forgotten, and Egypt has become one of the servile nations of the world.

Aaron the Elder, Moses the Greater. "These are that Aaron and Moses," says the sacred scribe of some far-off time, observing the order of their birth.[1] "These are that Moses and Aaron," says some later scribe—it may be Ezra—who revised the Sacred Canon, and who desired to place them in the rank of historical achievement.[2] For there are last which shall be first, and first that shall be last. The order of Nature is reversed by grace. The elder serve the younger, for that is not first that is spiritual, but that which is natural, and the Divine purpose must stand, not of works, but of Him that calleth. Moses might do his best to put Aaron forward as first and foremost in the challenge to Pharaoh, but inevitably he sank to the second position, and his illustrious brother, though meekest of all men, was compelled to assume the foremost place.

[1] Exod. vi. 26.　　　　　　[2] *Ibid.*, 27.

Moses, though Younger, First in God's Plans.

" And it came to pass on the day when the Lord spake unto Moses in the land of Egypt, that the Lord spake unto Moses, saying, I am Jehovah: speak thou unto Pharaoh king of Egypt all that I speak unto thee."

The Second Challenge. III. THE SECOND CHALLENGE. The brothers were to speak to Pharaoh and show their signs, with the clear knowledge that he would not hearken unto them, until Jehovah had laid His hand on Egypt, and brought forth the hosts of His people with great judgments. It was necessary that they should realise the need for patience. After long pondering some heaven-given programme at a distance from courts and camps, a man is apt to suppose that he has only to propose it, to see it carried into effect. He becomes unaware of the dead dull incubus of human inertness and indifference, to say nothing of obstinate resistance.

Moses might naturally have expected that Pharaoh would give way before his first miracle. He had to learn the necessity of a Divine patience; that much labour, apparently abortive, would have to be sunk before the roadway for the Exodus could be made; and that he must carry out his instructions in absolute indifference to the behaviour of the King, as the share cleaves the soil at the summons of the ploughman.

Two Issues Made Plain. Two things were made clear from the outset, first, that the hold of Egypt on Israel was to be loosened and overthrown by sublime manifestations of the Divine power; and second, that Pharaoh's heart would be gradually hardened in the conflict, till the waves of the Red Sea closed over him and his armies.

God's Dealings with Pharaoh. Why did not God crush Pharaoh by one terrific miracle? Because he never terrifies men into submission. He respects the understanding, the judgment, and the will-power, which He has given; and by appealing to these, He seeks to lead them to penitence, faith, and obedience. It is not to be wondered at that this descendant of a long line of kings, who were treated as demigods, should resent the interference and dictation of a race of slaves. For them great Egypt existed, and her peoples toiled. For them magicians and priests, philosophers and statesmen, generals and builders wrought. Their will was law; in their hands were life and death.

Pharaoh a Deeply Religious Man. At the same time the Pharaoh's were an eminently religious race. Behind the whole system of

Egyptian idolatry and animal-worship there was a profound reverence for the unknown Power which held the world in its grasp, and ruled in its palaces. If this had not been so, is it likely that the King would have been so dependent on his magicians? There was a mysterious awe in his deepest soul, begotten by the secret belief that these men were in touch with the One Being, to which the inscription on the Temple of Isis made reference:

A Wonderful Inscription. "I am that which was, and is, and shall be, and no man hath lifted my veil."

It was to this deepest principle in Pharaoh's nature, his sense that there must be something beyond the phenomena which he worshipped, his religious awe, that Jehovah made His appeal.

A Pauline Parallel. Moses did not accost Pharaoh as a heathen, but appealed to him almost precisely as, centuries after, Paul addressed the assembly on Mars Hill: "Men of Athens, I perceive that you are in every respect remarkably religious. For as I passed by, and observed the things you worship, I found also an altar bearing the inscription, TO AN UNKNOWN GOD. The Being, therefore, whom you, without knowing Him, revere, Him I now proclaim unto you."[1] It was as though Moses said, "You admit that there is a Power at work in Nature, beyond your furthest imaginings; but He is the God Who has sent us, to whom this people belongs, and who asks you to set them free. To prove that this is so, behold these wonders, wrought in the sphere of Nature, and mastering the very symbols and elements which you are wont to associate with your deities. Does not this prove that I, through whom these wonders are wrought, am the messenger and spokesman of the God of gods and the Lords of lords?"

All this was involved in Pharaoh's demand for a sign, in answer to which the rod was cast down, to become a serpent.

The Magician's Miracles—Were They of God? It is noticeable that in this and one or two of the earlier plagues, "the magicians of Egypt did in like manner with their enchantments—they cast down every man his rod, and they became serpents." This was permitted, because they possessed some knowledge of the Power behind Nature. The fact that they could work similar miracles to those of Moses seemed to prove that he and they were working in the same sphere. Perhaps also, legerdemain, in which they were adepts, accounted for their earlier successes.

[1] Acts xvii. 22, etc. (Weymouth).

The Magicians Defeated. But when Aaron's rod swallowed their rods, when the magicians could turn water to blood, but not blood to water, when presently they failed in the third great plague, when finally they cried, This is the finger of God, and retreated from the conflict,[1] there could be no reasonable doubt that there was none like unto Jehovah among the gods, none like unto Him, glorious in Holiness, fearful in praises, doing wonders: for what god was there in Heaven or on Earth, that could do according to these works, and according to these mighty acts?

[1] Exod. viii. 19; ix. 11.

THE NINE PLAGUES

Exodus 7:14-25;8:1-32;9:1-35;10:1-29

14. And the Lord said unto Moses, Pharaoh's heart *is* hardened, he refuseth to let the people go.

15. Get thee unto Pharaoh in the morning, lo, he goeth out unto the water; and thou shalt stand by the river's brink against he come; and the rod which was turned to a serpent shalt thou take in thine hand.

16. And thou shalt say unto him, The Lord God of the Hebrews hath sent me unto thee, saying, Let my people go, that they may serve me in the wilderness: and, behold, hitherto thou wouldest not hear.

17. Thus saith the Lord, In this thou shalt know that I *am* the Lord: behold, I will smite with the rod that *is* in mine hand upon the waters which *are* in the river, and they shall be turned to blood.

18. And the fish that *is* in the river shall die, and the river shall stink; and the Egyptians shall loathe to drink of the water of the river.

19. And the Lord spake unto Moses, Say unto Aaron, Take thy rod, and stretch out thine hand upon the waters of Egypt, upon their streams, upon their rivers, and upon their ponds, and upon all their pools of water, that they may become blood; and *that* there may be blood throughout all the land of Egypt, both in *vessels of* wood, and in *vessels of* stone.

20. And Moses and Aaron did so, as the Lord commanded; and he lifted up the rod, and smote the waters that *were* in the river, in the sight of Pharaoh, and in the sight of his servants; and all the waters that *were* in the river were turned to blood.

21. And the fish that *was* in the river died; and the river stank, and the Egyptians could not drink of the water of the river; and there was blood throughout all the land of Egypt.

22. And the magicians of Egypt did so with their enchantments: and Pharaoh's heart was hardened, neither did he hearken unto them; as the Lord had said.

23. And Pharaoh turned and went into his house, neither did he set his heart to this also.

24. And all the Egyptians digged round about the river for water to drink; for they could not drink of the water of the river.

25. And seven days were fulfilled, after that the Lord had smitten the river.

1. And the Lord spake unto Moses, Go unto Pharaoh, and say unto him, Thus saith the Lord, Let my people go, that they may serve me.

2. And if thou refuse to let *them* go, behold, I will smite all thy borders with frogs:

3. And the river shall bring forth frogs abundantly, which shall go up and come into thine house, and into thy bedchamber, and upon thy bed, and into the house of thy servants, and upon thy people, and into thine ovens, and into thy kneading troughs:

4. And the frogs shall come up both on thee, and upon thy people, and upon all thy servants.

5. And the Lord spake unto Moses, Say unto Aaron, Stretch forth thine hand with thy rod over the streams, over the rivers, and over the ponds, and cause frogs to come up upon the land of Egypt.

6. And Aaron stretched out his hand over the waters of Egypt; and the frogs came up, and covered the land of Egypt.

7. And the magicians did so with their enchantments, and brought up frogs upon the land of Egypt.

8. Then Pharaoh called for Moses and Aaron, and said, Intreat the Lord, that he may take away the frogs from me, and from my people; and I will let the people go, that they may do sacrifice unto the Lord.

9. And Moses said unto Pharaoh, Glory over me: when shall I intreat for thee, and for thy servants, and for thy people, to destroy the frogs from thee and thy houses, *that* they may remain in the river only?

10. And he said, To-morrow. And he said, *Be it* according to thy word: that thou mayest know that *there is* none like unto the Lord our God.

11. And the frogs shall depart from thee, and from thy houses, and from thy servants, and from thy people; they shall remain in the river only.

12. And Moses and Aaron went out from Pharaoh: and Moses cried unto the Lord because of the frogs which he had brought against Pharaoh.

13. And the Lord did according to the word of Moses; and the frogs died out of the houses, out of the villages, and out of the fields.

14. And they gathered them together upon heaps: and the land stank.

15. But when Pharaoh saw that there was respite, he hardened his heart, and hearkened not unto them; as the Lord had said.

16. And the Lord said unto Moses, Say unto Aaron, Stretch out thy rod, and smite the dust of the land, that it may become lice throughout all the land of Egypt.

17. And they did so; for Aaron stretched out his hand with his rod, and smote the dust of the earth, and it became lice in man, and in beast; all the dust of the land became lice throughout all the land of Egypt.

18. And the magicians did so with their enchantments to bring forth lice, but they could not: so there were lice upon man, and upon beast.

19. Then the magicians said unto Pharaoh, This *is* the finger of God: and Pharaoh's heart was hardened, and he hearkened not unto them; as the Lord had said.

20. And the Lord said unto Moses, Rise up early in the morning, and stand before Pharaoh; lo, he cometh forth to the water; and say unto him, Thus saith the Lord, Let my people go, that they may serve me.

21. Else, if thou wilt not let my people go, behold, I will send swarms *of flies* upon thee, and upon thy servants, and upon thy people, and into thy houses: and the houses of the Egyptians shall be full of swarms *of flies*, and also the ground whereon they *are*.

22. And I will sever in that day the land of Goshen, in which my people dwell,

that no swarms *of flies* shall be there; to the end thou mayest know that I *am* the Lord in the midst of the earth.

23. And I will put a division between my people and thy people: to-morrow shall this sign be.

24. And the Lord did so; and there came a grievous swarm *of flies* into the house of Pharaoh, and *into* his servants' houses, and into all the land of Egypt: the land was corrupted by reason of the swarm *of flies.*

25. And Pharaoh called for Moses and for Aaron, and said, Go ye, sacrifice to your God in the land.

26. And Moses said, It is not meet so to do; for we shall sacrifice the abomination of the Egyptians to the Lord our God: lo, shall we sacrifice the abomination of the Egyptians before their eyes, and will they not stone us?

27. We will go three days' journey into the wilderness, and sacrifice to the Lord our God, as he shall command us.

28. And Pharaoh said, I will let you go, that ye may sacrifice to the Lord your God in the wilderness; only ye shall not go very far away: intreat for me.

29. And Moses said, Behold, I go out from thee, and I will intreat the Lord that the swarms of *flies* may depart from Pharaoh, from his servants, and from his people, to-morrow: but let not Pharaoh deal deceitfully any more in not letting the people go to sacrifice to the Lord.

30. And Moses went out from Pharaoh, and intreated the Lord.

31. And the Lord did according to the word of Moses; and he removed the swarms *of flies* from Pharaoh, from his servants, and from his people; there remained not one.

32. And Pharaoh hardened his heart at this time also, neither would he let the people go.

1. Then the Lord said unto Moses, Go in unto Pharaoh, and tell him, Thus saith the Lord God of the Hebrews, Let my people go, that they may serve me.

2. For if thou refuse to let *them* go, and wilt hold them still,

3. Behold, the hand of the Lord is upon thy cattle which *is* in the field, upon the horses, upon the asses, upon the camels, upon the oxen, and upon the sheep: *there shall be* a very grievous murrain.

4. And the Lord shall sever between the cattle of Israel and the cattle of Egypt: and there shall nothing die of all *that is* the children's of Israel.

5. And the Lord appointed a set time, saying, To-morrow the Lord shall do this thing in the land.

6. And the Lord did that thing on the morrow, and all the cattle of Egypt died: but of the cattle of the children of Israel died not one.

7. And Pharaoh sent, and, behold, there was not one of the cattle of the Israelites dead. And the heart of Pharaoh was hardened, and he did not let the people go.

8. And the Lord said unto Moses and unto Aaron, Take to you handfuls of ashes of the furnace, and let Moses sprinkle it toward the heaven in the sight of Pharaoh.

9. And it shall become small dust in all the land of Egypt, and shall be a boil breaking forth *with* blains upon man, and upon beast, throughout all the land of Egypt.

10. And they took ashes of the furnace, and stood before Pharaoh; and Moses sprinkled it up toward heaven; and it became a boil breaking forth *with* blains upon man, and upon beast.

11. And the magicians could not stand before Moses because of the boils; for the boil was upon the magicians, and upon all the Egyptians.

12. And the Lord hardened the heart of Pharaoh, and he hearkened not unto them; as the Lord had spoken unto Moses.

13. And the Lord said unto Moses, Rise up early in the morning, and stand before Pharaoh, and say unto him, Thus saith the Lord God of the Hebrews, Let my people go, that they may serve me.

14. For I will at this time send all my plagues upon thine heart, and upon thy servants, and upon thy people; that thou mayest know that *there is* none like me in all the earth.

15. For now I will stretch out my hand, that I may smite thee and thy people with pestilence; and thou shalt be cut off from the earth.

16. And in very deed for this *cause* have I raised thee up, for to shew *in* thee my power; and that my name may be declared throughout all the earth.

17. As yet exaltest thou thyself against my people, that thou wilt not let them go?

18. Behold, to-morrow about this time I will cause it to rain a very grievous hail, such as hath not been in Egypt since the foundation thereof even until now.

19. Send therefore now, *and* gather thy cattle, and all that thou hast in the field; *for upon* every man and beast which shall be found in the field, and shall not be brought home, the hail shall come down upon them, and they shall die.

20. He that feared the word of the Lord among the servants of Pharaoh made his servants and his cattle flee into the houses:

21. And he that regarded not the word of the Lord left his servants and his cattle in the field.

22. And the Lord said unto Moses, Stretch forth thine hand toward heaven, that there may be hail in all the land of Egypt, upon man, and upon beast, and upon every herb of the field, throughout the land of Egypt.

23. And Moses stretched forth his rod toward heaven: and the Lord sent thunder and hail, and the fire ran along upon the ground; and the Lord rained hail upon the land of Egypt.

24. So there was hail, and fire mingled with the hail, very grievous, such as there was none like it in all the land of Egypt since it became a nation.

25. And the hail smote throughout all the land of Egypt all that *was* in the field, both man and beast; and the hail smote every herb of the field, and brake every tree of the field.

26. Only in the land of Goshen, where the children of Israel *were*, was there no hail.

27. And Pharaoh sent, and called for Moses and Aaron, and said unto them, I have sinned this time: the Lord *is* righteous, and I and my people *are* wicked.

28. Intreat the Lord (for *it is* enough) that there be no *more* mighty thunderings and hail; and I will let you go, and ye shall stay no longer.

29. And Moses said unto him, As soon as I am gone out of the city, I will spread abroad my hands unto the Lord; *and* the thunder shall cease, neither shall there be any more hail; that thou mayest know how that the earth *is* the Lord's.

30. But as for thee and thy servants, I know that ye will not yet fear the Lord God.

31. And the flax and the barley was smitten: for the barley *was* in the ear, and the flax *was* bolled.

32. But the wheat and the rye were not smitten: for they *were* not grown up.

33. And Moses went out of the city from Pharaoh, and spread abroad his hands unto the Lord: and the thunders and hail ceased, and the rain was not poured upon the earth.

34. And when Pharaoh saw that the rain and the hail and the thunders were ceased, he sinned yet more, and hardened his heart, he and his servants.

35. And the heart of Pharaoh was hardened, neither would he let the children of Israel go; as the Lord had spoken by Moses.

1. And the Lord saith unto Moses, Go in unto Pharaoh: for I have hardened his heart, and the heart of his servants, that I might shew these my signs before him:

2. And that thou mayest tell in the ears of thy son, and of thy son's son, what things I have wrought in Egypt, and my signs which I have done among them; that ye may know how that I *am* the Lord.

3. And Moses and Aaron came in unto Pharaoh, and said unto him, Thus saith the Lord God of the Hebrews, How long wilt thou refuse to humble thyself before me? let my people go, that they may serve me.

4. Else, if thou refuse to let my people go, behold, to-morrow will I bring the locusts into thy coast:

5. And they shall cover the face of the earth, that one cannot be able to see the earth: and they shall eat the residue of that which is escaped, which remaineth unto you from the hail, and shall eat every tree which groweth for you out of the field:

6. And they shall fill thy houses, and the houses of all thy servants, and the houses of all the Egyptians; which neither thy fathers, nor thy fathers' fathers have seen, since the day that they were upon the earth unto this day. And he turned himself, and went out from Pharaoh.

7. And Pharaoh's servants said unto him, How long shall this man be a snare unto us? let the men go, that they may serve the Lord their God: knowest thou not yet that Egypt is destroyed?

8. And Moses and Aaron were brought again unto Pharaoh: and he said unto them, Go, serve the Lord your God: *but* who *are* they that shall go?

9. And Moses said, We will go with our young and with our old, with our sons and with our daughters, with our flocks and with our herds will we go; for we *must hold* a feast unto the Lord.

10. And he said unto them, Let the Lord be so with you, as I will let you go, and your little ones: look *to it*; for evil *is* before you.

11. Not so: go now ye *that are* men, and serve the Lord; for that ye did desire. And they were driven out from Pharaoh's presence.

12. And the Lord said unto Moses, Stretch out thine hand over the land of Egypt for the locusts, that they may come up upon the land of Egypt, and eat every herb of the land, *even* all that the hail hath left.

13. And Moses stretched forth his rod over the land of Egypt, and the Lord

brought an east wind upon the land all that day, and all *that* night; *and* when it was morning, the east wind brought the locusts.

14. And the locusts went up over all the land of Egypt, and rested in all the coasts of Egypt: very grievous *were they*; before them there were no such locusts as they, neither after them shall be such.

15. For they covered the face of the whole earth, so that the land was darkened; and they did eat every herb of the land, and all the fruit of the trees which the hail had left: and there remained not any green thing in the trees, or in the herbs of the field, through all the land of Egypt.

16. Then Pharaoh called for Moses and Aaron in haste; and he said, I have sinned against the Lord your God, and against you.

17. Now therefore forgive, I pray thee, my sin only this once, and intreat the Lord your God, that he may take away from me this death only.

18. And he went out from Pharaoh, and intreated the Lord.

19. And the Lord turned a mighty strong west wind, which took away the locusts, and cast them into the Red sea; there remained not one locust in all the coasts of Egypt.

20. But the Lord hardened Pharaoh's heart, so that he would not let the children of Israel go.

21. And the Lord said unto Moses, Stretch out thine hand toward heaven, that there may be darkness over the land of Egypt, even darkness *which* may be felt.

22. And Moses stretched forth his hand toward heaven; and there was a thick darkness in all the land of Egypt three days:

23. They saw not one another, neither rose any from his place for three days: but all the children of Israel had light in their dwellings.

24. And Pharaoh called unto Moses, and said, Go ye, serve the Lord; only let your flocks and your herds be stayed: let your little ones also go with you.

25. And Moses said, Thou must give us also sacrifices and burnt-offerings, that we may sacrifice unto the Lord our God.

26. Our cattle also shall go with us; there shall not an hoof be left behind; for thereof must we take to serve the Lord our God; and we know not with what we must serve the Lord, until we come thither.

27. But the Lord hardened Pharaoh's heart, and he would not let them go.

28. And Pharaoh said unto him, Get thee from me, take heed to thyself, see my face no more; for in *that* day thou seest my face thou shalt die.

29. And Moses said, Thou hast spoken well, I will see thy face again no more.

PSALM CV. 27–35

27. They shewed his signs among them,
   And wonders in the land of Ham.
28. He sent darkness, and made it dark;
   And they rebelled not against his word.
29. He turned their waters into blood,
   And slew their fish.
30. Their land brought forth frogs in abundance,
   In the chambers of their kings.

31. He spake, and there came divers sorts of flies,
    And lice in all their coasts.
32. He gave them hail for rain,
    And flaming fire in their land.
33. He smote their vines also and their fig-trees,
    And brake the trees of their coasts.
34. He spake, and the locusts came,
    And caterpillars, and that without number,
35. And did eat up all the herbs in their land,
    And devoured the fruit of their ground.

THE NINE PLAGUES

Exodus 7:14-25;8:1-32;9:1-35;10:1-29

The Plagues and Their Purpose. Three months, or at the most six, is the period that must be assigned to the plagues. As we have seen, they were primarily intended to answer the question which Pharaoh had very naturally asked, "Who is Jehovah?" By entering into the spheres which were ruled by the gods of Egypt, and by overruling them; by predicting exactly what would happen, and by causing the prediction to come to pass; by leaving the magicians, with all their arts, out-distanced and ashamed; Jehovah, through His servants, answered that question to the full, and gave incontestable proof that He was God of gods. And further, when Pharaoh, knowing that he was now face to face with the demands of the great God of Nature, resented and resisted His claim, the Plagues set forth in the realm of Nature the horror and awfulness of sin. It was only as the evil of Pharaoh's heart was projected on the screen of the natural world, that he could be made to realise that he was in conflict with the natural order of the universe. Therefore these plagues were "signs."[1]

Miracles as "Signs". It is familiar to all students of the New Testament, that two words are used to describe our Lord's miracles. The Synoptics describe them as mighty acts of power, whilst the Fourth Gospel refers to them as *signs*.[2] There are these two aspects of the miraculous elements, whether we regard it simply as the calling into exercise of forces which are outside the ordinary course of Nature, or as the revelation, in a sudden flash, of the processes which are always at work around us. The miracle of Cana compressed into a moment the production of the juice of the grape, which through many months each year is formed in the vines of the South from the waters of rains and dews. The multiplication of the bread was not really more wonderful than the production of the annual harvest that goldens each autumn throughout the world.

[1] x. 2.   [2] John ii. 11.

Our Lord's Miracles Thus Viewed. Looked at from this point of view, the miracles of our Lord were indications of the Divine power which is latent in Nature around us, but which is so ordinary and gradual in its operations that its glory and divinity are hidden from our eyes. When compressed into a single flash, we recognise it, and cry, "This is the finger of God." But God's handiwork is equally present in the vineyard or cornfield, the formation of the eye in the babe, the healing processes of the human body, and the daily triumph of life over death. The Lord's miracles were signs, therefore, that the same divine power which was admittedly at the back of all these familiar processes, was in a unique and special manner resident in Himself.

What the Plagues Signified. What is true of the beneficent acts of Jesus is also true of the plagues. They were signs, i.e. they revealed in a flash of pain and distress, that self-will and pride are contrary to the Divine order of the world, and destructive of all human well-being. It would seem as though the Almighty withdrew the restraints which, in the present-time of discipline and probation, are holding back the immediate consequences of wrong-doing, so that men might be able to see what an evil thing sin is, and how terribly it injures their own best interests. For the most part, the processes of retribution are so gradual that we fail to connect them with their causes. For instance, in a vague way, we believe that luxury and debauchery ultimately destroy noble families, but, in our hurrying and migratory days, we do not stay long enough to be impressed with the certainty and terror of the Divine judgments. Given some overwhelming act of retribution, like the fate of Belshazzar on the night that Cyrus took Babylon, and the heart of humanity instantly recognises that there is One who judgeth in the earth.

The World Suffering Under Sin. As our bodies are affected by indulgence in sin, so probably the natural world, and even the brute creation, are powerfully influenced by the indulgence of human passion. Creation, says the apostle, groans and travails together with man; the revelation of the sons of God is to inaugurate her emancipation from the bondage of corruption.[1] The rending rocks and veiled heavens of the Crucifixion were the natural expression, in the earth-plane, of the love and hate which met in dread collision at Calvary. The prophet Jeremiah tells us that the land

[1] Rom. viii. 19–22.

mourns and the herbs of a whole country wither for the wickedness of them that dwell therein, and that even the beasts and birds are consumed.[1] It has never seemed remarkable that when the Puritan Commonwealth expired with Cromwell, so vast a revolution was accompanied by one of the most terrific storms that ever devastated Britain; or that on that momentous afternoon when the assembled conclave at the Vatican pronounced the dogma of Papal Infallibility, the reading of the decree was rendered almost inaudible by peals of reverberating thunder that shook the city.

Nature and Soul. By its constitution, Nature is sympathetic with the motions of the soul. Man acts on his environment, as his environment reacts on him. The scars on the world's surface, in many cases, are directly attributable to enormous crimes, such as the desolation of the Dead Sea, or the masses of scoriae that buried Pompeii. It is through such natural correspondences that God speaks to men, compelling their attention, and forcing them in these catastrophes in the world around to understand the perilous and harmful nature of sin.

Natural Calamities the Voice of God. His Hand is everywhere, sustaining and directing, but at times it is manifestly stretched out. His finger is always present, but sometimes it indicates its meaning with awful accuracy; and traces in characters of fire upon palace-walls the sentence of doom—"Thou art weighed in the balances, and art found wanting."[2]

Mercy in God's Severity. Granted that there is a great apparent contrast between the beneficence of our Lord's healing work, and the terrific strokes of these successive plagues; yet the Psalmist is undeniably right when he interludes his enumeration of the plagues with the refrain, "For His mercy endureth for ever." "To Him that smote Egypt in their first-born for His mercy endureth for ever." There is mercy in the severity, as in the goodness of the Lord. There is stern severity in the inevitable pain which follows on the violation of natural law, as when the fingers of your little child are blistered if it reaches out to the ruddy flame; but is not the Love greater which insists that it should learn to conform to those conditions on which the elements achieve their useful ministry to mankind?

The Exodus to Benefit Egypt Also. The ill-usage that Egypt was meting out to Israel, the overbearing insolence of the task-masters,

[1] Jer. xii. 4. [2] Dan. v. 27.

the indifference of the masses of the people who profited by their toils, the heartless cruelty of King, Court, and Priesthood, were really hurting Egypt more than Israel. In the best interests of each the intolerable situation had to be ended; and if these months of pain were comparable to the pangs of birth, surely the undoing of wrong and the birth of a nation to its rightful liberty were ample justification of the infliction of the plagues. With the froward God shows Himself froward, as with the merciful He shows Himself merciful. But this is His strange, unwelcome work.[1]

The Plagues and Their Order. The plagues[2]—and we use this word, as most familiar—have been divided into three triads, leading up to the last and most terrible, which naturally stands by itself. Each triad is severer than the preceding; and in each the successive blows culminate, like the third wavelet which runs further and breaks with a louder splash than the two preceding.

Each Series begins in the Morning. "And the Lord said unto Moses, Pharaoh's heart is stubborn, he refuseth to let the people go. Get thee unto Pharaoh *in the morning.*"[3] "And the Lord said unto Moses, Rise up early *in the morning,* and stand before Pharaoh."[4] "And the Lord said unto Moses, Rise up early *in the morning,* and stand before Pharaoh."[5]

The Triads. In the first triad—of the Nile, the frogs, and lice— all the land was smitten indiscriminately; but in the last two triads the land of Goshen enjoyed immunity from harm, showing that the successive strokes were not the result of a chance combination of the elements, but were directed by a presiding Mind.

In the first triad, Aaron is to the front; but in the second he falls into the background, and Moses leads the fight. In the third, the invariable formula employed by Jehovah to Moses is "Stretch forth thine hand toward Heaven." In the two first, he stretches out his rod, but in the last his hand only.

Similarities in Each Triad of Plagues. In each triad there is a long warning before the first stroke, a shorter one before the second, and none before the third. The announcement of what is about to happen, when given, is very precise; and these accurate forecasts of what no mortal prescience could foresee, and their exact fulfilment, compelled the frank confession of the College of Magicians, that the

---

[1] Ps. xviii. 26; Isa. xxviii. 21.   [2] ix. 14.
[3] vii. 14, 15.   [4] viii. 20.
[5] ix. 13.

portents were not casual, but catastrophic, and due to the direct interposition of God.

Plagues not Casual. Those who stood in Pharaoh's inner circle of advisers were certain that he was engaged in conflict with a greater Deity than any known to them, and founded their conclusion on the twofold ground, first, that the magicians themselves had been driven from the field; and, second, that nothing failed of all that Moses spoke.[1]

The First Triad. THE NILE IS TURNED TO BLOOD. The Nile was worshipped as a beneficent deity, in whose honour hymns were chanted by the priests. The papyri furnish the very words of those ancient odes. Probably Pharaoh's visits to the river at early dawn, which gave the Hebrew brethren the opportunity of an interview, were for purposes of worship. Not only did the Nile-water provide a daily beverage of exceptional sweetness, and an abundant supply for the ablutions in which the Egyptians excelled; but the annual inundation, when the river covered the adjacent lands with rich alluvial soil, transformed the arid sand into a broad riband of green verdure.

The River of Blood. What terror and horror must have smitten the universal heart of the people, when the waters suddenly became ghastly to sight, putrid and poisonous in the scorching heat, and impossible for any purpose! The ponds left by the receding tides, the pools or cisterns where water had been carefully stored, suffered equally with the river; only the wells sunk in the sands yielded a scanty supply of water; and this deprivation lasted for seven days.

The Frogs. A frog-headed deity has been discovered on the monuments. It was the symbol of fecundity and affluent life. Loathsome in appearance, tormenting with its incessant croak, hideous to trample on or touch, poisonous in the stench of its putrifying body when dead, the frog was the symbol of everything that could produce disgust in the cleanly and fastidious Egyptian. That frogs should cover their land and fill their homes, and be found in the bedchambers of the king, was unbearable. Ancient history tells of a tribe being driven out of their territory by a visitation of this sort. Small wonder, then, that Pharaoh, for the first time, gave signs of relenting. "Entreat the Lord, that He take away the frogs from me, and from my people; and I will let the people go, that they may sacrifice unto the Lord." Moses asked him to fix his own time,

[1] viii. 19; ix. 11; x. 7.

in order that the Divine aspect of the visitation might stand out in clearer relief; and in his reply of "to-morrow," Pharaoh intimated that there was sufficient ground for its infliction, so much so that he dared not ask for instantaneous respite.

The Lice. The frogs invaded their homes, the lice their bodies. Travellers in Egypt have described experiences in which the very dust seemed turned to lice. This, and the fact that lice would be extremely repulsive to the magicians and priests, who were accustomed to shave themselves every other day in order to avoid this very pest, incline us to accept the traditional view of this plague, rather than that it consisted of mosquitoes or midges. It was this that elicited the conviction of the magicians that they were in the presence of a new and greater deity.[1]

It is specially noticeable that beasts are mentioned here, as though the sacred animals themselves, in their sacred shrines, were smitten. Their glossy skins, kept with so much care by their attendants, were suddenly infested by the pernicious and insidious plague. How could the sacred bull-calf help its votaries, if it could not save itself? And what sanctity could attach to shrines, the walls and gates of which could not defend from these hideous intruders?

So the first triad closed, but "Pharaoh's heart was hardened, and he hearkened not; as the Lord had spoken."[1]

The Second Triad. The Flies. These "swarms of flies" are supposed by some to refer to the dog-fly; but more probably the phrase denotes the beetle, and refers specially to the sacred Scarabaeus beetle, an emblem of the Sun and of the abiding life of the soul. Every monument, every mummy-chest, innumerable amulets and charms bore the effigy of this revered symbol. But the multiplication of this creature became so intolerable, together with the swarms of other flying things that filled the air, that for a second time Pharaoh showed signs of relenting. He "called for Moses and for Aaron, and said, Go ye, sacrifice to your God in the land." So far he was prepared to admit that Jehovah was specifically the God of Israel—*your* God. But he intimated in this reservation that he did not admit that *he* was under the necessity of obeying Him. Further, he made the cautious condition that if they went into the wilderness, they were not to go far away. It was easy for Moses to convince him that it was impossible to conform to his first condition. The Egyptians would resent such profanation of their

[1] viii. 19.

sacred soil as blasphemy. It was certain that the feast must be celebrated beyond the limits of the land of Egypt.

The Murrain. The heavy strokes of Divine chastisement were to become heavier, as the king's obstinacy became more intelligent and reasoned. Hitherto they had been annoying and painful, but no life had been sacrificed. Now death appeared on the scene, and though at first beasts alone perished, before long there would not be an Egyptian home that should not have been entered and visited.

It is startling to find the beasts now included, directly and specifically, in the incidence of God's stern dealings with the land of Egypt; and yet is not their lot always intimately bound up with ours?

Man's Sins Infect the Beasts. Those who object to the plague of murrain that swept Egypt, as the Rinderpest has depleted parts of South Africa in recent years, must equally resent the entire scheme of Providence, which binds the lower orders of being in such extraordinarily close connection with the human family. The whole creation is bound together by invisible cords. None can sin or suffer alone. No man liveth or dieth to himself. Our sins send their vibrations through creation, and infect the very beasts. Our want of harmony with God jars on the music of the spheres.

It is not surprising therefore that the prophets speak of the rending of the veil that sin has cast over the whole creation, and which may stretch back into the dim past, as the efficacy of Christ's redemption does, for was not He the Lamb slain from the foundation of the world? Did not Isaiah catch sight of this truth when he said after his glowing fashion, that the lion shall eat straw like an ox, that the wolf shall lie down with the lamb, and that they shall not hurt nor destroy in all God's holy mountain?[1] In these directions we must seek the explanation of the murrain, which specially revealed the inability of the sacred animals to protect either themselves or their votaries.

The Boils and Blains. These were a further warning of the gathering vehemence of the fever heat of sin. The lice were loathsome, but these were loathsome and inflammatory sores, painful to endure and loathsome to behold. The magicians, who up to this point had endeavoured to keep up with Moses, though unable

[1] Isa. xi. 9.

to repeat their wonders, seem now to have abandoned the field, as though their own appearance was revolting to themselves as well as to others. We recall the awful descriptions of the Apocalypse, founded on this plague: "They gnawed their tongues for pain, and they blasphemed the God of Heaven because of their pains and their sores; and they repented not of their works."[1] So the second triad of signs and wonders came to an end, but still the king is obdurate. "He hearkened not unto them; as the Lord had spoken unto Moses."[2]

The Third Triad. The last and most tremendous blows were to be struck. Once more, in the early morning, the two brothers break in with their inexorable demand: "Thus saith the Lord, the God of the Hebrews, Let My people go, that they may serve Me." And following this challenge, with tremendous directness and urgency they foreshadowed the awful risks that the king was incurring for himself, his servants, and his people. He was told that he had been raised up for this very purpose, that God might show him His power, and that His name should be declared throughout the earth. This does not necessarily imply his overthrow at the Red Sea or his ultimate destiny, but simply that Jehovah desired to illuminate him, and through him the world of men, as to His supremacy and attributes. He had already done so, and if only Pharaoh had acted on the knowledge that he had already received, no further harm would have accrued. Up till now no human life had been sacrificed. The losses and privations already sustained, having accomplished their purpose, would have passed away. Israel would have been emancipated, and the world would have acquired a never-to-be-forgotten lesson. Instead of ten plagues, there would have been six, and probably these would have been always described as "signs."

A Change in the Character of the Plagues. At this point, however, we seem to be passing into a new chapter in the Divine dealings. Man had come into collision with the Divine Power, and what was intended for instruction and illumination suddenly became punitive and destructive. Pharaoh had been raised up to learn God's power, and enough had been done to make him acquainted with it; but he had misused his opportunity, and turned God's goodness into an occasion of ever-hardening resistance. The result was, that instead of being a monument of mercy, of the hearing ear and the under-

[1] Rev. xvi. 10, 11. [2] ix. 12.

standing heart, of the docility which is prepared to learn and obey, he became a beacon and a warning, a sign to all generations that if a man will not bend he must break, and that the soul may turn to poison what God intended should be for its nourishment and enlightenment.

Penalty for Misuse of God's Gifts. The sun sheds its beneficent light and heat on the world, the dews distil, the rains fall, the earth is prepared to provide food meet for our food and pleasure, but if, instead of planting corn and vegetables, we cultivate the land for the poppy, we have ourselves to blame for having diverted the beneficent processes of Nature to the undoing of human health and happiness.

Let it never be forgotten that if we are told that God hardened Pharaoh's heart and the heart of his servants, we are also told again and again that he hardened his own heart; and it is not difficult to understand how God may be described as doing what really was due to Pharaoh's resistance to a chain of providential dealings that were intended to enlighten and convert him.

The Hail. The explicit references to the crops affected by this visitation proves that it befell in the month of March, for the barley was in ear and the flax in blossom, though the wheat and spelt were as yet only green. Josephus says that not only had the land of Egypt never experienced such a storm, but that the like had never been known even in northern and arctic lands, more habituated to the violence of the elements. Thunder and lightning are not unknown in Egypt in spring; but a storm of this kind was unheard of. The terrific explosions of thunder, the flashing lightning, the electric fire as it ran along the ground, the violence of the hail that slew man and beast, and destroyed every tree and every herb, filled king and people with panic. Only the land of Goshen was immune.

But notwithstanding Pharaoh's confession that he had sinned, and his unconditional assurances that he would let the captive people go, so soon as, in answer to Moses' out-spread hands, the rain and hail and thunder ceased; he sinned yet more, and hardened his heart, he and his servants.

The Locusts. An invasion of locusts is probably the most terrible pest that a land can suffer. Their numbers darken the sun, and no green thing survives their passage. The King's advisers knew well that whatever had survived the hail would perish before these voracious hordes. And when they heard the brothers say that this visitation would exceed anything that their fathers, or father's fathers had heard of or seen, from the earliest days of man's history, they were profoundly moved. This was the reason of their very unusual interposition and remonstrance, "Let the men go, that they may serve Jehovah their God; knowest thou not yet that Egypt is destroyed?"

Pharaoh temporises in vain. Pharaoh was so far affected by their representations that he sent for the two brethren, and for a second time tried to enter into an arrangement. On the former occasion he stipulated that they should not go very far away; but on this he endeavoured to limit the numbers of those who should participate in the proposed feast to the men. Their little ones should remain as hostages! "No," said Moses; "we will go with our young and with our old, with our sons and with our daughters, with our flocks and with our herds; for we must hold a feast unto the Lord."[1] This so far exasperated Pharaoh that they were driven from his presence, and then the plague befell. The locusts darkened the ground with their brown bodies; they utterly destroyed every green thing; there was neither vegetable nor fruit in all the land. "Very grievous were they; before them there was no such locusts as they."

Again Pharaoh professed to repent. This time he confessed that he had sinned, not only against Jehovah, but against the two brethren. He asked them to forgive, and intercede on his behalf. But as soon as the stroke was removed he returned to his former hardness of heart.

The Darkness. It is supposed that this was caused by a hot desert wind, laden with vast whirlwinds of sand, that has been known to bury whole armies, leaving no trace. An Arab chronicler, about the end of the eleventh century, records a great storm, accompanied by darkness so intense that it was thought that the end of the world had arrived.[2] Again Pharaoh summoned the Hebrew leaders, and made one last effort at compromise. He was willing for Israel to go, both young and old, but their flocks and herds were to remain.

Moses Refuses to Bargain with Pharaoh. Not for a moment could the bargain be considered. "Our cattle shall go with us," said

[1] x. 7–11.
[2] Quoted by Dr. Geikie.

Moses, "not a hoof shall be left behind." At this the King broke out with angry threats, dismissing him from his presence, and assuring him that any further intrusion would be penalised with death.

But Moses, who, with every successive step in the conflict, had arisen to a more resolute and commanding attitude, before leaving his presence announced the doom that was about to close the conflict.

And Announces the Death of the Firstborn.

" Thou hast spoken well," he said, " I will see thy face no more. But thus saith Jehovah: About midnight will I go out into the midst of Egypt: and all the first-born in the land of Egypt shall die, from the firstborn of Pharaoh that sitteth upon his throne, even unto the first-born of the maid-servant that is behind the mill; and all the firstborn of cattle. And there shall be a great cry throughout all the land of Egypt, such as there hath been none like it, nor shall be like it any more. But against any of the children of Israel shall not a dog move his tongue, against man or beast: that ye may know how that the Lord doth put a difference between the Egyptians and Israel. And all these thy servants shall come down unto me, and bow down themselves unto me, saying, Get thee out, and all the people that follow thee: and after that I will go out."[1]

The Pause before the Passover.

Then a great silence settled down upon the land, like that stillness which precedes a tropical thunderstorm. The Egyptians were full of an awful dread of the threatened judgment, which their monarch's obstinacy had incurred. Their gods were discredited; their priests and magicians had retired from the conflict; the forces of Nature seemed arrayed against them; the King's policy had only landed them deeper and deeper into domestic loss and national misfortune.

The Discredited Egyptian Gods.

On the other hand, as the children of Israel beheld the gods of Egypt unable to defend their worshippers, but overwhelmed with eclipse and collapse, unable to save themselves or the country of which they were the tutelary deities, when they realised the immunity which the land of Goshen enjoyed for their sakes, when they remarked the power of Moses with God and man, the might of those outstretched hands and of that omnipotent faith, they cast aside the bonds of despondency and despair in which they

[1] x. 29; xi. 4–8.

had been held, and began to count confidently on their emancipation from their long bondage into the land which God had covenanted to give Abraham and his seed for ever.

During this pause, Moses issued his final instructions for the Feast of Passover, and the Exodus.

THE PASSOVER

Exodus 11:1-10;12:1-28,43-51;13:3-10

1. And the Lord said unto Moses, Yet will I bring one plague *more* upon Pharaoh, and upon Egypt; afterwards he will let you go hence: when he shall let *you* go, he shall surely thrust you out hence altogether.

2. Speak now in the ears of the people, and let every man borrow of his neighbour, and every woman of her neighbour, jewels of silver, and jewels of gold.

3. And the Lord gave the people favour in the sight of the Egyptians. Moreover the man Moses *was* very great in the land of Egypt, in the sight of Pharaoh's servants, and in the sight of the people.

4. And Moses said, Thus saith the Lord, About midnight will I go out into the midst of Egypt:

5. And all the firstborn in the land of Egypt shall die, from the firstborn of Pharaoh that sitteth upon his throne, even unto the firstborn of the maidservant that *is* behind the mill; and all the firstborn of beasts.

6. And there shall be a great cry throughout all the land of Egypt, such as there was none like it, nor shall be like it any more.

7. But against any of the children of Israel shall not a dog move his tongue, against man or beast: that ye may know how that the Lord doth put a difference between the Egyptians and Israel.

8. And all these thy servants shall come down unto me, and bow down themselves unto me, saying, Get thee out, and all the people that follow thee: and after that I will go out. And he went out from Pharaoh in a great anger.

9. And the Lord said unto Moses, Pharaoh shall not hearken unto you; that my wonders may be multiplied in the land of Egypt.

10. And Moses and Aaron did all these wonders before Pharaoh: and the Lord hardened Pharaoh's heart, so that he would not let the children of Israel go out of his land.

1. And the Lord spake unto Moses and Aaron in the land of Egypt, saying,

2. This month *shall be* unto you the beginning of months: it *shall be* the first month of the year to you.

3. Speak ye unto all the congregation of Israel, saying, In the tenth *day* of this month they shall take to them every man a lamb, according to the house of *their* fathers, a lamb for an house:

4. And if the household be too little for the lamb, let him and his neighbour next unto his house take *it* according to the number of the souls; every man according to his eating shall make your count for the lamb.

5. Your lamb shall be without blemish, a male of the first year: ye shall take *it* out from the sheep, or from the goats:

6. And ye shall keep it up until the fourteenth day of the same month: and the whole assembly of the congregation of Israel shall kill it in the evening.

7. And they shall take of the blood, and strike *it* on the two side posts and on the upper door post of the houses, wherein they shall eat it.

8. And they shall eat the flesh in that night, roast with fire, and unleavened bread; *and* with bitter *herbs* they shall eat it.

9. Eat not of it raw, nor sodden at all with water, but roast *with* fire; his head with his legs, and with the purtenance thereof.

10. And ye shall let nothing of it remain until the morning; and that which remaineth of it until the morning ye shall burn with fire.

11. And thus shall ye eat it; *with* your loins girded, your shoes on your feet, and your staff in your hand; and ye shall eat it in haste: it *is* the Lord's passover.

12. For I will pass through the land of Egypt this night, and will smite all the firstborn in the land of Egypt, both man and beast; and against all the gods of Egypt I will execute judgment: I *am* the Lord.

13. And the blood shall be to you for a token upon the houses where ye *are*: and when I see the blood, I will pass over you, and the plague shall not be upon you to destroy *you*, when I smite the land of Egypt.

14. And this day shall be unto you for a memorial; and ye shall keep it a feast to the Lord throughout your generations; ye shall keep it a feast by an ordinance for ever.

15. Seven days shall ye eat unleavened bread; even the first day ye shall put away leaven out of your houses: for whosoever eateth leavened bread from the first day until the seventh day, that soul shall be cut off from Israel.

16. And in the first day *there shall be* an holy convocation, and in the seventh day there shall be an holy convocation to you; no manner of work shall be done in them, save *that* which every man must eat, that only may be done of you.

17. And ye shall observe *the feast of* unleavened bread; for in this selfsame day have I brought your armies out of the land of Egypt; therefore shall ye observe this day in your generations by an ordinance for ever.

18. In the first *month*, on the fourteenth day of the month at even, ye shall eat unleavened bread, until the one and twentieth day of the month at even.

19. Seven days shall there be no leaven found in your houses: for whosoever eateth that which is leavened, even that soul shall be cut off from the congregation of Israel, whether he be a stranger, or born in the land.

20. Ye shall eat nothing leavened; in all your habitations shall ye eat unleavened bread.

21. Then Moses called for all the elders of Israel, and said unto them, Draw out and take you a lamb according to your families, and kill the passover.

22. And ye shall take a bunch of hyssop, and dip *it* in the blood that *is* in the bason, and strike the lintel and the two side posts with the blood that *is* in the bason; and none of you shall go out at the door of his house until the morning.

23. For the Lord will pass through to smite the Egyptians; and when he seeth the blood upon the lintel, and on the two side posts, the Lord will pass over the door, and will not suffer the destroyer to come in unto your houses to smite *you*.

24. And ye shall observe this thing for an ordinance to thee and to thy sons for ever.

25. And it shall come to pass, when ye be come to the land which the Lord will give you, according as he hath promised, that ye shall keep this service.

26. And it shall come to pass, when your children shall say unto you, What mean ye by this service?

27. That ye shall say, It *is* the sacrifice of the Lord's passover, who passed over the houses of the children of Israel in Egypt, when he smote the Egyptians, and delivered our houses. And the people bowed the head and worshipped.

28. And the children of Israel went away, and did as the Lord had commanded Moses and Aaron, so did they.

43. And the Lord said unto Moses and Aaron, This *is* the ordinance of the passover: There shall no stranger eat thereof:

44. But every man's servant that is bought for money, when thou hast circumcised him, then shall he eat thereof.

45. A foreigner and an hired servant shall not eat thereof.

46. In one house shall it be eaten; thou shalt not carry forth ought of the flesh abroad out of the house; neither shall ye break a bone thereof.

47. All the congregation of Israel shall keep it.

48. And when a stranger shall sojourn with thee, and will keep the passover to the Lord, let all his males be circumcised, and then let him come near and keep it; and he shall be as one that is born in the land: for no uncircumcised person shall eat thereof.

49. One law shall be to him that is homeborn, and unto the stranger that sojourneth among you.

50. Thus did all the children of Israel; as the Lord commanded Moses and Aaron, so did they.

51. And it came to pass the selfsame day, *that* the Lord did bring the children of Israel out of the land of Egypt by their armies.

3. And Moses said unto the people, Remember this day, in which ye came out from Egypt, out of the house of bondage; for by strength of hand the Lord brought you out from this *place*: there shall no leavened bread be eaten.

4. This day came ye out in the month Abib.

5. And it shall be when the Lord shall bring thee into the land of the Canaanites, and the Hittites, and the Amorites, and the Hivites, and the Jebusites, which he sware unto thy fathers to give thee, a land flowing with milk and honey, that thou shalt keep this service in this month.

6. Seven days thou shalt eat unleavened bread, and in the seventh day *shall be* a feast to the Lord.

7. Unleavened bread shall be eaten seven days; and there shall no leavened bread be seen with thee, neither shall there be leaven seen with thee in all thy quarters.

8. And thou shalt shew thy son in that day, saying, *This is done* because of *that which* the Lord did unto me when I came forth out of Egypt.

9. And it shall be for a sign unto thee upon thine hand, and for a memorial between thine eyes, that the Lord's law may be in thy mouth: for with a strong hand hath the Lord brought thee out of Egypt.

10. Thou shalt therefore keep this ordinance in his season from year to year.

THE PASSOVER

Exodus 11:1-10;12:1-28,43-51;13:3-10

Unity of Idea in the Passover and the Death of our Lord. The space given to the specification of the details of the Passover reminds us that a third of the Gospel is occupied with the narrative of the death of our Lord. Evidently it was intended that these two subjects were intended to bulk largely before the mind of coming generations; and if we go to the root of the matter, they are one. The dread anticipation with which our Lord viewed the approach of His decease, the rending rocks and veiled skies of Nature, the extraordinary results that have accrued from its proclamation to the world, attest that it was of paramount importance to mankind; and whether it was prefigured by the Passover, or commemorated by the Lord's Supper, it stands unapproached and unapproachable— a monolith on the sands of Time.

Conflict between the Head and the Heart perpetual. There are two organs of inquiry by which we can approach the meaning of that death, the Head and the Heart. The conflict between them is as old as the world. The head says: "I am higher, and see further"; the heart answers: "I am deeper, and know more truly by my swift intuitions." When the heart has accused the head of being unconverted, the head has retorted on the heart for being foolish. But what God has joined together, let no man put asunder. It is in the combination of these two, like the lenses of a binocular, that we shall be led to apprehend the truth.

This Conflict and the Signification of Calvary. It must never be forgotten, when we speak of this interaction between the intellectual and the intuitive processes of our nature, that they must combine to discover the significance of Calvary in the realm of conscience. Any solution that moves on a lower level must be dismissed at once. The Cross speaks of Sin, Righteousness, and Judgment. Every interpretation, therefore, which endeavours to shift its significance from the moral and spiritual into the mere physical sphere is to be refused. The battle that our Lord fought on the cross was not primarily in the sufferings of His body, except in so far as they reflected and registered the Divine and hidden transactions of His soul. Though, by the contemplation of the wounds of Christ, we succeeded in transferring them to our flesh, yet if we did not also apprehend and assimilate the deeper aspects of His Passion, we should miss its profoundest helpfulness.

The Virtue of the Death of Christ. There has been a strong endeavour to make the virtue of the death of Christ consist in the inner death, the inner crucifixion, the crushing-out of the self-principle; and who can deny that this is the teaching of Rom. vi. and Col. ii.? But there is something prior to that. The objective precedes the subjective; and if you would really benefit by all the holy influences of His death, be sure that you believe first that Christ died for our sins, "according to the Scriptures"; *that* is objective; and the subjective follows naturally, "that we being dead to sin should live unto righteousness, for we were as sheep going astray, but are now returned."

Considerable light on the whole subject may be obtained by viewing it in the light of the Passover Supper—a view-point commended by the Apostle when he said, Christ, our Passover, has been sacrificed for us: therefore let us keep the Feast.[1] Three words will help us:

The last Plague Really a Judgment. "Against all the gods of Egypt will I execute judgments." Up to this moment the signs (or plagues) had been illuminative. They were intended to answer Pharaoh's question, "Who is the Lord?" and to convince Egyptians and Israelites that Jehovah was God of gods and Lord of lords. But the last plague was a stroke of awful judgment and punishment. Egypt had to be punished for its inveterate stubbornness and obstinacy by the death of the first-born. Pharaoh had hardened his heart—"he and his servants"—the whole nation was guilty, and on the whole nation, because of its essential solidarity, was inflicted the inevitable judgment which compelled it to realise and repent of its sin in the enforced slavery and hard bondage of the Hebrews.

God had to Maintain the Moral Order of the World. It was not that Jehovah had any personal or selfish motive in this, but because it

[1] 1 Cor. v. 7, 8.

was necessary for Him to maintain the moral order of the world. In every state or commonwealth the honour of the king or judge must be protected and enforced. If the circulation of scurrilous statement and slanderous reports is not challenged, and the person of the ruler be traduced, there is but a single step to the rupture of the foundations of society and order. Society defends its head because he is the representative and embodiment of its highest sanctions; if he is set at naught, there is urgent fear lest justice and righteousness may be murdered in the daylight in the open street.

Similarly, suppose men persistently profane and refuse the claims and call of God, as Pharaoh and his people did, knowing that He is God, but flouting His edicts and demands, the ultimate dissolution of society is within view, for its order is based on morality, and morality ultimately is based on the recognition and admission of the authority of God.

When matters reach such a crisis, there is no alternative but judgment. For the sake of Egypt herself, and for the sake of mankind generally, Pharaoh and his people must undergo judgments of so distinct and startling a nature, that all the world should be compelled to give heed.

What is Judgment? But what is Judgment? It is admitted that a miracle is the compression into a moment's flash of natural processes that otherwise consume weeks or months. When the Lord changed the water into wine at Cana, He hurried into a moment processes that ordinarily consume the greater part of the year, during which the vines distil their juices from dews and rain. When He multiplied the bread, He compressed into a single act all the procedure of a cornfield, from the ploughing of the autumn to the ingathering of August. The healing miracles of the Gospel epitomise the remedial processes which are always at work to repair the wounds and wastage of current life.

Various Judgments Reviewed. *Similarly, Judgments compress into a sudden flash the inevitable results of wrong-doing.* They are like the lightning flash at night revealing the precipices yawning before the feet of the unsuspecting traveller. They are terrible and painful, but they startle and convict and impress. The judgment of Sodom revealed what must befall communities who trifle with impurity. The judgment of Babylon revealed the overthrow that must overtake empires which are as indifferent to the claims of humanity as that ruthless empire was. The judgment of Jerusalem, when it was overthrown by Titus, revealed the fate that follows on the divorce of religion from morality. The judgment of the Napoleonic dynasty at Sedan revealed the hollowness of any rule which is based on treachery and blood. So the judgment of the Red Sea revealed the certain dissolution of all human power which defies the will of the Supreme.

All Egypt was Guilty. "By men kings rule" is fundamental to the order of the world; and it was to reaffirm this, and announce its eternal validity, that the firstborn of Egypt were stricken and Pharaoh overthrown at the Red Sea. All Egypt was guilty, but all Egyptians were not slain. Only the firstborn of each household was smitten, from the firstborn of Pharaoh that sat on the throne to the firstborn of the maid-servant, that was behind the mill, and all the firstborn of cattle, including those of the sacred beasts which Egyptians worshipped as gods. That night was to be remembered.

The Judgment on Egypt Compared with Christ's Offering for Sin. It was a night of judgment. The judgment Egypt deserved fell on its firstborn; and the judgment which, for many sins and much corruption, was merited by Israel fell, not on its firstborn, but on the lamb. Our Lord is both Firstborn of the Race and Lamb.

A Light thus Thrown on the Cross. These thoughts may throw some light on the Cross. Suppose that, for reasons dictated by His love, God resolves to forego the punishment of the world, so as not to destroy it, He must find somewhere other guarantees than those which would accrue through the execution of His verdict. If the judgment which, either gradually or suddenly, will destroy wrong-doers is not to take place, another judgment, of like or even greater awfulness, must be substituted. This is indispensable, for without it the proclamation of grace would do away with the distinctions between good and evil. But this problem was solved by the Cross of Christ, wherein God, in the person of Christ, took on Himself, and bore, the judgment due to sin.

Calvary a Concentrated Judgment. At Calvary, into those hours of suffering, was concentrated the judgment which is the inevitable concomitant of sin. It was the judgment of this world, as our Lord said. The veil was withdrawn, and men could see the horror, the shame, the dissolution that sin can produce. And if such sufferings were experienced in the green tree of Christ's pure nature, which only knew sin by close sympathy with the race He had assumed, what would not be the effect on the dry tree of the individual sinner!

Again, then, we reaffirm our faith that as Egypt was judged in the death of the firstborn, and as Israel's firstborn was judged and yet saved through the substitution of the lamb, so the world has been judged in the death of Christ, its Firstborn, its noblest and best, and we are saved through the Lamb of God, who has borne away the sin of the world.

The Passover Feast. SUBSTITUTION. "A lamb for an household." On the tenth day of Abib, which henceforth was to mark the beginning of the religious year, each family was to set apart a kid or lamb, which must be a male, without blemish and in its prime. If a household were too small to consume the whole, members of another might join, but none save a Hebrew or a proselyte to the Hebrew faith was eligible to partake. Four days later, between sunset and the appearance of the stars, the whole congregation, as by one act, killed the victims thus selected. The blood was sprinkled from a sprig of hyssop on the doorposts and lintel, as the parts most readily seen; and the household within the shelter thus provided, secure from the judgment abroad in Egypt, gave itself to the first Passover Feast.

The Judgment Falls on the Egyptians. Presently the judgment befell. It was midnight, the hour of silence, repose, and tranquillity. No one anticipated evil. The fears that Moses' words had aroused in Pharaoh's heart had probably been allayed by the delay. Suddenly, and without warning, death was everywhere.

The Silence of Death in the Stillness of Night. Probably there was no pain, no struggle, no dying groan, but the marble, the chill, the silence of death. The Angel of Death passed through the land, striking the eldest son of the palace and the slave hut, and of the domestic and sacred beasts. Only where the blood showed that the lamb had died was there deliverance. "And there was a great cry in Egypt; for there was not a house where there was not one dead."

The Ordinance of Unleavened Bread. Another ordinance was combined with that of the Passover. Unleavened bread was to be eaten for seven days, to remind them of having been thrust out of Egypt so suddenly that they had to take the dough before it was leavened, and to bind up their kneading-troughs with their clothes upon their shoulders. As the bitter herbs recalled the bitterness of their afflictions and the salt of their tears, so the unleavened bread, eaten for seven days after the Passover, reminded them that the hot haste of their flight hindered them from preparing their food.

These were as signs upon their hands and as frontlets between their eyes, and they were observed in their season, year by year. But the prominent note throughout was that of the substitution of the lamb for the child.

Substitution a Human Instinct. Why is it that substitution has fallen into discredit in these days? It is because we do not think in accordance with reality. We think of every human being as an individual by itself, and that humanity is a multitude of separate sand-grains. But a closer study of our world, of our national and political existence, and of our family-life, ought to convince us to the contrary. Ninety-nine per cent. of what we are, and think, and do, is not our own production. We share our possessions with the race, and any spontaneity or individuality that an individual may manifest will always be insignificant in comparison with what is due to the totality of the human family. Do we not all acknowledge this? Why does a father save for his children? Why does a mother rear her little ones? Why do men expend themselves for their fellows in every walk of life? They are not obliged to, but they are moved by an irresistible human instinct and impulse. What does the sense of responsibility mean, except that we are led almost instinctively to substitute our thought, our care, our suffering, to relieve another?

Jesus Man's Substitute, because He was King, and More. The higher we ascend in the scale of being, the deeper and intenser become our sense of responsibility and the scope of substitution. There is a difference whether Leonidas or one of his three hundred is killed, for Leonidas is the leader. There is a difference whether a beggar or King Lear wanders along the heath, for Lear is the King. When the fortunes of war rob a whole nation, the leader of the nation feels it most. The king suffers more deeply, because he knows that he is responsible for the fate of his people, and therefore his personal feelings are incomparably heavier than those of the entire nation. But Jesus was conscious of being the Head of Humanity and the King of Men. If He had not been He could not have stood for us. But because He was all that, and more, He was able to become the propitiation, not for our sins alone, but for those of the whole world.

Jesus Pre-eminently the Sacrificial Lamb. He also was in His prime; no moral blemish had ever defiled His pure heart or extorted a confession; He was set apart from before the foundation of the world; His sufferings were bitterness itself. Pre-eminently He was the

Lamb of God, and He was sacrificed for us. Let us reckon ourselves judged in Him. The Judgment which has befallen Him has settled the great question of sin. He was wounded for our transgressions, bruised for our iniquities, the chastisement of our peace was upon Him, and with His stripes we are healed.

The Eucharist of Joy. "Let us keep the Feast!" *That implies the Joy of Redemption.*

The anguish of Egypt must have been bitter. It was the absorption of the Egyptians in their bereavement and in the burying of their firstborn that gave Israel the opportunity of going forth "with a high hand in the sight of all the Egyptians."[1] But what a contrast was presented by the Hebrews, as they knew that the destroying angel could not enter the blood-besprinkled door!

The Joy of Redemption. A similar joy is experienced when we realise that our sin has been judged and put away in Christ. It has been so in the purpose and intention of God; and as soon as we accept His assurance as true, and rest upon it, our "mouth is filled with laughter, and our tongue with singing." We reckon that if we have been judged in Christ, we have passed to the other side of the thunderstorm, and are living under the blue skies of God's acceptance and grace, on which the storm-clouds can never again gather. "There is no condemnation to them which are in Christ Jesus." "Being justified by faith, we have peace with God through our Lord Jesus Christ." If the moral law of the universe has been vindicated, if the character of God has been honoured, if His Name is hallowed by the obedience of Christ, as our Surety and Head, even unto death, there is absolute remission of sin. It is gone, as far as the East is from the West; it is buried deep as a stone in mid-ocean. The terror has passed, and we go forth into freedom and Life indeed. Christ our Passover is sacrificed for us, and we keep the Feast, i.e. all life becomes henceforth festal. The feast lasts as long as life lasts. The early Church called the Lord's Supper a Eucharist, so joyous were the emotions with which they celebrated their deliverance by Christ. But, in point of fact, all life may be eucharistic, full of praise and thanksgiving.

The Joy of Satisfaction. But there is more than the Joy of Forgiveness, there is *the Joy of Satisfaction.* The lamb or kid, the blood of which had been sprinkled without, was eaten within. It was roasted entire, the bones unbroken, and the flesh shared among all

[1] Num. xxxiii. 3.

the members of the household. No foreigner might partake, and no part might be applied to profane purposes. "It was holy to Jehovah." Probably it was believed that He ate with His people. It was the Lord's Passover. We also must feed in daily fellowship and communion on Christ. He that eateth His flesh and drinketh His blood after a spiritual and mystical fashion, abides in Him, and He in him. There is no other way for the nurture of the Divine life and the storage of the strength needed on life's journey.

The Joy of Anticipation. There is also *the Joy of Anticipation.* The Israelites stood around the table, sandals on their feet, staff in hand, and their flowing robes girt up around their loins, as those who were starting for a journey, a race or a battle. The light of an immortal hope was in their eyes, and their hearts beat high with expectation. At any moment the trumpet might ring out on the silent night, with its signal to be gone.

Not less do we rejoice at the severance wrought by the Cross between us and the old creation. The world is crucified unto us, and we unto the world; and we, according to His promise, look for new heavens and a new earth, in which dwelleth righteousness.

" Wherefore girding up the loins of your mind, be sober and set your hope perfectly on the grace that is to be brought unto you at the revelation of Jesus Christ. . . . knowing that ye were redeemed, not with corruptible things, with silver or gold, from your vain manner of life handed down from your fathers; but with precious blood, as of a lamb without blemish and without spot, even the blood of Christ."[1]

All Old Leaven to be Got Rid Of. OUT OF ALL THIS COMES THE PUTTING AWAY OF THE LEAVEN. "There shall be no leaven seen with thee, in all thy borders." "Purge out the old leaven!" "Let us keep the feast, not with old leaven, neither with the leaven of malice and wickedness, but with the unleavened bread of sincerity and truth." So careful were the Jews to avoid the possible contamination of leaven, before the Passover, that the Pharisees would not enter Pilate's palace on the eve of the feast. We need to be equally scrupulous, not as to the outward rite, but the inward spirit.

For us the leaven must stand for the selfness which is characteristic of us all, through the exaggerated instinct of self-preservation and the heredity received through generations, which have been a law to themselves, serving the desires of the flesh and of the mind. We are by nature self-confident, self-indulgent, self-opinionated; we

[1] Pet. i. 13, 18, 19.

live with self as our goal, and around the pivot of I our whole being revolves.

Like the Old Leaven, Self must be Abandoned. As time passes, however, we begin to question the wisdom or safety of this policy. We find ourselves dissatisfied, and pierced with many sorrows. We resemble the natives of a volcanic island who find the coast-line trembling beneath the tremors of earthquakes; they move inland, and detect them there; they climb the mountain, and feel them there. At last they leave the island, and settle on the mainland.

Similarly we, by the grace of God, have been led to abandon the isolated life of self, and settle on the continent of God's love in Christ. We were once darkness, but are now light in the Lord. We have been translated out of the kingdom of darkness into that of God's dear Son. And as the light gets brighter from the glimmer of dawn to the growing splendour of the perfect day, we become increasingly aware of the leaven of evil that still remains. We judge ourselves with increasing exactness and scrupulosity. Merciful to all others, we are merciless to every manifestation of the self-life. The Love of Christ constraineth us, for if one died for all, then all died, that they which live should henceforth not live unto themselves, but unto Him.

"A Night to be Much Observed"

Exodus 12:29-51;13:1-2,11-16

29. And it came to pass, that at midnight the Lord smote all the firstborn in the land of Egypt, from the firstborn of Pharaoh that sat on his throne unto the firstborn of the captive that *was* in the dungeon; and all the firstborn of cattle.

30. And Pharaoh rose up in the night, he, and all his servants, and all the Egyptians; and there was a great cry in Egypt; for *there was* not a house where *there was* not one dead.

31. And he called for Moses and Aaron by night, and said, Rise up, *and* get you forth from among my people, both ye and the children of Israel; and go, serve the Lord, as ye have said.

32. Also take your flocks and your herds, as ye have said, and be gone; and bless me also.

33. And the Egyptians were urgent upon the people, that they might send them out of the land in haste; for they said, We *be* all dead *men*.

34. And the people took their dough before it was leavened, their kneading-troughs being bound up in their clothes upon their shoulders.

35. And the children of Israel did according to the word of Moses; and they borrowed of the Egyptians jewels of silver, and jewels of gold, and raiment:

36. And the Lord gave the people favour in the sight of the Egyptians, so that they lent unto them *such things as they required*. And they spoiled the Egyptians.

37. And the children of Israel journeyed from Rameses to Succoth, about six hundred thousand on foot *that were* men, beside children.

38. And a mixed multitude went up also with them; and flocks, and herds, *even* very much cattle.

39. And they baked unleavened cakes of the dough which they brought forth out of Egypt, for it was not leavened; because they were thrust out of Egypt, and could not tarry, neither had they prepared for themselves any victual.

40. Now the sojourning of the children of Israel, who dwelt in Egypt, *was* four hundred and thirty years.

41. And it came to pass at the end of the four hundred and thirty years, even the selfsame day it came to pass, that all the hosts of the Lord went out from the land of Egypt.

42. It *is* a night to be much observed unto the Lord for bringing them out from the land of Egypt: this *is* that night of the Lord to be observed of all the children of Israel in their generations.

43. And the Lord said unto Moses and Aaron, This *is* the ordinance of the passover: There shall no stranger eat thereof:

44. But every man's servant that is bought for money, when thou hast circumcised him, then shall he eat thereof.

45. A foreigner and an hired servant shall not eat thereof.

46. In one house shall it be eaten; thou shalt not carry forth aught of the flesh abroad out of the house; neither shall ye break a bone thereof.

47. All the congregation of Israel shall keep it.

48. And when a stranger shall sojourn with thee, and will keep the passover to the Lord, let all his males be circumcised, and then let him come near and keep it; and he shall be as one that is born in the land: for no uncircumcised person shall eat thereof.

49. One law shall be to him that is homeborn, and unto the stranger that sojourneth among you.

50. Thus did all the children of Israel; as the Lord commanded Moses and Aaron, so did they.

51. And it came to pass the selfsame day, *that* the Lord did bring the children of Israel out of the land of Egypt by their armies.

1. And the Lord spake unto Moses, saying,

2. Sanctify unto me all the firstborn, whatsoever openeth the womb among the children of Israel, *both* of man and of beast: it *is* mine.

11. And it shall be when the Lord shall bring thee into the land of the Canaanites, as he sware unto thee and to thy fathers, and shall give it thee.

12. That thou shalt set apart unto the Lord all that openeth the matrix, and every firstling that cometh of a beast which thou hast; the males *shall be* the Lord's.

13. And every firstling of an ass thou shalt redeem with a lamb; and if thou wilt not redeem it, then thou shalt break his neck: and all the firstborn of man among thy children shalt thou redeem.

14. And it shall be when thy son asketh thee in time to come, saying, What *is* this? that thou shalt say unto him, By strength of hand the Lord brought us out from Egypt, from the house of bondage:

15. And it came to pass, when Pharaoh would hardly let us go, that the Lord slew all the firstborn in the land of Egypt, both the firstborn of man, and the firstborn of beast: therefore I sacrifice to the Lord all that openeth the matrix, being males; but all the firstborn of my children I redeem.

16. And it shall be for a token upon thine hand, and for frontlets between thine eyes: for by strength of hand the Lord brought us forth out of Egypt.

"A NIGHT TO BE MUCH OBSERVED"

Exodus 12:29-51;13:1-2,11-16

Pharaoh Concedes the Right to Go. *"This is that night of the Lord to be observed of all the children of Israel in their generations"* (xii. 42). On this night, the processes which had been quietly working out the Divine purpose, foreshadowed to Abraham centuries before, came suddenly to a head.[1] It became, therefore, as the margin suggests, a "a night of watching unto the Lord."

THAT NIGHT SAW PHARAOH CONCEDE THE DEMAND MADE IN THE NAME OF JEHOVAH. "Thus saith the Lord, the God of Israel, Let My people go, that they may hold a feast unto Me in the wilderness." It was afterwards intimated that they must go at least a three days' journey into the wilderness that they might sacrifice unto Jehovah, lest their worship should be contaminated by the evil associations of Egypt, or arouse the fanaticism of the Egyptians.

The Demand Right and Reasonable. Viewed in the light of after-events, it has been suggested that this demand concealed the real intention of returning no more. But this would impeach the Divine veracity, and base the whole movement on falsehood. There is, however, no sufficient ground for these suggestions. The demand was eminently right and reasonable. No monarch is justified in depriving his people of their rights to worship after the dictates of their own consciences. Not only had Pharaoh ground down the Hebrew race by oppression, but he had taken from them the opportunity of observing, in a proper manner, the festivals and rites of their religion. He needed to be reminded of this, and requested to concede at least this point of fair treatment. If he had yielded this modicum of elementary justice, he would have been probably willing to consider more favourably the wider demand, which was soon afterwards proposed.[2]

[1] Gen. xv. 14. [2] Exod. vi. 11.

The Demand a Test-Case. This was a test-case. To have granted this would have established new conciliatory relations between himself and the two brethren, which would have widened out until the whole question of Hebrew bondage had come under consideration, and become the subject of amicable negotiations. But in refusing this modest request, which appealed to his sense of humanity, fairness, and religion, he put himself hopelessly in the wrong.

The Demand Met by Temporising. Pharaoh met the demand of the Hebrew leaders first by contemptuous insult, as we have seen,[1] and then by a series of attempts to compromise. *First,* he offered permission for them to worship Jehovah, wherever they pleased within the limits of Egypt.[2] A foolish offer, which might have led to riot and civil war. *Next,* he was willing to allow them to go forth to worship in the wilderness, only they must not go very far away.[3] *After this,* he proposed that they should go three days' journey into the wilderness, only they must leave their families behind.[4] He did not realise how dear children are to God, and that they were a necessary part of the nation! *Finally,* he was willing that they should go three days' journey into the wilderness, taking their families with them, if only they would leave their cattle.[5]

Compromise Leads to Surrender. Moses had no option but to reject each of these offers. Indeed, the religious man must always regard with suspicion every proposal to take less than the Divine standard presents. Compromise in religion almost invariably leads to the surrender of some particular, Divinely ordered or instituted, for the sake of some supposed advantage or convenience. It is for this reason that our Lord spoke so earnestly about breaking one of these least Commandments, and teaching men so.

The End of Efforts to Soften Pharaoh's Heart. All these efforts at compromise, and especially the last, lay broken and torn on the ground. Pharaoh had broken up the interview with violence, and had threatened Moses with death, and there was nothing more to be done than set him aside from the way of the execution of the Divine purposes. On this night, therefore, there was a culmination of the long struggle. One subterfuge after another was swept away, the true character of the king had become revealed, the last effort to bend him had proved abortive; there was nothing more to be done

[1] Exod. v. 4, etc.   [3] viii. 28.
[2] viii. 25.   [4] x. 8–11.
[5] x. 24.

than achieve through his overthrow what might have been accomplished with his co-operation. "Behold, a watcher and an holy one came down from heaven. He cried aloud, and said thus, Hew down the tree, and cut off his branches, shake off his leaves, and scatter his fruit: let the beasts get away from under it, and the fowls from his branches."[1]

Pharaoh's Conduct Reviewed. THE HARDENING OF PHARAOH'S HEART ALSO HAD REACHED ITS CLIMAX. The process is carefully noted, and may be set forth thus:

I will harden Pharaoh's heart, that he shall not let the people go (iv. 21).

I will harden Pharaoh's heart, and multiply My signs and My wonders (vii. 3).

After the rod was changed to a serpent, his heart was hardened (vii. 13; see R.V.).

It was so after the waters had been turned to blood (vii. 22).

He showed signs of yielding when the frogs came, but when there was respite, "he hardened his heart" once more (viii. 15).

When his magicians were compelled to admit the finger of God in the third plague, "his heart was hardened, and he hearkened not" (viii. 19).

When the fourth plague was removed, "he hardened his heart at this time also, neither would he let the people go" (viii. 32).

After the plague of murrain, again we are told that his heart was hardened (ix. 7).

But in the following plague, we are told definitely, *for the first time*, that the Lord hardened his heart, as He had foretold Moses would be the case (ix. 12).

Did the Lord Harden Pharaoh's Heart? After the visitation of hail, Pharaoh appeared to make an absolute surrender; but no sooner had it ceased than the hardening returned (ix. 35).

The Lord is said to have hardened his heart before and after the plague of locusts (x. 1; 20), and after that of the awful darkness (x. 27). The same sentence is repeated, generally, at the conclusion of the conflict (xi. 10); and thrice again in the narrative of the overthrow of Egypt in the Red Sea (xiv. 4, 8, 17).

Impenitent Hearts Accumulate Wrath. In this series of quotations it should be noticed that there is no statement that God hardened Pharaoh's heart till after the sixth plague. The apparent exception

[1] Dan. iv. 13, 14.

of vii. 13 is not really so, as the R.V. clearly proves. At first we are told that Pharaoh hardened his own heart; or the fact is simply stated that his heart was hardened. The first steps in this dread process of heart-ossification take place at the instigation of the sinner himself, and it is the hardened heart that perverts to its own hurt all the goodness which would conduct it to repentance. When water turns to ice, its ice converts to thicker ice the thin film of water which is poured over it, when the last skater has left the pool. It is possible, as Paul tells us, for men so to abuse the long-suffering of God, which would lead them to repentance, as to turn to evil what God intended for good. In this way hard and impenitent hearts accumulate to themselves wrath against the day of wrath.[1]

It is not difficult, as it seems to the present writer, to understand how in the rich Oriental speech God may be said to have hardened Pharaoh's heart,—and it must be admitted, of course, that there are necessary limitations in all human speech, which expose to criticism any statement in popular phrase of the inner operations of the soul. This book was not written for Psychologists!

Goodness May Render Evil More Evil. Suppose a Christian woman awakes to find that she has married a man who has no sympathy with either her religious beliefs or consistent character. She is at a loss how to treat him; but following the bent of her loving and tender nature, she sets herself to win him from his evil courses by wifely unselfishness and gentle consideration. The contrast between her goodness and his baseness seems, however, only to madden him and drive him to excesses of cruelty, which he would never have dreamt of with a wife who repaid hate with hate, and unkindness with indifference. First, he hardens himself against her gentle ways, and finally, as the result of resisting her daily influence, he deteriorates more rapidly, and becomes more utterly degraded than would have been otherwise credible. May it not be said that she hardens his heart, though her whole endeavour is to turn him from his evil courses?

A New Testament Illustration. Or take that striking illustration in Hebrews vi. No one will deny that the rain is one of the most necessary and beneficent gifts of God. That the moisture needed by the thirsty earth should be diffused so gently and softly is one of the incidental evidences of the design of the Creator. Beneath the soft vernal showers, the cultivated earth, "which drinketh in

[1] Rom. ii. 4, 5.

the rain which cometh oft upon it," brings forth fruit for those for whose sake it is tilled. But the same rain, falling upon the common and the waste, covers them with thorns and briars, and brings upon them a curse and burning. The rain, therefore, may be said to secure these sad disasters! No! Not the rain, but the land, which turned the good gifts of the Creator into noxious growth. If we turn to death the commandment which God meant for life, to poison what God meant for health, to cursing what God meant for blessing, it may be possible, from one point of view, to credit God with the evil consequences that have accrued; but, as a matter of fact, they would not have accrued unless we had misapplied His good and perfect gifts.

Why do Souls Differ. The sun that melts wax hardens clay; but the difference between these two results is due, not to any variableness in the sun's nature, but to the trend and direction which each substance supplies. Thus contact with the same Spirit of God made Moses the meekest, and Pharaoh the proudest and strongest of men; but the difference was in the texture and quality of their respective souls.

Why souls differ thus is an enquiry which probably will never be solved in this life. That there are reasons, and that they are consistent with infinite Justice, we believe, but as yet they are not revealed, and we await the unveiling in patience. All that we can see is, that those whom God foreknew, He predestined to be conformed to the image of His Son.[1]

The Final Blow Falls. Whatever influence it was that had brought the Pharaoh of that time to this pitch of hardihood, it is clear that nothing more could be gained by delay, and the final blow fell. "And it came to pass at midnight, that the Lord smote all the firstborn in the land of Egypt, from the firstborn of Pharaoh . . . unto the firstborn of the captive that was in the dungeon. . . . And Pharaoh rose up in the night, he, and all his servants, and all the Egyptians; . . . for there was not a house where there was not one dead."[2]

"Spoiling" the Egyptians. THAT NIGHT LED ALSO TO THE GREAT ENRICHMENT OF ISRAEL. When the Almighty spoke first to Abraham, He said, "That nation whom they shall serve, will I judge: and afterward shall they come out with great substance."[3] In the original

[1] Rom. viii. 29.   [2] Exod. xii. 29, 30.

[3] Gen. xv. 14.

announcement of His purpose, Jehovah also told Moses that He would give the people favour in the sight of the Egyptians, so that, when they went forth, they should not go empty; but every woman was to ask of her neighbour and of her that sojourned in her house, jewels of silver, and jewels of gold, and raiment, which were to be placed upon their sons and their daughters; and the Egyptians would be spoiled.[1] On the eve of the Exodus, Moses was reminded of this injunction:

"Speak now in the ears of the people, and let every man borrow of his neighbour, and every woman of her neighbour, jewels of silver, and jewels of gold."[2]

" And the children of Israel did according to the word of Moses; and they asked of the Egyptians jewels of silver, and jewels of gold, and raiment: and the Lord gave the people favour in the sight of the Egyptians, so that they let them have what things they asked. And they spoiled the Egyptians."[3]

Referring to this incident, which took place during the night of the Exodus, the Psalmist of a much later date sang:

" He brought them forth with silver and gold; and there was not one feeble person among his tribes."[4]

A Mistranslation. A large amount of misconception has been introduced into this incident by the mistranslation of King James' Version, which repeatedly employs the words "borrow" and "lent". "They *borrowed* of the Egyptians." "They *lent* unto them." The Revised Version substitutes "asked" for "borrowed," and "let them have" for "lent."

Not "Spoils," but Freewill Offerings. It is plain that these were free-will gifts, which the Egyptians proffered, and the Hebrews received, as a final wage for long years of enforced and unremunerated service. Thus good comes out of evil. Had Pharaoh yielded at the first, the Egyptians would have felt no special sympathy for the captive race. But the opposition of King and Court, the long-deferred hope, the often-repeated disappointment elicited a vast amount of sympathy for the harried race. Also "Egypt was glad" of their departure, for they were afraid of them.

[1] Exod. iii. 21, 22.
[2] xi. 2.
[3] xii. 35, 36.
[4] Ps. cv. 37.

Tabernacle Built from the Spoils. These rich spoils were opportune, and of special value for the construction of the Tabernacle, which could never have been so gorgeously equipped with precious stones and priceless hangings, except for this spoiling of the Egyptians.

An Epoch and an Offering. THAT NIGHT WAS TO BE THE BEGINNING OF MONTHS.[1] It was the time of the "earing" of the wheat—about our April; and henceforth the month Abib—"the earing"—would open the ecclesiastical year. The Egyptian calendar began when the Nile was rising in the summer solstice; but all connection with Egypt must be broken, and the new year was to begin with the Passover, which commemorated the deliverance of their firstborn sons from the sword of the destroying Angel.

The Passover. On the tenth day of the month, as we have seen, each family was to set apart a kid or a lamb, which must be a male, without blemish, in its prime. If a household were too small to consume it, members of another might join, but no foreigner might partake, and no part of the sacrifice might be carried out of the house or left over for the morning meal. Four days after the selection of the lamb, between sunset and starlight, it was killed. The blood sprinkled on the doorposts and lintels suggested that the household were hiding behind it to escape the stroke of the destroying angel; whilst the feast within doors suggested that Jehovah had condescended to eat with His people and become their guest. Each house was a temple, each father was a priest, each firstborn son was saved by blood.

The Hebrews Are Ready. In the meanwhile the whole Hebrew population were ready at a moment's notice to set forth. They stood with sandalled feet, staff in hand, their loins girded, and they ate in haste. At the dread hour of midnight, the firstborn of Egypt died; and shortly after every Hebrew family was hurrying, by the light of the full moon, to the rendezvous previously appointed, where the tribes were mustering. The babes and young children, the aged and sick, were borne on asses; the man drove his cattle or sheep; the woman carried her kneading-trough and unleavened dough on her shoulder.

The Exodus Begins. Each village contributed its confluent streamlet to the swelling river of fugitives. As they advanced, they were joined, not only by the crowds of their own race, but by a great

[1] xii. 1, 2.

mixed multitude of aliens, of the disaffected, of deserters and slaves. They converged finally on Rameses, were separated into detachments or divisions, and marched forth as in battle-array, or, as the margin suggests, "by fives in a rank."[1] Ewald suggests that this signifies that they were marshalled in five divisions—the van, the centre, two wings, and the rearguard.

The Number of the Israelites. More than once we are told that there were 600,000 men able to bear arms, that is, between twenty and sixty years of age; and this would yield a total of no less than two millions of men, women, and children.

The First-born Belong to God. Our attention is specially drawn to the firstborn of every house, whose lives had been forfeited, except for the blood of the lamb, that bespoke salvation. From that hour the firstborn of man and beast belonged to God; and when any child in coming years asked why the firstborn of all animals, except the ass, were offered in sacrifice, he was told that it was to commemorate the slaying of the firstborn of Egypt, and the sparing of the firstborn of Israel.

And Are to be Priests of God. All firstborn sons were redeemed from the death that was meted out to the firstborn of the animals, by the sacrifice of a lamb, and were expected and required to act as an army of priests unto the Lord.[2]

In subsequent generations firstborn sons were redeemed, not by the sacrifice of a lamb, but by a money-payment of five shekels: but it must always have been a solemn thought to the boys of each successive generation, that they had been redeemed to serve, that either a lamb had died that they might live, or that money had been paid down for them in their unconscious hours of earliest infancy.[3]

The Levite Made Priests. Before the camp broke up from Sinai, the tribe of Levi was substituted for the eldest sons of the race, as priests to serve in the Tabernacle. "The Lord spake unto Moses, saying, Take the Levites instead of all the firstborn among the children of Israel; and the cattle of the Levites instead of their cattle, and the Levites shall be mine; I am the Lord."[4] What a blessing it would be in each household of God's people, if the eldest son was taught to account himself as devoted to the service of the Most High! How good it would be for every Hannah to say to her Samuel, so soon as he was able to understand, "My little son, thou art not

[1] xiii. 18.
[2] xiii. 1, 11–16.
[3] Num. xviii. 15, etc.
[4] Num. iii. 44, etc.

mine, but God's. I know not yet what work He has for thee, but He will make it clear. I have given thee to the Lord, and as long as thou livest thou must be His!" When will every family be a Missionary Society, the father and brothers working to maintain the missionary son or brother, the mother and sister living a life of prayer and intercession on his behalf, and holding the ropes of loving sympathy?

The Birthnight of Modern History. What crowded memories gathered around that memorable night, which Bunsen says was the birthnight of modern history, when, bearing with them the bones of Joseph, which had remained unburied, awaiting this hour, which he desired thus to share, the sacramental host of God's firstborn, the elect of our race, marched forth to become a nation, under the tutelage of their great leader!

THE WAY OF THE WILDERNESS

Exodus 13:17-22

17. And it came to pass, when Pharaoh had let the people go, that God led them not *through* the way of the land of the Philistines, although that *was* near; for God said, Lest peradventure the people repent when they see war, and they return to Egypt:

18. But God led the people about, *through* the way of the wilderness of the Red sea: and the children of Israel went up harnessed out of the land of Egypt.

19. And Moses took the bones of Joseph with him: for he had straitly sworn the children of Israel, saying, God will surely visit you; and ye shall carry up my bones away hence with you.

20. And they took their journey from Succoth, and encamped in Etham, in the edge of the wilderness.

21. And the Lord went before them by day in a pillar of a cloud, to lead them the way; and by night in a pillar of fire, to give them light; to go by day and night:

22. He took not away the pillar of the cloud by day, nor the pillar of fire by night, *from* before the people.

THE WAY OF THE WILDERNESS
Exodus 13:17-22

Rameses the Scene of the Miracles. "GOD LED THE PEOPLE ABOUT." It is supposed that Rameses, from which the Israelites started,[1] was the same place as Tanis or Zoan, now San. It had been rebuilt by Rameses II, was a place of great importance, and the common residence of the Court of that Period. It is probable that the miracle of Moses and his interviews with the Egyptian King took place in this city, and strong probability is given to this supposition by the statement of the Psalmist that the miracles were wrought in "the field of Zoan."

The direct road from this city to Palestine lay along the coast of the Mediterranean, through the land of the Philistines. It was by this way that Jacob "went down" to Egypt, and by which the funeral procession "went up" to lay him in the sepulchre of his fathers. The journey from Rameses to Gaza would consume about ten days. This road was easy, rapid, and safe; but it was not the route selected by Moses, under the guidance of the Lord.

The "Desert," What it was Like. The other route I will describe in as few words as possible. The extreme boundary of Palestine on the South is a vast, monotonous limestone plateau, about two thousand feet above sea-level, extending from the Mediterranean to the Dead Sea. South of this, again, is the triangle between the Red Sea and the Gulf of Akaba, in which are piled the great mountains of Sinai, of which the highest peaks reach an elevation of ten thousand feet. They compose a scene of solemn grandeur and sublimity, not paralleled probably by any other mountain range in the world. The formation is of rich red sandstone, mingled with granite and porphyry, and has excited the enthusiastic comments of all thoughtful travellers, notably of Dean Stanley. Between the limestone desert and this triangular mass of mountains is an irregular

[1] Exod. xii. 37; Num. xxxiii. 3.

broad-stretching plain, and this great desert valley was the path trodden at the Exodus.

A "Wilderness" of Green Pastures. We must dismiss from our minds, when we use the words "desert" or "wilderness," the idea of desolate wastes of sand. The Pentateuch has very few references to sand. The fact is that sand is the exception in the desert or wilderness which Israel traversed for forty years. It will be remembered that the Psalmist sings of "the pastures of the wilderness." We must, therefore, imagine a tract of country in which, though there are no cornfields or vineyards, yet there would be abundance of pasture for nomad tribes wandering with their flocks; and sometimes the broad open wastes, like our downs or commons widens out into scenes of splendid luxuriance and beauty.

The Law of God's Dealings with Us. It was along this path that God led His people. But is not this the law of His dealing with us all? "God led the people about." "By the way of the wilderness." These words expound the whole philosophy of human life.

The Philistine Barrier. I. THE BARRED PATH. "Not by the way of the Philistines." This people was highly disciplined and thoroughly equipped, a strong and martial race; and though, of course, they must have yielded before the right hand of the Most High, as they did in after centuries, yet at that time, and Israel being what they were, the Philistines effectually barred the progress of the host in that direction. The five important cities of Gaza, Ascalon, Ashdod, Gath, and Ekron formed an impassable barrier.

Hindrances that Help. But the barriers of life may be ranked among its great benedictions. To borrow a suggestion: In his poem, "The Day-Dream," Tennyson describes the spell cast on castle and maiden, till it was broken by the prince's kiss; then the fountain, which had suffered from long repression, leapt up to twice its former height. How often has this been the case! Demosthenes became the consummate orator of Time, because in early life oratory did not come easily and naturally to him—he stammered. The men who lisp in numbers do not make the greatest poets, and the sons of rich men, born with silver spoons in their mouths, are more often than not failures who need to be spoon-fed all their days. The smaller kingdoms of the world whose area has been limited, like Tyre or Greece or Great Britain, have, as the rebound from their limitations and restrictions, leapt up into superb careers of colonisation and world-power. Thomas Carlyle suffered from the pressure of poverty in his early life, but it made his soul the stronger, and possessed his moral nature with thews of steel. It is the effort of the bee to emerge from the narrow confining cell that breaks the delicate membrane which confines its wings.

The Barred Path not necessarily a Closed Path. Many who read these words can recall the hard experiences of their earlier life, when obstacles, apparently insuperable, threatened to bar their progress; but in these things, as Hezekiah said, they found the life of their spirits. If you are passing through such an experience, be of good courage, the barred path is not the closed one. God will go before you, and make the crooked places straight and the rough places smooth, so that His glory may be revealed. Storms are the triumph of His art, for the training of mariners that shall dare to cross stormiest seas.

Early Delay often Means Quick after Progress. Suppose that the winning of this world for Christ had been a holiday-parade, and that the Cross had only to be uplifted, or the message of salvation announced, to win instant acknowledgment, where would have been the splendid patience and heroic victory of the Church? What scope for her prayers, her passion, her tears and toils? The loss to the annals of Christian character, heroism, and faith would have been incalculable. May we not suppose that the great cloud of witnesses are deriving sacred lessons, as they behold the noble patience and illustrious triumphs of the Church? God is showing them also evidences of His manifold wisdom.

The Way of the Church. So in the slow progress of the centuries! If the Church had been rapt away at the Fall of Jerusalem, instead of having to watch through the long night until cock-crowing and the dawn-break, she never would have realised and revealed those great qualities which have been evinced by the noble army of martyrs, the goodly company of prophets, the wonderful achievements of missionaries, reformers, and statesmen in their conflict against evil, and their efforts to build the New Jerusalem on the plains of Time. The barred path has been best.

How Barriers Are Made. Our Lord said significantly to His Apostle, "Thou canst not follow Me *now*." The barrier was, in fact, raised by Peter's own petulance and vehemence. Thus our barriers are often created by our follies and sins, and we have ourselves to blame for them. But the barrier was none the less salutary to that eager nature: for he is the one Apostle who speaks of the girding up of the loins of the mind, not to do some great deed, or run in some historic race, but to set our hope perfectly for the grace to be brought unto us at the revelation of Jesus Christ.

The Value of the Delay. Sometimes when spring is yet young, there comes a spell of hot summer weather. As we walk through the gardens or woodlands, we can almost detect the growth of Nature. There are the building of the woody fibre of the plants, the deepening of their roots, the busy life-blood hurrying along the veins. You almost expect to-morrow to see the deep-red flower blazing on the stem. The very plant seems aware of the coming flower, and feels its fire already in its tumultuous sap. But when to-morrow dawns, the clouds veil the sky, the sun is hidden; the wind has changed to east, Nature shivers. The mistaken birds put off their marriage-plans, and all the glad movement springwards is arrested. But when summer and autumn come there will be gratitude for the very set-back which led to the greater health and wealth of the year.

The Education of the Waiting Hour. So in life! Granted that Philistines bar the way. They shall not do so always. One day their champion will bite the dust, and their squadrons will flee, as broken clouds before the gale. In the meanwhile, as you stand against the barriers, let your patience, your faith, your hope and love strike their roots downwards, and reach their heads higher. They that sow in tears shall reap in joy. The barred way is not permanently closed.

What Divine Guidance Means. II. THE CIRCUITOUS ROUTE. "God led the people about." Is not this true of the human race? Carry your mind back to the opening chapters of the Bible. Do not the opening pages present a striking illustration of this very truth? On the failure of Adam and Eve, did their Almighty Friend condone their offence, retain them in Eden, and continue that fellowship which He was wont to permit at the time of the breathing of the evening breeze? No, certainly.

" Unto Adam he said, Because thou hast hearkened to the voice of thy wife, and hast eaten of the tree, of which I commanded thee, saying, Thou shalt not eat of it: cursed is the ground for thy sake; in sorrow shalt thou eat of it all the days of thy life: thorns also and thistles shall it bring forth to thee. . . . So he drove out the man, and he placed at the east of the garden of Eden the Cherubim, and the flame of a sword which turned every way, to keep the way of the tree of life."[1]

[1] Gen. iii. 17, 18, 24.

An even more striking illustration of God's treatment of His sons is furnished by the example of our Lord, of whom it is recorded,

> " Straightway the Spirit driveth him forth into the wilderness. And he was in the wilderness forty days tempted of Satan; and he was with the wild beasts." [1]

All the pilgrim-host has to travel by this path, with the long stretches of monotonous stepping, and just a few soft resting-places which are meant for rest, but not for abiding.

Spiritual Power the only Safe Guide. But why the wilderness-route? When in Œnone Wisdom dissuades the youth from accepting the tempting offer of earthly kingship, with all that this carried with it—fleets, armies, towered cities, and territory—she shows how illusory that promise is, unless combined with inward and spiritual power. We often make a similar mistake. We think that if we were to revolutionise our circumstances, we should revolutionise ourselves. But it cannot be. We may change our place, our dress, our house, our surroundings; but all will be unavailing unless we change ourselves. Power lies not without us, but within. This couplet, which sums up the advice of wisdom, deserves to be written on the heart of each young man and woman as they enter the lists of the battle:

> " Self-Reverence, Self-Knowledge, Self-Control,
> These three alone lead life to sovereign power."

But how and where are these three to be acquired save in the wilderness?

Things Only Acquired in the Wilderness. Therefore it was said of old time: "Thou shalt remember all the way which the Lord thy God hath led thee these forty years in the wilderness, that He might humble thee, to prove thee, to know what was in thine heart, whether thou wouldest keep His commandments, or no."[2]

Self Knowledge! How little did Israel realise, when the ransomed hosts stood in the rapture of fresh deliverance beside the Red Sea, all the seeds of evil that lay slumbering in their hearts, and that were to flower forth at Marah, and Sinai, and Kibroth-hataavah.

Self-Reverence!—The first step towards self-reverence is to see God, to worship Him, to bow down before Him, to know that He

---

[1] Mark i. 12, 13.　　　　　　　[2] Deut. viii. 2.

is God alone, and then we begin to reverence the nature made in His image, which we are to hold sacred for His sake.

Self-Control!—This cannot be acquired in an instant. To learn to say No, and to say it instantly, almost before the evil suggestion has had time to form upon the retina of the inner sight; to persist in saying it, though, like Joseph, solicited to evil every day; to possess it because we have learned to hand it over to Jesus Christ; to be self-controlled because we are Christ-controlled—*this* does not come easily or at once. Only through long years of temptation and failure, and faith, do we come at last to learn that we are nothing, and can effect nothing, and hand over the entire control and management of the inner life to Him Who is able to keep us from falling, and present us before the throne of His glory with exceeding joy.

The Tempter in the Wilderness. In the wilderness the Tempter comes to us. In his first temptation, when he advises us to use for ourselves the powers entrusted us for others, we learn to control our appetites. In his second temptation, when he suggests that we should cast ourselves headlong, we learn to reverence the bodies that God has given us, and the holy laws which He has laid down for our guidance. In his third temptation he drives us to know ourselves in all our weakness, and we have no resource save to bid him get behind us, lest if he linger he should prevail.

The wilderness finds us out, humbles us, brings us down from the high pinnacle of self-sufficiency and self-glorification. Beaten, baffled, disappointed, dependent for our manna and water on His constant bounty, suffered to hunger, and then fed with Heaven's own food, athirst, and satisfied from the rocks, fighting but vanquished till the arms of faith and prayer are uplifted, we come to know God, and to know ourselves: to reverence God and reverence ourselves; and to hand over the control and keeping of our souls to a faithful Creator.

The difficulties of our lot also reveal the many-sided help of God. We discover and appropriate Christ in a new aspect.

The Everpresent Guide. III. THE UNERRING GUIDE. "The Lord went before them by day in a pillar of cloud, to lead them the way; and by night in a pillar of fire, to give them light; that they might go by day and by night." That cloud probably always hid within its folds a heart of fire; but only when night fell on the world was it apparent.

Jesus has Become the Pillar of Cloud Fire. *It was an emblem of* *the presence of God.* In ancient warfare fire and smoke signals were used by the commanders to show that they were present. Similarly, whether moving majestically forward, or brooding over the Tabernacle in after days, Israel felt assured that the Lord of Hosts was with them, and that the God of Jacob was their refuge. Ages have passed since then. The glory has ceased from between the Seraphim, but Jesus fulfils for all the ages that sacred emblem. The cloud, His veiling flesh; the fire, His Godhead. "The Word was made flesh, and dwelt among us, and we beheld His glory, the glory as of the Only-Begotten of the Father"; and we welcome His Promise: "Lo, I am with you alway."[1]

We must not Precede our Guide. *It was an Infallible Guide.* The Book of Numbers makes very emphatic references to this, and tells us how absolutely the marches and halts of Israel were controlled. When it was taken up, they journeyed; when it settled down, they encamped. As long as it lay spread above the Tabernacle, there they stayed. No impatience, chafing at the long delay, could force the march. The camp might be pitched in a desolate place, far from Elim, and invaded by serpents, but there it must remain, whether for days or months, until the cloud gathered up its fleecy folds, and sailed magnificently forward. We have as our sufficient Guide neither pillar of cloud nor fire, but the Light of the World, who said, "He that followeth Me shall not walk in the darkness."[2] He guides us with His eye. Only let us not precede Him. There should always be a space between the guiding cloud and you, "about two thousand cubits by measure." And when He says by the intimation of the Spirit within, or His Providence without, "Let us go hence," let us be sure that neither the warmth of the camp-fire, nor the attractiveness of the site retain us. Oh, to be able to say with the Psalmist: "My soul followeth hard after Thee!"

Pillar and Cloud—Sun and Shield. *It was both Sun and Shield.* When the excessive heat made it necessary for Israel to march at night, the light of the Fiery Pillar was enough to light the way: and when in the day the scorching glare of the sun was blinding, the cloud spread itself abroad like a great umbrella, so that the women and children could travel in comparative comfort.

" The Lord God is a Sun and Shield. He will give grace and glory. No good thing will He withhold from them that walk uprightly."

[1] See Neh. ix. 19; Matt. xxviii. 20.   [2] John viii. 12.

Yes, and at times He will be a wall of defence, as when the cloud settled down between Israel and Pharaoh's hosts, so that the one came not near the other all the night.[1]

"God With Us." May the Lord Jesus be to each one of us a cloud and smoke by day and the shining of a flaming fire by night, and over all the glory may He spread His wings as a canopy, so that His Presence may be a pavilion for a shadow in the daytime from the heat, and for a covert from storm and rain till we reach our Father's Home, and rest in Paradise for ever![2]

[1] Exod. xiv. 19, 20.   [2] Isa. iv. 5, 6.

The Salvation of the Lord

Exodus 14:13

13. And Moses said unto the people, Fear ye not, stand still, and see the salvation of the Lord, which he will shew to you to-day: for the Egyptians whom ye have seen to-day, ye shall see them again no more for ever.

THE SALVATION OF THE LORD
Exodus 14:13

Judgment and Mercy. "STAND STILL, AND SEE THE SALVATION OF THE LORD." "Behold then," cries the Apostle, "the goodness and severity of God; on them which fell severity, but towards thee, goodness." Surely the chapter before us presents a notable illustration of the truth of his words. Towards Egypt, severity indeed, but for Israel goodness, which has kept their heart singing for generations. It would ill repay us to enter into topographical details. The supreme importance of the fact remains, although the exact locality has been probably obliterated by the shift of the sand and an alteration in the configuration of the shore.

The First Stage in the Exodus. At first the direction of the Exodus was S.E., but suddenly the guiding-cloud took a course due S., along the western shores of the Bitter Lakes. By this route, five or six days after setting forth, the Israelites found themselves in the extreme point of a wedge. On one side the Red Sea, on the other the wilderness, and in front an insuperable barrier of mountains. There was no natural egress from that *cul de sac*, except they turned back on their course.

A Supreme Test of Moses' Faith. Probably it was the supreme test of Moses' Faith. He knew perfectly well what was happening, and the extreme peril into which he was leading this helpless flock of human beings; but he maintained an absolutely untroubled composure. He knew that God had pledged His word to deliver His people, and if He seemed to take them into an impossible labyrinth, there must be a solution and a way out. He knew in Whom he had believed; his heart was fixed, trusting in the Lord.

Pharaoh's Decision. In the meanwhile Pharaoh had recovered from his extreme alarm. No further deaths had followed on the destruction of the firstborn, and he might have thought that Jehovah had expended all His arrows, and that there was nothing more to fear. Moreover he realised how great a loss he and his people would sustain in the exodus of so vast a body of slaves, many of whom were highly skilled in the arts of that age. When therefore he heard of the change of route, and knew that Israel was entangled in the land, he mustered all the troops available, and marched in pursuit with six hundred chariots and perhaps 100,000 footmen, all trained and disciplined soldiers, and habituated to warfare. What chance had these fugitive slaves against that seasoned host!

" And when Pharaoh drew nigh, the children of Israel lifted up their eyes, and, behold, the Egyptians marched after them; and they were sore afraid. . . . And Moses said unto the people, Fear ye not, stand still, and see the salvation of the LORD, which He will work for you to-day; for the Egyptians whom ye have seen to-day, ye shall see them again no more for ever " (xiv. 10, 13).

Egypt a Type of the Cunning World. The Salvation of Israel from Pharaoh and his hosts cannot be viewed as an isolated fact. As the Apostle says: "Now these things happened unto them by way of example; and they were written for our admonition, upon whom the ends of the ages are come."[1] Egypt is the invariable type of the cunning, thoughtless, wanton world, out of which in all ages God is calling His sons. The infant Jesus was called out of Egypt, and to every son of God a similar summons arrives: "Arise ye, and depart; for this is not your rest." You too are called to an Exodus. You are called to arise from your enslaving passions, your love of gain or applause, the leeks, onions, and garlics of this enervating world, where self-gratification is the one law of life. You are summoned to come forth to the wilderness, the holy mount, the spiritual rock, the heavenly food. Be loyal to the Divine voice; strike your tents, and follow. Though the Egyptians pursue, they shall not overtake. The Lord will be your rearguard. He shall fight for you and save you; and the Egyptians whom you have seen to-day, you shall see them again no more for ever. We are justified therefore in tracing a close analogy between the deliverance and salvation of the chosen people and our own.

The Pursuit. I. THEY WERE SAVED BY A DIVINE WORK. There were four stages in it.

(1) *The Movement of the Cloud.* It was sundown when the Egyptians, after a long and hasty march, arrived on the ridges of the desert hills overlooking the Israelite camp below them on

[1] 1 Cor. x. 11.

the seashore. They could watch every movement, hear every sound, and were truculently sure of their quarry. But suddenly the cloud removed from the head of the Israelite column and settled as a wall behind and around them. This movement altered the entire aspect, because it spread a thick darkness over the Egyptian lines, and presented an apparently impenetrable barrier to their advance; Israel, on the contrary, enjoyed a brilliant glow of light, which turned the darkness of the midnight into broad day. "It was a cloud of darkness to the one, while it gave light by night to the other."

(2) *The Strong East Wind.* Probably it contained a large ingredient of south as well as east, which drove back towards the land the upper waters of the shallow bay, now silted up, whilst at the same time a strong ebb-tide may have drawn the lower waters southwards, so that a pathway a mile or more in length was cleft across the sands. "With the blast of thy nostrils, the waters were gathered together, the floods stood upright as an heap; and the depths were congealed in the heart of the sea."

(3) *The Storm.* When the Egyptians saw the wall of cloud slowly moving forward, and realised that Israel was escaping, that their camping-ground was being vacated and the sea-bed entered, their rage knew no bounds; and they hurled themselves in pursuit. "The enemy said, I will pursue, I will overtake, I will divide the spoil; my lust shall be satisfied upon them; I will draw my sword; my hand shall destroy them."

The Host Overthrown. So they pursued, and went in after them into the midst of the sea, even all Pharaoh's horses, his chariots, and his horsemen. And it came to pass that in the morning watch the Lord troubled the host of the Egyptians. Josephus explains that showers of rain began to descend, with thunder and lightning and flashes of fire, "nor was there anything wont to be sent by God as indicating His wrath, which did not happen to them on this occasion." The Psalmist thus describes the situation: "The clouds poured out water; the skies sent out a sound. Thine arrows also went abroad. The voice of Thy thunder was in the heaven; the lightnings lightened the world: the earth trembled and shook."[1] Then as the Egyptians, stricken with panic, turned to flee, their chariot wheels sank deep in the soft ooze of the sea-bed, so that rapid movement and therefore escape became impossible.

(4) *The Returning Tide.* When Moses stretched out his hand

[1] Ps. lxxvii. 17–18.

over the sea the second time, the wind lulled and the waters which it had upheld towards the land fell and rushed back, while from the south the tide turned and raced furiously forward. Those who know anything of the treacherous sands of the Wash, where King John lost his treasure, or of the Solway Firth or Morecambe Bay, will be able to form a fairly true conception of the situation. The parted waves leapt together, and, encumbered by their heavy armour, the Egyptians "sank as lead in the mighty waters."

An Act of God. Explain it as you will, there can be no reasonable doubt that the deliverance of Israel from the clutches of their foes was a conspicuous act of Divine power in answer to the faith and prayer of Moses, and through the operation of natural law.

> " By faith they passed through the Red Sea as by dry land: which the Egyptians assaying to do were drowned."
>
> " Thy right hand, O Lord, is become glorious in power, Thy right hand, O Lord, hath dashed in pieces the enemy. In the greatness of thine excellency Thou hast overthrown them that rose up against Thee; Thou sentest forth Thy wrath, which consumed them as stubble. . . . Who is like unto Thee, O Lord, among the gods? who is like Thee, glorious in holiness, fearful in praises, doing wonders? "[1]

—Prefiguring the Soul's Salvation. But no less Divine is the salvation of every soul of man. It is from beginning to end of God. The grace that prompts to redeem, the work of the Cross by which our redemption was effected, the tender wooings and strivings of the Holy Spirit which first suggested that we should wish to be redeemed, the patience which has never surrendered the conflict with the evil of our nature—all are of God.

> " Knowing that a man is not justified by the works of the law, but by the faith of Jesus Christ."[2]
>
> " Not by works of righteousness which we have done, but according to His mercy He saved us."[3]
>
> " I am not ashamed of the Gospel of Christ, for it is the power of God unto salvation to every one that believeth."[4]

Only God Can Work This. Unless your salvation depends on a Divine work, it may well be said to rest on a basis of sand. Unless your righteousness is God's righteousness, it can never stand the searching scrutiny of the white light of the Throne. Unless your robe has been woven on the Divine loom, it will never bear the

---

[1] Heb. xi. 29; Exod. xv. 6, 7, 11.   [3] Titus iii. 5.
[2] Gal. ii. 16.   [4] Rom. i. 16.

inspection of the King when He comes in to see His guests. Shut in there, between your heredity on the one hand and your temptations on the other, with your old taskmaster-sins blocking your retreat, what hope is there, unless your soul can stand still, and see your salvation achieved *for* you on the Cross by the Son of God, and accomplished *in* you by the efficiency of the Holy Spirit? Stand still in Gethsemane with its shadowing olives, on Calvary amid its apparent desertion, and in the garden-sepulchre amid the rending rocks of Eastermorn, and see the salvation of God. "Behold God is my salvation. I will trust, and not be afraid, for the Lord Jehovah is my strength and song."

Sacrifice the Basis of that Work. *That Divine Work was based on Sacrifice.* "Moses called for all the elders of Israel, and said unto them, Take you a lamb according to your families and kill the Passover. . . . And it shall come to pass that when your children shall say unto you, What mean ye by this service? that ye shall say, It is the sacrifice of the Lord's Passover, when He smote the Egyptians and delivered our houses."

An Unexplained Mystery. Was not a Lamb slain for us also? Verily. We worship Him Who by His own blood entered in once into the Holy Place and obtained eternal redemption. Behold the Lamb of God, Who was brought as a Lamb to the slaughter. There is no other hope against the day of days. Not that we have been moral and blameless in the eyes of our fellows, not that we have met the requirements and standards around us, but that the Lamb was slain before the foundation of the world. We cannot explain this mystery. And if we elect to stay outside the Holy of Holies until we understand, we shall never enter. But the contrite, penitent, and obedient heart, that has no words of excuse or palliation, will understand and live on the precious words which assure it that the blood of Jesus Christ, God's Son, cleanseth from all sin. Remember that He said Himself, in the most solemn hour of His life: "This is the cup of the Covenant in My Blood, shed for many unto the remission of sins."

The Blood the Greatest Gift Possible. It is enough. We know that blood is the life, and represents the love, the heart, the innermost element of human existence. This has been shed for us, and represents the uttermost self-giving of the Son of God. By His stripes we are healed. We do not attempt to bar the window or lock the iron door between us and the menacing blow, we shelter beneath the Cross.

> " Not all the blood of beasts,
>   On Jewish altars slain,
> Could give the guilty conscience peace,
>   Or wash away the stain:
> " But Christ, the heavenly Lamb,
>   Takes all our sins away,
> A sacrifice of noble name,
>   And richer blood than they."

Final Parting of Hebrew and Egyptian. *God's salvation is also characterised by Finality.* "The Egyptians whom ye have seen to-day, ye shall see them again no more for ever." The hostility of Hebrew and Egyptian had lasted for centuries. Again and again the Hebrews may have rebelled against their intolerable sufferings; but even if they were successful for a time, the old tyranny closed in upon them, like manacles clasped again on the hand of the escaped but recaptured slave. Now, at last, the Egyptians, who had made their lives bitter, lay dead on the seashore. They looked for the last time on those hard, cold, stony faces, and then took their journey into a land wherein the Egyptian would have no part. They might have to encounter Midianites and Moabites; but Egyptians—*never.*

The Dead Egyptians. It has been truly remarked that the sands of time are strewn with dead Egyptians, who once held the hearts and minds of men in thrall. The dominion of the priest over the human conscience, the ownership of man by man, the use of torture to extort the needed lie, the praise of ignorance as the safeguard of order, the habitual degradation of womanhood, the massacre of child-life. But they have lost their power. They are dead Egyptians. It is even difficult for us to imagine a world in which they were once supreme.

There are a few Egyptians left! War, vast armaments born of fear and hate, greedy money-competition, impurity, the slavery of the Congo basin, the opium traffic, which Great Britain forced on the reluctant Chinese, the nefarious sale of British spirits to the natives of Nigeria. But the conviction is gaining ground that these also shall perish, as other great evils have perished before them, and we shall be permitted to see these also dead upon the seashore of Time.

What is your Egyptian? Some besetting sin that has been your taskmaster for years. Long ago it made you its slave, or perhaps it enslaved your father before you. In former days you struggled valiantly for freedom; but all your efforts were in vain. Of late you have renounced the conflict, and have allowed yourself to yield at your tyrants' imperious behests. Perhaps you cherish the hope that some day the ebbing forces of your life, or even satiety, will emancipate you from your servitude. But it is a weary prospect. Not for you the perfect peace, the erect head, the cheery tone, the victor's shout, "Thanks be to God, who giveth the victory!"

Now, from this hour, will you not begin to cherish the anticipation of complete deliverance, not hereafter, in old age and in heaven, but now and here? Not because of your resolutions, or strivings, or agonies, but because you will stand still and see the salvation of God, because the Lord shall fight for you, and you will hold your peace.

Sin and its Dominion. (1) *Sin is not an inevitable part of our nature.* It is not indigenous, but an alien and intruder. What smallpox and measles are to the fair flesh of a little child, that sin is to our nature. The Scripture says that it was not present in our first parents. Certainly it was not in Christ, who was perfect man, and it will not be in the perfected humanity of the future. There is no necessity that sin should have dominion over you, any more than that Israel should serve Egypt. Dare to believe that the enemy may die; that the jealousy, envy, passion, greed may absolutely pass out of your experience; and that you shall be able to say with Paul, "The law of the Spirit of life in Christ Jesus hath made me free from the law of sin and death."

Sin is an Intruder. The great message of Christianity is that sin has no business in human hearts. It is an intruder who is to be expelled, and can be expelled. Not that man can be sinless in this mortal life, because even if we are delivered from positive trespass, we shall always be coming short of the glory of God; but that there need be no perpetual conscious self-condemnation for those who are in Christ Jesus; because God has sent forth His own Son in the likeness of sinful flesh, and as an offering for sin, and has neutralised sin in the flesh, that the righteousness of the law might be fulfilled in us.

Our Red Sea. (2) It was *on the far shores of the Red Sea* that the Israelites saw the dead bodies of their ancient foes. This also suggests the lesson that it is on the other side of the Cross and the grave, in which we have been crucified and buried with Christ, that we really find entire deliverance. Do not be content to confine your Christian experience to the belief that the Saviour's Cross is only for your beholding; it must also be for your participation. You must be crucified with Him, lie in the grave with Him, and rise with Him, from the dead; and then, standing on the other, the Easter, side of death, you will know that the old Egyptian taskmaster has no longer control.

Set about a new life. Believe that old things are passed away, and that all things are become new. Do despite to yourself! Not only avoid selfishness, but act unselfishly. Not only fight pride, but assume the girded towel of humility. Not only repress words of criticism and hate, but fill your life with pure love and charitable constructions. Not only put off the old man, but put on the new. The easiest way to do the former is by all means to do the latter. You will put off the old best when putting on the new, as the sap of spring, pulsing through the branches of evergreens, pushes off the faded leaves of the previous summer.

Dare to Believe. First, dare to believe that you were never meant to be the man that you have been so long; and next, step out of your grave under the blue sky and on the fresh soil, and live there as one alive from the dead, yielding your members unto God for ministry to man in His dear Name and in His power.

Two closing words. First: Remember Moses' repeated injunction that the people should borrow (the word in the Hebrew suggests *asking*, with no thought of return) of their neighbours jewels of silver and jewels of gold. It was only befitting and right that there should be some remuneration for their long toils. The dead Egyptian not only provided armour and weapons for their subsequent fight against other foes, whom they must surely meet, but enriched them, so that the very Tabernacle glittered with the flashing splendour of those jewels. Similarly, your whole life hereafter may be enriched by your present experiences. The patience, faith, love, purity, which will shine so radiantly in your character presently, will be the inalienable inheritance of this glad hour.

The once Bondman becomes Deliverer. Secondly: remember that you were once a bondman. Even if you are now delivered, Egypt still exists, and your brethren and sisters are there enslaved. Do not vaunt yourself over them, but in all humility and tenderness help the captive to freedom and the prisoner to breathe the air of liberty. Bear ye one another's burdens: and restore the fallen in a spirit of meekness, considering yourselves.

The Twofold Song

Revelation 15:1-8

1. And I saw another sign in heaven, great and marvellous, seven angels having the seven last plagues; for in them is filled up the wrath of God.

2. And I saw as it were a sea of glass mingled with fire: and them that had gotten the victory over the beast, and over his image, and over his mark, *and* over the number of his name, stand on the sea of glass, having the harps of God.

3. And they sing the song of Moses the servant of God, and the song of the Lamb, saying, Great and marvellous *are* thy works, Lord God Almighty; just and true *are* thy ways, thou King of saints.

4. Who shall not fear thee, O Lord, and glorify thy name? for *thou* only *art* holy: for all nations shall come and worship before thee; for thy judgments are made manifest.

5. And after that I looked, and, behold, the temple of the tabernacle of the testimony in heaven was opened:

6. And the seven angels came out of the temple, having the seven plagues, clothed in pure and white linen, and having their breasts girded with golden girdles.

7. And one of the four beasts gave unto the seven angels seven golden vials full of the wrath of God, who liveth for ever and ever.

8. And the temple was filled with smoke from the glory of God, and from his power; and no man was able to enter into the temple, till the seven plagues of the seven angels were fulfilled.

THE TWOFOLD SONG
Revelation 15:1-8

The Revelation and its Readers. Turn from Exodus to the Revelation. The Book is variously interpreted. For certain minds there is a perfect fascination in the attempt to fasten some particular interpretation on this or the other mysterious symbol. One questions sometimes whether the Book is not like the mysterious writing of the Hittites—a vanished race—for which we are only now finding the clue,[1] which was certainly known to the Christians of the first era. The very diversity of the interpretation, whether praeterist, presentist, or futurist, seems to establish this beyond doubt. Probably the visions do include what these eager and ingenious minds see in them, but certainly they include a great deal more, and touch all those events beneath which the same great principles lie. The special examples which are so frequently quoted are but part of the universal movement of Divine Providence.

But though we cannot read the Book of the Revelation as others do, in the light of accomplished fact, it does not follow that it is devoid of meaning and use. To adopt the words of another: The highest value of anything is its moral and spiritual value; and we do well to penetrate beneath the symbolism, however magnificent, in order to reach that which is of eternal significance and comfort. It is certainly so with the passage before us. Let us consider then the position of the singers, their history, and their song.

This Vision: The Singers. *The Position of these Singers.* "They stood beside the sea of glass." I saw, says the Seer, a sea of glass mingled with fire, and they that had gotten the victory stood on its shores. It is impossible not to trace the direction of the Apostle's thought. When the morning broke after the Exodus the redeemed hosts stood on the eastern shores of the Red Sea. The sky was bathed in the glow of the crimson-dawn, and the sea had returned to

[1] See Sayce's *Hittites* (R.T.S.).

its strength. Its calm, placid, glassy expanse gave no sign of the agony of the previous midnight. Around its shores were strewn the mailed bodies of the Egyptian chivalry. But its very texture seemed bathed in fire, the fire of the dawn that dyed its waters. Lying there in its big, broad basin, it was a veritable sea of glass mingled with fire. So, as the saints of God review the way by which they have passed, and the great tribulation out of which they have come, it will seem to them as if it were a sea of glass mingled with fire.

The Mystery of God's Wisdom. It stands for three things: (1) *Illumined Mystery.* The sea to the Jew was always the emblem of mystery. "Thy judgments are a mighty deep." "Thy way is in the sea, and Thy path in the great waters, and Thy footsteps are not known." "O the depth of the riches both of the wisdom and of the knowledge of God! How unsearchable are His judgments, and His ways past finding out." And the comparison is not unnatural. What lies beyond the rim of that horizon, where the white sails come up? what is covered by those mighty waters, which swallow up our treasures and give no account? But here the dark abysses are lit up with flame. Who is not conscious of an even deeper mystery in each human life? Some of these mysteries have been caused by the limitation of our faculties, and others by the incompleteness of the revelation given us. There are knots we cannot untie, questions we cannot answer, riddles we cannot solve. But some day the sea will be mingled with fire. Those sunless depths will be illuminated. Those subterranean caves will be radiant. We shall know as we are known, and see face to face.

The "Sea of Glass" a Type of Peace and Strength. (2) *Peace through Trial.* The sea of glass without a ripple dimpling it is the type of repose, of rest, of peace. And fire, which tests, purges, and purifies, is always and everywhere the emblem of sharp trial. The sea of glass, then, mingled with fire, must stand for the Peace and Strength which are ours, as the result of the testing flame. Take the peace on the face of a child, where there is no freckle or wrinkle, and contrast it with that on the face of a man who has fought his way through doubt, and disputation, and conflict. The one is the sea of glass, the other is the sea of glass mingled with fire. Take the passiveness of some mean character which has no energy to combat evil, and contrast it with the patience of one who has learnt it through awful experiences which have tested him to the quick. The one is the sea of glass, the other is the sea of glass mingled with fire. Contrast Samuel, the innocent boy, running to old Eli and asking for his blessing, with the old prophet before he surrendered his weary burden. The one is the sea of glass, the other is the sea of glass mingled with fire. We know not what we shall be when truth and love have become the very atmosphere and home of our souls, but probably we shall always remember the ordeal through which we have passed. Even in heaven we shall remember from what we were saved by the grace of God. Though our peace shall be as a sea of glass, our very peace will be dyed with the fire of pain and anguish and sorrow.

First Morning of Israelite History. (3) *The Everlasting Morning.* "The sea returned to its strength when the morning appeared." Ah, what a morning was that! The first morning in Asia, the first morning of freedom, the first morning of Israelite history. The flush of that glory on the crystal sea was the reflection of the herald beams of the greatest day that had ever broken on their race. Not the day when Abram left Ur of the Chaldees, nor the day when Joseph was raised from the prison to the palace, nor the day when Moses was found by the king's daughter, had been as momentous as this. But the day which we anticipate is more radiant far, since it will usher in the timeless glory of eternity. We shall see it some day. The nights will have passed with their weeping and loneliness, and the redeemed of the Lord shall return with singing unto Zion. Everlasting joy shall be unto them. They shall obtain gladness and joy, and sorrow and sighing shall flee away.

> " The morning shall awaken,
>   The shadows shall decay,
> And each true-hearted servant
>   Shall shine as doth the day."

The Mystic Number of "the Beast." *The Singers.* "They had gotten the victory over the Beast." We cannot state in full what is included in the term "The Beast." One large school says that it means the Church of Rome, and another used to make it stand for Napoleon the Third, and compelled the mystic number 666 to spell out his name. But may we not say that it stands for the blind passion of instinct, unrestrained and unregulated by the high intention and rule of our moral and spiritual nature?

What "the Beast" Stands For. The Beast stands for all that is low and degrading, for whatever endeavours to pull us down from our standing in Christ Jesus, for whatever is inconsistent with our high calling as sons of God. He opens his mouth in blasphemy against God, to blaspheme His name, and His tabernacle, and them that dwell in heaven. He makes war with the saints, and overcomes them. He rules over all those whose names are not written in the Book of Life of the Lamb slain from the foundation of the world.

The Beast Within Us. The Beast is in ourselves, in us all; and only as you learn to overcome it can you hope to stand upon that sea of glass, having one of the harps of God. We must fight and overcome all that is of the beast, with an unrelenting hatred. We must mortify the flesh with its affections and lusts. We must return good for evil, love for hatred, mercy for ill-deeds. We must put on the Lord Jesus Christ, and make no provision for the flesh, to fulfil the lusts thereof. We must not content ourselves with repelling the attacks of evil upon us. It is never safe to remain only on the defensive, we must sally forth and do despite to our worst selves. With Divine courage and unflinching faith we must make inroads upon the ranks of evil, and break them to pieces in the name of the Lord.

The Beast Around Us. The Beast is around and without, in society. In the cruelty and hatred, in the jealousy and malice, in the scenes that fill our streets with riot on Saturday night, in the awful revelations of the police courts, and in the evil literature that brings a pile of gold into the tills of the purveyor, at the cost of the letting loose of the vilest passions and the blighting of whole gardens of innocence and modesty, we have abundant evidence of the presence of the Beast.

The Fight against the Beast. We must fight against these beast-like evils. Against the wolf of cruelty, and the Satyr of foul impurity, and the Fox of cunning, and the Vulture which delights in blood. Let us resolve that life shall be one determined struggle in the effort to free others from the dominion of these lower propensities and passions by which Earth's Edens are too often turned into very shambles of blood. And in proportion as we do this we shall find ourselves dwelling beside that sea of glass bathed with fire, and having in our hands the harps of God, i.e. harps which God has prepared and attuned. Do you want its peace? Carry peace into the warring strifes and tumults of the world! Do you want its touch of fire? Go and love men with the love of God! Do you want its harp and song? Then do your best to kindle hope and joy in other breasts than those of your own loved ones!

Only One Way of Victory. There is only one way of victory.

"They overcame him by the blood of the Lamb, and by the word of their testimony."[1]

The Blood of the Lamb is the supreme gift of God. It is self-giving in sacrifice, and it is impossible to follow in the footprints of the supreme sacrifice of Calvary without sharing finally the bliss of association with Him in His Victory and Glory. And as to the word of your testimony—never be ashamed of testifying to your own deliverance. Let the redeemed of the Lord say so, whom He has brought out from under the hands of the oppressor, and made them free with the freedom of the sons of God. It is the loyal confession of your King that will help you and others to escape from the enemy and destroyer, as it was Moses' perpetual affirmation of God that broke down the power of Pharaoh.

These, then, are the singers. They were redeemed from among men. Their names are written in the Book of life of the Lamb, slain from the foundation of the world. They love not their lives unto the death. They follow the Lamb whithersoever He goeth. They overcome by the blood of the Lamb, and the word of their testimony.

The Song and its Burden. "It is the song of Moses the servant of God, and the song of the Lamb."

Music the Highest Language. The life of the redeemed is represented as a Song. This is very suggestive. Order and Beauty naturally express themselves in music. Human language cannot express all the thoughts and hopes and affections of the heart, but music can. Music is the highest language with which we are acquainted. Words fail, even looks fail, and gestures and tears, but not music. When, therefore, we are told that in the next life they sing, we realise that they are superlatively happy.

The Law of Human Life. But when in addition we find that allusion to the harps of God, we are driven to the further conclusion that in the other life we shall be in perfect accord with God as our environment. To be in tune with the Infinite is the real goal of all human aspirings. It is not so now. Unfulfilled desire for God is the law of human life. In our best moments we want to attain to that ineffable Being Who is so near and yet so far, so intimate and yet so transcendent, so humble and loving and yet so awful.

" Like tides on a desert sea-beach,
When the moon is low and thin,

[1] Rev. xii. 11.

> Into our hearts high yearnings
> Come welling and swelling in."

We want to get out of ourselves into God, to lose ourselves in Him. Men and women fly to money, or art, or human love for satisfaction, but in vain. But we shall never rest until we reach the crystal sea which lies spread out at the foot of the Throne of God: and there we shall burst out into song, as the child does who is thoroughly happy.

Song Denotes Perfect Union. But song also denotes perfect union. The battle song, martial music, the wild notes of the pibroch, have a marvellous effect in unifying vast masses of men. This was probably John's conception. He conceived of a vast society gathered from all ages, all dispensations, and from all lands, filled with one purpose, animated by love to God and to one another. In that one perfect society he saw the fulfilment of the hopes of the saints of the Old Testament and of the New, of those who trembled under Sinai, as of those who had rejoiced beneath the touch of Pentecost.

The Song of Moses. *Let us consider the Song of Moses.* It is contained in Exodus, ch. xv.: "Then sang Moses and the children of Israel this song unto the Lord, saying, I will sing unto the Lord, for He hath triumphed gloriously: the horse and his rider hath He thrown into the sea."

A Song of Deliverance. From beginning to end, *it was praise of God.* There is no mention of Moses, though so much was due to his faith and courage, his wise foresight, and peerless leadership. The whole strain of the song was an ascription of praise to Jehovah. *It celebrated the entire overthrow of the enemy.* "The waters covered their enemies: there was not one of them left."[1] How those words must have sounded when afterwards sung by the Levitical choirs! The soloist would utter the air, "Not one of them left." It might be sung as a duet, "Not one of them left." It would be tossed to and fro in the chorus. "Not one of them left."

—Of Victory. *It commemorated the ease of victory.* "Thou didst blow with Thy wind, the sea covered them. They sank as lead." If man had gone to work to destroy the hosts of Egypt, what a multitude of deadly engines he would have required! But God had only to breathe with His lips.

—Of Confidence. *It anticipated the future.* God would not be

---

[1] Ps. cvi. 11.

content with bringing the people out. He would also bring them in, and plant them in the mountain of His inheritance, where He would reign over them for ever and ever.

Each of these ingredients will be found in the life of heaven. There, too, we shall have no note save of praise to God: unto Him that loved us! There, too, we shall celebrate the total overthrow of all that exalted itself in opposition: He shall put down all authority and power. There we shall commemorate the ease of the Victory, and anticipate the eternal reign of love.

The Song of the Lamb. *Let us consider the Song of the Lamb.* It is written in Rev. v.: "And they sung a new song, saying, Thou art worthy to take the book, and to open the seals thereof; for Thou wast slain, and hast redeemed us to God by Thy Blood out of every kindred, and tongue, and people, and nation; and hast made us unto our God kings and priests."

The Blended Words. *Let us consider the blending of these two in the words before us.* "Great and marvellous are Thy works, O Lord God, the Almighty; just and true are Thy ways, Thou King of the ages." When we look back on the history of the world, with the overthrow of its Pharaohs; when we consider the entire plan of God's dealings with men, as it will appear in all its integrity and beauty; when we review the story of our own lives, that now seem so tangled and incomprehensible, we shall not only agree that God's works were great and marvellous, but that His ways were right and true. The righteousness, or rightness, of His acts will then be made manifest. It is not always manifest now. Many stumble at God's dealings with them, and accuse Him of injustice and inequality. But one day His righteous acts will be made manifest.

Mourning Turned to Music. Think of it, the very things that now weigh thee down and oppress thee will one day be set to music. Thou are setting up the type from which the songs of eternity are to be printed off. The dark lines of thy spectrum will be shown to be incandescent metal. Thy weights, thy wings. Thy misereres, thy magnificats. Thy dark sorrows, the pearls of light and glory. Keep vigil in perfect faith through the long dark night. He will give thee songs at break of day.

THE WELLS OF BITTERNESS

Exodus 15:23-26

23. And when they came to Marah, they could not drink of the waters of Marah, for they *were* bitter: therefore the name of it was called Marah.

24. And the people murmured against Moses, saying, What shall we drink?

25. And he cried unto the Lord; and the Lord shewed him a tree, *which* when he had cast into the waters, the waters were made sweet: there he made for them a statute and an ordinance, and there he proved them,

26. And said, If thou wilt diligently hearken to the voice of the Lord thy God, and wilt do that which is right in his sight, and wilt give ear to his commandments, and keep all his statutes, I will put none of these diseases upon thee, which I have brought upon the Egyptians: for I *am* the Lord that healeth thee.

THE WELLS OF BITTERNESS
Exodus 15:23-26

A Wilderness Episode. In the same chapter that records Israel's triumphant ode we have the story of their experience at the Bitter Wells. Of course it is only a coincidence, and yet how true to human life! We sing our songs of triumph one day, and within three days we have touched the bottom of disappointment and despair.

Three Days into the Wilderness. "Moses brought Israel from the Red Sea, and they went out into the wilderness of Shur."

Character of the Wilderness. We must repeat what has been said already that the word wilderness does not imply a waste of sand, but a broad open expanse, which affords pasture enough for a nomad tribe wandering with their flocks. Waste and desolate so far as human habitations are concerned, the traveller will only encounter a few Bedouins. But everywhere the earth is clothed with a thin vegetation, scorched in summer drought, but brightening up, as at the kiss of the Creator, into fair and beautiful pastures, at the rainy season and in the neighbourhood of a spring.

It is quite true that it was no Eden, and the soil yielded no such profusion of vegetable life as made the valley of the Nile a riband of green. But it was at least the land of freedom, besides being the vestibule of the Land of Promise. Moreover, it was the school for the necessary discipline of the sons of God.

The First Day's March. We can almost picture the march of *the first day.* When they had sung their great song of Liberty, they saw the majestic cloud gathering itself up and moving slowly forward and the vast host began its march, with one last look on the faces of their dead masters. At the first sense of freedom, the greatness of their deliverance, the consciousness of God's guiding presence sustained and cheered them. On their right lay the deep waters of the Red Sea, on their left the mountains which support the great inland central plateau of the desert. It is quite likely that Moses and the leaders, with the armed men, would keep together, whilst the remainder of the great host of two million souls would spread themselves far and near, moving slowly, the women and children and aged perched on asses, whilst the able-bodied would talk together of the achievements of the past night, or break into snatches of their ode of victory.

The Second Day. *The second day,* judging from the reports of travellers, must have tried them greatly. They turned away from the sea into a labyrinth of mountains. The way lay over a white limestone plain, the dust of which had become caked into a hard surface, hot to the feet and dazzling to the eye. Treeless, waterless, shadowless! After Marah, we are told that there is hardly a single day's march that does not bring the traveller to some green oasis, or some tiny thread of watercourse; but there was nothing of this sort in that dusty waste. At last the evening drew its shadows over the blazing sky, the stars shone brilliantly above them, the night breeze refreshed them; they still had water in their water-skins, which they had filled at the Wells of Moses, and had provision enough for their hunger, so they slept and hoped for better things on the morrow.

The Third Day. But *the third day* was as monotonous and tiresome as the preceding. All the morning and afternoon they toiled on, not without many hard expressions and harder thoughts of Moses, whose noble service they were inclined to forget in the toilsomeness of the way. Benefactors must not count on gratitude. The mob broke the windows of Apsley House, the residence of the Duke of Wellington, though he had won Waterloo for them.

Disenchanted and Grumbling. This again is human life. The young lad who leaves school at sixteen or seventeen congratulates himself that he is free of restraint and lessons and the sense of inferiority. He is to go to business, to be apprenticed, or articled, to prepare for medicine or the bar. He sings his song of emancipation; but within three weeks or months he finds that the way of the new life blisters his feet and hems him in with restraint and compulsion. So rough is the wilderness that he is half-inclined to wish himself back at school.

Our Wilderness Experiences. A young man who has won the confidence of his employer, is one day suddenly commissioned to start within a few days for Shanghai or Tokio, as superintendent or manager of the business there. He is filled with a perfect ecstasy of joy. Here is his chance. At first the sense of freedom, the voyage, the interest of novel surroundings, lift him into a new world; but as he becomes familiar with the severe difficulties of the situation—the cunning native, the trying climate, the letters from the firm whose demands he cannot satisfy—he looks wistfully back to the evenings when the desk was closed till the morrow, and he went forth with absolutely no care upon his soul. All through life we have the wilderness experience.

—In the Christian Life. Is it not so in Christian life? We have known what it was to pass through a memorable experience of the love and power of Christ. From the vantage-ground of a Transfiguration mountain we have seen the open door of Paradise. We have learned how to pray: have acquired the secret of victory; have become energised by the Holy Spirit. Emotion has risen to flood-tide. It has seemed as though we could never fail Christ again. Henceforth we should have hinds' feet, and walk on our high places. But after a while we become aware that the light is dying off the landscape. There is hardly enough left to guide our steps. The roughness of the path hurts our feet, its difficulty appals us. We have to live in our will. We are led up into the wilderness to be tempted of the devil. We have such revelations of our own evil heart that we are tempted to despair. We cry out with the prophet, as we learn to know ourselves, "Woe is me, for I am undone!" and with the apostle, "Depart from me, for I am a sinful man, O Lord!" All this is the way of the wilderness.

Marah. *The Wells of Bitterness.* Towards the afternoon of the third day, on the sky-line there appeared a sign of verdure, which inspired new hope. It was like the white sail of a ship to the castaway on a lonely island in mid-ocean, or the flag of a relieving squadron to a beleaguered fortress. The inspiration of hope flashed in every eye, and quickened every step. Men said to one another, "Moses was right after all." Women told their children that Jehovah had been mindful of them. The very beasts seemed to forget their languor and their loads. They pressed to the wells, and cast themselves down beside them for long refreshing draughts. "And when they came to Marah, they could not drink of the waters of Marah, for they were bitter. And the people murmured against Moses, saying, What shall we drink?"

The "Marahs" of Ordinary Life. They were disheartened and disappointed. For three days when no wells were in sight they had kept up bravely. But when a well appeared to be within reach, but proved a failure, they were maddened with the sudden set-back to their hopes. A man may brace himself to live without human love; but when it comes almost within his reach, and then eludes him, he becomes broken with perpetual heartache, that darkens every subsequent day. Another may be perfectly content with a modest income and his pretty home, till he learns that he is the possible heir of an immense fortune. Only at the last moment is he suddenly deprived of his expectations, by the appearance of another heir, more closely akin to the testator. But from that moment the old zest in his more meagre lot is gone.

Or yet again, we may in our journey have reached the pools that promised us satisfaction, only to find them brackish. That marriage, that friendship, that new home, that partnership, that fresh avenue of pleasure, which promised so well turns out to be absolutely disappointing. Who has not muttered "Marah" over some desert well which he strained every nerve to reach, but when reached, it disappointed him!

Wordsworth tells us of the disheartenment and disappointment which befell him after the French Revolution. He had counted on the great issues of that stormy time. He had hoped for the birth of brotherhood and freedom. He thought that the race would slough off its evil past and rise to the dignity of man. But when instead of all these the tumbrel carried its daily contingent to the guillotine, and the streets of Paris for months ran blood, he says:

> " I lost
> All feeling of conviction, and in fine
> Sick, wearied out with contrarieties,
> Yielded up moral questions in despair."

Are you there to-day? Are you at Marah to-day? At least suspend your judgment. Don't murmur against Moses, and don't judge God. This is no time for a well-balanced verdict upon the way that you are being brought. Strike out if you will, but don't sum up. Remember, also, that others are probably suffering as heavily as you are, and more so. You are only one and by yourself, that man has a wife and children. Is his lot not worse than yours? In the theatre of ancient Greece, the actors depicted the great sorrows of their greatest heroes, and those who saw them, feeling that their heaviest griefs were inferior, returned to their homes to bear them nobly. The best thing to do, when you are despondent and sad, is to go forth and brighten the lot of some one else.

The Tree not a Special Creation. *The Tree.* And Moses "cried unto the Lord; and the Lord showed him a tree, which when he had cast into the waters, the waters were made sweet." We are not to suppose from these words that a tree had been created for this purpose. The answer to Moses' prayer came not in creating but showing the tree.

Travellers tell us that several trees are used by the Arabs for this very purpose. There is especially the bark of a certain tree, which has power to precipitate the mineral particles which embitter the waters, so that they become sweet and clear. It is a beautiful provision of Nature, an illustration of that wonderful law of compensation which is always cropping up from the divine foundations of the world.

The Antidote always near at Hand. In Nature the antidote grows near the poison, the dock-leaf beside the nettle. No need to travel far for healing. And for every sorrow to which we are subject there is a swift and sufficient cure. The tree grows near the Marah pool. For every sin there is a ready salvation. The word is nigh thee, even in thy mouth, and in thine heart. There is no need to ascend into the heavens, or descend into the depths. The Lord is always at hand, a very present help in time of trouble.

The Purpose of Miracles. But we need to be shown! "The Lord *showed* him the tree." When Hagar, in the dire need of her dying child, cast him under a shrub, and went and sat her down over against him a good way off, as it were a bowshot, God opened her eyes and she saw a well of water, from which she filled her empty bottle-skin with water. It had been there all the while, but she was too blinded with grief to behold it. We need, similarly, to receive not the spirit of the world, but the Spirit which is of God, that we may know the things that are freely given to us of God. All around us there are deliverances waiting for our appropriations and comfort. Cry to God; in the cry there is relief, and in answer to it He will show thee the balm in Gilead, the healing for thy wound, the fountain for thy thirst. This is probably the design of miracles, to point the way, and reveal what we had been otherwise too stupid to discern.

But surely to us the tree is that on which Jesus died. In evident allusion to the ancient word, "Cursed is he that hangeth on a tree," the apostle says, "His own self bear our sins in His own body on the tree."[1] How little did the tree of which the Cross was made realise the high honour for which it was intended as it grew in some

[1] 1 Peter ii. 24.

deep forest-glade! But probably before His birth our Lord had seen it planted, and had watered it with His rain and nurtured it with His sun. This is the tree which, cast into the fountains of the world's bitterness, makes them sweet.

> " Bane and blessing, pain and pleasure,
> By the Cross are sanctified;
> Peace is there that knows no measure,
> Joys that through all time abide."

Christ the Tree that sweetens all Bitterness. Look to the Cross, disappointed soul. Did not Jesus suffer more than ever thou hast done? Look unto Him, the Author and Finisher of Faith, who instead of the joy that was set before Him, endured the Cross, despising the shame. Consider Him that endured such contradiction of sinners against Himself, lest thou be wearied and faint in thy mind. Besides, the Cross stands for self-denial, self-sacrifice, self-giving. Learn so to renounce and give thyself, that the hard lessons acquired in the school of sorrow may pass into action, and so into the experience of others. In addition, the Cross was the way to the Father's bosom. When the cup had been drained to the dregs, and the perfect obedience finished, the Father bade the Crucified sit with Him by His side.

Joy in the Looking Forward. In the light of that heaven of bliss, how small become the aches and pains of Time! Be of good cheer, then! If you have shared His griefs, you shall share His joys. If you have been crucified you shall reign. The sorrows of the present are not worthy to be compared with the glory to be revealed. Our light affliction, which is but for a moment, shall work out a far more exceeding and eternal weight of glory. Your Marah shall never be named or brought to mind, when you find yourself beside the river of water of life that proceeds out of the Throne of God and of the Lamb. There you shall hunger no more, neither thirst any more; the sun shall not light on you, nor any heat; for the Lamb Who is in the midst of the Throne shall feed you, and shall lead you to living fountains of waters, and God shall wipe away all tears from your eyes.

It is remarkable that at Marah God took to Himself a new name. "I am the Lord that healeth thee."

God gives Himself a New Name at Marah. We do not find Him giving Himself a new name at Elim, but at Marah. The happy experiences of life fail to reveal all the new truth and blessing that await us in God. It was after the pursuit of Chedorlaomer and the kings, and when there was fear of reprisals, that Jehovah's word came to His servant, saying, "I am thy shield and thine exceeding great reward." It was in the agony of the conflict with Amalek that Israel knew Jehovah as Jehovah-Nissi—i.e. The Lord my banner.

Come to the Lord for Healing. It was as though He said: The tree has healed the waters, but its virtue was in Me. God has implanted healing properties in drugs and balsams and waters, that we might look through them all to Himself. Whether in physical, mental, or spiritual maladies, let us climb past the channel to the source, away from the ritual, the ministry, even the Cross, to Him who forgives all our iniquities, heals all our diseases, redeems life from the daily destructions that threaten it, and crowns us with loving kindness and tender mercy.

Let us come to our Lord for healing, with whatever disease we have in this complex nature of ours. When once the spirit receives the inbreathing of His perfect health, it spreads to the soul, and even the body experiences quickening through His Spirit that dwelleth in us.

The Arrival at Elim. *After Marah, Elim.* "And they came to Elim, where were twelve wells of water, and threescore and ten palm-trees: and they encamped there by the waters."

They say that Elim must have been the Wady Ghurundel, where a considerable spring wells out at the foot of a sandstone rock, forming a pool of clear water, around which quite a considerable amount of vegetation clusters. This forms a welcome contrast to the wilderness. We can easily realise the satisfaction with which the weary host flung themselves on the grass, beneath the shadow of the palm-trees, and drank refreshing draughts to the full.

The Elims follow the Marahs. There are many Elims in life's pilgrimage. The Home, the Weekly Rest-Day, the House of God, the quiet beauty of the countryside, the interspace of rest that comes to most of us amid the stress of our life-work. And those hours of fellowship with our Saviour, when we are fed on the hidden manna, and drink of the spiritual rock, and are healed by the leaves of the tree of life—these again are green oases. But remember the Elims follow the Marahs, because Christ's soldiers must be taught that life is stern and real, and that the intervals of rest are not the goal, but the arbour on Hill Difficulty, where we stay for a brief interval, ere we again brace ourselves for the climb.

THE FOOD FROM HEAVEN

Exodus 16:1

1. And they took their journey from Elim, and all the congregation of the children of Israel came unto the wilderness of Sin, which *is* between Elim and Sinai, on the fifteenth day of the second month after their departing out of the land of Egypt.

THE FOOD FROM HEAVEN

Exodus 16:1

The Rest at Elim. Elim with its twelve springs of water and seventy palm trees had been a welcome resting-place after the three days' journey into the wilderness; but it could be nothing more. That small pool of clear water, with its grassy margin, its tamarisk and dwarf palm trees and other shrubs, which is still pointed out as the Elim, must have been very attractive to thirsty lips and weary feet, but it could not be for long the abiding-place of the heirs of promise.

Our Elims. It has been truly said that God does not multiply our Elims, for He cannot trust us there. He gems the earth with them, to teach us that it is not all blasted, and that we are not a cursed race in a cursed world. He sets them before our eyes as witnesses that there are worlds where there is no bitterness in the fountains of life. He causes us to lie down in them, only that we may be better able to tread in the paths of righteousness in which He leads us. He suffers us not to linger there, but summons us forth, that privation and toil may brace our moral muscles, and make us fit to join the pilgrim race. Rest in Elim, but never ungird. Drink, but like Gideon's men, who lapped in haste. Slumber if you will, but let your lamps be trimmed and your staff ready to your hand, that at the first movement of the cloud by night or day you may start again on the wilderness-march.

In the Wilderness of Sin. On leaving Elim, the way lay at first through a labyrinth of rich sandstone, like the outer avenues of some great temple; and indeed they were on the outskirts of a Temple not made with hands, where they were to meet God. There is much wonderful scenery between Elim and the wilderness of Sin, notably at that spot alluded to in the itinerary recorded in Numbers[1]: "They removed from Elim, and encamped by the Red Sea." It was there, as Dean Stanley reminds us, that they had their final glimpse

[1] Num. xxxiii. 10, etc.

of Egypt on the farther shores of the bright sea that formed the base of the view.

The Threatened Famine. "And they removed from the Red Sea, and pitched in the wilderness of Sin." It was a toilsome journey, in part along the strand, and then through scorching valleys; but the general distress was greatly augmented by the failure of their stores of food. Famine threatened the host. Moses and Aaron were assailed with angry murmurs; and regrets were freely expressed that they had not remained in the slavery of Egypt, where at least they had flesh-pots and bread to the full. It was under such circumstances that the Lord said to Moses, "Behold I will rain bread from heaven for you."

The Manna. THE MIRACLE OF THE MANNA. *It was a distinct act of God.* He spread the table for them in the wilderness, which they had deemed to be impossible. They had spoken against Him, saying, "Can God furnish a table in the wilderness?"[1] But He did more, He gave them to partake of the corn of heaven, and man did eat angels' food. He thus gave evidence of His inexhaustible resources, and showed Himself willing and able to supply all their physical need, whilst they learned His great lessons.

What was Manna? Many theories have been advanced to account for this great miracle. Some have ascribed it to the honey dew which falls in the desert, and refreshes the exhausted traveller; others to the tree-manna which exudes from the tamarisk tree; others again have made much of an edible lichen which grows in the desert; but none of these hypotheses meet the conditions of the case. For instance, how can these theories account for the abundance of the manna, its cessation on the seventh day, its perennial provision for forty years, or its sufficiency as the staple of human life? We are quite prepared to admit that there was a substratum of Nature beneath the miracle, as there was in the gift of quails, in the feeding of the five thousand, and in all the miracles; but in the last resort there can be no doubt that it was the act of God, calling into operation, as He invariably does, some far-reaching natural laws and processes.

The Feeding an Act of Grace. *But it was a supreme act of Grace.* It is an astonishing fact that there was not, on God's part, a single severe word in reproof of the people's murmurings, far less any punishment. At a later period, when they had been longer under

[1] Ps. lxxviii. 19.

His training, they were severely punished when they gave way to a similar outburst of complaint.[1] "Some of them also murmured, and were destroyed of the destroyer,[1] but in this preliminary stage of their education God made allowances for them, large and merciful in extent. Both here and at Rephidim, when they tempted and proved Him, He did not chide, but bore with them as a father with his querulous child. Surely He knew their frame, and remembered they were but dust. He put the gentlest construction on their wild speeches, on their forgetfulness of the great benefits they had received, on their ingratitude, on their accusations and reproaches to His servants, on their exaggerated estimate of Egypt, on their distrust and unbelief of Himself. In the touching words of the Psalmist: "He remembered that they were but flesh; a wind that passeth away, and cometh not again."[2] He wrought for His Holy Name's sake.

—**As well as a Test.** *The daily gift was intended as a test.* "The people shall go out and gather a certain rate every day, that I may prove them, whether they will walk in My Law, or no."

The gift of manna during forty years, many of which were stained by sinful murmuring and disobedience, was a perpetual exhibition of God's patience, long-suffering, and fidelity to His promise. But the rules prescribed for the gathering of the manna were a prolonged test of their obedience. They were also trained to dependence, and self-control, and care for one another, as they stooped daily over the desert-floor.

—**And a Divine Revelation.** *The gift of manna was connected with a Divine Theophany.* "And Moses spake unto Aaron, Say unto all the congregation of the children of Israel, Come near before the Lord: for He hath heard your murmurings. And it came to pass, as Aaron spake unto the whole congregation of the children of Israel, that they looked toward the wilderness, and, behold, the glory of Jehovah appeared in the cloud."

Aaron took the initiative, probably because Moses was withdrawn in the secret chamber of prayer. But how remarkable that revelation of God's glory appears, when we compare it with the theophany that closes the Book of Job, or the look that our Lord cast on Peter as He left the council-chamber! There are times in all religious experiences, when the thought that God is, that God is near, that God can, that God will, and that God does, is enough to silence

[1] Num. xxi. 6; 1 Cor. x. 10.   [2] Ps. lxxviii. 39.

every murmur and hush every fear. God is here in this wilderness with me, and I dare not renounce hope or utter a word of complaint.

The Abundance of Quails. *He did more than supply the necessary support of life.* "He rained flesh also upon them as dust, and feathered fowls like as the sand of the sea: and He let it fall in the midst of their camp, round about their habitations."[1]

Quails still pass over the Sinaitic Peninsula in vast migratory flocks on their way from the interior of Africa. They can easily be secured, because, exhausted with their journey, they fly near the ground, on which they often fall through sheer weariness. Tristram tells us that in Algeria also he has found the ground covered with them over many acres, and they were so fatigued that they scarcely moved until almost trodden upon. The miracle, therefore, lay in the timeliness of their advent. God always uses existing Nature as His basis, modifying and altering as slightly as possible, augmenting the quantity, but not exerting more supernatural power than needful, or departing further from the established course of Nature than required. How suggestive it is that He did not confine Himself to the gift of the necessary manna, but added the luxury of quails! We are reminded of the preparation by our Lord of fish as well as bread at that memorable morning meal beside the calm waters of the lake.

God responsible for His Followers. This God is ours to-day. When He is directly responsible for our circumstances, we shall find him faithful. Is not this a particular instance of that great law? If the people had gone wantonly and wilfully into the desert, there would have been no obligation on God to supply their need. But God had led them there. His moving cloud was directing every step. Even Moses was not responsible for the route. Obviously, then, He could not leave them to starve in the wilderness. When once we have started forth at His command, and have gone on His providentially-indicated way, we may say it reverently that God cannot refrain from assisting us, save at the loss of His dearest attributes. It is quite true that we have to obey His laws. We must go out and gather: we must observe the laws of rest: we must not gather more than we need: we must care for our families and homes. But these observances do not touch the primal and gracious faithfulness of the Father of lights, in whom is no variableness, neither shadow cast by turning.

But Obedience Necessary. Trust Him absolutely. After all, every meal comes from above. Our Father in Heaven gives us our daily

[1] Ps. lxxviii. 27, 28.

bread. Every day we are sitting at His table. Though our bread comes through the sweat of our brow, we only gather what He has provided. Come to His table every morning, and sit there till He spread it. He may keep thee waiting for a little, but watch and wait. "Behold the fowls of the air, they sow not, neither do they reap, nor gather into barns, yet your Heavenly Father feedeth them. Are ye not much better than they?"

The Cry of Humanity. THE MYSTICAL APPLICATION OF THE MIRACLE. We learn from John vi. that the manna was a type of the Son of Man, and that He was "the true bread from heaven." *If this be so, we must infer that the whole race for which He stands must be stricken with hopeless hunger.* The cry of the prodigal in the far country, which may have been Alexandria, Ephesus, or Rome, is the cry of humanity,—"I perish with hunger." The insatiable passion for pleasure and money, the restlessness of modern life, with its incessant cry for something new, the weary look on so many faces in the fine carriages of the parks or the crowds in the streets, tell the same tale of those who would fain appease the cravings of their appetite with husks fit for swine, but still are perishing with hunger. Is not this a fact in the heart-life of every individual, who is thoughtful and experienced enough to diagnose his true condition? And it is because of this hunger, as an indispensable element in the life of man, that we have absolute confidence in a great future for the religious life of mankind.

Indifference to Religion only Temporary. We have been told lately that the whole of our civilisation is slipping away from the religion out of which it sprang. Men are forsaking the churches where their fathers worshipped, are ceasing to pray, are shutting out God from all their thoughts. We have not yet gone the length of the French Revolutionists, who sought to blot out the name of God from literature, and to alter every name of day and street that referred to ancient religious observances. Practically, however, tens of thousands are doing what amounts to the same thing. But this is only a temporary phase. Ultimately our race will be tired of the husks, tired of spending money for that which is not bread, and labour for that which satisfieth not. Again these places of worship will be filled with teeming crowds.

" Thy children shall make haste; thy destroyers and they that made thee waste shall go forth of thee. . . . For thy waste and thy desolate places, and the land of thy destruction, shall even now be too narrow by reason of the inhabitants, and they that swallowed thee up shall be far away."[1]

Man Really Hungers for God. But let us be quite sure as to what it is that men hunger for. It is not for mere formularies, even though these may express truths. It is not for theories concerning inspiration or eternal punishment. It is not for this or that ecclesiastical system. No; the heart of man, made for God, hungers for God. It will accept a false religion rather than none, if it presents but a modicum of the knowledge of God. But with how certain an appetite and avidity will the heart of man accept the Gospel of Christ, when it is freed from adventitious circumstances, and presented in all its native beauty, not only to the mind, but to the heart!

Truth Alone not Enough. Beyond this, however, it must be said that Truth alone is not enough to satisfy the heart of humanity. We crave the concrete. We desire that the Absolute should clothe itself in tangible flesh and blood. And has not this natural yearning been met abundantly in Christ, Who is Himself the Truth?

True Religion Known by its Fruits. This is the ultimate evidence of the Divine origin of Christianity. "The bread of God is that which cometh down from heaven, and giveth life unto the world." Show us that which is capable of giving life unto the world. Not to an individual here or there, or to this or that community, but *to the world.* Show us a religion which gives life to those who are dead in trespasses and sins; and that does this irrespective of national and racial distinctions; and you have produced a religion which must have come down from heaven.

The effect of all our fellowship with Christ should be "more life and fuller." We do not need the emotional or intellectual, but the building up of spiritual force, so that we shall be strong to suffer or to wait, strong to do or dare, strong to minister to the sorrows and sins of men. These fruits are the inevitable criterion of right feeding. Where they are absent, nothing will convince us that you are feeding on Christ; whereas if you feed on Him there will be no "impossible" in your vocabulary, no "peradventure" in your outlook.

Jesus Satisfied the Apostles. LET US TAKE A PARTICULAR INSTANCE OF THE FEEDING OF THE HUNGER OF THE HEART. The Apostles furnish

[1] Isa. xlix. 17, 19.

a precise illustration of the way in which Jesus satisfies the soul. As young men they hungered for the Bread of God. For this they left their native haunts beside the Lake of Galilee, and came down the Jordan valley to the spot where John was baptising. He had caught a glimpse of the coming Christ, which he passed on in burning speech. But this failed to satisfy those eager souls, and when the Lord was manifested they turned to Him, and fed on His every word. His words were found, and they did eat them, and they became the joy and rejoicing of their hearts all through those happy months of fellowship.

A Keener Spiritual Hunger. But as they knew Him better they became hungry with a more refined appetite, hardly knowing what they wanted. Therefore they plied Him with questions: Whither goest Thou? Show us the Father! How wilt Thou manifest Thyself to us, and not unto the world? All these were suggestive of a deeper and more passionate hunger than would be satisfied by a physical presence, however beloved and fair. And this also was met when He tarried with them, being seen of them forty days, and speaking of the things pertaining to the Kingdom of God. Though they had known Christ after the flesh, from henceforth they knew Him so no more. They had become joined to the Lord by a spiritual affinity, and ate of the spiritual manna, and drank of the spiritual Rock.

But even that was not enough. When they beheld Him return to the Father, leaving them alone in the midst of the world, and when a full realisation of the need of the world broke on them, they began to hunger after a fresh fashion. Their soul followed hard after Him. They longed to be endued with His power, to go forth to continue and consummate His work, and to win the world for His sceptre.

Hunger and Thirst in Heaven. It is said that in heaven they neither hunger nor thirst. Every longing heart shall be satisfied. And yet even there the Beatitude must hold good, "Blessed are they that hunger and thirst after righteousness for they shall be filled." Oh blessed hunger! Always perfectly met and satisfied, and yet always breaking out with new appetite and desire for things not seen as yet!

An Application to Ourselves. THERE IS A PARTICULAR AND PERSONAL APPLICATION OF ALL THIS FOR US ALL. Has not God humbled us, and suffered us to hunger, and fed us with manna, that He might make us know that man doth not live by bread alone, but by every word that proceedeth out of the mouth of God? Are you feeding on that Bread? You have been laying up for yourselves treasures which moth and rust corrupt: you have been building big barns, and saying to your soul, Soul, thou hast much goods stored up for many years, eat, drink, and be merry. But how vain it all is! "Labour not," saith the Master, "for the meat which perisheth, but for that meat which endureth unto everlasting life, which the Son of Man shall give unto you."[1]

The Manna an Emblem. Was the manna needful for the body? Even more urgently is Christ needed for the soul. Alas, that our spiritual health is so impaired that we have lost our appetite!

Was the manna given freely for all the camp of Israel? Even so is Christ given for all. He is the bread of life for the world. Every one that seeth the Son, and believeth on Him, may have eternal life.

Was the manna so accessible that the people had only to stretch forth the hand to take it? The word of eternal life is nigh thee, in thy mouth and in thy heart. There is no need, therefore, to climb into heaven or descend into the depth.

Was the manna white in colour, and sweet to the taste? A master-mind in our days has made his hero, a well-disposed heathen, see in Christ, even before he could believe in Him, "the *White* Christ."

Did the manna distil noiselessly in the night? So Christ cometh not with observation—not in the wind, the fire, the earthquake, but when other voices are hushed.

Our Own Part. Was it needful to gather the manna? So Christ calls Himself bread, to bring this point out strongly, not only what He is, but what we must do with Him. He must be received, fed upon, inwardly appropriated. As the mouth receives, and the digestive organs assimilate and transform our food into vital force, so we must feed spiritually upon our Lord, until He be formed in us.

Except ye eat and drink the blood of the Son of Man, ye have no life in you. But if you come to Him you shall never hunger; if you believe in Him you shall never thirst. Take thy fill, then, eat the fat and drink the sweet. The Body of the Lord Jesus, given for thee, shall preserve thy body and soul unto everlasting Life. Take then and eat, to thy great comfort, strength, and encouragement!

[1] John vi. 27.

Rephidim

Exodus 17:1-15

1. And all the congregation of the children of Israel journeyed from the wilderness of Sin, after their journeys, according to the commandment of the Lord, and pitched in Rephidim: and *there was* no water for the people to drink.

2. Wherefore the people did chide with Moses, and said, Give us water that we may drink. And Moses said unto them, Why chide ye with me? Wherefore do ye tempt the Lord?

3. And the people thirsted there for water; and the people murmured against Moses, and said, Wherefore *is* this *that* thou hast brought us up out of Egypt, to kill us and our children and our cattle with thirst?

4. And Moses cried unto the Lord, saying, What shall I do unto this people? they be almost ready to stone me.

5. And the Lord said unto Moses, Go on before the people, and take with thee of the elders of Israel; and thy rod, wherewith thou smotest the river, take in thine hand, and go.

6. Behold, I will stand before thee there upon the rock in Horeb; and thou shalt smite the rock, and there shall come water out of it, that the people may drink. And Moses did so in the sight of the elders of Israel.

7. And he called the name of the place Massah, and Meribah, because of the chiding of the children of Israel, and because they tempted the Lord, saying, Is the Lord among us, or not?

8. Then came Amalek, and fought with Israel in Rephidim.

9. And Moses said unto Joshua, Choose us out men, and go out, fight with Amalek; to-morrow I will stand on the top of the hill with the rod of God in mine hand.

10. So Joshua did as Moses had said to him, and fought with Amalek: and Moses, Aaron, and Hur went up to the top of the hill.

11. And it came to pass, when Moses held up his hand, that Israel prevailed: and when he let down his hand, Amalek prevailed.

12. But Moses' hands *were* heavy; and they took a stone, and put *it* under him, and he sat thereon; and Aaron and Hur stayed up his hands, the one on the one side, and the other on the other side; and his hands were steady until the going down of the sun.

13. And Joshua discomfited Amalek and his people with the edge of the sword.

14. And the Lord said unto Moses, Write this *for* a memorial in a book, and rehearse *it* in the ears of Joshua: for I will utterly put out the remembrance of Amalek from under heaven.

15. And Moses built an altar, and called the name of it Jehovah-nissi:

REPHIDIM

Exodus 17:1-15

The Approach to Sinai. On leaving the seashore the march had turned eastwards towards the great mass of mountains known generally as Sinai. The route is described as inexpressibly grand. On each side of the narrow passes rise peaks and precipices of every form and colour. Grey, red, brown, green, chalk-white, and raven-black are the hues of those entrance-gates of the most august temple of the world. Here, from before Abram left Haran, the Egyptian Government had worked mines of copper and turquoise by convict labour. It is not improbable that there were many Hebrews amongst these wretched beings, and if so, the host may have been led by this route in order to have the opportunity of freeing them from a slavery, compared with which I should suppose and hope that there is nothing in the world of to-day so bad.

The Israelites Disappointed and Thirsty. Up to this point the sufferings of the pilgrim-host, though trying, had not been insupportable; but on leaving Dophkah[1] and entering the Wady Feiran, the whole camp, man and beast, became severely pressed. The oases which had varied the monotony of the desert failed them; the granite walls on either hand reflected an intolerable glare and heat, and the failure of the supply of water threatened to drive the whole camp to frenzy. At Marah the water had been unpalatable; here there was no water at all. The brook which at times waters the valley was dry, as it often becomes still; and perhaps the presence of vegetation along the empty water-course made the disappointment more tantalising. The word Rephidim signifies "resting-places," and everyone had been buoyed up during the stiff experiences of the last two days with the happy expectations which that name suggested. Obviously, therefore, the contrast between hope and reality was the more exasperating.

[1] Num. xxxiii. 12.

"And the people thirsted there for water." Hunger is bad enough to bear, but it affects only one organ of the body, whereas thirst sets the whole being on fire. It mounts to the brain and burns like fever in the blood. The little children were drooping like flowers; the cattle were on the verge of exhaustion, and lay panting on the ground. The scouts searched everywhere for water in vain, and came back with but one report—that there was no water anywhere to be found.

Discontent and Rebellion. THE TEMPTING OF MASSAH. At first the people chode, or strove, with Moses, wilfully ignoring the fact that their route was determined by the cloud; then their murmurings became so threatening that Moses really feared for his life; and finally they began to question whether the Lord were among them or not. "They tempted the Lord," i.e. they doubted Him, questioned His love and care, impeached His righteousness, and finally suggested that He had deserted them, and all because He did not act in the way they expected. Ignoring the lessons of the plagues, the marvels of the Exodus, the triumphal passage of the Red Sea, they actually questioned whether God were with them at all. In the Gospels the same spirit was always challenging Christ for signs. Not content with His spotless holiness, His words and deeds, His fulfilment of ancient prediction, they were always asking for the outward and sensible evidence of God's presence and power.

Modern Questionings. In our own time the same demand is made, the same challenge repeated. Men are not satisfied with the moral evidences of the Being and providence of God, they point to the physical evils around, the hunger and thirst, the poverty and misery, the pollution and self-will of our times, crying—If there be a God, why does He permit these things? Why does He allow suffering and sorrow? Why does He not interpose? And then, when the heavens are still silent, they infer that there is no God, that the sky is an empty eye-socket, and that there is nothing better than to eat and drink, because death is an eternal sleep.

Our Rephidim. Has not something of that spirit infected our own peace? We have served Him from our youth, have even kept His Glory and Kingdom before our eyes, have denied ourselves for His sake, have had many an answer to prayer, have reckoned that there was a very special alliance and friendship between Him and us. Then suddenly we have been brought to our Rephidim, in which there has been no drop of water. We have come into some bitter situation of personal or relative suffering, we have cried out for help, but the heavens have seemed as brass, and we have been inclined to doubt whether our religious life has not been one long deception.

When Faith is Relaxed. Does God care for me? Does He hear prayer? Is He with me, as I thought? Instead of saying, God is with me, He is steering the boat, He is leading the pilgrimage, He is adequate for this emergency. He has borne me on eagles' wings from Egypt, and cannot desert me now—we say, Is He among us or not? It becomes then a debatable question, Aye or Nay; and when once faith has relaxed its unswerving affirmation, we are on an ocean without chart or compass, or trying to cross a quaking quagmire.

Life's Difficult Hours. Life is full of these difficult hours, when we are tempted to forget all the past, and question everything that we had once most steadfastly believed. Instead of doing that, we ought to fall back on all that God had been to us, and insist that He is still all that He was. The incident which confronts us may be difficult, but it shall not rob us of our faith. We will still trust, and not be afraid.

> " His love in time past forbids me to think,
> He'll leave me at last, in trouble to sink,
> Each sweet Ebenezer I have in review,
> Confirms His good pleasure to help me right through."

Gathering Wealth for Experience. Suppose you are descending a mountain after a long day in its heights, and are following a stream which has been increasing with every hundred yards. Finally you emerge from the woods, and begin to pass the farms which, one below another, climb down to the valley. To you as you pass them in their snug enclosures of green vegetation, they seem to be utterly and absolutely distinct. But they are not. The stream runs through them, and more; the rains are always washing down the alluvial soil of the upper to the under. Melting snows, spring rains, the very attritus of the ground, makes each of them richer and richer still, and the bees flying from one to another mix their products. So it is with life. Some men pass from one experience to another, as though there was no connection between them; but others are always gathering wealth and richness from the earlier experiences to help them in the later. They say, "God was with me in my boyhood, He will not desert me in my age: He was with me in six troubles, and will not leave me in the seventh: He that spared not His own Son, will in His own good time and way, with Him freely give all else." Such never say, Is God? but God is. They that come to God believe that God is. Such is the new order of them that diligently seek Him.

The Purpose of Suffering. STILL THE QUESTION RETURNS ON US, WHY DID GOD ALLOW HIS PEOPLE TO SUFFER? Without doubt, one reason is that suggested afterwards, He wished to reveal them to themselves, that they might know the evil of their hearts. "Know therefore," was the incontestable reproof of their leader in after days, "that the Lord thy God giveth thee not this good land to possess it for thy righteousness; for thou art a stiff-necked people. Remember, forget thou not, how thou provokedst the Lord thy God to wrath in the wilderness: from the day that thou wentest forth out of the land of Egypt."[1]

Intentional Discipline. This stern discipline was also intended to make them rely on God, rather than on Moses or circumstances. He suffered them to thirst, that He might make them know that man doth not live by rains and rivers only, but by God's provision, however it may come. Take, for instance, the child of some rich inheritance, whose estates, stocks, shares, and bank-balance, are a fourfold wall against the intrusion of want. For that child, the Providence which gives our daily bread is a nonentity. It is when all these have passed out of his life, and he is compelled to hang hour after hour on the care of God, with no obvious means of support, that he offers the fourth petition of the Lord's Prayer with absolute sincerity.

Inhabitants of the Sinaitic Region. But there was a deeper reason than these. At the time of the Exodus the Sinaitic peninsula was mainly peopled by two tribes of Bedouin. The Kenites, chiefly pastoral and inoffensive, claimed descent from Abraham, and were closely connected with Israel through Moses' marriage with the daughter of one of their chiefs.

The Amalekites. The Amalekites were one of the great nations of antiquity. Balaam said, "Amalek was the first of the nations."[2] Their traditions assert that their earliest home was the neighbourhood of the Persian Gulf, from which they were driven always southwards by the advancing power of Assyria. At this time they covered the country with their extensive flocks.

[1] Deut. ix. 6, 7.   [2] Num. xxiv. 20.

They did not challenge the hosts of Israel on their emergence from the Red Sea, either because they understood their destination to be Canaan, the route to which would soon take them out of their territories, or because they had left the seaboard for the mountain pastures, clothed at that period in their most attractive and abundant dress. But when Israel, as we have seen, marched southwards, their progress was eyed with the utmost jealousy and suspicion. It was extremely distasteful to the Amalekite chiefs to learn that these aliens were enjoying the abundant pastures and palm-groves of an oasis like Elim. Probably a council of war was held, at which it was unanimously agreed that measures must be concerted for the arrest and turning back of the march.

Cutting Off the Stragglers. After the manner of the East, messengers had been sent out far and wide, to summon all the available forces of the peninsula to the conflict: and until they were assembled, orders were issued that light-armed troops, on swift camels, should hang on the rear of the Israelite host, cutting off its stragglers, pillaging its baggage, and doing as much damage as possible.

" Remember what Amalek did unto thee by the way as ye came forth out of Egypt; how he met thee by the way, and smote the hindmost of thee, all that were feeble behind thee, when thou wast faint and weary; and he feared not God."[1]

Preparing for the First Battle. As God looked down on the land through which the people were slowly making their way He beheld these gathering hosts. He saw them mustering from the rock-dwellings of Petra, from the rich pasture-lands of Kadesh, from the rolling downs in which the mighty Lebanon range sinks into the sand-wastes of the desert. It may be that at the very hour when this murmuring outbreak occurred these marshalled hosts were within an hour's march of the camp of Israel. He knew it all, and suffered them to thirst, that on the background of their pain He might work a supreme miracle of power, which would be their fortress and stronghold in the day of Amalek's attack.

The composure with which Moses prepared to resist Amalek; the absolute confidence with which Israel fell in with his measures of resistance; and the courage with which these undisciplined troops fought their first fight, would be absolutely inexplicable, unless we had the record of the slaking of their thirst by the smiting of the Rock.

[1] Deut. xxv. 17, 18.

Moses Composed. *Consider the composure of Moses.* Hitherto in his difficulties he has cried unto the Lord, not of course in despair, but as urgently needing Divine help. Here, however, he does not hesitate a moment, but bids Joshua select the most promising of the armed men for the fight, and announces that he will stand on an adjoining hill with the rod of God in his hand.

The Ground of His Courage. He betrayed no sign of discomposure! Why? Because yonder across the valley was the Rock which like a cistern had yielded streams of water; because he had seen God standing there before him on the Rock; and because at that moment he could hear the gurgle of the streams as they poured down those water-courses, as though from the melting snows of Lebanon. Could he doubt that the Lord of Hosts was with them, and that the God of Jacob was their refuge? Though an host should encamp against him, his heart would not fear; though war should rise against him, in this he would be confident!

The Miracle that Banished Mistrust. *Consider the confidence of the people in his leadership.* Suppose that Amalek had come out against them in an earlier part of the march, and before these miracles of power had been wrought, through the instrumentality of Moses and his wonderful rod, might there not have been a good deal of questioning, whether it was well to leave him in uncontrolled command? There might have been an attempt to substitute a council of war, and to wrest from his aged hands the direction of the battle. But after what they had witnessed of his fellowship with Jehovah and of Jehovah's answer to his appeal, they had neither the will nor the opportunity to dispute his authority. He had deserved well of them: he stood right with God: his rod was the symbol of victory. Had it not smitten the flinty rock, so that the rock had been turned into a pool of water and the flint into a spring?[1] They too saw that stream, and heard the music of those waters, and even their murmurings were silenced and their mistrust banished.

The Courage of the Hebrew Warriors. *Consider also the courage of these chosen warriors.* Yesterday they were complaining that Moses had brought them into the wilderness; now they are actually adventuring their lives against a highly equipped and disciplined foe. They were strong in a confidence of which Amalek could form no conjecture. These ancient masters of the peninsula had said among themselves, "We shall easily prevail over this rabble of escaped slaves.

[1] Ps. cxiv. 8.

They have no water, do not understand the country, and possess few arms. They are harried, discouraged, and will easily fall our prey." Little did they know that God's people were nourished from secret springs, not of water alone, but of courage and faith. All these traits were directly due and traceable to the anguish out of which Israel had been so recently delivered by the Almighty.

But is that not the key to much of the experience that falls to our lot? Does not God lead us into sore straits, and deliver us, that we may be prepared for greater troubles which He sees ahead? He smites rocks of granite, to touch which blisters our hands, and makes even these yield supplies, that when presently we descry the troops of Amalek drawn up to dispute and arrest our progress, we may be of good courage, and know that the Lord will fight for and deliver us.

The Uplifted Rod of Prayer. THE LESSON OF THE UPLIFTED ROD. We are told that "Joshua discomfited Amalek and his people with the edge of the sword"; but the edge of the sword would have been unavailing, had it not been for that uplifted rod.

At the opening of the battle, the great leader was seen by the troops ascending a spur of rock, well within view, first standing and then sitting, with the rod of God in his hand. Hour after hour, he remained there with the rod uplifted; and as the afternoon advanced in that long hard-fought day, it was noticed that on either side a venerable man upbore his wearied arms. "Aaron and Hur stayed up his hands, the one on the one side and the other on the other, until the going down of the sun."

Prayer is Labour. That attitude has always been interpreted as significant of intercessory prayer. There are many among us who cannot go down into the battle, but can sit on their chair or lie on their couch and pray. Prayer is labour! We are told of Epaphras, when far from his people, that he laboured in prayer for the Colossian Church. Without doubt, prayer of the right kind means strenuous and exhausting labour. It is the most exhausting exercise that the soul can possibly sustain. But prayer makes all the difference in our fight against principalities and powers. When the arms of the Church are uplifted, her troops prevail, and when let down, they are defeated. Amalek could not connect the two, but Israel connected them. The outside world cannot understand why, just now, the Church is losing her hold on the masses, and so few additional adherents swell her ranks; but we know—her arms are sunken to the ground. If only they were uplifted, the legions of the Cross would advance with their ancient prowess, and victory would attend their arms. Why do you fail in your Christian life? Because you have ceased to pray! Why does that young Christian prevail? Ah, in the first place, he prays for himself; but also, there are those in distant places, mothers, sisters, grandparents, who would think that they sinned, if they ceased to pray for him, and they will not fail to lift up their hands for him until the going down of the sun of their lives!

A Symbol of God's Presence. But though that is all true, it is not all the truth. There is no word about prayer in the narrative, and sitting is not precisely the attitude of prayer. Were not that uplifted hand and rod rather the symbols of the presence and help of God? Moses not only prayed that God would help them, but affirmed that He was helping, that He was in the field, that Amalek was being driven before the Lord and before His host. Faith, says Coleridge, is an affirmation and act, that makes eternal Truth be fact.

Jehovah-Nissi. This interpretation is confirmed by the subsequent action of Moses in building an altar, and calling it Jehovah-Nissi, "the Lord is my Banner." When we speak of a banner, we think of a flag, the piece of drapery which is attached to the banner-pole. But the ancients had only a pole with a bright metal ornament at the top. Moses' rod, then, was a banner in the Oriental use of the term. But a banner for what? For the host of Israel? No, but for that other host, the host of God's unseen embattled warriors that were riding to the fray. It was at that moment that Joshua must have received the first inkling of the great truth, which broke on him on the plains of Jericho, when the Angel of the Covenant said, "I am come as captain of another, a *third* host, of the Lord's host."

The Key of Victory. This is the key of victory. You may be peevish and petulant to-day, because you look only to Moses, i.e. to human strength and help; but directly you look beyond Moses to God, you become strong and glad, and in that very spot of Rephidim, the name of which you had changed into Meribah and Massah, you shall gain the victory of your life.

> " Lord, what a change within us one short hour
> Spent in Thy presence will prevail to make,
> What heavy burdens from our bosoms take,
> What parchèd grounds refresh as with a shower!
> We kneel, and all around us seems to lower;
> We rise, and all the distant and the near,
> Stands forth in sunny outline, brave and clear;
> We kneel—how weak! We rise—how full of power."

THERE IS A MYSTICAL SIDE TO ALL THIS. (1) Israel represents the Church in her warfare against the religions of darkness, the wicked spirits that rule in the Heavenlies. She, with her Lord, is engaged in putting down all rule, authority, and power till God is all in all. "We wrestle not against flesh and blood, but against principalities and powers."

Symbolism of the Smitten Rock. (2) The Smitten Rock is surely our Lord Jesus, smitten for us. "They drank of that spiritual Rock that followed them: and that Rock was Christ."[1] He was smitten for our offences, bruised for our iniquities! One of the soldiers pierced His side, and there came out blood and water! "Rock of Ages, cleft for me!"

(3) The Church must drink of that Rock-water, flowing clear as the Holy Spirit of Pentecost; so only will she be able to cope with her spiritual foes. Drink, ye thirsty souls, drink, yea, drink abundantly and deeply, for Amalek will be upon you to-morrow; but he will have no power at all against those who have cleansed themselves in the healing streams of the blood and have learned to drink of the living water.

> " Let the water and the blood,
> From Thy riven side which flowed,
> Be of sin the double cure,
> Save me from its wrath and power."

[1] 1 Cor. x. 4.

THE ECONOMY OF FORCE

Exodus 18:1-27

1. When Jethro, the priest of Midian, Moses' father-in-law, heard of all that God had done for Moses, and for Israel his people, *and* that the Lord had brought Israel out of Egypt;

2. Then Jethro, Moses' father-in-law, took Zipporah, Moses' wife, after he had sent her back,

3. And her two sons; of which the name of the one *was* Gershom; for he said, I have been an alien in a strange land:

4. And the name of the other *was* Eliezer; for the God of my father, *said he*, *was* mine help, and delivered me from the sword of Pharaoh:

5. And Jethro, Moses' father-in-law, came with his sons and his wife unto Moses into the wilderness, where he encamped at the mount of God:

6. And he said unto Moses, I thy father-in-law Jethro am come unto thee, and thy wife, and her two sons with her.

7. And Moses went out to meet his father-in-law, and did obeisance, and kissed him; and they asked each other of *their* welfare; and they came into the tent.

8. And Moses told his father-in-law all that the Lord had done unto Pharaoh and to the Egyptians for Israel's sake, *and* all the travail that had come upon them by the way, and *how* the Lord delivered them.

9. And Jethro rejoiced for all the goodness which the Lord had done to Israel, whom he had delivered out of the hand of the Egyptians.

10. And Jethro said, Blessed *be* the Lord, who hath delivered you out of the hand of the Egyptians, and out of the hand of Pharaoh, who hath delivered the people from under the hand of the Egyptians.

11. Now I know that the Lord *is* greater than all gods: for in the thing wherein they dealt proudly *he was* above them.

12. And Jethro, Moses' father-in-law, took a burnt-offering and sacrifices for God: and Aaron came, and all the elders of Israel, to eat bread with Moses' father-in-law before God.

13. And it came to pass on the morrow, that Moses sat to judge the people: and the people stood by Moses from the morning unto the evening.

14. And when Moses' father-in-law saw all that he did to the people, he said, What *is* this thing that thou doest to the people? why sittest thou thyself alone, and all the people stand by thee from morning unto even?

15. And Moses said unto his father-in-law, Because the people come unto me to enquire of God:

16. When they have a matter, they come unto me; and I judge between one and another, and I do make *them* know the statutes of God, and his laws.

17. And Moses' father-in-law said unto him, The thing that thou doest *is* not good.

18. Thou wilt surely wear away, both thou, and this people that *is* with thee: for this thing *is* too heavy for thee; thou art not able to perform it thyself alone.

19. Hearken now unto my voice, I will give thee counsel, and God shall be with thee: Be thou for the people to Godward, that thou mayest bring the causes unto God:

20. And thou shalt teach them ordinances and laws, and shalt shew them the way wherein they must walk, and the work that they must do.

21. Moreover thou shalt provide out of all the people able men, such as fear God, men of truth, hating covetousness; and place *such* over them, *to be* rulers of thousands, *and* rulers of hundreds, rulers of fifties, and rulers of tens:

22. And let them judge the people at all seasons: and it shall be, *that* every great matter they shall bring unto thee, but every small matter they shall judge: so shall it be easier for thyself, and they shall bear *the burden* with thee.

23. If thou shalt do this thing, and God command thee *so*, then thou shalt be able to endure, and all this people shall also go to their place in peace.

24. So Moses hearkened to the voice of his father-in-law, and did all that he had said.

25. And Moses chose able men out of all Israel, and made them heads over the people, rulers of thousands, rulers of hundreds, rulers of fifties, and rulers of tens.

26. And they judged the people at all seasons: the hard causes they brought unto Moses, but every small matter they judged themselves.

27. And Moses let his father-in-law depart; and he went his way into his own land.

THE ECONOMY OF FORCE

Exodus 18:1-27

Jethro's Suggestion. There is a noteworthy parallel between the circumstances narrated in this chapter and those of which we are informed in Acts vi. Here the Hebrew people, emerging from centuries of slavery and oppression, which had almost obliterated the spirit of nationality, suddenly assumes a highly organised condition. Out of Jethro's suggestion sprang an organisation which laid the foundations of the national polity, and has existed with more or less permanence amid all the other changes that have swept over that remarkable race. In Acts vi a similar movement was necessitated by the immense increase of converts.

> " In these days, when the number of the disciples was multiplying, there arose a murmuring of the Hellenists against the Hebrews. . . . And the Twelve called the multitude of the disciples unto them, and said, It is not fit that we should forsake the word of God, and serve Tables. Look ye out therefore, brethren, from among you seven men of good report, full of the Spirit and of wisdom, whom we may appoint over this business."[1]

In each case the increased organisation was a sign of vitality, and led to the immediate strengthening and increase of the entire movement. It is a great forward step in evolution, when the bony case which had been exterior, as in the crab, becomes interior, as in the mammal. Life always tends towards increased complexity in organisation.

Jethro's Arrival. *There is little to detain us in the circumstances which led up to this great step of advance.* Whether Jethro was the father-in-law or brother-in-law of Moses is still undecided by the experts, and does not greatly concern us. The Hebrew word may mean either. He had given shelter to Zipporah and her two sons until he heard of the Exodus; and then crossed the peninsula from

---

[1] Acts vi. 1-3.

the extreme east to the Mount of God, somewhere in the near neighbourhood of Horeb. First, he desired to renew the friendly relations which had subsisted during the forty years of companionship in pastoral and tribal interests; and secondly, he desired to restore the wife and boys whom he had received as a sacred trust.

His Meeting with Moses. The meeting was thoroughly Oriental. On the announcement of his approach, Moses went out to meet him, knelt down and touched the ground with his forehead, then kissing his relative's hand, he rose and kissed him on both cheeks. Each asked the other of his welfare with the minuteness and prolixity still characteristic of the sons of the desert, with whom time is a less precious commodity than with ourselves. The greetings of husband and wife, of father and children, would probably be reserved for the privacy of the tent.

As Moses told of the marvellous dealings of God with Israel, not only in delivering them from Pharaoh, but during all the travail of their journey, Jethro rejoiced for all the goodness which Jehovah had shown, and burst out into an ascription of adoration and praise.

Declaration of the Supremacy of God. Perhaps, up to that hour, like the generality of the heathen, he had believed in a plurality of gods, and regarded the God of Israel as only one among many equals. But under the marvellous recital given by Moses, he renounced that creed, and declared his belief that Jehovah was supreme over all gods. How much might be done, if only religious men to-day would recount their experiences! Many a wavering scale would be turned in favour of true religion, if only you would begin to tell of God's dealings with your own life. "Go home to thy friends," said our Lord, to the man from whom He had cast a legion of demons, "and tell them how great things the Lord hath done for thee."

Orders of Religious Life. It is remarkable that Jethro appears to have acted as priest in the sacrifice which followed. We have already been told that the sheikh was also the priest of Midian.[1] Like Melchizedek he was the priest of the Most High God. The fact of Moses and Aaron and the elders of Israel participating in the sacred feast which followed shows that they recognised orders of religious life and priestly administration outside the limits of their own race: and this confirms us in the view, which surely needs no arguing, and which Malachi so clearly teaches: For from the rising

[1] iii. 1.

of the sun even unto the going down of the same, God's name is great among the Gentiles, and in every place incense is offered in His name, and a pure offering.[1]

A Striking Spectacle. The spectacle he witnessed on the following day was remarkable. From morning till evening he beheld Moses sitting in the midst of a great throng of people, slowly ploughing his way through an immense number of causes, which were submitted to his adjudication. Even if we pare down the numbers of the Exodus to half, or a quarter, of a million of people, it is easy to see what an overwhelming task lay on the Lawgiver, who was called upon in his single person to combine the legislative and judicial functions.

The Hebrew Character. The difficulty lay, not only in the quantity but the quality of the people. The Hebrew character has always been stiff-necked and intractable. But, in addition, they had just emerged from generations of slavery, with all its debasing and demoralising effects. There were as yet no Decalogue nor code of laws. The very effect of their recent emancipation was to induce the idea that they were free to do as they chose. The first experiences of the French Revolution were bewildering and disappointing to all thoughtful souls. How Wordsworth laments it! It seemed as if all hope of Liberty, Equality, and Brotherhood was to be drowned in a deluge of sensuality and bloodshed. So with Israel, they were no longer under the despotic rule of Pharaoh and his myrmidons. Their knowledge of Jehovah was extremely vague. There was no general standard of appeal. The very rebound from centuries of oppression was in the direction of self-assertion and lawlessness. In addition the recent rout of Amalek may have left in the possession of the victors an immense amount of costly property, as in the experience of Gideon afterwards.[2] Disputes about the proper division of these may have greatly added to the weight of that day's business.

Weight of Responsibility Too Great. In any case, at the end of the day, Moses was absolutely worn out, and even then the people were not satisfied. There was therefore justice in Jethro's remark: "Wasting thou wilt waste away, both thou and this people that is with thee."

Jethro's Plan Adopted by Moses. Jethro therefore suggested a division of labour, founded on the system still in vogue among the

[1] Mal. i. 11. [2] Judges viii. 25, etc.

Arabs. Causes were in the first instance to be judged by rulers of tens,—which recalls our own tythings,—from which there was an appeal to the rulers of fifties, from them to the rulers of hundreds, and finally to the rulers of thousands. Difficult causes, which the rulers of thousands felt themselves incompetent to decide, were reserved for the judgment of Moses. After referring this to God, as was his wont, Moses adopted this good advice, and by this arrangement the whole nation profited immensely.

Its Advantages. *The advantages were obvious.* Moses was henceforth able to concentrate himself on the higher branches of his great calling. He was for the people *God-ward*, as mediator, looking into the bosom of God, where, as Hooker says, "Law hath her seat." He had also time to bring the difficult causes to God. Then, turning to the people, he taught them the statutes and the laws, and showed them the way wherein they should walk and the work they should do.

Calling Out Latent Talent. Next, it immediately developed a large number of men whose very existence had, up to that moment, been hardly realised. In every community there is an untold wealth of latent talent; to every man grace is given according to the measure of the gift of Christ. The King gives each of his servants the charge of talents, and none is absolutely destitute. It must have been rather surprising, however, to Moses to discover that there was a complete equipment for all the offices that had to be filled. "He chose able men out of all Israel." These men might have developed into critics and schemers; but from the moment that they were entrusted with responsibility, they became staunch and useful allies. Not only were their talents saved from wastage and developed in useful directions, but the men themselves were redeemed and purified, their noblest qualities were evoked, and their characters saved from that prostitution of the best which always becomes the worst.

Advantage to the Congregation. The congregation also profited greatly by the swiftness with which disputes and quarrels were dealt with. Nothing is more hurtful to the individual or community than to leave a sore open. The longer a controversy lasts, the worse the tangle becomes, the more hot words are spoken, the more bystanders become involved. "Agree," said our Lord, "with thine adversary quickly, whiles thou art in the way with him."

There are three directions in which we may apply this subject: Church Administration; Christian Service; and Missionary Organisation.

A Lesson for the Churches. I. CHURCH ADMINISTRATION. It is a mistake for any one person, be he minister or layman, to monopolise many offices. Some ministers insist on keeping every department of Church life and Church work under control; some Sunday-school superintendents have apparently never learnt to educate their teachers to maintain the order of the school, or the children to feel that they may fill useful offices; and some Church officials, in their true desire to serve the Church, prefer to undertake more duties than they can perform satisfactorily, instead of setting to work to create or develop the younger men and women about them.

Mr. Moody's Shrewd Saying. Mr. Moody said shrewdly: It is better to set a hundred men to work, than do the work of a hundred men. You do a service to a man when you evoke his latent faculty. It is no kindness to others or service to God to do more than your share in the sacred duties of Church life. For the hand to do the work of the foot, or the eye intrude into the province of the ear, is to introduce anarchy and discord into body and soul. We are told that when Saul saw any mighty man or any valiant man he took him unto himself.[1] This is the law of Church consolidation and expansion.

The Men We Want. We must have in every Christian community our Moses, Aaron, and Hur, men who give themselves to prayer and the ministry of the Word, men who are to God-ward, men who can inquire of God, who can teach statutes and laws, who can show the way in which we should walk, and the work we should do.

In every Christian community we must have men of affairs, whose character is admirably summed up in Jethro's words, *Men of ability*! Jethro evidently expected that there would be one man in ten who would commend himself as exceptionally able, and though to-day's standard of ability is higher than ever, the estimate is not too sanguine. They must be *men of piety*! "Such as fear God!" He who fears God will regard man; the unjust judge did neither. The Apostles asked for "seven men of good report, full of the Holy Spirit and wisdom." *Men of truth!* There can be no real piety without truthfulness, so that this qualification is in fact included in the last, and yet there is a semblance of piety which is not over-scrupulous as to veracity. This, however, is a bastard growth. *Men of uncorruptible honour*! In the East it is rare to find the office of judge exercised without a strong susceptibility to bribes. Like the sons

[1] 1 Sam. xiv. 52.

of Samuel, the judges turn aside after lucre, take bribes, and pervert judgment. At whatever cost, let our nation preserve the great traditions which have always attached to our bench and legal profession! In all walks of life unbiased impartiality is of priceless worth to the community which is thus endowed.

The Rank and File. We must also in every Church have our warriors, who can encounter Amalek; our workers, whose deft fingers can build our Tabernacle; our financiers, who will see that no part of the Church-finance suffers; our singers; our aged men and women, who can sustain the duties of perpetual intercession; our boys and girls, inspiring us with their boundless hope and inexhaustible activity; our sufferers, who teach us tenderness and patience. Some must open the doors, some light the lamps, some lead the service of song, some preach, and others teach. There is no one who is not his neighbour's superior in some respect. There is no one from whom his neighbour may not learn something. It was necessary for Jethro to cross the desert to give Moses the conception of this organisation, which, one would suppose, ought to have occurred to him during his own ponderings over his failure to discharge his enormous tasks. "The eye cannot say unto the hand, I have no need of thee; or again, the head to the feet, I have no need of you."[1]

Christ's Awards. Some day we shall stand before our Lord, Who at His own judgment-seat—which must be distinguished from the judgment of the Great White Throne—will allot our rewards. At such time He will pursue a far different method than that adopted amongst even the best of us. We applaud the man who reaps the results, but He will equally congratulate those who ploughed and sowed to produce them. We allot the crown and palm to the pastor or evangelist whose fervent appeals win the largest number of accessions to the Church, but Christ will not forget the verger and the charwoman, the treasurer and the secretary, the organ-blower, and those who bring refreshment to the harvest-field. The players on instruments shall be there as well as the singers, and he that sowed shall rejoice with him who reaped. To each the reward will be apportioned, not according to the apparent results, but to the faithfulness with which each fulfilled his humble task. The smallest wheel in a big machine is able by its precision to promote, or its inexactitude to impair, the entire movement, just as a dispute among

[1] 1 Cor. xii. 21.

a few girls or in one class of operatives may throw out of employment hundreds of thousands, and affect a whole district. It is necessary, therefore, in adjudicating the rewards, that none be overlooked who have contributed, however slightly, to the general result.

Personal Witness Necessary. II. THE SAME PRINCIPLE APPLIES IN THE SPREADING OF THE KNOWLEDGE OF CHRIST. There is too strong a tendency in most congregations to leave the work of saving the lost to a salaried class. The plan of sending substitutes may have its advantages for heathen lands, but it cannot become universal, without serious loss to individual believers, as to the Church and the World. Your personal witness for Christ is an imperative obligation. You cannot evade it by any excuse as to your temperament, your nervousness, or your circumstances. The King makes no exceptions. His command is decisive. If we belong to His Church, we are bound to proclaim His love and death to every creature within our reach. You must speak of Him to your brother, your neighbour, and your fellow-citizen, saying, Know the Lord. He that heareth must say, *Come.* In this respect the converts on the mission fields set us a notable example, as we gather from the reports handed in to the recent Edinburgh Missionary Conference.

Testimonies of Missionaries. Bishop Tucker of Uganda wrote: The work of winning the souls of the people of this country to Christ is really being done by the natives themselves, under the supervision of the foreign missionaries. Dr. John Ross stated that of the 20,000 Church members in Manchuria, less than 100 had been led to Christ solely by the missionaries, and the remainder, 19,900, by the devoted labours of these newly-converted souls. Dr. Moffett of Korea has stated that the Korean Christians for the last ten years have been bringing in the converts faster than the missionaries have been able to provide instruction for them.

It is quite common, says Dr. Mott, in Korea, in Manchuria, and in other parts of China, for Christians to pledge themselves to give a certain number of days to the work of public preaching, as well as to speaking to individuals one by one, subscribing their time, just as we in the homelands subscribe our money. At one meeting, one Church member promised to devote to work of this kind, during the following year, one hundred and eighty days; and in reporting at the annual meeting a year later, he apologised because he had been able to give only one hundred and sixty-nine days.

A Personal Call. In view of these facts, shall we not, each one, from to-day, dedicate ourselves to Christ for this service? Is it impossible to promise our Lord, that if He will open the door of opportunity, and give us a tongue and wisdom, which cannot be gainsaid, that we are willing to speak to some one daily on His claims? We shall not then have to assume any yoke of mere legalism, nor shall we force the matter on unwilling ears, but, as the opportunity offers, we shall look for the uprising impulse and the needed message. It is not what we do for Him, but what He does by us, that really tells.

> " Wherever in the world I am,
> In whatsoe'er estate,
> I have a fellowship of hearts,
> To keep and cultivate.
> And a work of lowly love to do
> For Him on Whom I wait."

How to Find a Good Investment. It is the duty of the Chief Shepherd to call out His servants, who shall bear with Him the burden of the cure of souls; but it is His pleasure also to show each one in His Church the way in which he should walk, and the work which he should do. If you are in doubt as to the use that you should make of your one talent, at least bring it to the bankers, i.e. to the leaders of the Christian congregation with which you are connected, and they will show you how to invest it, that the Lord at His coming may receive it back with interest.

The Work for Modern Apostles. III. THE SAME PRINCIPLE MAY BE APPLIED TO MISSIONARY ORGANISATION. It is heart-rending to find how much of the precious time of missionaries is occupied in keeping accounts, attending to the repair of mission premises, and adjudicating matters which could as easily as not be dealt with by a godly layman. Every group of missionaries ought to have one competent business man attached to them, who could relieve them of these details.

It is clear, also, that missionaries, as the years go on, will have to avail themselves increasingly of the services of native converts. During my journey through India I came on one remarkable and godly man, whose service consisted in gathering around him a number of young men, with whom he ate and slept and lived, with the one object of reproducing himself in them, and sending them forth to tell out the Gospel. The Apostolic Peters of our time must concentrate themselves on the Corneliuses and the Priscillas on Apollos.

Alexander Duff, the pioneer missionary statesman, said that when the set time arrives, the real reformers of Hindustan will be well-qualified Hindus. Mackay said the same of Uganda, and Dr. Nevins of China.

The Layman's Missionary Movement. But without doubt all these questions, and similar ones, will be solved through the Layman's Missionary Movement, which is quite the most remarkable development of our time. It was inaugurated in New York in 1905, and has spread with amazing rapidity. Its aim is to interest laymen in the subject of Missions, and to lead them to recognise and accept responsibility to promote the cause of Missions, primarily in connection with their own Churches.

In Toronto, taking the five principal Christian Communions, we are told that in two years the contributions to foreign missions have practically doubled; £35,000 have become £70,000. But better, the movement has developed the lay leadership of the Church. Literally, and I can corroborate Dr. Mott's testimony on this point, thousands of laymen throughout the United States and Canada, who formerly had no interest in the subject, are now making speeches on Missions, leading Mission-study Circles, guiding missionary organisations, and conducting financial canvasses.

This is the far-away result of the spirit that animated Jethro in his advice to Moses, at the conclusion of which "he went his way into his own land."

A Desirable Epitaph. It is a pathetic conclusion to the chapter, but it is the epitaph which we may all desire to have recorded at the close of life. That we came for a few short days or years into the wilderness: that we had the grace to reverence and rejoice in all of good that we heard and saw: that we spoke words which lingered long after we were gone: that we relieved Moses from wasting away, initiated salutary reforms, and called out scores and hundreds of noble men, spoiling for want of work: and that we went our way back into our own country, in the Land o' the Leal.

The Preparation for the Giving of the Law

Exodus 19:1-25

1. In the third month, when the children of Israel were gone forth out of the land of Egypt, the same day they came *into* the wilderness of Sinai.
2. For they were departed from Rephidim, and were come *to* the desert of Sinai, and had pitched in the wilderness; and there Israel camped before the mount.
3. And Moses went up unto God, and the Lord called unto him out of the mountain, saying, Thus shalt thou say to the house of Jacob, and tell the children of Israel;
4. Ye have seen what I did unto the Egyptians, and *how* I bare you on eagles' wings, and brought you unto myself.
5. Now therefore, if ye will obey my voice indeed, and keep my covenant, then ye shall be a peculiar treasure unto me above all people: for all the earth *is* mine:
6. And ye shall be unto me a kingdom of priests, and an holy nation. These *are* the words which thou shalt speak unto the children of Israel.
7. And Moses came and called for the elders of the people, and laid before their faces all these words which the Lord commanded him.
8. And all the people answered together, and said, All that the Lord hath spoken we will do. And Moses returned the words of the people unto the Lord.
9. And the Lord said unto Moses, Lo, I come unto thee in a thick cloud, that the people may hear when I speak with thee, and believe thee for ever. And Moses told the words of the people unto the Lord.
10. And the Lord said unto Moses, Go unto the people, and sanctify them to-day and to-morrow, and let them wash their clothes.
11. And be ready against the third day: for the third day the Lord will come down in the sight of all the people upon mount Sinai.
12. And thou shalt set bounds unto the people round about, saying, Take heed to yourselves, *that ye* go *not* up into the mount, or touch the border of it: whosoever toucheth the mount, shall be surely put to death:
13. There shall not an hand touch it, but he shall surely be stoned, or shot through; whether *it be* beast or man, it shall not live: when the trumpet soundeth long, they shall come up to the mount.
14. And Moses went down from the mount unto the people, and sanctified the people; and they washed their clothes.
15. And he said unto the people, Be ready against the third day: come not at *your* wives.

16. And it came to pass on the third day in the morning, that there were thunders and lightnings, and a thick cloud upon the mount, and the voice of the trumpet exceeding loud; so that all the people that *was* in the camp trembled.

17. And Moses brought forth the people out of the camp to meet with God; and they stood at the nether part of the mount.

18. And mount Sinai was altogether on a smoke, because the Lord descended upon it in fire: and the smoke thereof ascended as the smoke of a furnace, and the whole mount quaked greatly.

19. And when the voice of the trumpet sounded long, and waxed louder and louder, Moses spake, and God answered him by a voice.

20. And the Lord came down upon mount Sinai, on the top of the mount: and the Lord called Moses *up* to the top of the mount; and Moses went up.

21. And the Lord said unto Moses, Go down, charge the people, lest they break through unto the Lord to gaze, and many of them perish.

22. And let the priests also, which come near to the Lord, sanctify themselves, lest the Lord break forth upon them.

23. And Moses said unto the Lord, The people cannot come up to mount Sinai: for thou chargedst us, saying, Set bounds about the mount, and sanctify it.

24. And the Lord said unto him, Away, get thee down, and thou shalt come up, thou, and Aaron with thee: but let not the priests and the people break through to come up unto the Lord, lest he break forth upon them.

25. So Moses went down unto the people, and spake unto them.

THE PREPARATION FOR THE
GIVING OF THE LAW

Exodus 19:1-25

Was the Earth Made for Man? To read the descriptions given by modern travellers of the scenery of the Sinaitic Peninsula, and especially of the heart of it, alluded to in this chapter, and to compare them with the events that took place there, creates the impression that it was prepared for this very purpose.

In the ages of Creation, the Divine Hand set itself to construct the localities which were to be specially associated with man's moral and spiritual development. Palestine, like a nest in the recesses of the hills, yet hard by the highway of the nations; Jerusalem, upraised on its rocky plateau, amid the hills—"the joy of the whole earth"; the seven hills on which Rome sat, as mistress of the world through so many centuries,—these are illustrations of the work of the Divine Artificer, Who built our earth as the platform on which scenes were to transpire that were to affect the powers and principalities in heavenly places.

God's Preparatory Actions. If the moulding hand of God's purpose is manifest in these historic sites, may we not still more conclude that the action of glaciers, the rush of torrents, the deposits on the floor of oceans through uncounted aeons, the volcanic throes that rent and tore the surface of the earth and built up rocks of every hue, must have supplied the titanic implements employed by the Creator, Who was also the Judge of men, and desired to prepare a Tribune from which to announce His Law, and a Sanctuary in which to teach His people to worship?

Arrival at Er Râheh and Sinai. Leaving Rephidim, the pilgrim-host, led by the cloud, travelled slowly along the Wâdy-es-Sheykh, which still forms the great highway of the desert, running due east and west, from the Red Sea to the Gulf of Suez, until they came on the plain *Er Râheh*, which means "the palm of the hand." It lies outspread from north to south two miles long and half-a-mile wide, nearly flat, and dotted over with tiny shrubs. On either side are mountains far higher than the loftiest mountain in Britain, composed of black and yellow granite, and at the end, blocking the southern extremity of the plain, rises the sheer precipice of Sinai, 1,200 to 1,500 feet in height—the Mount of God.

God's Pulpit. The peculiarity about this huge cliff is that it resembles, as nearly as possible, a colossal pulpit. It springs perpendicularly from the level of the plain, and might easily be touched, as though it were a wall, and in front are some slight alluvial mounds, on which the artificial railing was probably placed. From this pulpit on which the cloud brooded, the Almighty spake, in words that linger still upon the trembling air. Clouds and darkness were round about Him, and justice and righteousness were the habitation of His throne.

An Ideally Chosen Spot. No spot on earth, it has been affirmed, combines in a more remarkable manner the conditions of commanding height and of a plain in which the sights and sounds described here could reach the assemblage of two million souls. "That such a plain should exist at all in such a place," says Dean Stanley, "is so remarkable a coincidence with the sacred narrative as to furnish a strong internal argument, not merely of this being the actual scene of the giving of the law, but of it having been described by an eye-witness. All the surroundings suit the narrative. The awful and lengthened approach, as to some natural sanctuary, the long retiring sweep of the plain enabling the people to remove and stand afar off, the cliff rising like a huge altar, and visible against the sky in lonely grandeur from end to end of the whole plain." Those who, in Switzerland, have heard the shepherds and mountaineers speaking to each other across the valleys, quite a mile in width, will have no difficulty in understanding that even a human voice might be heard down that plain in the dry and quiet air.

The Camp. That part of the Peninsula abounds in water-springs, which are never dry; and though the heights are bare and wild, there are innumerable valleys of exceptional richness, and there must have been therefore an abundance of provision for the people and their cattle. Here the host encamped, little realising the long sojourn that was before them, and the world-wide, time-long importance of the events in which they were to take part. So far in the history of the world nothing has happened, with the single exception of Bethlehem and Calvary, so august, so momentous, so sublime as the giving of the Law of God Himself at Sinai.

God's Purpose about to be Explained. THE OBJECTS FOR WHICH ISRAEL WAS BROUGHT INTO THIS VAST NATURAL TEMPLE WERE MANIFOLD. (1) *God desired to assure them of their unique relationship to Himself.* They had already seen what He had done for them. He had given Ethiopia and Egypt for them, had borne them on eagles' wings, had fed them with manna, had smitten the flinty rocks for them, had delivered them from Amalek, and now He desired to assure them that, as the children of Abraham His Friend, they were peculiarly dear to Him. They were to be a peculiar treasure among all peoples, a kingdom of priests, and an holy nation.

Do you look wistfully back on the privileges which were thus proposed for the chosen people? Remember that they were called with an earthly calling, whilst we with a heavenly. The Grace of God hath appeared, and our Saviour Jesus Christ hath given Himself for us, that He might redeem us from all iniquity and purify unto Himself a people for His own possession, zealous of good works.[1] And so Peter said to the sojourners of the dispersion and to us, Ye are an elect race, a royal priesthood, a holy nation, a people for God's own possession, that ye may show forth the praises of Him Who has called you out of a blacker darkness than that of Egypt to a gladder inheritance than of Canaan.[2]

The Third Covenant. (2) *God desired to enter into Covenant with them.* Scripture tells us of two Covenants that had already been made with man—the first with Noah, the second with Abraham. A third was now to be enacted, in fulfilment of pledges made four hundred and thirty years before.

A covenant is an understanding, a working basis, an agreement between the two covenanting parties, so that for each side may be stated their mutual rights and obligations. Does it seem, at the outset, altogether incredible that God, Whom the Heaven of Heavens cannot contain, should condescend to enter into a compact with sinful man? It may seem so, if you degrade humanity and account men as worms or atoms. But if you realise, apart from sin, the greatness of man, his moral worth, his likeness to God, his creative powers, his patience, his hope, his love, then it will seem less wonderful that God should subordinate all else for the education of a being

[1] Titus ii. 14.   [2] 1 Pet. ii. 9.

who is capable of eternal fellowship with Himself, and who is doubly bound to Him, first by original creation and then by the blood of the Cross. How shall He not with Christ freely give us all things?

The Covenant with the Israelites. Still, God's covenant is with them that fear Him. Our Lord became the great Shepherd, because He sealed with His blood the new covenant which is opened and extended to each soul of man who will avail himself of its privileges and step out on its provisions. But how different is our covenant from theirs! That rested on the obedience of the people, an obedience which egregiously failed on that very spot; whereas ours rests on the obedience of Him in Whom we stand.

—And with Us. That consisted in *doing*, but ours in believing, which leads to doing. That for its reward had blessings largely temporal, whilst ours presents for our acceptance those which are incorruptible, undefiled, and unfading.

Israel Governed by a Theocracy. (3) *God desired to lay down the fundamental principles of His Government.* Israel was to be governed, not by a democracy, the rule of the people; nor by an aristocracy, the rule of the few; but by a theocracy, the rule of God; and here their Divine King announces the principles on which He is about to govern His people. No human sovereign could have been more careful for his people's welfare, or at more pains to lay down the beneficent requirements of his reign.

A Method of Grace. The Divine method is full of grace. First, God reveals Himself as the God of their fathers, then reminds them of all the goodness and mercy which He had shown, and finally challenges their faith and love. Had He commenced by uttering the Ten Words of the Law, or the precepts and statutes which follow, He might have aroused criticism and resistance. This is always the first effect of the Law. But there was nothing of this. No mutter of thunder, no blast of trumpet, no flash of the lightning's flashing sword. Nothing was attempted to frighten or compel the people's obedience. In His most winsome aspect their fathers' God reminds them of the mighty past, tells them of the relationship which He designs for them, and finally challenges their loyalty. It was only afterwards, when the people had declared that they would do as He had spoken, that the trumpet rung out its thrilling blast, and the requirements of God's holy law were enumerated.

What the Giving of the Law Did. But the giving of the Law had an aspect to the whole world. The Divine law is engraven on the moral nature of man. The work of the law, says Paul, is written in men's hearts, their consciences bearing witness therewith, and their thoughts excusing or accusing them.[1] Else how could God judge the world? There must be one standard of appeal, one common denominator, one code of morality, not only set up in high heaven, but duplicated in each human breast. Otherwise it would not be possible to bring in all the world guilty before God. But it was necessary that these convictions of righteousness should be set forth authoritatively, in clear-cut and single majesty. Sir Walter Scott, in his *Old Mortality*, has depicted the peregrinations of a son of the Covenanting race, as he travelled throughout Scotland, removing the moss and lichens that had obliterated the inscriptions on the tombs of the mighty dead. This is precisely what the giving of the Law did. It would have had, comparatively speaking, small effect, if it had now been promulgated for the first time, as a new code of Morals. It is because God's code so precisely reflected and echoed man's deepest convictions, that the Decalogue, and the statutes which follow, have commanded universal respect.

The Law but Repeating Dictates of Conscience. It is wrong to steal, or murder, or covet, not primarily because these sins are forbidden by the Decalogue. They are forbidden by the Decalogue, because they were previously forbidden by conscience; and they are forbidden by conscience because they are forbidden by the nature of things; and the nature of things is God. It is right to love God with all our being, and our neighbours as ourselves, not because the Mosaic code says so, but because conscience says so; and conscience says so, because in the nature of things it is so, and because God is so. Thus Sinai is a pulpit whence God has addressed mankind.

Why the Jews were Singled Out. (4) *God desired also to impress on them the great truths which they were also to communicate to mankind.* He remembered that all the earth was His. Had He not made it, and put man upon it? Were not all souls His? Was He not responsible for them, as a shepherd for His flock? He could not rid Himself of the heavy burden which Creatorship had imposed. He had made, and therefore He must bear. When He said, "You shall be a peculiar treasure to Me," it was not that He proposed to monopolise that treasure for Himself, but that He might enrich the whole world by their words and songs, their character and gifts. When He said,

[1] Rom. ii. 15.

"Ye shall be a kingdom," it was not that they were to be merely a great realm ruled by Him, but that they were to go forth to reign in the earth. All were to help Him as kings and priests, calling back mankind to His Supremacy and ennobling them by their purity and prayers. If Israel were God's firstborn, then all the children were also His, and Israel were specially privileged that all the world might be brought into the close intimacy and high honour of the family of God.

Why God Appeared as a Formless Cloud. Consider how much light these thoughts cast on the Theophany of Sinai. All mankind at this time was deeply infected with idolatry. God as the Divine Spirit was seeking that men should appreciate His monotheism, and worship Him in spirit and in truth. If He had adopted any outward form, they would have seized upon it at once, reproduced it, and placed it in their shrines as an object of veneration. It was necessary that they should be thoroughly convinced of His Presence, and yet that there should be no outward form. Therefore, though Mount Sinai was altogether in a smoke, because the Lord descended there, yet as Moses said afterwards they saw "no similitude."[1]

A Sublime Creed. How rich a revelation was this, and what a momentous effect it has had on all subsequent history! The Hebrew, the Christian, and the Moslem are to this hour existing to perpetuate this sublime Creed. The Lord our God is one God: a Spirit Who must be worshipped in spirit and in truth: and they repudiate all worship of images whatsoever, as likely to deteriorate the spirituality of the soul's fellowship with the Eternal.

Covenant and Mediator. It should be noticed also that the Covenant was promulgated through a Mediator. Paul says: "It was ordained through angels by the hand of a mediator."[2] Three times apparently Moses went and came. As soon as the camp had been pitched, we were told that "Moses went up unto God." It was as though there had been some previous appointment that he should do this, and he was met by the voice of God telling him of the preciousness of Israel to Himself, and pleading for obedience—"If obeying, ye obey."

Moses' Three Interviews with God on Sinai. A second time he returns to God to bear the answer of the people: and a second time he was bidden to go down and bid the people prepare to meet their God when He came down. One of the results of that coming was

[1] Deut. iv. 11, 12.   [2] 1 Gal. iii. 19.

to be that the people should hear Jehovah speaking to him, and so believe him for ever. He went down to sanctify the people, to bid them wash their clothes, and put bounds and barriers around the mount, that none might touch it.

Yet once more, on the third day, when the smoke of Sinai ascended like the smoke of a furnace, and the whole mount quaked greatly, because the Lord had come down, the Lord called His servant to the top of the mount, and said to him again, "Go down, charge the people, lest they break through unto the Lord to gaze, and many of them perish, and let the *priests* also sanctify themselves, lest the Lord break forth upon them."

People Forbidden to Approach Sinai. It was absolutely necessary for mankind to learn the nature of holiness, and the awful contrast between God and humanity, between the Holy God and His sinful creatures. How could this lesson be impressed by mere words? They would convey no distinct or permanent impression. So God chose out of the human family one nation, which was separated and cleansed, so far as outward rites went. But even this people were deemed absolutely unfit to approach Him. Barriers must be erected, to keep them at a distance, which only one of their number might pass, and he their leader and saint. But even he exceedingly feared and quaked. No animal was to stay there under penalty of death, because the animal creation is closely related to man. If a man were to touch that mount, he would meet death; but no hand must touch him, he must be stoned or shot through. If even the priests broke through the barriers, they might be stricken with death. No lesson could have been more impressively taught: and it is for all time. Who would not fear Thee, Great God, glorious in holiness, fearful in praises, doing wonders? surely Holiness becometh Thy house. How shall we be thankful enough for Jesus Christ, in whom the Holiness of God shines so transcendently! and yet He is touched with the feeling of our infirmities and is acquainted with our temptations and griefs. He lays His hands upon us both. "There is one God, and one Mediator between God and men, the man Christ Jesus."[1]

Contrast between God and Man. This after all is always the first step in the soul's deepest union with God. We must somehow be brought to the point of realising and admitting the awful contrast between God and ourselves. There must be the bowed head, the

[1] 1 Tim. ii. 5.

hushed voice, the reverent obeisance, and the broken heart. We must see ourselves, because we have seen God. We must see the King in His beauty, and cry, "Alas! I am undone!" We must behold Him as Job did, when he exchanged the hearing of the ear for the seeing of the eye. We must, like the publican, beat on our breast, as we go up to the Temple in prayer, saying, "God be merciful to me, the sinner." Only from such experiences at Sinai can we pass on to the beatific experiences of acceptance and peace.

God's Awful Appearance. It must have been a great spectacle on that third day. The dense clouds veiling the mountain-peaks and riven with lightning! The thunder like the rattle of an army of angel drums or salvoes of heavenly artillery, announcing the approach of God! The furnace flames that cast a lurid light upon the scene! The thrilling notes of the trumpet, "exceeding loud!" Only once again will the ear of man hear that resonant voice, "for the Lord Himself shall descend from heaven with a shout, with the voice of the Archangel and with the trump of God, for the trumpet shall sound, and the dead shall be raised incorruptible, and we shall be changed."

But we are not come to the mount that might be touched and that burned with fire, or unto blackness, and darkness, and tempest! No, the blackness hid the face of God from the eyes of our dying Lord! The darkness was the midnight in which He cried, "Why, My God, hast Thou forsaken Me!" The tempest is that which broke on the Cross and exhausted itself! Thank God, we are to the windward of the storm . . . for we are to come to Jesus, the Mediator of a new covenant, and to the blood of sprinkling.

THE TEN WORDS

Exodus 20:1-17

1. And God spake all these words, saying,
2. I *am* the Lord thy God, which have brought thee out of the land of Egypt, out of the house of bondage.
3. Thou shalt have no other gods before me.
4. Thou shalt not make unto thee any graven image, or any likeness *of any thing* that *is* in heaven above, or that *is* in the earth beneath, or that *is* in the water under the earth:
5. Thou shalt not bow down thyself to them, nor serve them: for I the Lord thy God *am* a jealous God, visiting the iniquity of the fathers upon the children unto the third and fourth *generation* of them that hate me;
6. And shewing mercy unto thousands of them that love me, and keep my commandments.
7. Thou shalt not take the name of the Lord thy God in vain; for the Lord will not hold him guiltless that taketh his name in vain.
8. Remember the sabbath day, to keep it holy.
9. Six days shalt thou labour, and do all thy work:
10. But the seventh day *is* the sabbath of the Lord thy God: *in it* thou shalt not do any work, thou, nor thy son, nor thy daughter, thy manservant, nor thy maidservant, nor thy cattle, nor thy stranger that *is* within thy gates:
11. For *in* six days the Lord made heaven and earth, the sea, and all that in them *is*, and rested the seventh day: wherefore the Lord blessed the sabbath day, and hallowed it.
12. Honour thy father and thy mother: that thy days may be long upon the land which the Lord thy God giveth thee.
13. Thou shalt not kill.
14. Thou shalt not commit adultery.
15. Thou shalt not steal.
16. Thou shalt not bear false witness against thy neighbour.
17. Thou shalt not covet thy neighbour's house, thou shalt not covet thy neighbour's wife, nor his manservant, nor his maidservant, nor his ox, nor his ass, nor any thing that *is* thy neighbour's.

THE TEN WORDS

Exodus 20:1-17

The Decalogue for all Mankind. The scene of the Giving of the Law is unparalleled in the history of our race. There is no single moment in the history of the nations—of Egypt, Babylon, or Rome, that can bear comparison with this august event. Search the annals of any nation under heaven, and there is but one report from every quarter. "Here were temples, pyramids, and palaces, wars and triumphs, discoveries and achievements, mythologies and ceremonials, but never is it recorded that God declared with audible voice His will." This event was not for the Jews alone, but for mankind, not for an hour, but for all time.

The Ten Words. The phrase "Ten Commandments," is suggested by our Lord's words to the young ruler, "Keep the commandments."[1] The Hebrew phrase for these Divine utterances is "The Ten Words."[2] But they are also described as The Law, the Covenant, and the Tables of Testimony. They are distinguished from all other words, even of inspiration, by these three characteristics, (1) They were spoken by God Himself; (2) they were written by the finger of God on the Tables of Stone; and (3) they set forth His will for our human life, as He wrote it originally on the heart of man, and as He is writing it always in our hearts and lives by the regenerating grace of His Spirit.

Distinction between Right and Wrong. THE FOUNDATION OF LAW. What is the ultimate source of the distinction between Right and Wrong? Why is it wrong to steal, to commit adultery, or to do murder? Many might answer that question by saying: These actions were forbidden by God's voice on Sinai: they are wrong, because He said *Thou shalt not.* But suppose that He had never said "Thou shalt not," would they not still have been wrong? Or, travel back

[1] Matt. xix. 17.　　　[2] Exod. xxxiv. 28; Deut. iv. 13, marg.

to the long ages which preceded the giving of the Law, were they not equally wrong, though as yet Sinai had never trembled beneath the utterance of "the fiery law?"[1] Or go to lands and peoples that have never heard of Sinai, is it not clear that for them also these things are wrong? Clearly then, Rightness and Wrongness do not depend on the Law of Sinai.

God Uttered Himself. What then is the basis of the distinctions between right and wrong? For this we must go beyond the scene on Sinai, beyond the utterance of God, to the nature of things, older than Creation, older than the oldest angel, as old as eternity, i.e. from everlasting. These words were spoken here, because they had already been uttered by the Eternal Word; and He uttered them because they were in the foundations of His own Being. They were engraven on stone, because they had always been graven on the Universe. Is not this what the Psalmist meant, when he said, "Judgment and righteousness are the habitation of Thy throne?" It is for this reason that though Heaven and Earth pass away, one jot or one tittle shall in no wise pass from the law until all be fulfilled; and it is on this ground also that God is able to judge the world. As each of us carries a watch which declares for us privately and individually the time which is measured by the revolutions of worlds, so each moral being has first-hand knowledge of right and wrong. The moral law is written on the heart; and Sinai is a convenient epitome of the great sanctions within us, which bless each act of obedience, crying, "Blessed are ye," and which denounce their curse, when we fail to continue in all things written in the Book of the Law.

The Law not Arbitrary but Necessary. These rewards and punishments are therefore not arbitrary but necessary. Just as man, whilst an inhabitant of this world, is bound and limited by certain conditions, which are known as natural laws, to infringe any of which is to incur instant suffering, not by an arbitrary act of God, but in the nature of things: so if anyone infringes these great Words, defying them against the remonstrances of conscience and the acknowledged standards of rectitude, there is but one result—he must suffer. There cannot but be for him the fiery indignation of offended righteousness. He that has sinned against the laws of fire, of electricity, of gravitation, of health, dies without compassion; of how much sorer punishment, think ye, will they be thought worthy,

[1] Deut. xxxiii. 2.

who have trodden under foot the remonstrances of conscience, and have done despite to the Spirit of Grace!

Heaven and Hell Necessary Outcomes of Conduct. Men sometimes argue as though Heaven were an arbitrary gift, and hell an arbitrary infliction, as an estate to a loyal supporter of the monarchy, or the gaol for a felon. No! Each is the necessary outcome of a life. We go like Judas to our own places. Feathers float up, lead sinks down. They that by patient continuance in well-doing, seek for glory, and honour, and incorruption, cannot but enjoy eternal life. It is theirs in the nature of things. They are factious, and obey not the truth, but obey unrighteousness, begin forthwith to suffer tribulation and anguish by the very nature of things.[1]

Hooker's Dictum. Again, therefore, we are reminded of Hooker's immortal dictum: "Of law there can be no less acknowledged, that her seat is in the bosom of God; her voice the harmony of the world." To be out of harmony with that voice, is to be out of harmony with oneself, with all holy beings, with the nature of things, and with God, whose Being is the Fountain of Grace and Blessedness. That discord is hell.

Fourth Commandment. It might at first sight seem that the Fourth Commandment, demanding the observance of the seventh day as the Rest-Day, were an exception to the assertion that the Decalogue is founded on the nature of things. Is this a matter of conscience? Does this rest on eternal and unalterable sanctions? Will its violation entail necessary rather than arbitrary penalty?

There is no difficulty in answering these questions in the affirmative. The Law of the Rest-Day is engraven on the physical nature of man. Even when the revolutionists of France determined to abolish every trace of the Christian faith, they felt that humanity must have a respite from incessant toil, and appointed one-rest-day in ten, which had afterwards to be altered back to the older arrangement.

Man a Seven-Day Clock. Man is a seven-day clock. He must be wound up with regular accuracy; and his soul needs time to adjust itself equally with the spirit. The sanctions for Sabbath-keeping lie deep in the heart of Nature, and for this reason it was included with the rest in the Ten Words.

Majesty and Love. THE INTRODUCTORY SENTENCE. "I am the Lord thy God, that brought thee up out of the land of Egypt, out of

[1] Rom. ii. 7.

the house of bondage." At Sinai, men have been wont to discern only the sterner and more terrible sides of God's nature, but in view of this tender preface it is difficult to maintain that view. Granted that the opening phrase, "I am Jehovah thy God," declares the majestic authority of the Eternal, does not that tender sequel, "that brought thee up out of the land of Egypt," recall the love that espoused the nation when cast out "to the abhorring of their person"?[1]

The Law Given for Man's Sake. Mark the order. It is that of the Gospel. First, God saves, and then delivers His law. Because He had brought them out of darkness into marvellous light, therefore, as a return, He pleaded with them to remember His commandments to do them, not for His sake alone, but that it might be well with them during all their generations. It is out of love for us that God pleads with men. "The Lord commanded us to do all these statutes . . . for our good always that He might preserve us alive, as at this day."[2]

God's Order in Dealing with Israel. Had He propounded these laws to Israel in Egypt, they would have turned from them in despair. Crushed with oppression, smarting under the lash of the taskmaster, with a sense of being forgotten and out of mind, they would not have hearkened, for bitterness of spirit. They could not have respected the will of a God who seemed powerless against the might of Pharaoh! Either the God of their fathers could not, or He would not help them, and in either case was not calculated to win or hold their respect.

But God did not begin by proclaiming His law in Egypt. He began by manifesting His greatness in actions that appealed powerfully to the imagination of the people whom He had set about redeeming. Why He had seemed to sleep so long, they knew not, but they had seen His mighty arm awake and make itself bare in the eyes of the heathen, and they were now prepared to listen to His voice, since those thunders and lightnings that played about Sinai had been launched on their foes, and had brought terror into the heart of Pharaoh and his advisers.

"If Ye Love Me." He had brought them as on eagles' wings to Himself. His manna was each morning awaiting their search, His waters were flowing from the flinty rocks, His guiding pillar was before their eyes. What more could they desire to show His love?

[1] Ezek. xvi. 5.   [2] Deut. vi. 24.

But before us shines the more tender embodiment of God in Christ. He stoops to our mean life, treads our pathways, drinks of our cup, and is baptised with our baptism, then turns to us saying, "If ye love Me, keep My commandments." He redeems us from the power of darkness, translates us into the kingdom of His dear Son, gives us His Son and Spirit, makes us heirs of an incorruptible inheritance and co-heirs with Christ, and then entreats us to walk in His ways and do His will.

The Whole of Man. With such a preamble, shall we not meditate on these words, as our Lord must have done till they nourish our innermost soul? "Man shall not live by bread alone, but by every word that proceedeth out of the mouth of God." Let us also remember those great words of the Preacher at the close of the Book of Ecclesiastes: "This is the end of the matter; all hath been heard: fear God, and keep His Commandments; for this is the whole of man."[1] Not "the whole duty of man," as it is in the A.V., but "the whole of man." That is to say, if a man will fear God and keep His commandments, not to be redeemed, but as redeemed, not to win love, but because he is loved, not to be saved, but because he is saved—then he is a whole man, and therefore a holy one. All else is empty and vain, as the soap bubbles that break in the air. "Vanity of vanities," says the Preacher, as he passes in review the kingdoms of the world, and the glory of them. "The world passeth away, and the lust thereof; but he that doeth the will of God abideth for ever."[2] "I beseech you therefore, brethren, by the mercies of God, that ye present your bodies a living sacrifice, holy, acceptable to God, which is your reasonable service. And be not fashioned according to this world: but be ye transformed by the renewing of your mind."[3] Because He has freed you, and brought you from the house of bondmen, render this your free and glad service.

Division of the Decalogue. THE CONTENTS OF THE DECALOGUE. *Note the divisions.* That there were ten is clear from Deut. x. 4, but opinions have differed as to how the material should be divided in order to give just *ten*. The division that we follow is that of the Prayer Book, the Greek Church, and the Reformed Church; but the Roman Church and the Lutherans combine our first and second into one, and break up our tenth into two. But this division does not acknowledge or emphasise the clear difference between having

[1] Eccles. xii. 13.   [2] 1 John ii. 17.
[3] Rom. xii. 1–2.

another God than Jehovah, which is one form of sin, and making an image of Him, which is another.

It has been thought by some that since there were two stone-tables of the divine inscription, the ten commandments were equally divided between them, five on each. If this were so, the law about our honouring our parents would be on the same level with the four that refer to God, and this might be justified by the reflection that in honouring them we really honour Him, in Whom every family in heaven and earth is named. But on the whole the old Division is better into four and six, the first regarding our duty to God, and the second our duty to man.

Duty to God First. *Note the position of these two divisions.* Duty to God stands first, and lays the needful foundations for the right discharge of our duties to man. The Love of God is the foundation of all love to our fellows. Neglect the duties of piety, and you will soon neglect your duties to your neighbour. The Scripture does not ignore the distinction between Religion, i.e. the duties we owe to God, and Morality, i.e. the duties implicated through earthly relationships, but it unites the two in the deeper idea that all duty must be done to God, Who is above all, through all, and in all. The precepts of the first Table enjoin that God be honoured in His being, worship, name, and day. The precepts of the second follow naturally, requiring that he who loves God should love his brother also, who is made in the image of God; and surely that love implies that he will refrain from injuring him in deed, in word, and in thought, and neither in his person, his wife, his property, nor his reputation.

Love and the Law. *The whole of the Ten Words are gathered up in the one word Love.* Love is the fulfilling of the Law.[1] If a man should love God perfectly, but have never seen the Decalogue, and if after years of holy communion with God, he should suddenly meet with this enumeration of the Divine Code, there would be no new feature that he would have to introduce into his behaviour, and no newly discovered wrong that he would have to avoid. On the other hand, it is certain that, apart from love, obedience to the law of God is impossible. The heart of the Ten Words is contained in verse 6: "Showing mercy unto thousands that love Me and keep My commandments." It is in proportion as we love Him, that we can obey Him! Whatever of outward service or obedience we render

[1] Rom. xiii. 8–10.

to God or man, if love is withheld, the law is not fulfilled. "If I bestow all my goods to feed the poor, and if I give my body to be burned, but have not love, it profiteth nothing."

The Supreme Necessity of Love. It is impossible to worship God in spirit and in truth, to reverence His Name, or delight in His Day, unless we love Him. It is impossible to keep the heart free from malice, hate, covetousness, and passion, except as it is possessed and filled by the opposite principle of love. Therefore when in answer to the challenge of His critics, our Lord refused to particularise any one of the Ten Words, but summed up the first table of the Law by saying, "Thou shalt love the Lord thy God with all thy heart, and with all thy soul, and with all thy mind, and with all thy strength"; and summed up the second by saying, "Thou shalt love thy neighbour as thyself," we can repeat the comment of His interlocutor, and say, "Master, Thou hast well said! There is none other commandment greater than these!"

The Decalogue a Unity. *The Decalogue is therefore a Unity.* In the Epistle of James, we are told by that austere son of the Law that "whosoever shall keep the whole law, and yet stumble in one point, he is become guilty of all."[1] It seems a severe utterance. We are apt to think that if we obey nine out of the ten Commandments our obedience will be put to our credit, even though we fail in the tenth. But in thinking thus, we ignore the fact that the ten words of Sinai are not ten separate enactments, having no connection with each other, except that they are included in the same code.

Ten Aspects of God. Remember that they are ten aspects of the Holiness of God, as it looks out on different phases of human life. If then we infringe one particular, we are proved to be deficient in perfect holiness. A perfectly good man cannot fail in any single point; just as a man cannot make a single provincialism in his speech, without betraying himself to be a Galilean. We only live, as we ponder and obey *every* word that proceedeth from the mouth of God.

The Law a Revealing Power. *These ten words imply that sin is in the world.* Looked at from this standpoint, what a revelation is this of the evils of our hearts! You can judge of a nation by its statute-book, and you may judge of the heart of humanity by these ten words. Evidently it finds it hard to worship the one God apart from some symbol, it turns aside to vanity, it ignores His worship

[1] Jas. ii. 10.

and rest, it is full of uncleanness, and hatred, of coveting and theft. "Out of the heart of men," said our Lord, "evil thoughts proceed, fornications, thefts, murders, adulteries, coverings, wickednesses, deceit, lasciviousness, an evil eye, railing, pride, foolishness."[1] Judging from our knowledge of ourselves, and of the world around us, we are quite prepared to accept this enumeration, for there is not one of this terrible catalogue that is not included in these prohibitions. Is it not a grievous thing, that such a nature is ours by inheritance? How eagerly we need to utter the old prayer: "Cleanse the thoughts of our hearts by the inspiration of Thy Holy Spirit, that we may perfectly love Thee, and worthily magnify Thy Holy Name." How gladly should we cling to the promise, "I will sprinkle clean water upon you, and ye shall be clean: from all your filthiness, and from all your idols, will I cleanse you. . . . And I will put My Spirit within you, and cause you to walk in My statutes, and ye shall keep My judgments, and do them."[2]

The Law becomes Death. *The Relation of the Law to the Gospel.* In his profound self-anatomy, the great Apostle says that the commandment is holy, just, and good, but that it slew him.[3] What was good in itself became death to him, i.e. when he came to realise its perfectness and purity, his hope of ever being able to fulfil it, or to win the favour of God by fulfilling it, died. To use Bunyan's figure,—before he realised the claims and spirituality of the law, his heart had resembled an unswept room, in which the dust of months, undisturbed by the broom, lies in thick layers, though to a superficial gaze, viewing it in the twilight, it appears swept, cleansed, and garnished. But when the full light of the law fell on him and searched him, when he stood face to face with the mirror of eternal truth, and saw himself as he really was, he knew that he could never fulfil its high and holy demands. He died to self-confidence, died to self-satisfaction, died to the hope of ever gaining eternal life. Nay, more, the law even stirred up the slumbering evil of his nature by its prohibitions. Tell a child not to do a thing,—not to open a cupboard, not to break the seal of a letter—and you at once stir its whole nature to revolt. So Paul says sadly, "Sin revived, and I died." This is the invariable experience of those who observe carefully the phases of experience through which the soul passes.

Law from Moses, but Grace by Christ. What hope is there? None

---

[1] Mark vii. 21, 22.   [2] Ezek. xxxvi. 25, etc.
[3] Rom. vii. 11.

from man, but everything from Christ. We are, as the Apostle says, shut up to Him. The Law came through Moses, but Grace and Truth came by Jesus Christ.[1] "For what the Law could not do, in that it was weak through the flesh, God sending His own Son in the likeness of sinful flesh, and as an offering for sin, condemned sin in the flesh."[2]

First our Lord fulfilled the obligations of the Law to the last detail. He was made under the Law for this very purpose. He magnified it by His absolute obedience to all its jots and tittles. Not only did He abstain from its negative prohibitions, but He realised its positive requirements. When He died on the cross, He bore the sin and guilt of the world, and bearing them, delivered us from their curse. "Christ hath redeemed us from the curse of the Law, being made a curse for us."[3] Dare to believe that He bare thy sins on His own body on the tree, and freed thee for ever from the house of thy sad and weary bondage. "Be it known unto you therefore, brethren, that through this man is proclaimed unto you remission of sins; and by Him every one that believeth is justified from all things, from which ye could not be justified by the law of Moses."[4]

Then, when we are redeemed, the Lord by His Spirit comes to live within us, and the Spirit of His life repeats in us His own life, His life of love and obedience and righteousness. "Do we then make the law of none effect through faith? God forbid; nay, we establish the law."[5]

[1] John i. 17.
[2] Rom. viii. 3.
[3] Gal. iii. 13.
[4] Acts xiii. 38, 39.
[5] Rom. iii. 31.

The Mount that Might Be Touched

Exodus 20:18-21; Hebrews 12:18-22

18. And all the people saw the thunderings, and the lightnings, and the noise of the trumpet, and the mountain smoking: and when the people saw *it*, they removed, and stood afar off.

19. And they said unto Moses, Speak thou with us, and we will hear: but let not God speak with us, lest we die.

20. And Moses said unto the people, Fear not: for God is come to prove you, and that his fear may be before your faces, that ye sin not.

21. And the people stood afar off, and Moses drew near unto the thick darkness where God *was*.

18. For ye are not come unto the mount that might be touched, and that burned with fire, nor unto blackness, and darkness, and tempest,

19. And the sound of a trumpet, and the voice of words; which *voice* they that heard intreated that the word should not be spoken to them any more:

20. (For they could not endure that which was commanded, And if so much as a beast touch the mountain, it shall be stoned, or thrust through with a dart:

21. And so terrible was the sight, *that* Moses said, I exceedingly fear and quake:)

22. But ye are come unto mount Sion, and unto the city of the living God, the heavenly Jerusalem, and to an innumerable company of angels.

THE MOUNT THAT MIGHT BE TOUCHED

Exodus 20:18-21; Hebrews 12:18-22

The People at Sinai. The Hebrew people had seen a great sight, in which no other people have shared. As they stood massed in the level plain at the foot of Sinai, they had beheld the Divine Theophany.

> " The earth trembled,
> The heavens also dropped at the presence of God:
> Even yon Sinai trembled at the presence of God, the God of Israel."

Such is the description of the Psalmist (Ps. lxviii. 8).

> " When God of old came down from Heaven,
> In power and wrath He came:
> Before His feet the clouds were riven,
> Half darkness, and half flame."

Such is the description of our modern time.[1]

Their Dread. The effect produced on the people by these accumulated terrors was panic-stricken flight. "They removed and stood afar off." They thought that they must die. They requested that Moses would act as mediator. "They said unto Moses, Speak thou with us, and we will hear: but let not God speak with us, lest we die." They were glad to participate in God's merciful providence, and to believe that He was the unseen background of their life. They had sung His praise on the shores of the Red Sea; they had thankfully appropriated the supplies with which He enriched the desert wastes; they had rejoiced in the shadow of the brooding-cloud by day, and the light of the pillar of fire by night. But there they stayed. They were unwilling that the naked beam of the Deity, unveiled and undiluted, should shine forth upon their mortal vision.

Man and the Divine Scrutiny. This tendency is characteristic of us all. We are quite prepared to admit the existence and providence

[1] Keble: *The Christian Year*, "Whitsunday."

of God, but we do not desire that He should obtrude His presence too obviously. The mass of men turn and hide their faces, or run away when the profounder aspects of life present themselves, much as a sensitive person will hurry past when there has been a terrible accident in the street, with which he feels incompetent to deal. Men do not object to think of God in His high heaven, but they object to conceive of each common bush as being aflame with the Divine fire.

The Reluctance of the Religious Professor. *Take the normal religious man.* True religion welcomes God's life and light into the innermost recesses of the soul, yields to Him the key of every department of life, views His hand in each particular providence, believes that no hair falls from the curly head of the child or the thin locks of age without the Father. But the typical church-goer of the time shrinks in alarm from such a Divine interpenetration of life. "Not so near!" he cries in apprehensive tones; and then bids his priest or minister, his creed or sacrament, his church or meeting-house become his Moses, to mediate God and supply the smoked glass, that the tempered light may be mitigated for his seeing. "Speak thou with us, and we will hear: but let not God speak, lest we die."

What a contrast is this to the condition of soul that says with Samuel, "Speak, Lord, for Thy servant heareth," or, with David, "Be not silent unto me, lest if Thou be silent unto me, I become like unto them that go down into the pit." We are thankful for Moses, thankful for the Creed and the Church, but we cannot be content with these; our heart and our flesh cry out for the living God— "When shall we come and appear before God?"

The Reluctance of the Men of Science. *Take the case of science.* There is, of course, a noble army of scientific men who have passed up the shining staircase of Nature into God's pavilion. But with many others it is not so. They set themselves to ascertain the facts of the universe, to arrange those facts into laws, to describe the action of the dynamic forces that operate through those laws. But there they stay their footsteps. When the light of a personal intelligence and will beyond Nature begins to glimmer on their souls, they draw back, and begin to talk of laws, of forces, of an eternal something not themselves. Their feet are on the mountain-path that culminates in God, but they turn aside, when they are on the verge of the greatest discovery of all. "Let not God speak to us, lest we die!"

The Reluctance of the Politician. *Take the case of modern politics.* No one thinks of quoting the Bible in the chamber of legislation, or enforcing an argument with the teaching of Christ. When we argue for the rest-day, it is not because God made and hallowed it, or because our spiritual nature requires an opportunity for worship but because our physical nature requires for its efficiency a periodic rest. When we speak of ameliorative legislation, it is not because the love of God demands the love of man, but because we would provide against revolution. And even if missions are argued for, it is because they exert a civilising influence and promote trade. Are not these methods of expression which are artfully designed to evade the profoundest aspects of human life, the noblest sanctions of human conduct? "Let not God speak to us, lest we die."

A Contrast. We cannot help contrasting this attitude of mind and speech with the conduct of that much-misunderstood and thoughtlessly abused body, of whom Macaulay wrote: " They were men whose minds had derived a peculiar character from the daily contemplation of superior beings and eternal interests. Not content with acknowledging in general terms an over-ruling providence, they habitually ascribed every event to the will of a Being, for whose power nothing was too vast and for whose inspection nothing was too minute. . . . Instead of catching occasional glimpses of the Deity through an obscuring veil, they aspired to gaze full on His intolerable brightness, and to commune with Him face to face. . . . The Puritan therefore was never alarmed, when he was bidden to stand still and listen to the voice of God. His closet and his church were full of the reverberations of that awful, gracious, and beautiful voice for which he listened. He made little of sacraments and priests, because God was so intensely real to him. What should he do with lenses, who stood in the full torrent of the sunshine!"[1]

Causes of this Reluctance. This reluctance, on the part of ordinary men, to recognise the near presence of God arises from *three remediable causes*, which will repay our careful consideration.

The Purpose of our Existence Misunderstood. (1) *We are in danger of mistaking the true intention of our existence.* Existence is from the Latin *ex*, out, *sto*, to stand. We have been called into existence that we may live, and move, and have our being in God, and *know* that we were doing so. We were made for God. Our soul was intended to communicate with the great Spirit, through our

[1] Essay on Milton.

spirit. What the water is to the fish, what air is to the bird, what sunshine is to the eagle, that God's nature was intended to be to ours. As well might the fish ask not to be thrown into the water, or the bird ask that its cage-door might not be opened, admitting it to the air, or the eagle fly into a darksome cage, away from the glorious sunlight, as that any man should say, "Let God not speak to me, lest I die." The exact contrary is true: If God does not speak to us, we shall die; for the Speech of God is Jesus Christ, THE WORD.

—**From our Contact with the World.** But the soul has yielded to the binding, blighting influences of the world, the flesh, and the devil, that antipodean trinity below which is the antithesis of the blessed Trinity above. Through the senses of the body, the soul has come under the dominion of the earth-sphere, and so by long and evil habits has lost its sensitiveness to the spiritual and eternal. The eyes of the heart have become blinded, lest the light of the knowledge of the glory of God should shine in upon the soul. It is as though a man had been so long imprisoned in darkness, that when liberty is at last granted him, he preferred to remain in his cell, to bearing the glare of sunshine or mixing in the unaccustomed life of his fellows. Many of the animals in our Zoological Gardens have become so accustomed to their unnatural conditions, that they would soon perish, if emancipated, and set to find the means of livelihood for themselves. Similarly the soul of man has dwelt so long and habitually in the life of the senses, that the spiritual function has become starved, perhaps atrophied. "The Egyptians are men, and not God, and their horses are flesh, and not spirit." Men forget that they came from God, that they need God, that they are akin to God, having been made in His image and after His likeness, and that they can never be truly at rest till they rest in Him. It is for such reason that they cry, "Let not God speak with us, lest we die!"

—**Remedied through Christ.** All this is altered in Christ. He comes to the sepulchre of sense, where the spirit lies entombed, and bids it awake, arise, and come forth. "You hath He quickened, who were dead in trespasses and sins." We are born again of the Spirit, and that which is born of the Spirit is spirit. The soul begins to use the wonderful apparatus of the spirit towards God, as formerly it used only the apparatus of the physical body towards the material world. And suddenly it awakens to see things which the physical eye had not seen, and to hear things which the physical ear had not heard, and to enjoy delights which the heart of the ordinary man has never conceived of; but which God has prepared for those who live in the Spirit, and walk in the Spirit, and are therefore endowed with spiritual discernment. The things of Christ are not known, save by those who are born of the Spirit, for they are spiritually discerned. Only the twice-born can see the things which are hidden from the wise and prudent and revealed to babes. But when once the soul has seen them, it counts all things but loss for the excellency of that knowledge, and reckons them but dross in comparison. Then the cry becomes: "To whom shall we go? Thou hast the words of Eternal Life."

The Consciousness of Sin is Powerful. There is yet another reason: (2) *We are deeply conscious of sinnership.* The holiest are most conscious of their failure. They have done what they ought not, and have not done what they ought. They know that there is no health in them. There is not one who has not missed the mark. So many resolutions have been like spent arrows, so many have flown wide of the golden centre. "I was shapen in iniquity," says one, "and in sin did my mother conceive me." "Among whom," says another, "we all had our conversation in time past, and were by nature children of wrath, even as others."

But those who are yet in their sins, swept before temptation, as leaves before the autumn breeze, are also deeply conscious of sinnership. It is for this reason that they contrive, if possible, never to be alone, and that they rush through an unending series of diversions. Yes! that is the word—*diversion.* Everything must be sought and tried that promises to divert their thoughts from themselves. These people, as our Lord said, hate the light, and refuse to come to the light. They avoid the society of good people, will change seats on an ocean-going steamer rather than face for a week at meals a minister of religion; will banish from their houses the godly servant-maid, and from their shelves the religious book.

The Reminder of God Resented. And why all these precautions? Because the presence of anything that reminds them of God hurts their conscience, as daylight a diseased eye, or salt an open wound. "Where shall I go from Thy presence? or whither shall I flee from Thy Spirit?" is a question they put from quite other motives than animated the Psalmist. If the wings of the morning, or the uttermost parts of the sea; if hell itself; if the darkness of the darkest cave; if rocks and mountains would only hide them from the face of Him that sitteth on the throne, and from the Lamb,—how gladly would they face any sacrifice, any distance, any other deprivation! It is for such reasons that they cry, "Let not God speak with us!" The strange thing is, that these people should desire to go to heaven when they die. What incongruity of thought! To be so afraid of the revealed presence of God here, and yet to desire the place of all others where "they see His face." But even in heaven it is improbable that they would see Him. A blind man might be face to face with a king without seeing him. A deaf man may sit amid ravishing music, and not hear a chord.

The Remedy in Christ. But our Lord has altered that. He has taught us that all sin and guilt are put away instantly and for ever for those who are penitent and believing. They shall not be remembered nor brought to mind; not even mentioned from the judgment throne; obliterated as a cloud from the summer sky; lost as a pebble in the depths of the sea! He clothes us in the white robe, frees us from the law of sin and death, puts a new song in our mouth, and presents us to the Father without spot or wrinkle or any such thing. The supreme end and aim of our Saviour's work on our behalf is to bring us to God (1 Peter iii. 18).

Man is Deemed More Merciful than God. There is, lastly (3), *a lurking belief in the heart of man that man is more merciful than God.* It is for this reason that men have created priests, who might bear gently with the ignorant and erring, because they themselves were compassed with infirmity, and needed to offer sacrifices for themselves. It was for this reason that the worship of the Madonna obtained so wide a vogue, especially in the Middle Ages.

—But God's Mercy is Revealed in Christ. And it is for this reason, knowing our frailty and accommodating Himself to our weak faith, that God manifested Himself in human flesh. "It behoved Him to be made like unto His brethren, that He might be a merciful and faithful High Priest, and make intercession for the sins of the people." Remember also how He said Himself to the despairing appeal of Philip, "He that hath seen Me hath seen the Father; and how sayest thou then, Show us the Father?" No woman's heart is so tender, no mother's hand is so gentle, no father's care of his helpless babes is so pitiful as God's. He who made the dove's tenderness for her nestlings, or the sensitive watchfulness of the fallow-deer for her fawn, is surely more sensitive than either. He who causes the dew to distil, the light to fall so gently on our earth after its swift flight from the sun, and the soft rain to drop so lightly that it does not break the petals of an overblown rose, cannot be devoid of a similar delicacy to those who are weary and heavy laden, or as the feebly smoking flax and the bruised, broken reed. Is it not written in the same chapter, that He who sustains the stars in their mighty orbits, and calls them by their names, in the greatness of His power will also gently lead the ewes that are with young?

Let Us, then, Draw Near. Therefore the sacred writers cry exultingly, "Let us draw near with boldness, having our hearts sprinkled from an evil conscience, and our bodies washed with pure water"; and again, "Ye who were once afar off are made nigh by the blood of Christ"; and again, "Ye are not come to the mount that might be touched, or to blackness, and darkness, and tempest . . . but ye are come to Mount Sion, the city of the Living God, the heavenly Jerusalem; to an innumerable company of angels; to the Church of the First-Born; to God the Judge of all; to the spirits of just men made perfect; to Jesus, the Mediator of the New Covenant, and to the blood of sprinkling, that bespeaketh better things than that of Abel." This is the ladder let down from heaven to earth. Let us reverse it, beginning from the last clause, and climb through the glowing links of this sublime sentence till we are permitted to dwell habitually in the City of God!

THE SUMMONS TO WORSHIP

Exodus 20:22-26

22. And the Lord said unto Moses, Thus thou shalt say unto the children of Israel, Ye have seen that I have talked with you from heaven.

23. Ye shall not make with me gods of silver, neither shall ye make unto you gods of gold.

24. An altar of earth thou shalt make unto me, and shalt sacrifice thereon thy burnt offerings, and thy peace offerings, thy sheep, and thine oxen: in all places where I record my name I will come unto thee, and I will bless thee.

25. And if thou wilt make me an altar of stone, thou shalt not build it of hewn stone: for if thou lift up thy tool upon it, thou hast polluted it.

26. Neither shalt thou go up by steps unto mine altar, that thy nakedness be not discovered thereon.

THE SUMMONS TO WORSHIP
Exodus 20:22-26

The Covenant. Here begins the first paragraph in the Book of the Covenant which continues through the following chapters to xxiii. 19. The contents were communicated to Moses on the Mount, at the request of the people: "Speak thou with us, and we will hear: but let not God speak with us, lest we die." "And Moses came and told the people all the words of the Lord, and all the judgments: and all the people answered with one voice, and said, All the words which the Lord hath said will we do." Moses wrote all the words of the Lord in a book, and afterwards took the blood of sacrifices and sprinkled it on the people.

The Code of Laws. This book was therefore the first draft or nucleus of the Book of Exodus, as we now have it. There is much in it of most significant value, as bearing on the early history of the Hebrew people, and on ourselves. As to the former, we may say, in the words of Professor Maitland, "There can, so we think, be no doubt that the stage of civilization of which these laws speak to us is marvellously high. This may be the oldest Code of Laws in the world; but it is very far from being the most archaic."

Their Origin. It may be that these commands are really a codification of laws which had been handed down to Israel from the days of their fathers. It may be that they had been in vogue not only through the Egyptian bondage, but in the tents of Abraham. Here they are presented in a succinct and impressive form, with the solemn sanctions of Jehovah and the ratification of the people's voice. Moses probably set forth in them the principles on which he had been accustomed to administer justice, and the principles on which his co-assessors were to administer it.

Their Authority. But there was an altogether new authority communicated to these "judgments," or *decisions*, by the fact that God had announced them, and the people had received them, as the basis of their national life. "The gold had been lying about before, but it was now collected and coined into the currency of the kingdom. Old coins had been gathered in. All had now passed through the mintage of the Heavenly Sovereign, and bore the image and superscription of the King of the new theocracy."

The first of the three chapters contains laws regarding the person, the next laws regarding property, and the third miscellaneous laws, mostly regarding religious observances.

Ordinances as to Worship. Here in the forefront of all stand these ordinances as to worship. There is repeated the prohibition of the manufacture of idols, and the worship of Jehovah under the symbolism of either Egypt or Assyria. Then follows the injunction for the altar of earth on which burnt-offerings and peace-offerings were to be offered. As yet the place of Divine Worship had not been fixed, and would not be, until God placed the tent of Shiloh amongst His people. But in the interim these provisions were made for the erection of an altar at which the devout worshipper might approach the Heavenly Father. The patriarchal altars had evidently been of this description, and it was now provided that the same usage should continue. Elaborate structures of hewn and decorated stonework were not allowed, lest the objects carved on the stones should become objects of idolatrous worship.

The Offering. The burnt-offering of course stands for our entire surrender and consecration to God; whilst the peace-offering was a sacramental meal, in which the worshipper ate of the same sacrifice with his God (Lev. i and iii). The sacrifices offered by Abraham, Isaac, and Jacob had been of this character, because the sacrifices which bespoke atonement were not as yet permitted to be offered by ordinary men. They awaited the further development of the Priesthood and the Ritual, to which the following pages bear witness.

Let us deeply ponder the suggestion of this initial paragraph, that worship stands in the forefront of our relationships to God, and to each other. "In the beginning, God."

The Idea of Worship: The Sinai Stage. There were several stages in the development of the idea of worship among the Hebrew people. The first may be summarised as that of *Sinai*. When the mighty God descended there, clouds brooded over it, as we have seen, with forked lightning glancing to and fro amid the blackness, darkness, and tempest. Even Moses said, as he approached it, "I do exceedingly fear and quake." Very few of the children of men have had so pure a bosom as Moses, the man who seems to have been raised above the rank and file of men into a spirituality and purity of which the virgin peaks of Sinai were a symbol, and if the effect on his nature was so awe-inspiring, what must not have been that revelation of the Divine Majesty!

—In Modern Life. But are there not some lives still that are represented by Sinai? They are always living under the brooding cloud, their religious sentiments are full of dread, their experience is sombre, dark, and uninviting. For them death is the leaving behind of the sunny landscape, and the threading of a dreary mountain pathway to the lonely desolations of Sinai, with its thunder and storm. It is not impossible that the words of Moses aptly describe your own life. "I exceedingly fear and quake when I come in contact with a religious man, and I do my best to avoid him; I exceedingly fear and quake when a religious subject is quoted in my proximity; I exceedingly fear and quake when I anticipate the act of death; I exceedingly fear and quake at the thought of living for ever. Religion is a burden, sorrow, and torment to me." Ah, any who speak thus need to ponder *over*, and ask God's inward teaching on those words of the Apostle: "The Word became flesh, and tabernacled among us (and we beheld His glory, the glory as of the Only Begotten of the Father), full of grace and truth." "Of His fulness have all we received, and grace for grace" (John i. 14, 16). Directly you see that God was more perfectly revealed in the winsomeness of Jesus than in the terror of Sinai, you will pass in a moment from the Sinai conception of worship.

The Shiloh Stage. God next recorded His Name in *Shiloh*. "The whole congregation of the children of Israel assembled together at Shiloh, and set up the tent of meeting (i.e. the Tabernacle) there" (Joshua xviii. 1). Shiloh stands for the worship in symbol and outward form. The tabernacle, with its two sanctuaries, the holy and the most holy, the ark and altar, the veil and outer court, the high-priest and the priests, was a parable for all time. Very obviously it could not give real relief to the conscience. There was no direct contact between the worshipper and God. All he could hope for was that his representative would not forget to put his case before the Eternal and Almighty Father, when they were face to face. From first to last, the service stood only in meats and drinks, and divers washings and carnal ordinances. There was the shadow of good things to come, not the very image of the things; and there was a remembrance of sins made year after year, with no consciousness of absolute remission and relief.

—**In Modern Life.** This, again, is the type of the religion of not a few. They have no spiritual vision, no spiritual touch. Their highest aim is to fulfil diligently and conscientiously their religious duties, as prescribed by their religious directors and counsellors. They are regular and punctual, scrupulous and minute. So far as the outward observance and the inner desire to perform all that is required by the Church and her ministers, they are without reproach; and yet they never feel satisfied. The veil is never withdrawn. Always touching the garment's hem, they never get a glimpse of the face of the Wearer. Without a doubt these obtain the virtue of the Risen Life of Christ. But they have no assurance, no consciousness of childship, no witness of the Spirit. As it was in the days of Shiloh's sanctuary, when Samuel ministered there, so for them: "The Word of the Lord was precious (or rare) in those days; there was no open vision." There is something better for thee. "Having therefore, brethren, boldness to enter into the holy place by the blood of Jesus, by the way which He dedicated for us, a new and living way, through the veil, that is to say, His flesh; and having a great Priest over the house of God; *let us draw near* . . ." (Heb. x. 19–21, R.V.).

The Jerusalem Stage. God next recorded His Name in *Jerusalem*. For the full story of the overthrow of Shiloh and its causes, and of the transference of the seat of worship to Jerusalem, we must turn to Psalm lxxviii. 57–72 and 1 Kings vi., etc. Beautiful for situation, the joy of the whole earth was Mount Sion, the city of the Great King; but the special attraction which drew the crowds of devout men from every nation under heaven was the fact that God had said: "This is My rest for ever, here will I dwell, for I have desired it." Jerusalem was the city of the Great King, mainly because the Temple arose above all other buildings like a dream of white marble. Try and imagine the fascination of those great annual gatherings. The cornfields were bare, the vines had yielded their ruddy juice, and all the land was resting from the labours of the year. The villages yielded the beginnings of the pilgrim-host, which were swollen by confluent streams as every village and mountain-valley yielded their tributaries; and presently fathers, mothers, and children, greyheaded sires and aged women, with boys and girls of the third and fourth generations, that made hill and valley ring with laughter and song, crowded through the gates of the beloved city. The fathers told again to their children the great stories of the past, that they might pass them on to their children. They thronged the Temple-courts, participated in the holy rites, thrilled before the sacred words that were read or sung, and gave themselves up to all the holy associations that religion and patriotism could inspire. And even when darkness fell, and the clouds of Sennacherib's attack gather around the beleaguered city, Isaiah and others said, "There is no need of fear. God is in the midst of her, she shall not be moved, God shall help her, when the morning breaks."

—**In Modern Life.** This is a phase of religious experience of which we all know something. The great festal crowds, the vast convocations, the uplifting volume of praise and prayer, the thrill of the mighty audience reacting upon each unit, the stirring sermon —all this is helpful, especially in the early stages of our religious life; and though, thank God, it is possible for any one of us to worship Him in the privacy of our own apartment, yet we all know some-thing of the telepathy of common worship, and of the influence that passes from heart to heart in the emotion of a great audience. We should prize such opportunities. Probably we never realise how much we owe to them, until in long weeks of sickness, or in the comparative isolation of protracted journeyings, we are deprived of their impulse and consolation.

A Difficulty. There is always a difficulty, however, in deciding how much of the helpfulness of these services is due to the emotions, and how much to the felt presence of God. Our nature is so mysterious and intricate in its mechanism that we are not always aware as to the true origin and therefore true worth of what we take to be religion. It may only be an emotional fervour, and if so, it will lose its intensity, and have no vital effect on our inner life. It was to the people of Jerusalem that the prophet addressed, in God's Name, the words: "Bring no more vain oblations; incense is an abomination unto Me; new moon and sabbath, the calling of assemblies,—I cannot away with iniquity AND the solemn meeting" (Isa. i. 13, R.V.). Notice that *and*. It is very emphatic. The solemn meeting is not sufficient to deliver the soul from its iniquity, because its effect may only be skin-deep.

The Stage of the Well or Spring. There was a fourth phase of which our Lord spoke, when He sat at noon beside the well, and which we may describe as *the Worship of the Well or Spring.* Let us recall those memorable words (John iv. 21–26, R.V.): "Jesus saith unto her, Woman, believe Me, the hour cometh, when neither in this mountain, nor in Jerusalem, shall ye worship the Father. . . . The hour cometh, and now is, when the true worshippers shall worship the Father in spirit and truth." Then almost pathetically He adds, as though God were turning away dissatisfied from all the vain worship of the Temple, "For such doth the Father seek to be His worshippers."

Our True Temple. The true temple is the spirit of man. Not there, but here: not without, but within: not far away, but in thy mouth and in thy heart. Thou mayest find, as Plato said, that though thou dwellest within the walls of a city, thou mayest be as in a shepherd's fold on a mountain. The same thought occurs frequently in the writings of Marcus Aurelius. Men seek for themselves private retiring-places, as country villages, the seashore, mountains; and no thoughtful person would throw a slight on the acquisition of such opportunities when possible. Our Lord loved and chose to frequent mountains, gardens, and the sea. Divine pleasures are found in solitude. With more power over our own spirits, we may return thence to the business of the world. But where this is not possible we may still worship God in the very beauty of holiness. At any time whatsoever, it is in our power to retire within ourselves and be at rest.

> " Heart, heart, awake! the love that loveth all
> Maketh a deeper calm than Horeb's cave,
> God in thee, can His children's folly gall?
> Love may be hurt, but shall not love be brave?
> Thy holy silence sinks in dews of balm;
> Thou art my solitude, my mountain calm.
> Brood Thou around me, and the noise is o'er;
> Thy universe my closet with shut door,
>   The heart."

The Ordinances and Ourselves. The *altar of earth* is our humility that casts itself down in profound penitence and heart-break. Our *burnt-offering* is the consecration and devotement of spirit, soul, and body. "A body Thou hast prepared for me: behold I come to do Thy will, O God." Our *peace-offering* is our deep fellowship with God, as we commune with Him on the glory and beauty of the Only-Begotten Son. *The place* where He records His Name, and whither He comes to bless us, is within; and where the Shekinah shines in any heart, however humble, the commonest texture becomes transfigured, even as our Lord's simple homespun did, of which it is said, that His raiment became white and dazzling. We need to lift no tool to sculpture aught; no gods of gold or silver are required; the prohibition not to make any likeness of God is not for us, for have we not beheld the glory of God in the face of Jesus Christ? No need to say, "Little children, keep yourselves from idols," when we have seen Him who is the brightness of the Father's glory and the express image of His Person.

Our Praise. And when we worship thus, praise is our chief employ. We are not wholly indifferent to the command to make known our requests, but they are more frequently requests for other people than for ourselves, or, if we ask for ourselves, we include all with whom we live. We confess our sins, but we adore the Love that forgives and redeems. Whether in the aisle of pine-trees, or in the tiny garden, or by the margin of lake or river, we walk to and fro, saying aloud, "We praise Thee, O God, we acknowledge Thee to be the Lord." And suddenly we find ourselves part of the Holy Church throughout the world, irrespective of boundaries and divisions, as she joins her voice with the cry of the glorified hosts of perfected spirits before the throne. Then suddenly the glory of God shines over the humble plains of our daily life, and we hear a great multitude of the heavenly host praising God, and saying, "Glory to God in the highest, Peace on earth, Goodwill toward men."

THE RIGHTS OF THE INDIVIDUAL

Exodus 21:1-32

1. Now these *are* the judgments which thou shalt set before them.

2. If thou buy an Hebrew servant, six years he shall serve: and in the seventh he shall go out free for nothing.

3. If he came in by himself, he shall go out by himself: if he were married, then his wife shall go out with him.

4. If his master have given him a wife, and she have born him sons or daughters; the wife and her children shall be her master's, and he shall go out by himself.

5. And if the servant shall plainly say, I love my master, my wife, and my children: I will not go out free:

6. Then his master shall bring him unto the judges; he shall also bring him to the door, or unto the door post; and his master shall bore his ear through with an aul; and he shall serve him for ever.

7. And if a man sell his daughter to be a maidservant, she shall not go out as the menservants do.

8. If she please not her master, who hath betrothed her to himself, then shall he let her be redeemed: to sell her unto a strange nation he shall have no power, seeing he hath dealt deceitfully with her.

9. And if he have betrothed her unto his son, he shall deal with her after the manner of daughters.

10. If he take him another *wife*; her food, her raiment, and her duty of marriage, shall he not diminish.

11. And if he do not these three unto her, then shall she go out free without money.

12. He that smiteth a man, so that he die, shall be surely put to death.

13. And if a man lie not in wait, but God deliver *him* into his hand; then I will appoint thee a place whither he shall flee.

14. But if a man come presumptuously upon his neighbour, to slay him with guile; thou shalt take him from mine altar, that he may die.

15. And he that smiteth his father, or his mother, shall be surely put to death.

16. And he that stealeth a man, and selleth him, or if he be found in his hand, he shall surely be put to death.

17. And he that curseth his father, or his mother, shall surely be put to death.

18. And if men strive together, and one smite another with a stone, or with *his* fist, and he die not, but keepeth *his* bed:

19. If he rise again, and walk abroad upon his staff, then shall he that smote *him* be quit: only he shall pay *for* the loss of his time, and shall cause *him* to be thoroughly healed.

20. And if a man smite his servant, or his maid, with a rod, and he die under his hand; he shall be surely punished.

21. Notwithstanding, if he continue a day or two, he shall not be punished: for he *is* his money.

22. If men strive, and hurt a woman with child, so that her fruit depart *from her*, and yet no mischief follow: he shall be surely punished, according as the woman's husband will lay upon him; and he shall pay as the judges *determine*.

23. And if *any* mischief follow, then thou shalt give life for life,

24. Eye for eye, tooth for tooth, hand for hand, foot for foot,

25. Burning for burning, wound for wound, stripe for stripe.

26. And if a man smite the eye of his servant, or the eye of his maid, that it perish; he shall let him go free for his eye's sake.

27. And if he smite out his manservant's tooth, or his maidservant's tooth; he shall let him go free for his tooth's sake.

28. If an ox gore a man or a woman, that they die: then the ox shall be surely stoned, and his flesh shall not be eaten; but the owner of the ox *shall be* quit.

29. But if the ox were wont to push with his horn in time past, and it hath been testified to his owner, and he hath not kept him in, but that he hath killed a man or a woman; the ox shall be stoned, and his owner also shall be put to death.

30. If there be laid on him a sum of money, then he shall give for the ransom of his life whatsoever is laid upon him.

31. Whether he have gored a son, or have gored a daughter, according to this judgment shall it be done unto him.

32. If the ox shall push a manservant or a maidservant; he shall give unto their master thirty shekels of silver, and the ox shall be stoned.

THE RIGHTS OF THE INDIVIDUAL
Exodus 21:1-32

The Law of the Covenant. "The Book of the Covenant," which extends to xxiii. 19, was a peculiarly sacred document. It contained the conditions on which the peculiar relationship between Israel and Jehovah was based. If they obeyed His voice indeed, and kept His covenant, they would become His peculiar treasure among all people, "a kingdom of priests and a holy nation" (xix. 6).

It is quite likely, as I have already suggested, that many of the laws and judgments in these sections are a codification of existing customs, which had sprung up in the previous centuries, and may have dated from the days when, with his women-folk perched high on the backs of camels and a great retinue of household servants, Abram took his journey across the unoccupied territories between Ur of the Chaldees and Damascus.

Moses and Hammurabi. Strong confirmation to this suggestion is afforded by comparing these enactments with the Code of Hammurabi, probably the Amraphel of Gen. xiv. 1, one of the most important personages in the history of Western Asia.[1] He lived about 1900 B.C.; and in A.D. 1902 his monument—"a block of black diorite, nearly eight feet high"—was discovered. The inscription on this precious stone contained a collection of the laws of his empire. There are many interesting points of agreement between the two codes; but there is nothing to prove that the great Hebrew Legislation was copied or borrowed from Hammurabi's, but rather that they emanated from some common source, which was probably the traditional law and custom prevailing throughout the ancient East at a very distant period. Wherever possible, as here, God takes up and endorses those conclusions to which the Spirit of Truth has led mankind.

[1] *The Century Bible*, p. 13.

The Conditions Reflected in the Laws: Civilisation. As we pass we must notice the simplicity of *the state of civilisation* which these laws reflect. The ox and ass figure largely in the enumeration of property, the one for the toils of agriculture, the other for burden-bearing. There are no fences on the broad pasture-lands and commons on which the cattle graze, hence the peril of persons being gored (28, etc.).

Justice. *The administration of Justice was equally simple.* There were no gaols, and the act of requital for wrongdoing had to be automatic and summary. Ordinarily, the rule was one of strict retaliation: "Eye for eye, tooth for tooth, hand for hand, foot for foot, burning for burning, wound for wound, stripe for stripe" (24, 25; Lev. xxiv. 20; Deut. xix. 21). This principle lay at the basis of Solon's administration of Athens, and of the Twelve Tables of early Roman law; and there was a *primâ facie* appearance of justice in it which captivated simple people; but in practice it is uneven in its operation; and it would be obviously unwise for the sake of early society, where man was constantly engaged in fighting for his own, to increase the numbers of mutilated bodies, therefore the principle of preliminary compensation crept in and was legalised (19, 22, 30, 32). But a clear distinction was drawn between the sudden act of passion—"stone or fist," and the premeditated act of revenge— "lying in wait" (14, 18).

The Office of the Göel. In the early stages of human society the avenging of crime and wrong is the allotted work of the göel. To avenge the death of a kinsman was more than a right—it was a religious duty; and so strongly was this idea entertained that, long after the State had interfered, and made murder a matter of public prosecution, the nearest kinsman was imperatively bound to set the State procedure in motion. There is a trace of this in verse 13, which doubtless referred, in the first instance, to a part of the camp, known as the Sanctuary, where a manslayer might find respite until it was determined whether he was guilty of homicide or murder. This arrangement became afterwards extended into the appointment of six refuge-cities. But side by side with this ancient institution, judges were evidently assuming responsibility on the part, and in the name, of society (22).

The Honour of Womanhood. A new conception of *the honour of womanhood* also begins to appear. The national conscience is instructed, not on the respect due to a princess or priestess, such as Deborah or Miriam, but to a humble and unknown female slave, i.e. of a poor girl sold by her parents into slavery. She would be placed in a position—which is of course in this Christian age unthinkable—of a kind of secondary wife. Our Lord says that this custom was permitted by the Mosaic Code, because of the hardness of the uninstructed heart (Matt. xix. 8); but He swept away these concessions, by the one authoritative sentence which reinstituted the primal law of marriage,—"Have ye not read, that He which made them at the beginning made them male and female?" i.e. the one man for the one woman, and the one woman for the one man, the only admissible exception being the commission of the one act which dissolves faith. God's way is not catastrophic, but by the gradual method of education and evolution, as the eye is prepared by the gradual dawn of daylight to endure the full glare of noon. But the Mosaic legislation, as set down here, was as immensely in advance of anything known in the world of that time as it was beneath the Christian standard. It had, however, the certain promise of woman's complete emancipation, because for the first time it conferred rights on the poor girlslave (7–11).

Slavery. The legislation before us deals largely with the question of *slavery*, which was an integral part of the social economy of that age. It would have been useless to prohibit it, until conscience had become educated to a certain level. In the first approach to complete emancipation, all that was possible was to regulate the conditions of slavery, and insert in the national code principles which would ultimately render it impossible for slavery to continue. We cannot forget that, not so very long ago, many members of the Christian Church justified slavery as the best condition for child-races, and that men in high standing as Christians held slaves. The Scriptures, however, have made the system impossible, not only because of the evils which are almost inevitable, but because of its fundamental doctrine, that all men were created by one God, redeemed by one precious blood, and intended to form one great family.

The Message to Ourselves. As we study these ancient laws, it becomes us to ask ourselves whether this Mosaic Code contained in the Book of the Covenant may not have a message for ourselves, in regard to our relations to our fellows, and especially to God.

Consideration for Servants. *Our relations to servants and others* must always be considered in the light of our attitude towards God. The *maidservant*—not now, thank God, a slave—but able to leave the household if she will, should always be kindly considered. She too is the centre of a little world, far away in some Lowland village or Highland glen, and the post bring no news that fills her soul with joy or sorrow, but which she must probably keep to herself. She has her life to live which is as much to her as yours and mine. Without undue interference, the mistress is somewhat responsible to some distant mother for the company she keeps and the way she spends her leisure. Do not forget that she sometimes needs a little colour in the drab of the kitchen-life. Put her in touch with a Bible-class or church, if possible. For her sake, if for no other, maintain the family-altar. At your hands, the soul may be required, though you have only such rights in these matters as love and courtesy concede. But if you ignore her and such as she is, take care lest the temptations that master sons, and break mother's hearts, do not come back to you from her or her class.

Teach your children, and especially your sons, to honour the domestic servant, who is always at their beck and call. Not to give needless trouble, not to be unreasonable in our demands, not to be fretful, rude, passionate, and exacting, such are among the courtesies of a Christian home, and it is an invariable rule that those families are best served where the most courtesy and consideration are given to the servants. But be it remembered that it is no kindness to allow slackness, or permit rightful and necessary duties to be neglected. God Himself in His discipline of His children tempers goodness and exactitude. He comes to reckon with His servants, and does not shrink from inflicting heavy punishment on the unfaithful.

Charity in Thought and Speech. The prescriptions against sins of violence remind us that there are other ways of smiting men than with fist or stone. We remember the Psalmist's description of the assaults of his enemies: "Their words are spears and arrows, and their tongue a sharp sword." If you cannot speak kindly of people, it is better to refrain from speaking of them. Look out for the good and favourable points in the characters of those around you; and always remember that your alertness in discerning faults arises from your own liability of committing the same. In condemning them you betray yourself. It may be necessary to warn people against them; but always tell God first what you are going to do, and ask Him to show exactly the time and place. Never do it casually, or be betrayed into it. Whenever you go into society, or are thrown with your confidential friend, offer the prayer: "Set a watch, O God, over my mouth, guard the door of my lips."

Sins of the Tongue. And if there has been undue licence in speech, to the detriment of any absent one, there should always be compensation, in the confession of the wrong done, or where that is not possible, in the reparation for the wrong by an additional meed of praise. Be exacting and rigorous with yourself in these matters. "Pay for the loss of his time, character, or prestige, and cause him to be thoroughly healed!"

—Their Punishment. There is a profound truth contained in the ancient *Lex Talionis*, "An eye for an eye," etc. Every thought to which we give expression affects not only the person against whom we speak, but ourselves. Indeed, if a person stands fast in truth and love, we cannot harm him; our darts fall blunted to the ground. He is hidden as in a pavilion from the strife of tongues. No weapon that is formed against him can prosper, and every tongue that rises in judgment against him is condemned. If only God's servants, when they are maligned, would keep still and refrain from going hither and thither to explain and vindicate themselves, they would find God bringing forth their righteousness as the light and their judgment as the noon-day. But cruel and unkind statements come back to the person from whom they have emanated like the Australian boomerang. "Curses," the proverb says, "come home to roost." Every evil, malicious, and untrue word leaves its poison in the soul from which it emanates, and we reap the result of our idle words, until our own soul is sick and faint and poisoned. How little do the backbiters and gossipmongers of drawing-room or kitchen realise this!

Parents and Children. Of the honour and reverence due to parents we need hardly speak. Obedience is the law of a happy childhood; but it gradually passes into fellowship which, in a sense, is equally commanding. Parents do wisely, when they assist the process. They lose nothing by becoming the close companions and loving advisers of their grown sons and daughters. There is hardly anything more lovely than the mutual confidences of mothers and sons, of fathers and daughters: but it is a mistake when the parent forgets that children of twenty-five or thirty require different handling from that which was perfectly wise and right in their early teens: yet mothers have been known to order their grown daughters about as if they were children. This brings irritation and misunderstanding into what might be a very happy relationship.

Love the Fulfilling of the Law. That we are liable for any hurt which may be indirectly caused by us is an axiom which hardly needs to be emphasised; but as we turn from these injunctions, let us remember that Love is the fulfilling of the Law, and that in the Love of the Spirit we shall not only avoid these wrongs, but think on and practise whatsoever things are just, pure, lovable, and of good repute. We shall take care to practise not the negative, but the positive sides of the divine requirements. We shall realise that the Love of God begets a love for man which is infinitely sensitive.

The Case of the Bondman. We cannot turn from the remarkable paragraph with which this section opens, without recalling the use made of it in subsequent Scriptures. The seasons have been unkindly and the harvests have failed. The locust or mildew, the Nab or landlord have been too much for the small landowner. Vintage and olive-yield have been disappointing and disastrous. Bankruptcy can no longer be evaded. From the pressure of creditors, and the cries of hungry children, the farmer, distracted and hopeless, finally concludes to approach some rich neighbouring landowner, whose estate covers many far-extending acres. He obtains an interview, states his case, and asks for help. It is finally arranged that for the next six years he shall make over his land to be held by the great landlord, whilst his family and he become part of his household to be provided and cared for. Debts and creditors are referred for payment to his patron, and all legitimate requirements are met. The husband and father gladly gives his service to secure so great returns, always realising that in the seventh year he may go forth free. Even though at first the necessity to do another's behests might seem irksome, the consciousness of relief and security was prepondering and immense. The husband and father would look into the faces of his dear ones, filling out with happier conditions and regular nourishment, and be abundantly repaid. At the expiration of the six years, the small farmer might again seek an interview with the man who had befriended him, and explain his profound unwillingness to assume the anxieties and risks of his former life. He would propose that the arrangement which had worked out so happily should become a permanent one. On this, the magistrates would be called in, and whilst in their presence the petitioner repeated the prescribed formula, "I love my master, I will not go out free," his ear would be bored through with an awl to the doorpost of his master's house, making him his servant for ever.

The Psalmist's Application and Our Own. It is to this that the Psalmist refers in Psalm xl. 6, when he says: "Sacrifice and offering

Thou hast no delight in; mine ears hast Thou opened [marg. digged, or pierced for me]. . . . I delight to do Thy will, O my God,"— words the significance of which have a sublime exposition in Heb. x. 5–7. In our service of our Lord, these same words may be applied to us, as were so true of Him. We may serve Him under compulsion and constraint, because we see no other alternative, or we may serve Him with the devotion born of love. Oh for the latter! Oh to be constrained by the love of Christ! Oh to be able to say, deeply and gladly, "Bore my ear to Thy cross, dear Lord, and tie my wayward nature so closely to Thyself, that I may never be able to untie the knots. So I shall be for Thee, as Thou for the Father." And if you would know how the Lord Christ will treat you, His willing slave, read carefully the injunctions laid down for masters in Scripture, and remember that He will fulfil all those for you, and more also. Read, mark, learn, and inwardly digest Lev. xxv. 35–39; Col. iv. 1; and the Epistle to Philemon.

THE RIGHTS OF PROPERTY

Exodus 21:33-36;22:1-15

33. And if a man shall open a pit, or if a man shall dig a pit, and not cover it, and an ox or an ass fall therein;

34. The owner of the pit shall make *it* good, *and* give money unto the owner of them; and the dead *beast* shall be his.

35. And if one man's ox hurt another's, that he die; then they shall sell the live ox, and divide the money of it; and the dead *ox* also they shall divide.

36. Or if it be known that the ox hath used to push in time past, and his owner hath not kept him in; he shall surely pay ox for ox; and the dead shall be his own.

1. If a man shall steal an ox, or a sheep, and kill it, or sell it; he shall restore five oxen for an ox, and four sheep for a sheep.

2. If a thief be found breaking up, and be smitten that he die, *there shall* no blood *be shed* for him.

3. If the sun be risen upon him, *there shall be* blood *shed* for him; *for* he should make full restitution; if he have nothing, then he shall be sold for his theft.

4. If the theft be certainly found in his hand alive, whether it be ox, or ass, or sheep; he shall restore double.

5. If a man shall cause a field or vineyard to be eaten, and shall put in his beast, and shall feed in another man's field; of the best of his own field, and of the best of his own vineyard, shall he make restitution.

6. If fire break out, and catch in thorns, so that the stacks of corn, or the standing corn, or the field, be consumed *therewith*; he that kindled the fire shall surely make restitution.

7. If a man shall deliver unto his neighbour money or stuff to keep, and it be stolen out of the man's house; if the thief be found, let him pay double.

8. If the thief be not found, then the master of the house shall be brought unto the judges, *to see* whether he have put his hand unto his neighbour's goods.

9. For all manner of trespass, *whether it be* for ox, for ass, for sheep, for raiment, *or* for any manner of lost thing, which *another* challengeth to be his, the cause of both parties shall come before the judges; *and* whom the judges shall condemn, he shall pay double unto his neighbour.

10. If a man deliver unto his neighbour an ass, or an ox, or a sheep, or any beast, to keep; and it die, or be hurt, or driven away, no man seeing *it*:

11. *Then* shall an oath of the Lord be between them both, that he hath not put his hand unto his neighbour's goods; and the owner of it shall accept *thereof*, and he shall not make *it* good.

12. And if it be stolen from him, he shall make restitution unto the owner thereof.

13. If it be torn in pieces, *then* let them bring it *for* witness, *and* he shall not make good that which was torn.

14. And if a man borrow *ought* of his neighbour, and it be hurt, or die, the owner thereof *being* not with it, he shall surely make *it* good.

15. *But* if the owner thereof *be* with it, he shall not make *it* good: if it *be* an hired *thing*, it came for his hire.

THE RIGHTS OF PROPERTY

Exodus 21:33-36;22:1-15

The Code and Christian Morals Compared. We are apt to take our rectitude and goodness as a matter of course, and it will be good to linger for a little over these paragraphs, with the view of inquiring if our Christian morality is as quick and sensitive as that of this ancient code.

—**As to Careless Neglect** (vers. 33–36). The *first* case is that of water-cisterns, such as are very frequent in countries like Palestine, and are usually covered by a flat stone or a number of planks. To obtain water, it is necessary to uncover them; and it would be a gross act of carelessness to leave them so, lest animals, accustomed to come to them for water, should, on some hot and thirsty day, try to help themselves to drink, and should fall through the aperture. Whether the pit were full, or empty, or in process of construction, this would kill them. Obviously any person guilty of such gross carelessness would be held liable for the loss incurred. And the Christian must be equally careful lest any should suffer from his neglect.

If through his neglect to turn off a water-tap or a gas-jet, the property of an hotel-keeper is damaged, he must certainly own up to his neglect, and make good the damage. If his motor-car destroys a lamb or a fowl, he will certainly stay to make compensation. The Christian owner of property will see to it that the drains of his humblest cottage are in good condition, lest any harm accrue to a tenant's child; and if, through want of such care, a child should be ill and die of typhoid, he will unhesitatingly bear all the cost that can be fairly traced to his neglect. The Christian traveller will take care to leave the railway-carriage, hotel chamber, and other similar public resort in as good a condition as he would expect and desire, were he to be following next after himself. He will leave no pits behind him for the entangling of his fellow-travellers, because either he did not pay his accounts, or was discourteous and niggardly.

—As to Possible Injury or Annoyance. The *second* case is that of an ox that had been known to be of a vicious disposition. The owner was bound to keep him in, or pay for the damage caused to another's property: and the Christian neighbour will not keep dogs that worry their neighbours' sheep or frighten their children; and will not disturb the quiet peace of others by the incessant noise of a gramophone or the practice of some strident instrument of brass.

—As to the Law of Theft (xxii. 1–4). The general principle was that theft should be punished by a fine. There was moral fitness in this, since a man paid for his raid on his neighbour's property by the loss of his own. Ordinarily, he was to restore to the robbed man double what he had taken; but if his actions gave evidence of a malignant and deep-seated purpose, he would have to pay fourfold for a sheep and fivefold for an ox. If unable to pay, he might be sold as a slave to make good the loss he had caused. The burglar, who attempted a house by night, might be killed in self-defence, but not if his attempt were made by day.

We should repudiate the charge of theft in this literal sense. But have we never stolen a fragment of our neighbour's good name, reputation, and standing? Have we never diverted to ourselves some of the love, respect, and credit that were due to him? Have we never laid claim to his ideas, thoughts, speeches, sermons, which we have passed off, *literatim et verbatim* as our own? If so, let him that stole, steal no more, but rather let him labour, working with his own hands or brain the thing that is good.

—As to the Law of Trespass (vers. 5, 6). Next to theft, wanton damage of another's property is very reprehensible. The Israelite might turn his cattle into his neighbour's fields; or, either wantonly or accidentally, kindle a conflagration that would consume his corn, whether standing waiting for the sickle or already bound in shocks. Of course he must make the loss good. If we are animated by the Love of God, we shall take as much care of our neighbour's interests as of our own. We shall consider whether we cannot build our house so as not unnecessarily to spoil his view. We shall not allow our love of game to hurt his poultry-yards or crops; we shall abstain from all intrusive and obnoxious acts. "Love worketh no ill to his neighbour." Christian men should look not only on their own things, but also on the things of others.

Above all, we must remember that the tongue is a fire, set on fire by Gehenna, and capable of setting on fire a whole neighbourhood. Ah, how much damage professedly Christian people have done by starting a fire "in the thorns!" Have we done so? Then let us spend the rest of our life in making amends, by disabusing the minds of those whom we have poisoned, and by humble apologies to the individual we have maligned.

—As to the Law of Deposits (vers. 7–13). We are reminded of the sacred character of trusts, whether they consist of a secret entrusted on the pledge of inviolable confidence; or of a trusteeship of property made by a dying man to his choice friends for administration to widow or orphans and others; or of a wardship of young and immature children; or of manuscripts that need to be edited and published; or of funds given for investment. Few are there that have not come under one or other of these divisions! And it is well to observe the provisions here implied, and which may be summarised thus:

(*a*) In the case of loss which is not chargeable on the neglect of the trustee, the trustee is not liable.

(*b*) But if he take insufficient care, and damage ensues, he is bound to make good the injury caused by his neglect.

(*c*) If he should embezzle his trust, single restitution must be followed by condign punishment.

(*d*) In doubtful cases, the solemn assurance of the trustee that he had appropriated nothing should be accepted. The cause should come "before God," which may refer to the Court of Justice, where the trustee would be put on his oath.

Our Responsibility. As we entrust our souls to God, and expect Him to help that which we commit to Him, so we should accept no trust, whether of a secret, a child, a sum of money, or an office, without due deliberation. But when once undertaken, we should leave no *i* undotted and no *t* uncrossed, in our determined effort to fulfil the trust and confidence reposed in us.

This should especially be the case in the acceptance of public positions. Too many are absolutely reckless of the responsibility involved in giving their names to societies and institutions, or in assuming the honour associated with public functions, without fulfilling the duties that are involved. If you cannot honestly fulfil some public office, refuse to be pressed into it. If you cannot keep in touch with a society, have your name removed from the list of vice-presidents. If you will not inspect the report and balance-sheet, you are not justified in posing as sponsor, and gaining popularity or notoriety under false pretences. You are false to the trust which the public, unable to investigate for themselves, repose in you.

—**As to Borrowing** (vers. 14, 15). Not all of us are careful as to the duty of restoring borrowed articles with as little delay as possible, and in as good a condition as that in which we received them. How many books are there in your library that have been there an unconscionable time, so much that probably the owner has forgotten that they are in your possession! How many umbrellas, waterproofs, rugs, and other articles are being worn out by the borrowers until they are not worth returning! How much money we have borrowed for small expenses, which we have failed to repay! We forget that there is a text in the Psalms which says that it is *"the wicked"* who borroweth and payeth not again. We might object to applying that epithet to our borrowing friends, or having it applied to ourselves; but certainly the habit is wanting in the highest sanctions; and it would be very wholesome for us all if we would go through our household wares, discover all the books and other goods which are not ours, and return them to our friends with humble apologies. If we arrive at the altar, says our Lord, and remember that our brother has aught against us, we must leave our duty to God, in order first to address ourselves to performing our obligations to man.

The Importance of Detail. The things enumerated in this chapter may seem too small to mention; but after all nothing is small that touches character. The Master said that no jot or tittle should pass from the Law till all was fulfilled, and the fulfilment was to emanate from love and loyalty to Himself. Are we aware of the exactitude and minuteness of the demands of the Holy Spirit, His Spirit, the Spirit of Love? His word divides between joints and marrow. He notices cups of cold water, one idle word, one wayward look. The rocking-stones of great decisions impinge on very small points of rest. A whisper may start an avalanche. An aperture the size of a child's hand may wreck a dyke. We are not saved by attention to these minutiae, but if we are saved we shall not only be careful of the weightier matter of the law, but of straining out the gnats from the wine.

Miscellaneous Laws

Exodus 22:16-31;23:1-19

16. And if a man entice a maid that is not betrothed, and lie with her, he shall surely endow her to be his wife.

17. If her father utterly refuse to give her unto him, he shall pay money according to the dowry of virgins.

18. Thou shalt not suffer a witch to live.

19. Whosoever lieth with a beast shall surely be put to death.

20. He that sacrificeth unto *any* god, save unto the LORD only, he shall be utterly destroyed.

21. Thou shalt neither vex a stranger, nor oppress him: for ye were strangers in the land of Egypt.

22. Ye shall not afflict any widow, or fatherless child.

23. If thou afflict them in any wise, and they cry at all unto me, I will surely hear their cry;

24. And my wrath shall wax hot, and I will kill you with the sword; and your wives shall be widows, and your children fatherless.

25. If thou lend money to *any of* my people *that is* poor by thee, thou shalt not be to him as an usurer, neither shalt thou lay upon him usury.

26. If thou at all take thy neighbours' raiment to pledge, thou shalt deliver it unto him by that the sun goeth down:

27. For that *is* his covering only, it *is* his raiment for his skin: wherein shall he sleep? and it shall come to pass, when he crieth unto me, that I will hear; for I *am* gracious.

28. Thou shalt not revile the gods, nor curse the ruler of thy people.

29. Thou shalt not delay *to offer* the first of thy ripe fruits, and of thy liquors: the first-born of thy sons shalt thou give unto me.

30. Likewise shalt thou do with thine oxen, *and* with thy sheep: seven days it shall be with his dam; on the eighth day thou shalt give it me.

31. And ye shall be holy men unto me: neither shall ye eat *any* flesh *that is* torn of beasts in the field; ye shall cast it to the dogs.

1. Thou shalt not raise a false report: put not thine hand with the wicked to be an unrighteous witness.

2. Thou shalt not follow a multitude to *do* evil; neither shalt thou speak in a cause to decline after many to wrest *judgment*:

3. Neither shalt thou countenance a poor man in his cause.

4. If thou meet thine enemy's ox or his ass going astray, thou shalt surely bring it back to him again.

5. If thou see the ass of him that hateth thee lying under his burden, and wouldest forbear to help him, thou shalt surely help with him.

6. Thou shalt not wrest the judgment of thy poor in his cause.

7. Keep thee far from a false matter; and the innocent and righteous slay thou not: for I will not justify the wicked.

8. And thou shalt take no gift: for the gift blindeth the wise, and perverteth the words of the righteous.

9. Also thou shalt not oppress a stranger: for ye know the heart of a stranger, seeing ye were strangers in the land of Egypt.

10. And six years thou shalt sow thy land, and shalt gather in the fruits thereof:

11. But the seventh *year* thou shalt let it rest and lie still; that the poor of thy people may eat: and what they leave the beasts of the field shall eat. In like manner thou shalt deal with thy vineyard, *and* with thy oliveyard.

12. Six days thou shalt do thy work, and on the seventh day thou shalt rest: that thine ox and thine ass may rest, and the son of thy handmaid, and the stranger, may be refreshed.

13. And in all *things* that I have said unto you be circumspect: and make no mention of the name of other gods, neither let it be heard out of thy mouth.

14. Three times thou shalt keep a feast unto me in the year.

15. Thou shalt keep the feast of unleavened bread: (thou shalt eat unleavened bread seven days, as I commanded thee, in the time appointed of the month Abib; for in it thou camest out from Egypt: and none shall appear before me empty:)

16. And the feast of harvest, the first-fruits of thy labours, which thou hast sown in the field: and the feast of ingathering, *which is* in the end of the year, when thou hast gathered in thy labours out of the field.

17. Three times in the year all thy males shall appear before the Lord God.

18. Thou shalt not offer the blood of my sacrifice with leavened bread; neither shall the fat of my sacrifice remain until the morning.

19. The first of the first-fruits of thy land thou shalt bring into the house of the Lord thy God. Thou shalt not seeth a kid in his mother's milk.

MISCELLANEOUS LAWS

Exodus 22:16-31;23:1-19

It has been observed[1] that in this remaining section of the Book of the Covenant there is a want of method and logical sequence which makes it extremely difficult to arrange its precepts in a manner which would commend itself to the modern mind.

The Care of the Wards of Jehovah. We are, first, attracted by those who may be fairly described as *the wards or clients of Jehovah.*

—The Wronged Maid. Foremost among these is *the young girl* who has been cruelly wronged (vers. 16, 17). At any rate she shall be secure of an honourable marriage, either by her seducer, or by the payment of a worthy dowry, enabling her to contract a worthy match, notwithstanding the indignity she has suffered. The religious person, man or woman, is encouraged, therefore, to espouse the cause of girls like this, who in every age of the world have been induced to fling away the choice jewel of their purity.

The Stranger. Next in order is *the stranger* (ver. 21). The Hebrews were prone to forget that terrible Egyptian experience, when their fathers were strangers in the land of Egypt; and the stranger in their midst was in danger of being imposed upon, as elsewhere and always. Without friends, imperfectly acquainted with the customs and language of the people among whom he is stranded, compelled to trust himself to those who lie in wait for the unsophisticated and simple, the stranger is much to be pitied, and how often he has been accounted an easy and valuable prey! That he is so often referred to in the Pentateuch is not only a distinctive characteristic of its mild and noble spirit, but gives an incentive to ourselves. The alien who had been attracted to shelter, as Ruth did, beneath the wing of the God of Israel, was to share the Sabbath rest (xx. 10), might bring his offerings to the Tabernacle door (Lev. xvii. 8, 9), and was

[1] See *Pulpit Commentary on Exodus*, which has supplied several valuable suggestions for this chapter.

even assured of the love of God (Deut. x. 18, 19). So far, therefore, from vexing, the Israelites were bidden to love them.

—**Our Duty.** Ah! what blessing might accrue to the whole world if the Christian churches, through their members and adherents in the great centres of Christian civilisation, on either side of the Atlantic, could give a worthier welcome to the students that pour into them from all parts of the world to study in their universities, hospitals, and law courts! Instead of leaving our shores, for Burmah, India, China, or Japan, with a knowledge of our science, but contempt for our religion, how much might be done to attach them not only to ourselves but to the religion of Jesus Christ!

The Widow and the Fatherless. Next come *the Widow and the Fatherless* (vers. 22–24). The presence of this injunction on the statute-book furnishes melancholy evidence that these helpless ones, whose pitiful care is surely sad enough to melt hearts of stone, were not exempt from heartless cruelty and oppression. It is a very beautiful testimony, however, to the unique character of this legislation, that it so frequently emphasises Jehovah's solicitude for such. Throughout the Scriptures, the same spirit reveals itself. The widow and fatherless ate the tithe of the yearly produce (Deut. xiv. 29), and received their share in the rejoicings of the great feasts (xvi. 11–14). The widow's raiment might not be taken in pledge (xxiv. 17); and the gleanings of the harvest and the vintage were viewed as her perquisite (xxiv. 19–21). God sent Elijah to a widow-woman, beyond the precincts of Israel, that she should share in the provision prepared for His servant; and declared Himself to be the Father of the fatherless and Judge of the widow. The Saviour was urged by the widow's tears at Nain to recover her son to life and pure religion and undefiled before God the Father was declared by James to have this as its distinguishing note, that the widow is visited in her affliction. This is as dear to God as the unspotted purity of the holy soul. It is hardly necessary to inculcate on the Christian Church her duty to the widow. From the earliest days her desolate lot has engaged special solicitude (1 Tim. v. 3–9, 16). And let any widow who may read these words take comfort from the assurance given here, that her cry will *surely* bring about Divine interposition on her behalf (ver. 23).

—**The Poor.** *The Poor* also are specially mentioned (vers. 25–27). The reason of God's care for them is distinctively stated—"For I am gracious." Can Jesus Christ forget that His mother, when she presented Him in the Temple, could only bring two doves, because unable to afford more—this being in advance of the gifts of the Wise Men? The poor have only to cry, and He will hear. In the Israelite Commonwealth, not only were their richer brethren forbidden to make loans to them on interest, but they were expressly commanded to lend to them without (Deut. xv. 7–10). Those who had served as household slaves to extinguish their indebtedness, were to be dismissed full-handed (vers. 13, 14). The poor labourer's garment, needed to envelop him in its warm folds by night, was to be restored to him at the end of the day, on the morning of which he had pledged it for tools or food. He was not to have the misery of a sleepless night in addition to his other anxieties and privations. Do we sufficiently consider those homeless wanderers who may be spending the night in the streets whilst we are snug within our curtains? Not that it is good to give indiscriminate charity, or to make the way of the spendthrift and wrongdoer easy; but there are homeless ones who cannot be classed with these—especially women and children. Christians should inform themselves in Social Science and take part in movements for Social Reform. Radical and far-reaching schemes, dealing with modern conditions, are more urgently required than doles of charity. They cost more thought and take longer to evolve; but the result is more merciful and permanent. Poverty is due in its widest and largest aspects, not to wrongdoing, but to the preponderance of wealth in the hands of the few, instead of being evenly spread over the many. The goal of social reconstruction is that each human life should have a sufficiency of the great primal gifts of the Creator for its development and the realisation of its native possibilities.

—**Mercy to Dumb Animals.** But the kine, the sheep, and the goats, which had just given birth to their first-born, came equally under the thoughtful care of the great Lawgiver, who ordained that, for a week at least, the mother should have the pleasure and relief of suckling her offspring (xxii. 30). Thrice the Hebrews were forbidden to seethe a kid in its mother's milk (xxiii. 19; xxxiv. 26; and Deut. xiv. 21), probably to inculcate a tender appreciation of the natural order, and of the relation subsisting between the mother and her offspring. It was against nature to make the mother an accomplice in the death of her child. The precept is capable of wide application. Would that all mothers were equally careful for their children!

The Stringency of this Legislation. *The Stringency of this Legislation* is apparent in the enumeration of crimes which were visited by the death-sentence in vers. 18, 19, 20. It was also afterwards affixed to the sin named in ver. 28 (see Lev. xxiv. 16). Much discussion has been aroused by the sentence here passed on witches and witchcraft, which led to much cruelty in the Middle Ages, and immediately after the Reformation. Large numbers of innocent women were burned or hanged on the merest suspicion of the black arts, but certainly we have gone to the other extreme in the licence we give to crystal-gazers, to those who profess to read the future from the palm, or to summon spirits at their will. Beyond doubt, as the monuments prove, the Egyptians practised the use of the *planchette*; and every method was adopted by Moses to stamp out from the Hebrew race practices which invariably draw off the soul from the worship and service of God.

Our Duty. What have we to do with demons, we, who have first-hand rights to enter into the immediate presence of the Lord of all principality and power? When I accept the hospitality of a wealthy friend, who has troops of servants at his disposal, his welcome does not confer on me the right to command his servants. If I require their special assistance, it is a matter of honour and etiquette alike to request him to bid them help me. Whenever a soul becomes a member of the divine household, it has to deal not directly with the departed, the angels, or demons, but always with the Mediatorship of Christ. If *He* chooses to transmit a message to the beloved who have gone to be with Him, or to commission a ministering Angel to help us, it is for Him absolutely and only to take the initiative, and to do as He will among the armies of Heaven and the inhabitants of the earth. "*He* is the Head of all Principality and Power."

The Administration of Justice. *The provisions for the administration of justice are very precise* (xxiii. 1–9). They affect the witnesses, the judges, and the accuser or plaintiff. *Witnesses* are warned against inventing an untrue tale, or circulating one (vers. 1, 2). *Judges* are warned against being affected by the voice of the multitude, as Pilate was. They are not to be moved by the outcry of the mob, or the venom of a partizan press. They are not to be biased by sentimentality on behalf of the poor, or partiality for the rich. They are specially charged to see to it that the innocent should not suffer, that the wicked should not escape, that foreigners should get justice; whilst a bribe was not to be entertained for a moment (vers. 2, 3,

6–9). *Accusers* also are specially exhorted not to slay the innocent by making a false charge; which, even though it were disproved, might blight the defendant's name, soil his character, and shorten his days (ver. 7).

What a tender interpolation is that of verses 4, 5, with respect to the ox or ass of an enemy! We can almost see the pious Israelite meeting the wandering ox of a man who had done his worst to injure him, and leading it back to the homestead, just in time to meet the owner coming in search; or finding his enemy tugging in vain to get his fallen ass on his feet, and hastening to lift it. Their joint-act could hardly fail to bring the two men together and soften asperities. It was not Moses who said that the Hebrews were to hate their enemies. It was an unwarrantable conclusion which the rabbis founded upon his legislation. Here and in other places the glory of the coming dispensation had begun to shine on the jewels of the ancient breastplate of judgment.

The Feasts to be Observed. The Code closes with a *specification of the Religious Festivals which were to be observed by the people.* When they had attained to the goal of their long pilgrimage, and were settled in the good land beyond the Jordan, they were enjoined to allow the land to rest on each seventh year. In Egypt, where the soil was continually replenished by the overflow of the mighty Nile, the land could yield crop after crop without exhaustion; but in Canaan, where there was no such natural provision, and where the science of the rotation of crops and of artificial manuring was unknown, the land must have become prematurely exhausted, save for some such provision as this. Only by lying fallow through the septennial year could it retain its fertility as a land of corn and wine, of vineyards and oil-olive. The farmer learnt the necessity of care and forethought; the poor, who are specially mentioned, were allowed to help themselves to what grew of itself, as to the wild produce of woods and hedgerows; whilst the people generally had opportunity for thought and prayer, for religious exercises, and for domestic and social pleasure. It is not improbable also that in this year the festivals at the Tabernacle were prolonged for the solemn reading of the Law in the ears of all the people, as was the case in the days of Nehemiah (Deut. xxxi. 10, 11; Neh. viii. 1–15). From the reference in 2 Chron. xxxvi. 21 it would appear that this holy and wise arrangement had not been acted on; but for us how great a lesson is taught by the suggestion of this provision, followed as it is by that of the

Sabbath-rest! The question is whether the irreligion of our time may not be directly traceable to the unbroken drive and rush in which the modern world is living. We were not meant to work incessantly either at business or pleasure-taking. Long quiet days are necessary for the bliss of the family, the cultivation of the religious life, and for the growth of the soul in wisdom and strength. Otherwise we cannot be holy men unto God (xxii. 31).

Thrice each year the males were required to appear before God, and none was to appear before Him empty. All ancient religions had their festivals; and it is well that the children of God should maintain great convocations and conventions, when they feel the pulse of a great multitude engaged in praise, and prayer, and consecration. Heaven itself owes much of its delight to the great multitude, which no man can number, and to the vast orchestra of ten thousand times ten thousand voices. *The Feast of Unleavened Bread* fell in the early spring and commemorated the Exodus. *The Feast of Harvest* (or weeks) followed fifty days afterwards and commemorated the Giving of the Law; it was a peculiarly joyful occasion (Deut. xvi. 9–11), and for us is associated with the marvels of Acts ii. *The Feast of Ingathering* (or Tabernacles) began in the early part of October, when the olives had been gathered and the vintage was completed. The demand for this thrice-repeated visit to a common meeting-place was not tiresome, because Palestine was not bigger than Wales; and there was no better way of maintaining the Unity of the Nation in an age when there were no posts, telegraphs, telephones or daily Press.

Covenant and Character. As we conclude this brief review of the legislative contents of the Book of the Covenant, all the precepts of which the people definitely promised to fulfil, we can see from the crimes which were forbidden how much of heathen idolatry and custom still clung to the chosen race, which it would take long centuries of fiery ordeal to extirpate. But in this legislation we find the beginnings of their greatness; the genesis of that wonderful development which enabled them to furnish mankind with their sacred lyrics and epics, their unexcelled theology and ethics, their Psalmists, Prophets, Apostles and Teachers, and of whom, according to the flesh, came Jesus the Christ.

We cannot do better than close these chapters by the most eloquent passage in Lord Redesdale's Introduction to Chamberlain's *Foundations of the Nineteenth Century*—"The ancient Jew was not a soldier—foreigners furnished the bodyguard of his king. He was no sailor like his cousins the Phoenicians, indeed he had a horror of the sea. He was no artist—he had to import craftsmen to build his Temple—neither was he a farmer nor merchant. What was it, then, that gave him his wonderful self-confidence, his toughness of character, which could overcome every difficulty, and triumph over other races? It was his belief in the sacred books of the law, the Thora; his faith in the promises of Jehovah; his certainty of belonging to the chosen people of God. The influence of the books of the Old Testament has been far-reaching indeed, but nowhere has it exercised more power than in the stablishing of the character of the Jew. If it means so much to the Christian, what must it not mean to him? It is his religion, the history of his race, and his individual pedigree, all in one. Nay! it is more than all that: it is the attesting document of his covenant with his God."

The Prepared Place and the Angel-Guide

Exodus 23:20-33

20. Behold, I send an Angel before thee, to keep thee in the way, and to bring thee into the place which I have prepared.

21. Beware of him, and obey his voice, provoke him not; for he will not pardon your transgressions: for my name *is* in him.

22. But if thou shalt indeed obey his voice, and do all that I speak; then I will be an enemy unto thine enemies, and an adversary unto thine adversaries.

23. For mine Angel shall go before thee, and bring thee in unto the Amorites, and the Hittites, and the Perizzites, and the Canaanites, the Hivites, and the Jebusites; and I will cut them off.

24. Thou shalt not bow down to their gods, nor serve them, nor do after their works: but thou shalt utterly overthrow them, and quite break down their images.

25. And ye shall serve the Lord your God, and he shall bless thy bread, and thy water; and I will take sickness away from the midst of thee.

26. There shall nothing cast their young, nor be barren, in thy land: the number of thy days I will fulfil.

27. I will send my fear before thee, and will destroy all the people to whom thou shalt come, and I will make all thine enemies turn their backs unto thee.

28. And I will send hornets before thee, which shall drive out the Hivite, the Canaanite, and the Hittite, from before thee.

29. I will not drive them out from before thee in one year; lest the land become desolate, and the beast of the field multiply against thee.

30. By little and little I will drive them out from before thee until thou be increased, and inherit the land.

31. And I will set thy bounds from the Red sea even unto the sea of the Philistines, and from the desert unto the river: for I will deliver the inhabitants of the land into your hand; and thou shalt drive them out before thee.

32. Thou shalt make no covenant with them, nor with their gods.

33. They shall not dwell in thy land, lest they make thee sin against me: for if thou serve their gods, it will surely be a snare unto thee.

THE PREPARED PLACE AND THE
ANGEL-GUIDE

Exodus 23:20-33

"BEHOLD, I send an Angel before thee, to keep thee in the way, and to bring thee into the place which I have prepared" (ver. 20).

The Prepared Place for the Hebrews. I. *The Prepared Place.* In the dawn of history we see the patriarchal family leaving the Euphrates Valley and making across the desert for the land of which God had spoken. "The Lord said unto Abram, Get thee out of thy country, and from thy kindred, and from thy father's house, unto a land that I will show thee. . . . So Abram departed as the Lord had spoken unto him. . . . And the Lord said unto Abram, after that Lot was separated from him, Lift up now thine eyes, and look from the place where thou art, northward, and southward, and eastward, and westward; for all the land that thou seest, to thee will I give it, and to thy seed for ever" (Gen. xii. 1; xiii. 14, 15). This promise which Jehovah made with Abraham He now confirmed to Israel for an everlasting covenant, saying, "Unto thee will I give the land of Canaan, the lot of thine inheritance."

—And for us. "Now these things happened unto them by way of example, and they were written for our admonition, upon whom the ends of the ages are come" (1 Cor. x. 11, R.V.). For the Hebrews the prepared place was "the good land beyond Jordan, that goodly mountain, and Lebanon," of which Moses spoke so pathetically; the land flowing with milk because of its pastures, and with honey because of its flowers; "the glory of all lands," because of its fountains and springs, its mountains and vales, and its impregnable fastnesses. It gleamed before the eye of the pilgrim-host as the Highland valley to that of the far-travelled emigrant returning to see the place of his birth. It behoved them from afar to press on through vicissitudes and perils, undaunted and resolute.

For the young, the prepared place seems to be success, love, and home: when the results of strenuous toil begin to be assured, and the firm land appears. Thus in the story of Creation, when chaos began to give place to order and beauty, the smile of Paradise answered to the love of the one man for the one woman.

For the saint, it is, generally speaking, the place of which the Master said, "In my Father's house are many mansions, if it were not so I would have told you, I go to prepare a place for you, and if I go and prepare a place for you, I will come again, and receive you unto myself."

In that Land We shall be Perfected. The attractiveness of the fair land of Heaven arises from three anticipations. (1) *We shall be perfected.* There is not one of us that is not weary of the constant fret of the inward conflict. If only we could realise our ideals, if only we were always what we are in our best moments, if only the will were never uncrowned, if only the throne of conscience were never upturned. Our consciousness of God's presence is so fitful and the springs of eternity so intermittent. But there the vision of our Lord will be unimpaired. We shall see Him, and be like Him. We shall be perfectly good, desiring and realising only the best. Our whole being will be responsive to the summons of His will, and never get jangled and out of harmony. We shall hunger no more, neither thirst any more, because He will make us exceeding glad with His countenance.

—And shall be in Accord with Our Surroundings. (2) *We shall be in accord with the Nature of things.* Beauty is the remaining trace of the Creator's original workmanship. It is the hallmark of the Eternal. And when we are in perfect accord with Him, she drops her veil and makes us beside ourselves with ecstasy. Have you never walked to and fro, or sat quietly, amid some scene of natural beauty, like a summer morning on the hills, so intoxicated with the inner view of Nature that you hardly knew whether you were in the body or out? And have there not been other experiences, when the beauty of some natural law, or Divine handiwork, or moral splendour has broken freshly upon the eye of your mind, and you have been filled with speechless awe and reverence? These are rare and memorable experiences, and foreshadow the perfect unveiling of things as they are, when the mountains shall break forth into singing, and all the trees of the field shall clap their hands. Creation is now subjected to vanity. She groaneth and travaileth in pain, but when she is delivered from the bondage of corruption into the liberty of the glory of the children of God, when the sons of God are manifested, and the new heavens and earth are born, then God will destroy the face of the covering that is cast over all the peoples, and the veil that is spread over all nations, and will swallow up death in victory.

—**And shall have Fellowship with the Blessed.** (3) *We shall have uninterrupted fellowship with the blessed.* Without us they cannot be made perfect, and are awaiting us. To sit at the feet of Paul, to talk with John, to hear the story of Creation or Redemption from the lips of one of the Elders, like him who questioned about the great multitude—"one of the elders answered, saying unto me"—to greet the holy dead, to resume the long-interrupted converse, to take up the broken and snapped threads of friendship and fellowship, without the possibility of misunderstandings, heartbreaks or severance—surely all this, in the sweet society of Paradise, is enough to quicken our footsteps. Some lonely people amongst us may even thank God for their lonely hours, for *they* will realise the joys of heavenly fellowship as none else can. To no feet are grass and moss so soft as to those which have climbed long and arduously the difficult flint-paved path.

The Possibilities of the Present. Such are some of the thoughts that cluster around the place that Christ has prepared for them that love Him. But how great a mistake it is to postpone these blessings till we have passed through the Doors of the West! Many, for instance, read those inspiring words of 1 Cor. ii. 9, 10 as if they referred only and solely to the other life; they somehow miss the explanatory clause which follows immediately. Let us read the passage again: "Things which eye saw not, and ear heard not, and which entered not into the heart of man, whatsoever things God prepared for them that love Him. But unto us God revealed them through the Spirit" (R.V.). The latter words prove that they have been revealed to some, as is certainly on record; but if to some, why not to all? Why should we not receive, *here* and *now*, the Spirit which is of God, that we may know the things which are freely given to us by God? The one condition is that we should not be carnal, but spiritual, and that the eyes of our heart are enlightened that we may know. The trouble is, with most of us, that from the earliest infancy many loving friends have helped us to make use of the body, by which we know the world around us; and so few have helped us to recognise and use the Spirit, by which we come to know the Unseen, the Infinite, and the Divine.

Why Wait Till Death? It is not needful to wait for death ere we enter on the enjoyment of the good things prepared for us before the foundations of the earth were laid. Our eternity does not begin from death, but from the soul's second birth. We begin to live the religious life, which means that we live, and move, and have our being in the Presence of God, and in constant touch with Him. Forgiveness, Salvation, the New Birth are all preliminary to this. They are the vestibule to the Palace. Suddenly the soul finds that God is all and in all, that it is a child in the Divine Love, who need go no more out, and it hears the assurance which is borne in perpetually on its inner consciousness, "Son, thou art ever with me, and all that I have is Thine."

Then those three experiences, which we have located in the other world, begin to be habitual possession of the soul. In union with Christ, it comes to itself, it obtains the child's open vision of Nature, and it knows that it has become one with the Holy Catholic Church, and is admitted to the communion of saints. "All things are yours, whether Paul, or Apollos, or Cephas, or the world, or life, or death, or things present, or things to come: all are yours, and ye are Christ's; and Christ is God's" (1 Cor. iii. 22, 23).

The Angel-Guide. II. *The Angel Convoy.* This Angel was no ordinary or created angel. He is repeatedly identified with Jehovah Himself. God's name—His essential nature—is in Him. The martyr Stephen, in his defence, speaking of Moses, said, "This is He that was in the assembly in the wilderness with the angel which spake to him in the Mount Sinai" (Acts vii. 38, R.V.). Now, we know Who that Angel was, and what He said. "When the Lord saw that he turned aside to see, God called unto him out of the midst of the bush, and said, The place whereon thou standest is holy ground" (Exod. iii. 4, 5). Malachi describes Him as "the messenger of the Covenant" (Mal. iii. 1), whose way was to be prepared by John the Baptist. We can have no difficulty, therefore, in accepting the general consensus of Christian opinion, which has identified this Angel who was to help Israel in the way, and bring them to the prepared place, with Jesus Christ, the ever-blessed Son of God, to Whom is given the prerogative of pardoning or refusing to pardon sin.

—**For the Soul's Pilgrimage.** The Lord Jesus is the supreme Guide of the Soul's Pilgrimage. To abide in Him is to be saved from walking in darkness, and to have the light of life. He is the door and the way. As we yield ourselves to Him we are led into the deep things of God. But in order to appreciate Christ's guidance in "the Way"—the phrase by which Christianity was known in its earliest years (Acts ix. 2, R.V.)—we must be born of the Spirit, live in the Spirit and walk in the Spirit. The natural man lives only in the sensuous and intellectual realms. His outlook into the spiritual world is through a window of horn, or some similar almost opaque medium. The higher faculties, which the Apostle calls the eyes of the heart, must be opened before we know the hope of His calling, or the riches of the glory of His inheritance in the saints, or the exceeding greatness of His power toward them that believe. We can only know what Christ waits to unfold, as fast as and to the degree in which we increase in spiritual perception; and our spiritual faculties can only mature, as our physical faculties did, through use, i.e. through obedience.

Submission to His Control. If any man is willing and resolved to do His will, he shall know, and shall follow on to know the Lord whose advent and work are prepared as the morning. Take heed then to the Christ above you, and more especially to the Christ within you. Hearken unto His voice speaking in the Horeb-Cave of your soul. Be not rebellious against Him, for if you will indeed hearken to His voice and do all that He speaks, then you will be brought into union with God and the nature of things. The stars in their courses will fight for you. The mountains shall bring peace, and the little hills righteousness. God will be an enemy to your enemies, and an adversary to your adversaries. For Christ Himself shall go before you, and bring you in to possess those parts of your own nature which have hitherto been held by the Amorite, the Hittite, and the Perizzite, and the Canaanite, the Hivite, and the Jebusite. Those who obey Christ find Him to be as the Angel, whilst those who refuse Him discover Him to be as a hornet. God waits to bless, but if a man refuses and resists Him, He whets His sword.

Progress and Means. III. *The Royal Progress of the Soul.* The way to Canaan was infested by enemies, and the land itself was held by the nations already enumerated, but so long as Israel followed the Angel-Guide there was no power amongst them all that could resist them. The one condition was obedience—the hearkening to

His voice; and for us there is no other. Obey the voice that speaks in Scripture: obey the voice that speaks in moral intuitions: above all, obey the voice of the Good Shepherd, in the depths of the soul, of which Jesus said: "My sheep hear My voice, and I know them, and they follow Me." As we obey Him, we climb the mountain, and as we climb we see the ever-extending panorama of truth, which is a far-reaching continent, only trodden by those who are willing to go in and possess it by the obedient following of Christ.

But notice the promises which will be fulfilled in our experience. (1) *Guidance.* "Mine angel shall go before thee (ver. 23). It was superhuman guidance. He preceded them in the Pillar of Cloud and Flame, indicating the safest and directest of the desert-tracks, as no Arab or Bedäwin could; and wherever the cloud brooded the manna fell and the water flowed. The inner guidance of the Spirit of Jesus was of priceless value to Paul, as much in the paths He blocked as those He opened (Acts xvi. 6, 7, 10). And it is promised to every soul that will lay aside its own plans, and be still.

(2) *Material Blessing* (vers. 25, 26). There would be bread and water, immunity from disease, fertility of cattle, and the fulfilment of the term of life. It is not necessary to spiritualise all these, though they have their spiritual counterparts. But godliness has the promise of this life as well as of the next. It is a great word which is spoken of Abraham, when we are told that "Abraham died in a good old age, an old man, and *full.*" Surely this is what under normal conditions a child of God, who has followed the laws of Christ, may attain to—a full life, overflowing with grace and truth, strength and sweetness, and perfectly satisfied.

(3) *The Conquest of Canaan* (vers. 27, etc.). This was to be a gradual process, "little by little," but it would be sure. If the Israelites had been asked which they preferred, they would doubtless have replied, let it be done "at once." But that policy would have led to the incursion of wild animals and the deterioration of the cultivated soil, and it was better in every way for the Divine purpose to be executed with Divine deliberation. This made the conquest more thorough and lasting. It also enabled the Israelites to consolidate and organise their conquests, as they went from one point to another. "Little by little" does the work of God proceed through the individual soul. "Little by little" do the conquests of the Cross win over the world. "Little by little" is the unfolding purpose of Redemption made manifest to men and

angels. Supposing it were otherwise, and that as the result of some extraordinary outpouring of God's Spirit whole nations and continents should suddenly turn to Him, how impossible it would be for the Church to overtake, supervise, instruct, and consolidate. There would be profound peril of error creeping in, and of the wrong leaders coming to the front. It is not good for the whole responsibility of a Kingdom to be cast on a child, it is better for him to grow into it little by little. And the constant necessity for watchfulness, for discipline, and for the practice of the warrior's outfit, is a great asset. The fact that all our enemies are not suddenly extirpated forbids the sleep of the enchanted ground and the enervation of the heated plain. It is good even to have an incentive, and to be compelled to own "that we are not already perfect, but we follow on."

Needed Warnings. It should be noticed that the injunctions against idolatry are constantly repeated. We find them in verse 24 and again in verses 32 and 33. The stringency of these reiterated commands apparently could not be too strongly emphasised, because of the filthy rites with which the worship of Baal and Ashtoreth, of Chemosh and Rimmon, and of Canaanite deities was celebrated. It would be shameful even to mention the things that were done in their temples; and the emblems which the Israelites were commanded to destroy were highly indecent. Alas, that they disobeyed these commands, and that the story of the chosen people is one long series of provocations to the Angel of the Covenant. Thus the full limits of God's promise, mentioned here, were not realised until the reign of Solomon, and even then for but a little while, and it remains for yet another King to reign from the River to the end of the World. But let us take the warning seriously to heart, lest by our disobedience and failure we also limit the Holy One of Israel, and curtail the measure of influence, usefulness, and efficiency, which otherwise might be ours.

CONCENTRIC CIRCLES OF APPROACH

Exodus 24:1-18

1. And he said unto Moses, Come up unto the Lord, thou, and Aaron, Nadab, and Abihu, and seventy of the elders of Israel; and worship ye afar off.

2. And Moses alone shall come near the Lord; but they shall not come nigh; neither shall the people go up with him.

3. And Moses came and told the people all the words of the Lord, and all the judgments: and all the people answered with one voice, and said, All the words which the Lord hath said will we do.

4. And Moses wrote all the words of the Lord, and rose up early in the morning, and builded an altar under the hill, and twelve pillars, according to the twelve tribes of Israel.

5. And he sent young men of the children of Israel, which offered burnt offerings, and sacrificed peace offerings of oxen unto the Lord.

6. And Moses took half of the blood, and put *it* in basons; and half of the blood he sprinkled on the altar.

7. And he took the book of the covenant, and read in the audience of the people: and they said, All that the Lord hath said will we do, and be obedient.

8. And Moses took the blood, and sprinkled *it* on the people, and said, Behold the blood of the covenant, which the Lord hath made with you concerning all these words.

9. Then went up Moses, and Aaron, Nadab, and Abihu, and seventy of the elders of Israel;

10. And they saw the God of Israel; and *there was* under his feet as it were a paved work of a sapphire stone, and as it were the body of heaven in *his* clearness.

11. And upon the nobles of the children of Israel he laid not his hand: also they saw God, and did eat and drink.

12. And the Lord said unto Moses, Come up to me into the mount, and be there: and I will give thee tables of stone, and a law, and commandments which I have written; that thou mayest teach them.

13. And Moses rose up, and his minister Joshua; and Moses went up into the mount of God.

14. And he said unto the elders, Tarry ye here for us, until we come again unto you; and behold, Aaron and Hur *are* with you: if any man have any matters to do, let him come unto them.

15. And Moses went up into the mount, and a cloud covered the mount.

16. And the glory of the Lord abode upon mount Sinai, and the cloud covered it six days: and the seventh day he called unto Moses out of the midst of the cloud.

17. And the sight of the glory of the Lord *was* like devouring fire on the top of the mount in the eyes of the children of Israel.

18. And Moses went into the midst of the cloud, and gat him up into the mount: and Moses was in the mount forty days and forty nights.

CONCENTRIC CIRCLES OF APPROACH

Exodus 24:1-18

A Wondrous History. This is an amazing chapter with its four concentric circles of approach to the Most High; and, however true as an historical narrative, it is still more illuminating and inspiring when considered as conveying admonition and encouragement for ourselves.

It appears that Moses descended from the Mount bearing in his mind the first draft of the Book of the Covenant. With a summary of this he made the people acquainted, and on the following morning he ratified the covenant by special rites before he ascended with the elders, in harmony with the Divine Invitation, to one of the lower spurs of the mountain. He then again descended with them to the plain, where he received a further summons to ascend the mountain in company with Joshua, who was comparatively a young man at that time, though giving remarkable evidence of his sincere piety and devotion (xxxiii. 11).

The First Circle. I. *The Outer Circle formed by the Masses of the People.* They were still kept without the barriers. It is expressly said, "they shall not come near." Though they were included in the Divine purpose, they had a very unintelligent appreciation of its real significance or importance. Had they really understood either the one or other, surely the shameful scene of the worship of the golden calf would never have been enacted. When Moses first recited the conditions of the Covenant, they answered with one voice: "All the words which the Lord hath spoken will we do." But probably they were more attracted by the general suggestion of occupying the promised land than aware of the binding nature of the conditions on which the occupation was to be based.

The Blood Rite. It would appear that Moses committed the laws to writing that very night, and rose very early in the morning to ratify them with the most solemn ceremonial. From time immemorial men have bound themselves to each other by exchanging blood. There is no tie amid the Bedāwin more inviolable than this, and on this basis, though not exactly in the usual method, Moses sought to bind the people and Jehovah. An altar was built, twelve pillars were erected as a permanent memorial and young men selected from the firstborn sons of leading families, who officiated as priests until the family of Levi was set apart for that high office, offered burnt-offerings and sacrificed peace-offerings of oxen unto the Lord. It must have been a solemn scene, witnessed by a great concourse of people, who may even have climbed the mountain-slopes, other than those of Sinai, to witness it. Moses' actions were specially observed as he collected the blood in basins, sprinkling half of it on the altar, and reserving the remainder till he had read once more the enumeration of the law from the book, probably of papyrus leaves, like those which have been recently discovered in Egypt, and on the pages of which he had written the law. When, a second time, the people had cried, "All that the Lord hath spoken we will do, and be obedient," he took the blood which he had reserved, with water and scarlet wool and hyssop, and sprinkled both the book itself and all the people saying, "This is the blood of the covenant which God commanded to you-ward" (Heb. ix. 20, R.V.).

A Sacramental Union. By thus sprinkling both the altar, as representing God, and the people, who were the parties to the covenant on the other side, Moses made both parties partakers of the same blood, and so secured a kind of sacramental union. Yet within a few weeks it was trodden under foot in shameful orgies and dances, showing that however stoutly men asseverate their determination to keep their vows of consecration, even going so far as to write and sign them with their own blood, nothing will avail to keep them stedfast, short of the promise of the new covenant, in which God says: "This is the covenant that I will make with them after those days, I will put my laws on their heart, and upon their mind also will I write them, and their sins and their iniquities will I remember no more" (Heb. x. 16, 17, R.V.).

Promise but not Service. Too many professing Christians resemble these people. They are willing enough to receive all the benefits of religion, but are unchanged in heart and purpose; easily moved in this direction or that, like the waves of the sea, driven by the winds and tossed; fickle and passionate; crying "Hosanna" to-day and "Crucify" to-morrow; no real love, though much speech; quickly yielding the produce of the shallow soil, but beneath hard as adamant. They take the solemn sacrament in the morning, but have violated the solemnest sanctions of human life by night-fall. Of such the verdict of our Lord is only too true. "This people honoureth Me with their lips, but their heart is far from Me." They remind us of those who gathered round the Master during His earthly ministry, attracted by the eloquences of His teaching and the splendour of His miracles, but to whom He would not trust Himself, because He knew what was in man.

The Second Circle. II. *The next Circle was formed by the Seventy Elders, together with Aaron and his two sons.* They ascended the mountain-side, some distance beyond the barrier, at the express invitation of Jehovah. They were allowed a closer approach, but still the restriction remained—"Worship ye afar off."

The Vision. They were not allowed to come near. Israel beheld no similitude of God at the giving of the Decalogue (Deut. iv. 12, 15); but the narrative at this point suggests that these favoured men were permitted to behold some appearance of the Divine Being who had invited them for this purpose. Moses beheld the form of the Lord (Num. xii. 8), Isaiah saw the Lord sitting upon the Throne (Isa. vi. 1). For Ezekiel there was the appearance of a man upon the throne (Ezek. i. 26). What the Elders saw we cannot tell, but the mention of *feet* suggests a human form. Might not this have been an anticipation of the Incarnation? We are told that Melchizedek was made like unto the Son of God, and it may be that there are unexplored mysteries in those wonderful words of Genesis: "Let us make man in our image after our likeness!" But four interesting remarks are appended.

The Sapphire Pavement. (1) *"There was under His feet as it were a paved work of a sapphire stone."* The blue sapphire is one of the loveliest of jewels, reminding us of the deep azure of the sky, the blue of Geneva's Lake or the glacier-fissure, the bluebell and the Alpine flowers. Depth, distance, serenity, calm, gentleness, and peace shine in unrivalled beauty through the sapphire rays, as though pouring from exhaustless fountains. The evident intention was to set forth the milder glories of God's character, as reconciled with Israel, in contrast to those more terrible manifestations which accompanied the giving of the Law, and had filled the hearts of the people with awe. As we think of that sapphire work we are inclined to exclaim, Oh, the depth, not only of the wisdom, but of the Love of God! Above us is *Love in Excelsis*; beneath us is *Love in Profundis*; within are Love and Peace as an ocean; behind us is Love from everlasting; before us is Love to the uttermost. It besets us behind and before. It is about our path and our lying-down. It provided our mother's breast at birth, and will provide the soft bosom of mother-earth for our resting-place, when our spirit will have been received into the Father's Home, which Love hath gone to prepare. And in the meanwhile it paves our way thither with sapphire.

The Unclouded Splendour. (2) *"As it were the body of Heaven in its clearness."* Did not this represent God's transcendence, His superiority to the thunder-storms that darken the lower skies, His independence of the clouds, which at the best form His temporary vesture and hiding-place? The terrors of the Law were laid aside; here was unclouded clearness, light, love, and forgiving grace. All their sin was removed so far as the east is from the west, and blotted out as a thick cloud. Too often our vision of God is dimmed and beclouded by the earth-born clouds which originate in the misconceptions and sins of our own hearts. If only we were more careful to guard against these, and to keep an open firmament between the waters above and the waters below, dividing the Heavenly from the Earthly, and the spiritual from the sensual, how much more often would we dwell under the very heaven for clearness!

The Security of the Nobles. (3) *"Upon the nobles of the children of Israel He laid not His hand."* This sentence bespeaks some surprise. Evidently they had ascended with considerable alarm, and their families were awaiting their return with some anxiety. It is clear that if they had never returned nobody in the camp would have been very much surprised. We are always thinking that God will lay His hand on us. We take our pleasures sadly, because afraid to seem too happy. We love our dear ones with a nervous dread, lest if we love them too well they will be snatched from us. We speak of thunder and lightning and earthquake as "the act of God." We hardly dare think of a spell of unmitigated and unclouded delight, lest God should overhear our thoughts and hasten to mingle some sour with the sweet, some alloy with the pure gold. It is very sad, because such conceptions of God shed a sombre shadow on our life's landscape and shut out the sunshine. What a contrast there is between the thoughts of many children of God and the outbursts of the Psalms! Even Jeremiah in his Lamentations affirms that He doth not afflict willingly, *nor grieve the children of men!* Do let us put out of our minds these hard and hurtful thoughts. We are accepted in the Beloved, and ours is the God Who is *only good* (Ps. lxxiii. 1, R.V., marg.). Dare to believe that all is love, only love, pitiful and tender, rejoicing in human joy. Let us rejoice in every good thing which God gives, always believing that the last will be best, and that there will be sugar at the bottom of the cup. Do not believe that He will lay His hand on you, except to anoint and bless.

The Divine Condescension. (4) Also *they saw God, and did eat and drink.* Some people eat and drink without beholding God; others behold God, and are too shy or afraid to eat and drink; but evidently these seventy elders were perfectly at their ease. As they were engaged in the sacrificial meal, feeding, it may be, on the reserved remnants of the peace-offerings, slain earlier in the day (ver. 5), they became conscious of the near presence of God; and it did not affright them. When in the village inn, the Stranger who had so greatly commended Himself to Cleopas and his friend had taken the bread, and blessed, and broken it, their eyes were opened, and they knew Him; so was it as these elders ate of the peace-offerings, which were specially distinguished from the other offerings and sacrifices as being a feast of fellowship and communion between the human guests and the Divine Host. We are reminded also of Christ's words, Who tells us that He stands at the door and knocks, to be first assured that He will be welcomed, and that then He will come in to sup with us, and we with Him. But in this case He brings the sacred victuals with Him, as Melchizedek did, who met Abraham returning from the slaughter of the kings.

What Might Have Been. It was thus that these men, to whom Moses entrusted the care of the camp during his approaching absence, were prepared for the ordeal to which they were to be exposed. Abraham was prepared for the assault of the King of Sodom by the previous advent of Melchizedek. Our Lord—may we not say it reverently?—was fortified by the passion of the Passover which immediately preceded it. And if these elders had only realised the full significance of that meal, that vision, that consciousness of the Divine Presence, they would have stood like rocks against the clamour of the people for the golden calf. But it was not to be, and we can never forget that they at last perished in the desert, whilst Nadab and Abihu were consumed by fire on the very threshold of their priestly office. How near we may come to harbour, and yet be shipwrecked! Balaam desired to die the death of the righteous, and certainly he enjoyed unusual revelations of God, but he fell on an ignominious battlefield, and his name is handed down through the ages as an arch-tempter. "Wherefore let him that thinketh he standeth, take heed lest he fall." It is possible to pass from the communion table to perdition.

The Circle of Joshua. III. *The Circle represented by Joshua.* If the first and lowest circle represents those who are satisfied with the outward show of moving religious spectacles; and the second those who are capable of some glimpses into the eternal, which, however, have no permanent effect on character; this higher circle, with its solitary occupant, Joshua, may stand for the eager piety of many in the ranks of young manhood or womanhood, which lacks as yet the perfect vision of a Moses, but will be satisfied with nothing less. These have already fought and won their fight with Amalek. Amalek stands for the flesh, and Joshua had routed the Amalekite hosts before he came to Sinai, therefore he could stand nearer the centre than others, who were only occupied with the lower attractions of the meal, of which they ate and drank, apparently deriving nothing beyond. We must have met and conquered the Amalek of the flesh, if we are to see God. The child of appetite cannot climb to, and cannot breathe in, that rare atmosphere. Spiritual things are only discerned by spiritual senses, and our spiritual faculties are developed just in proportion as we crucify the flesh with its affections and lusts. But the spiritual force that is generated in obedience and conflict will carry the soul triumphantly through the forty years of wandering, and bring it into the land of Canaan, where it shall lead the hosts into the rest of God. Only Caleb and Joshua of all that host were destined to that supreme privilege!

The Circle of Moses. IV. *The last and highest circle of approach to God is represented by Moses.* "And the Lord said unto Moses, Come up to Me into the Mount, and be there. . . . And Moses rose up and his minister Joshua; and Moses went up into the Mount of God." But as they drew near the cloud which covered the Mount an arrest was placed upon their further advance. Though summoned, Moses went no further, until he received a further invitation. For six days the two waited, absorbed in prayer and meditation, and on the seventh Moses heard his name uttered from out of the midst of the cloud. Leaving Joshua to await his return, he entered the excellent glory, which to those beneath appeared like devouring flame; and as we see him enter we can only repeat the words of the

Psalmist: "Blessed is the man, O Lord, whom Thou choosest, and causest to approach unto Thee, that He may dwell in Thy courts!" When shall that day appear when we also shall see Thy face, and have Thy name written on our foreheads? Grant to us grace, when our name is called, to be so clothed in the righteousness of Christ that we may not be ashamed or turned back!

IN THE MOUNT WITH GOD

Exodus 25:1-9

1. And the Lord spake unto Moses, saying,

2. Speak unto the children of Israel, that they bring me an offering: of every man that giveth it willingly with his heart ye shall take my offering.

3. And this *is* the offering which ye shall take of them; gold, and silver, and brass,

4. And blue, and purple, and scarlet, and fine linen, and goats' *hair,*

5. And rams' skins dyed red, and badgers' skins, and shittim wood,

6. Oil for the light, spices for anointing oil, and for sweet incense,

7. Onyx stones, and stones to be set in the ephod, and in the breastplate.

8. And let them make me a sanctuary; that I may dwell among them.

9. According to all that I show thee, *after* the pattern of the tabernacle, and the pattern of all the instruments thereof, even so shall ye make *it.*

IN THE MOUNT WITH GOD

Exodus 25:1-9

The Import of Moses and the Cloud. When we finished our last chapter, the impression may have been left that the entrance of Moses within the cloud was an emblem of the moment of our passage at death from the earthly house of this physical body to the house not made with hands, eternal in the heavens. But that is not the lesson derived from this incident in the New Testament. It is used there as the emblem and symbol of that Divine fellowship to which we are summoned during this mortal life, when all, with unveiled face, may behold the glory of God in the face of Jesus Christ, and beholding, be changed into the same image, from glory to glory.

The Tabernacle. Great as had been the service rendered by Moses in the Exodus and the Red Sea, in the march through the wilderness and the giving of the Law, there was other and perhaps more important work to be done in the erection or ordering of the Tabernacle, and in translating into material forms the recondite and sublime spiritual truths which were to be enshrined there for centuries, and figuratively for all time. It was for this purpose that he was summoned within the encircling cloud. "Let them make me a sanctuary, that I may dwell among them."

The Preparation of Moses. Moses, Stephen says, was learned in all the wisdom of Egypt (Acts vii. 22), but that wisdom, which was intellectual and earthly, would not help him here, though it might be serviceable in translating into human thought and speech the mysteries that were to be communicated to the artificers and the crowd. But the natural (physical) man receiveth not the things of the Spirit of God, and he cannot know them, says the Apostle, because they are spiritually discerned. It was necessary, therefore, even for Moses to become aware of the things of the Spirit of God by another organ of cognition, namely the spiritual faculties, which alone are capable of receiving and understanding the things of the

Spirit. In modern parlance, this organ of spiritual cognition is described as *subliminal consciousness*, and in similar phraseology. But we prefer to use the expressions of the Apostle, which are clear and simple. He distinguishes between the wisdom belonging to this world and its leaders, who are soon to pass away, and the wisdom of God which is hidden from the wise and prudent, but revealed to babes, to those of the child-heart, who are spiritually-minded, who live and walk in the use of their spiritual vision, for there God's Spirit draws aside the veil, so as to reveal, intuitively and at a glance, the deep things of the Divine nature. Among human beings, pursues the Apostle, who knows a man's inner thoughts except the man's own spirit within him? and if we are to know God's inner thoughts it must be by His Spirit! But Spirit communicates only with Spirit, as in wireless telegraphy the transmitter and the receiver must be in perfect accord. It is clear, therefore, that the mind of Christ can only be made known by His Spirit to the spirits that have become percipient and receptive. We can now understand why Moses was left waiting for six days on the threshold of the great revelation, that he might lay aside his own wisdom and become perfectly attuned to the Spirit of Revelation, who was prepared to communicate the deep things of God.

Its Meaning for Us. Need we emphasise this profound lesson? By the new birth most, if not all, of the readers of these pages have been born of the Spirit, but probably they do not realise that, just as in natural birth they were born into the natural world, with an apparatus to apprehend it, so in the new or second birth they were born into the spiritual world, with an apparatus suited for it. The mistake, however, is that whilst they have never ceased to use the apparatus of the human body to receive through it the impressions of the outer world and react on it, yet they have allowed the senses and powers of these spirits to atrophy from disuse. Ah, the pity of it! Our mothers, nurses and friends did their best to train us in the use of the one, but we have had so few to help us to use the other. Like young eaglets, we have trembled on the edge of the nest, and if our Heavenly Father has threatened to break up our nest, and precipitate us out on the steeps of air, we have violently protested against His cruelty and have clung to the tattered remnants of the nest, dreading to use our enfeebled and useless wings, which might have borne us sunwards.

When Moses was entirely yielded to the Spirit's guidance and teaching he was able to discern things which before had been hidden. "The spiritual man discerneth all things, yet he himself is discerned of no man."

(1) The Plan of the Tabernacle. (1) *He beheld the perfect Plan.* "According to all that I show thee, the pattern of the tabernacle, and the pattern of all the furniture thereof, even so shall ye make it" (ver. 9). These words repeat themselves like an echo among the mountains. Sometimes at least they strike the ear from now until the Fall of the Second Temple was close at hand (Heb. viii. 5); and when Scripture in its comparatively narrow compass repeats one injunction so often, we may be sure that it deserves to be deeply pondered, and made one of the outstanding factors of life.

The whole Tabernacle, in all its courts and hangings, its altars and furniture, stood complete in the mind of God, and may have been represented by its Architect in a visible form. This at least is suggested by the use of that word *pattern.* Was some outward fashion of the Tabernacle presented to the eye of Moses, to help heart and mind to comprehend the Divine conception? Was some fairy shape created out of rainbow mist? Were curtains woven on the looms of wise-hearted angels? Were ark and altar, boards and hangings, table and laver reproduced of that same stuff of which dreams are made? Within the precincts of cloud, on some mountain level, did a visible pattern stand forth of what Moses was to reproduce upon the desert sand, that, carrying the picture in his eye, as well as in his soul, he might be able exactly and accurately to reconstruct it? If so, when the completed structure stood on the desert sand, he alone must have been disconsolate, amid the many rejoicing crowds, as he contrasted the very best that their united talents and gifts could produce, with what he had seen when he was on the Mount.

The Plan of our Lives. There is a profound lesson here. All our life has been preconceived in the mind of God, and every son and daughter is called, not only to see His face and live, but to behold the plan and pattern of life, which has to be reconstructed in actual living, so that we may say with our Lord, "The Son can do nothing of Himself—He can only do what He sees the Father doing; for whatever He does, that the Son does in like manner. For the Father loves the Son, and reveals to Him all that He is Himself doing. And greater deeds than these will He reveal to Him, in order that you may wonder. . . . The words I speak are those which I have seen in the presence of the Father" (John v. 19; viii. 38, *Weymouth*).

Three Attitudes Towards Design and Order. There are three sorts of men. First, those who care only for the forms of things. They have no ideals, they form no purpose. Without any upward or heavenward glance they day by day drift forward on the current of any whim or caprice, before the light and variable gales of fashion. To do the behest of the hour, in good form, and at the impulse of the moment, or at the call of routine and habit, is all they desire or concern themselves with.

There is a higher type of manhood than that. We know many who have some positive plan or programme of what they would like to make of their lives. The poet, the artist, the inventor of gems, the discoverer—each of these works more or less to a pattern which has been the dream of their boyhood, and with much witchery it has beckoned them to follow. They have seen a pattern, though it has not been shown them where Moses saw his, and they have not the driving-force on the one hand, or the sense of absolute assurance on the other.

A More Excellent Way. Each of these falls beneath the conception presented in the text, of the man who is accustomed to live in the presence of God, and who believes that of every year, of every month, and of every day there is a complete pattern. The ideal of his friendships is there, and he expects to be led from one stage into another of tender intimacy and ennobling intercourse. The ideal of his marriage, the ideal of his home, the ideal of his business-life, the ideal of each summer holiday, the ideal of the manner in which he is to pass home to God—each is there on the Mount, and he is at perfect peace, only desiring to build as near as may be to the pattern which lives in the thought of God. The same thought is contained in that assertion of Eph. ii. 10, R.V. "For we are His workmanship [the Greek word is *poiēma*] created in Christ Jesus for good works, which God afore prepared that we should walk in them."

The Secret of a Blessed Life. This is the secret of a blessed life. Do not be driven by circumstances; do not be shaped by Fate or Destiny; do not sullenly follow out your own plan and scheme, but continually hide yourself in God, wait your six days, as Moses did, and see the perfect pattern you are afterwards to reproduce. In some cases it is shown in early childhood, and from the first the young prophet, like Jeremiah, hears God saying: "Before I formed thee . . . I knew thee; . . . I have appointed thee a prophet unto the nations, . . . to whomsoever I shall send thee thou shalt go, and whatsoever

I shall command thee thou shalt speak." In other cases, the pattern is revealed piecemeal. We are asked to weave a curtain, or make an altar, or shape a plank, and we have no sort of idea what they will look like when all are placed together. It will be a discovery indeed when some faithful souls who lived by the day, doing just the day's work, will awake to see an invisible hand composing the disjointed pieces, and building them together as a fair temple for the habitation of God through the Spirit. Be of good cheer, you are building for Eternity!

If it be asked what we see when we are alone with God, we may answer with great reverence that we behold the nature of our Lord, standing forth as the perfect Exemplar, the Heavenly Pattern. His character, words, sufferings, most blessed obedience unto death, His absolute devotion to the Father's will—these are the pattern. He left us an example that we should follow in His steps. As the holy Apostle John puts it, we are to walk even as He walked, we are to purify ourselves as He is pure, we are to be righteous as He is righteous, and as He is, so are we to be in the world.

(2) **The Significance of its Details.** (2) *Moses saw also into the significance of the various parts of the pattern.* We are told in Exod. xxxi. 18 that when God had made an end of communing with Moses upon Mount Sinai He gave unto him the two tables of stone. That word *communion* is very significant, because it implies intercourse and reciprocity of thought.

—**How Revealed.** By its very nature, communion involves speech between two parties; and when we learn that God *communed* with Moses, it could not for a moment be implied that there was a monologue, and that God poured an uninterrupted stream of instruction into the mind of Moses, without a remark or response on his part. We must believe, on the contrary, that there was a perpetual interchange of question and answer. In this narrative, from this chapter to the verse just now quoted, Moses gives an account of what happened on the Mount, but makes no announcement of his share in it. He dwells only on what God said; but that word *communion* compels us to interpolate at nearly every paragraph the reverent inquiries, and probably the adoring ejaculations, of the human pupil.

A Reminiscence of Moody. Some years ago, when Mr. Moody, sitting in the porch of his home at Northfield, was talking with me about his British friends, he gave a very tender and appreciative characterisation of Dr. Andrew Bonar, whom he greatly admired and revered. He told me several things that Dr. Bonar had said, which had made a profound impression on his mind, and it is to that rich and devout imagination that the following paragraphs are due. They are the reproduction, in a very halting fashion, of faraway words, blurred and dimmed by the abrasion of many years. I admit that probably the conception is too materialistic, but it is at least vivid enough to live as a rich mosaic on the walls of our imagination.

The Questions of Moses. There stood the Tabernacle; in vision it may have been life-size. Moses may have been able to walk through the rainbow mists, the golden wreaths of light, in company with God, and to stand, so to speak, with God side by side in the Most Holy Place, or in the Holy Place, with its seven-branched candlestick and shewbread table. As they passed through, and paused at the laver, or the great brazen altar, or the furniture of the Holy Place, may we not suppose that Moses reverently questioned God as to the inner meaning of each separate item? He does not give us the inner significance in these chapters. It would have been unintelligible to that age, but, no doubt, God would explain it to His faithful servant.

The Cherubim. "Why, O Most Holy God, do those cherubim bend over that ark?" "It is because angels see, in that which the ark represents, mysteries which they desire to fathom."

The Lid. "And why is the ark covered by that golden lid?" "It is because the obedience of the Christ to the holy law will one day meet and cover its entire demand, as contained in those tablets of stone beneath."

The Veil. "And why this heavy veil?" "Because the worshipper must, in the first instance, be excluded, and only after centuries have passed will it be rent, so that those that love Me may come and enjoy the fellowship thou art enjoying now."

The Candlestick. "And why that seven-branch candlestick?" "To set forth the light which must shine through Israel to the world."

The Table. "And why that shewbread table?" "Because the life of the Christ is to be the bread of the whole world."

The Incense. "Why this incense?" "Because as the fragrance of the incense is grateful to the nostrils, so the prayers of My people are pleasant and delightful to Me."

The Laver. "But why this great laver?" "Because those who come near Me must ever wash themselves, their feet and hands, which had become befouled."

The Altar. "And this brazen altar standing here, why so large, why those horns?" "Ah," the answer might have been, "that is to represent the supreme act where My love is to make an Atonement for the sins of the world."

Do not you think therefore, that God was led by Moses' questions, as they communed together, deeper and deeper, to interpret the very heart and mysteries of the Atonement, until Moses understood, as perhaps no other man has understood, even in New Testament times, the whole drift, and plan, and conception of God's redeeming love? What a marvellous talk that must have been! It seems almost as if the Spirit anticipated the Epistles to the Hebrews, the Romans, the Ephesians, and the Colossians, and the deep and holy teaching of St. John.

A Present Possibility. "They communed together". That is possible for us still—communion with God—not simply to read the Bible and to take chapter after chapter in the order in which they stand, but that we should commune with God through the Word, standing on our Sinai every morning, face to face, in communion with Him, asking Him questions about all things which perplex and startle us, and receiving the plan of life and duty.

(3) **The Men for the Building.** (3) *Moses also beheld the agents through whom the Fabric of the Tabernacle was to be constructed and the source of the necessary materials.* It is more than probable that Moses had no knowledge of the genius and skill which were maturing in Bezalel and Aholiab. Their unique qualifications were a complete discovery when he heard of them from the Spirit of God. The very phrase *See*, with which their names were first uttered, seems to denote that they were to break on Moses with a kind of startlement: and it must have been bewildering to learn that there was in the camp a sufficiency of material for the execution of the work, and still more a disposition to make over these riches for such an object. Had he been thrown on the resources of his intellect and experience, Moses would have been at his wits' end to discover either artificers or materials for the gigantic task, which would cost at least a quarter of a million of pounds sterling. Like Andrew, he would have wondered, "Whence shall we buy bread?" But as he stood there with God in the Mount of Vision, all was disclosed. We will deal with these at length in future chapters, but in the meanwhile to any who stand bewildered before some great programme, which requires workers and materials, we would say, Do not worry and yield to nervous misgiving, but go and stand with God upon the Mount.

THE ARK OF THE COVENANT

Exodus 25:10-22

10. And they shall make an ark *of* shittim wood: two cubits and a half *shall be* the length thereof, and a cubit and a half the breadth thereof, and a cubit and a half the height thereof.

11. And thou shalt overlay it with pure gold, within and without shalt thou overlay it, and shalt make up on it a crown of gold round about.

12. And thou shalt cast four rings of gold for it, and put *them* in the four corners thereof; and two rings *shall be* in the one side of it, and two rings in the other side of it.

13. And thou shalt make staves *of* shittim wood, and overlay them with gold.

14. And thou shalt put the staves into the rings by the sides of the ark, that the ark may be borne with them.

15. The staves shall be in the rings of the ark: they shall not be taken from it.

16. And thou shalt put into the ark the testimony which I shall give thee.

17. And thou shalt make a mercyseat *of* pure gold: two cubits and a half *shall be* the length thereof, and a cubit and a half the breadth thereof.

18. And thou shalt make two cherubims *of* gold, *of* beaten work shalt thou make them, in the two ends of the mercy seat.

19. And make one cherub on the one end, and the other cherub on the other end: *even* of the mercyseat shall ye make the cherubims on the two ends thereof.

20. And the cherubims shall stretch forth *their* wings on high, covering the mercyseat with their wings, and their faces *shall look* one to another; toward the mercyseat shall the faces of the cherubims be.

21. And thou shalt put the mercyseat above upon the ark; and in the ark thou shalt put the testimony that I shall give thee.

22. And there I will meet with thee, and I will commune with thee from above the mercyseat, from between the two cherubims which *are* upon the ark of the testimony, of all *things* which I will give thee in commandment unto the children of Israel.

(See xxxvii. 1–9 for the realisation of this pattern.)

THE ARK OF THE COVENANT

Exodus 25:10-22

The Tabernacle an answer to Man's need. There is much in the earlier paragraphs of this chapter to startle us, because it seems as though a backward step had been taken in the education of the chosen people. When they emerged from the land of Egypt, they worshipped the Almighty without Tabernacle or Temple. The stars lit the way to fellowship and communion; and under the expanse of the sky, with its depths of fathomless blue, they worshipped the Father Who is in heaven. Was it not a retrograde policy on the part of Moses to erect a Tabernacle in which God should dwell, and in which He should hold fellowship with His people? Not so, because what is vague and insubstantial will fail to grip and hold the heart and conscience of man. He needs not the universe only, but a home; not an extended vault of sky, but some holy spot where the bush burns with fire. It is profoundly important for man to have a definite and concrete thought of God, in order that he may rise from that to the abstract, and discover the fire of God burning at every point and pinnacle of existence. For such reasons God said to Moses, "Let them make Me a sanctuary, that I may dwell among them" (ver. 8).

The Structure of the Ark. In the inmost recess of that house Moses was ordered to place the throne from which God's presence would be immediately revealed, and the lambent flame of the Shekinah shine with pure and awful radiance. We need not enter upon prolonged discussion of the construction of the Ark. It was a box of acacia-wood, three feet nine inches long, two feet three inches wide, and two feet three inches deep. Upon the lid lay a slab of solid gold, valued at £25,000 of our money, which was shadowed by the wings of the bending cherubim, as they knelt apparently looking together into the mysteries of which that slab of gold spoke.

The remainder of the Ark was gilded within and without with gold, and the whole must have become encrusted with blood, as the High Priests, year after year, besprinkled it with the blood of the victims slain on the Day of Atonement.

Its Import. All this was a parable for that time and for all time, "the Holy Spirit thus signifying" (Heb. ix. 8). That quotation is very pertinent to the understanding of these symbols, because of the distinct statement that there was a divine intention in their construction. Are we not told that God spake of old time by divers portions and in divers manners (Heb. i. 1)? This is one of those manners. He spake to man in the Holy Scriptures, on the history of the chosen people, and in the very apparatus which is so minutely furnished in these pages.

An Abiding Meaning. We must remember that God is One, and that His Truth is One. He did not pursue one method of salvation with the Hebrew and another with the Christian. There is no variation in the essential principles of moral or spiritual truth, whether stated in the Old Testament or the New. There may be an ever-growing and clearer appreciation and understanding of truth, but truth is immutably the same. As, therefore, we look into these symbols we shall encounter the same eternal facts of Redemption as those that underlay the death of the Cross, and which must underlie for evermore the Divine attitude towards those who shall have been redeemed from among men. God is the same, His years fail not, the thoughts of His heart shall endure for ever, and in studying these old-world emblems we shall be treading in the first steps of the Creator, Redeemer, and Moral Ruler of men.

There is an incidental lesson here for us all. The Tabernacle with its contents was the subject of much Divine thought and care. It was not a poor hut run up in an hour. It was not the creation of human fancy. Man was not the creator, but the executor of the Divine programme and plan. It was thus that God made the heavens and the earth. He was alone when the foundations of the heaven and earth were laid. To Him alone must be attributed, also, the pattern of the human life of our Lord, in which the Tabernacle was duplicated in flesh and blood. And He is intimately concerned in the fashioning of all our life. In the minutest details He is immediately interested; and in the Most Holy Place of our nature, within the veil, there is a shrine, where angels might tread with reverence, because His holy presence is there.

The Ark as a Symbol. I. *The Ark of the Covenant.* This wooden box, underlaid and gilded with gold, was the symbol of God's presence with His people. Its presence in the camp, as we shall see, indicated that the God of their fathers was amongst them, their fellow-pilgrim across the desert waste, sharing their anxieties, fighting their battles, sorrowing in their griefs, entering into that sympathetic companionship which was a perpetual source of inspiration and comfort. In all life there must be movement and change. We go forward because the Cloud beckons, and to linger behind would forfeit the manna and the safeguard. But the foreign becomes familiar, and the lonely is peopled with loving presences when God's sensible presence is with us.

The Ark at Jordan: and its Lesson. When Israel came to the swellings of Jordan, before the touch of the feet of the priests who bore the Ark of the Covenant, the floods fled right and left, leaving a passage for the hosts. They had not passed that way before, but the way was cleft for them. Do you ever ask what will you do at the swellings of Jordan? Do you fear that heart and strength will fail? Do you dread the touch of the cold water? Do you wish that you had lived in days when bushes burned with fire, when voices spoke from the Mount, when the Angel seemed visibly to precede the host, when the Captain of the Lord's host stood with drawn sword, and One like the Son of Man walked the glowing embers with His faithful witnesses? There is no need to cherish such backward yearnings. There is a Presence with us, a Divine Companionship, the Angel of the Covenant, the Christ of God! Like a voice ringing down a mountain-ravine, we hear His imperishable words, "Lo, I am with you all the days, even unto the end." Shall we not answer: "Yea, though I walk through the valley of the Shadow of Death, I will fear no evil, for Thou art with me"? Even if our emotions have not yet realised the experience, yet let our faith affirm the fact with unfaltering emphasis.

The Ark at Jericho: and its Lesson. When Israel approached Jericho, and the high walls, built up to heaven, threatened to be an impassable barrier, "Joshua called unto the priests, and said unto them, Take up the ark of the covenant, and let seven priests bear seven trumpets of rams' horns before the ark of the Lord." "And the ark of the covenant of the Lord followed the priests." "And the rearward came after the ark." "So the ark of the Lord compassed the city." It was not the march of the priests, nor blast of the horns, nor the shout of the people, but the presence of the Ark of the Lord of the whole earth that levelled those mighty obstacles.

So will it always be for those who abide in the secret of the Lord. For them the mountains and the hills shall be made low, before them difficulties shall be dissipated as heaps of chaff. When the soul, in dismay, as it faces the walled cities, asks, "Who will bring me into the strong city? Who will lead me into Edom?" it turns with strong faith to the Almighty Christ, saying, "Wilt not Thou, O Son of God?" and as the result, the triumphant cry rings out: "Through Him we shall do valiantly, for He it is that shall tread down our adversaries."

The Ark in Captivity: and its Lesson. When Israel had grievously sinned, and the Ark of the Covenant was forfeited to the Philistines —as though, since the Divine presence had departed, the symbol must also depart—wherever the Ark was borne, it carried destruction to the idols and populations of Philistia. Dagon was found on successive mornings fallen upon his face to the earth before the Ark of the Lord, and only the stump was left. The people were smitten with sore diseases, so that they said, "Send away the ark of the God of Israel, and let it go again to His own place" (1 Sam. v. 11). It was necessary for Jehovah to vindicate the symbol of His presence, and the fear and awe of Him falling on the Philistines laid them open to the sore ravages of the plague. It is the presence of God in the Church which is the sole talisman of victory. When we realise that He is in our midst, we cannot be moved, nay, we are more than conquerors. "Behold, the Lord rideth upon a swift cloud, and shall come into Egypt; and the idols of Egypt shall be moved at His presence, and the heart of Egypt shall melt in the midst of it" (Isa. xix. 1). In these days of religious declension, throughout professedly Christian nations, we are too apt to say that the situation has passed beyond our powers to retrieve it. "And there ran a man of Benjamin out of the army, and came to Shiloh the same day with his clothes rent, and with earth upon his head. And when he came, lo, Eli sat upon his seat beside the gate, watching the way [marg.], for his heart trembled for the ark of God. And when the man came into the city, and told it, all the city cried out" (1 Sam. iv. 12, 13, R.V.). Then the venerable judge fell backward and died, and the wife of the slain priest bore a son, and named him Ichabod, saying, "The glory is departed from Israel, for the ark of God is taken." But when Israel had resumed its ancient attitude towards God, all this was altered. The Ark was replaced, because God was replaced in the affection of His people; and the power of Philistia was absolutely and permanently broken by the successive victories of David and Joab.

How is it with You? How is it with you? Have the inward foes been too strong? Have they desolated your peace? Have they robbed you of the sense of God's redeeming grace? Dare to believe that whatever has transpired cannot break the Divine Covenant. It was *the Ark of the Covenant*, remember, which was seen by the divinely-instructed John when the Temple of God was opened in heaven, and there was seen in His Temple the Ark of His Covenant, (Rev. xi. 19). The Ark, of which we are speaking, may have perished when the Babylonians took the Holy City and burned the Temple; but the reality, of which it was the symbol, abides with the Church and the individual soul. God cannot break His Covenant. Though we believe not, *He* abideth faithful. He cannot deny Himself; and it is our Father's *good pleasure* to give us the Kingdom, *i.e.* victory over the power of appetite and passion. He will not give it grudgingly, or with niggard hand. He is only too glad to see us walking in the light of an unaccusing, uncondemning conscience. Only dare to affirm it. Dare to believe that notwithstanding all your failures and sins, He stands by His ancient promises, and that if you will but believe, even *you* shall see the glory of God in your restoration to that fair image which He conceived for thee before the worlds were made. Dare to step out on these immutable facts, which can no more be altered by your sinful changes than clouds can deflect the heavenly bodies in their constant order.

The Symbol Transient: the Facts Enduring. The symbol may pass, and must. Indeed, its transience was clearly foretold: "And it shall come to pass, when ye be multiplied and increased in the land, in those days, saith the Lord, they shall say no more, The Ark of the Covenant of the Lord; neither shall it come to mind: neither shall they remember it; neither shall they visit it; neither shall that be done any more" (Jer. iii. 16, R.V.). But the essential spiritual fact abides, to which the Apostle refers in that sublime series of questions, for which there is only one reply: "Who shall separate us from the love of Christ?"

The Mercy-Seat as a Symbol. II. The Ark was not only the symbol of the Divine Presence, *the Mercy-seat furnished a remarkable symbol of Divine Redeeming Grace.* The word rendered "Mercy-seat" really means "a covering," with special reference to the forgiveness and covering of transgression and sin. The same word occurs in the Greek of the New Testament, where we are told by the Apostle that the Father hath set forth Christ to be a *propitiation*, through faith, by His blood, and in the passing over of sin (Rom. iii. 25, R.V.). The same Greek word is used in the Epistle to Hebrews to designate "the Mercy-seat" (Heb. ix. 5). So that we might render the first-quoted passage thus: "The Redemption that is in Christ Jesus, whom God set forth to be a Mercy-seat."

Christ and the Mercy-Seat. In Jesus Christ the Divine and the human meet perfectly. It has been said, indeed, that the word Christ conveys the idea of Deity endowed with a familiar human element. Christ is the Divinely human, and the humanly Divine. "There are two words: God and man. One describes pure Deity, the other pure humanity. Christ is a word not identical with either, but including both. It is the Deity in which humanity has part, it is the humanity in which Deity resides. It is that special mediatorial nature which has its own double wearing of both, the ability to stand between and reconcile the separated manhood and Divinity."[1]

There is so strong a trace of the same Greek word in that familiar passage of John's First Epistle: "He is the propitiation for our sins" —that there also we might read it, "He is the Mercy-seat for our sins, and not for ours only, but also for the sins of the whole world." We can better understand, therefore, the inner meaning of the Divine Spirit, when, speaking of the Mercy-seat, He says, "There will I meet with Thee, and I will commune with Thee from above the Mercy-seat, from between the two Cherubim which are upon the Ark of the Testimony."

Emmanuel: God With Us. When the High Priests entered within the veil, or the ordinary priests ministered before it, and they thought of the Shekinah shining above the Mercy-seat, they knew that God was there, not only in the terror of His majesty, purity, and holiness, but in His tender, redeeming, forgiving grace. His glory was there, not to slay, but to illumine, not to abash, but to attract. In fact, they might almost have adopted words afterwards to be spoken: "God was in Christ, reconciling the world unto Himself, not imputing their trespasses unto them" (2 Cor. v. 19). How good it would be if timid, doubting souls could take this to their hearts! They dread Him, stand aloof, feel that they are cut off and banished, whereas the love of God in Jesus Christ awaits them; broods in gentle, holy and

[1] Philips Brooks: *The Mystery of Iniquity.*

unabated light; waits to unfold the riches of His grace; and does not impute trespasses to the penitent and believing soul.

The Sprinkled Blood. The Mercy-seat must have become encrusted with blood, as, in successive years, succeeding High Priests, who were not permitted to continue by reason of death, sprinkled there the blood of the victims slain on the great Day of Atonement. Those slain were the perpetual remembrance of the atonements which had been made and accepted. So we think of Calvary, where precious blood was freely shed, and we remember that Christ, our Passover, was sacrificed for us, and that when He had offered one sacrifice for sins for ever, sat down on the right hand of God. "In whom we have redemption through His blood, the forgiveness of sins." Let us dare to believe, then, that God does not impute our iniquities to us, and let us draw near with a true heart, in fullness of faith, having our hearts sprinkled from an evil conscience.

God's Abundant Mercy. It is a sweet word! A seat of mercy, baptised in mercy, from which mercy flows forth. Not wrath, not judgment, not indignation, but mercy is pouring forth from its original fountain in the heart of God. Compute the mercy around us in Nature, in the adaptation of music to the ear, of light to the eye, of savoury food to the palate! Consider the comfort and beauty of the world, the tender joys of home, the daily providence and care! Recall the mercy that burst forth into fresh expression at the manger-bed, and streamed from the wounds inflicted on the cross! Great and wonderful are all these, but they are crowned in the risen Christ. Let us realise, then, that the glorified nature of the Lamb in the midst of the throne, of the Lamb that was slain, is the trysting-place where God's mercy meets our sin and sorrow, our pain and grief, our fear and dread with infinite tenderness and sufficiency.

The Tables of the Law. III. Underneath the Mercy-seat and at the bottom of the Ark lay *the Tables of the Law* (Deut. x. 5). When the people sinned against God, and made the golden calf, the Law of God leapt from crag to crag, as though descending in a hurricane of judgment; but that was abnormal. Its usual position was to lie unseen and still beneath the Mercy-seat. How true a symbol this! Beneath all in God's universe—in the world, in the Church, and in God's dealings with men, there is the silent presence of law. Whatever storms sweep the sky, they do not disturb the silent beauty and order of Nature. Beneath the changes of the evolutions and revolutions there is the immutable precision of natural law, on which man counts with absolute certainty. And what is true in Nature is true also in Religion. The Divine Mercy is exercised in accordance with Justice.

Mercy and Justice. Two Apostles insist on this. Paul says God showed forth His *Righteousness* when He set forth Jesus Christ to be a propitiation; and John says that He is faithful and *just* when He forgives sin. Our Saviour in His life and death magnified the Law and made it honourable. Not one jot or one tittle is allowed to pass unfulfilled. There is no fear that it will ever arise to take by the throat and demand payment from any whom God has accepted. If we may put it so materially—the gold of our Saviour's obedience even unto death is of the exact size and pattern of the demand of the moral law. When He said, "*It is finished*," He meant that nothing more need be added or subtracted, and that what He had done, He had done, mediatorially and sufficiently for us all. Does not this explain the presence of the blood-marks? Where the law comes in collision with our fallen race, there are always blood and tears, not only of each individual, but of one for another, and most of all by Him who stood as our Representative, who was wounded for our transgressions, bruised for our iniquities; on whom was the chastisement of our peace, and by whose stripes we are healed. Mercy and truth are met together, righteousness and peace have kissed each other.

Free from Law and Bound by Law. But though we are free from the law in one sense, we are subject to it in another. We have not to meet either its exactions or penalties, in the matter of our personal salvation. Its demands were met, its inflictions suffered, on our behalf, by the great Representative Man, in whom we stand. But we are under the law to Christ. "Do we then make void the law through faith? God forbid: yea, we establish the law" (Rom. iii. 31). "Christ is the end of the law for righteousness to every one that believeth" (Rom. x. 4). "For what the law could not do, in that it was weak through the flesh, God, sending His own Son in the likeness of sinful flesh, and for sin, condemned sin in the flesh, that the righteousness of the law might be fulfilled in us, who walk not after the flesh, but after the spirit" (Rom. viii. 3, 4). Directly we accept the Mercy-seat, we bind ourselves more closely than ever to keep that law which is summed up in the one word, *Love*. We desire more than ever to please God. We do not obey to earn salvation, but being saved we obey. We do not work up to the Cross, but down from it. The Holy Spirit writes the law, not upon tables of stone, but upon the fleshly tablets of the heart, so that we say with the Psalmist, "I delight to do Thy will, O my God, yea, Thy law is within my heart."

The Cherubim. Space forbids me to expatiate on the bending forms of the cherubim. They represented at once guardianship, reverence, inquiry, and worship. The Israelites were taught that their experiences, their lessons, their progress in the knowledge of God were of absorbing interest to beings beyond their ken. The very angels desired to look into the mysteries connected with their redemption (1 Peter i. 12). And we remember that on us also similar interest is concentrated; that as the drama of human history unfolds, the process is watched with absorbing interest by other eyes than man's; and that now to the principalities and powers in the heavenly places is being made known through the Church the manifold wisdom of God, according to the eternal purpose which He purposed in Christ Jesus our Lord.

The Table of the Presence-Bread

Exodus 25:23-30; Leviticus 24:5-9

23. Thou shalt also make a table *of* shittim wood: two cubits *shall be* the length thereof, and a cubit the breadth thereof, and a cubit and a half the height thereof.

24. And thou shalt overlay it with pure gold, and make thereto a crown of gold round about.

25. And thou shalt make unto it a border of an hand-breadth round about, and thou shalt make a golden crown to the border thereof round about.

26. And thou shalt make for it four rings of gold, and put the rings in the four corners that *are* on the four feet thereof.

27. Over against the border shall the rings be for places of the staves to bear the table.

28. And thou shalt make the staves *of* shittim wood, and overlay them with gold, that the table may be borne with them.

29. And thou shalt make the dishes thereof, and spoons thereof, and covers thereof, and bowls thereof, to cover withal: *of* pure gold shalt thou make them.

30. And thou shalt set upon the table shewbread before me always.

5. And thou shalt take fine flour, and bake twelve cakes thereof: two tenth deals shall be in one cake.

6. And thou shalt set them in two rows, six on a row, upon the pure table before the Lord.

7. And thou shalt put pure frankincense upon *each* row, that it may be on the bread for a memorial, *even* an offering made by fire unto the Lord.

8. Every sabbath he shall set it in order before the Lord continually, *being taken* from the children of Israel by an everlasting covenant.

9. And it shall be Aaron's and his sons'; and they shall eat it in the holy place: for it *is* most holy unto him of the offerings of the Lord made by fire by a perpetual statute.

(See xxxvii. 10–16 for the realisation of this pattern.)

THE TABLE OF THE PRESENCE-BREAD

Exodus 25:23-30; Leviticus 24:5-9

The Table of Shew-bread: its Structure. The Table of Shew-bread, as we generally call it, stood on the right-hand side of the Holy Place, as the priests entered it. It was three feet long, a foot and a half broad, and two feet three inches high. It was thus quite a small table, narrow for its length, and rather below the ordinary height. It seems to have been regarded as of primary importance, because in this chapter its description follows immediately on that of the Ark. It was, like other articles, of acacia-wood, overlaid with pure gold; the surface was surrounded by an edging or border; and the legs were held together by a broad flat bar, which strengthened their framework. This is described as "the border of an hand-breadth round about." At the corners, or ends, of the legs, were rings, through which the staves were placed for its carrying, as is represented in the bas-reliefs on the Arch of Titus. The spoons, or incense-cups, the flagons and chalices were all of gold, and were employed for the libations and the burning of incense, which accompanied the weekly presentation of the twelve loaves, or cakes of bread.

The Shew-bread. These were renewed on each Sabbath-day, the stale ones being consumed by the priests in the Holy Place. The loaves were specially made of fine flour, and were known as "the bread of face," or "bread of presence," because they were set before the face or presence of God, who dwelt in the Holy Place, and the intention, so far as we can spell it out, was to suggest that, as man feeds upon the bread, which God gives in answer to his daily prayer, so man must provide the Divine Nature with food on which the Divine Spirit also may feed. Man cannot exist without the impartation of God's nature, and in turn must minister to Him what shall afford Him satisfaction. We are to walk worthy of God unto all pleasing. Our bodies are to be a living sacrifice acceptable to God. Probably the Lord's Supper was intended to convey this dual thought. Whilst we eat of the bread and drink of the wine, which God has given to us in Jesus Christ, He also draws near to commune with us. Our Lord is His beloved Son, in whom He is well pleased; and our faith, love, obedience, and adoration provide Him with profoundest satisfaction.

Its Symbolism. The injunction was very precise: "Thou shalt set upon the table the Presence-bread before Me alway." In two passages it is described as "the continual bread" (Num. iv. 7; 2 Chron. ii. 4). When the trumpet gave the signal for the march, the loaves and vessels were left undisturbed in their accustomed places, and over them all three coverings were placed, of blue, of scarlet, and of sealskin. There was therefore no interruption of the continued symbolism of *the Unity of the chosen people*.

This thought pervades the Scriptures. If we go back to the days of the Judges, when the land was repeatedly swept by whirlwinds of judgment, when every man did as seemed right in his eyes, and there was no unity of government or authority, we find that the Presence bread was still offered with undeviating regularity. This is established by the incident told of David, when he sought the hospitality of the High-Priest at Nob, and "did eat the shew-bread, which is not lawful to eat but for the priests" (Mark ii. 25, 26). Evidently, through those stormy centuries the twelve loaves still stood before God, an emblem of the essential unity of Israel. When, afterwards, schism came, and the ten tribes, under the leadership of Jeroboam, broke away from the house of David, still upon the holy table, in Solomon's temple, the twelve loaves were presented, representing an unimpaired oneness.

So when Elijah repaired the altar of the Lord, that had been broken down by Jezebel's orders, he took *twelve* stones, "according to the number of the tribes of the sons of Jacob, unto whom the word of the Lord came, saying, Israel shall be thy name." In the prophet's thought, as in God's, the sorrowful strife and alienation between the northern and southern groups were as though they were not, in view of the Eternal Covenant, ordered in all things and sure.

A Witness to the Unity of the People. When the ten tribes were carried into captivity, and scattered far and wide through Babylonia, Persia, and Asia Minor, still each Sabbath the priests brought the twelve loaves, and placed them on the Table of Presence, as though God knew well where to find his scattered people, and in His judgment they continued one. Then followed the captivity of the seventy years, and afterwards the return to the Temple of the priests, the people, and the holy bread. And in our Lord's time, though Israel was rent and scattered, and Simeon and Dan had long since disappeared, still the twelve loaves were presented; and in a remarkable sentence Paul, speaking before Agrippa of the promise made unto the fathers, expressed his belief in the unbroken number of the tribes, when he said: "Unto which promise *our twelve tribes*, earnestly serving God, night and day, hope to attain." In the opening of his epistle, James sends greeting to the twelve tribes of the dispersion. Our Lord assured His Apostles, that in the regeneration they should sit on twelve thrones, judging the twelve tribes of Israel. On the twelve gates of the New Jerusalem are written the names of the twelve tribes of the children of Israel. Dan is indeed missed out of the enumeration of Rev. vii., but the sacred associations of twelve are still maintained by the dual representation of Joseph. Remember also Ezekiel's unfulfilled prophecy (xxxvii. 15, etc.).

The Unity of Christ's Church. Throughout this is one of those deep and subtle suggestions of the way in which the objective ideal of the Church, as an undivided and sacred unity, stands before God, upon the pure table of our Lord's nature, in which the gold of Deity and the shittim-wood of humanity blend. Amid all the storms that have swept the world since our Lord constituted His Church, throughout those disastrous periods of division and distraction, there have still been, in the Divine estimation, "one body, and one Spirit, one Lord, one faith, one baptism, one God and Father of all, who is over all, and through all, and in all." Always the twelve loaves, the wine of His blood, and the frankincense of His merit, for we are made "accepted in the Beloved."

—Not Necessarily a Visible Unity. It need hardly be remarked that this unity was never intended to be organic, because Jesus prayed that His own might be one as the Father and He were one. "Holy Father," He said, "keep them in Thy Name which Thou hast given Me, that they may be one, even as we are." But the unity of the Godhead is clearly not physical, or visible, or organic. It is mystical and spiritual. It is therefore certain that those who suppose that the unity of the Church must be patent to the senses have wholly misconceived the Divine ideal. The members of the body of Christ were never intended to be gathered into one organisation, to repeat one formulary, or march in military array. Uniformity is far removed from unity; and you may have perfect unity apart from uniformity. A tree is a unity, though there is a vast diversity between the gnarled branches and the cones which it tosses on the forest-floor. A house is a unity, though there is no similarity between the gabled roof and the deep-laid foundations. A body is a unity, but the eyelash differs widely from the bones of the skeleton.

Uniformity is impossible where there is life, as the most superficial consideration of the autumnal produce of orchard, field and garden proves. Wherever, therefore, Uniformity has been insisted on, death has ensued. Just before the Reformation of the sixteenth century, it seemed as though the Inquisition had extinguished every trace of nonconformity with the tenets and practices of the Roman Catholic Church. Indeed, she might have almost literally adopted the proud boast of Babylon: "As one gathereth eggs that are forsaken, so have I gathereth all the earth; and there was none that moved the wing, or that opened the mouth, or chirped" (Isa. x. 14, R.V.). But at this period it is incontestable that the religious life of Christendom was dead; except where the limited Piedmontese, in the high Alps, kept a spark burning amid the grey ashes.

External Uniformity Unattainable. The same mistake is perpetrated by those who demand uniformity of creed as by those who insist on uniformity of ritual. You cannot make all men climb alike, or express identical conceptions in identical words. A creed is, after all, an intellectual effort, whereas religion is not the creature of the mind or reason, but of the heart and spirit. It is a life, the importation and reception of the divine nature, the inauguration of that eternal condition of existence which will be still young when all human formularies and conceptions have been put away, as a man puts away the things of childhood. If your soul is united to the Head of the Church by a living faith, through which the life of Christ enters and pervades it, you must be reckoned a member of the Body, though you may have passed through none of those ecclesiastical systems which at the best are but broken lights, reflecting the sunlight at different angles.

Variety Within the Church of Christ. In the Church there is room, therefore, for an infinite variety. Each brings his own contribution; and we must gather *with all saints*, if we would comprehend the length, and breadth, and depth, and height of the love of Christ. You cannot see the whole sky, the whole mountain, the whole broad ocean, nor can I; but I will tell you what I have seen, tasted, and handled of the Word of Life, and you shall tell me what you have experienced. Thus our spirits shall have fellowship one with another. There will be a mutual exchange in commodities, as we report our discoveries of the unsearchable riches of Christ. For none has exactly the same view-point as another has; and none exactly the same definition or formula. Be yourself! Make your own discoveries of the manifold grace of Christ. If you cannot bring grapes from Eschol, bring pomegranates or figs. Bartimaeus and the man born blind had different stories to tell of the way in which they were healed, but they both saw, and owed the sight which revealed the world to the same voice and touch. Whether you swam to shore or floated on a broken piece of ship-furniture, or a spar, makes very little difference, so long as you have been saved from the storm, and stand there with the rest in the circle round the fire lighted because of the cold. You are probably right in what you affirm, but wrong in what you deny. You are justified in holding firmly to your special fragment of Truth, but be willing to admit that you have not everything, and that others may be as conscientious, as true to truth, and as eager for its maintenance and diffusion as yourself. Seek to gain from others whatever will perfect your religious life, rounding it to a more complete circle, and touching it to finer issues. "I long to see you," said the Apostle, "that I may impart unto you some spiritual gift . . . that I with you may be comforted in you, each of us by the other's faith" (Rom. i. 11, 12, R.V.).

Christ the Bond of Unity. Christ is the bond of unity to His Church—Christ in each individual, and each individual in Christ. Let us never forget that gracious reciprocity. The sponge must be in the ocean and the ocean in the sponge. Each believer is written in the Lamb's Book of Life by the same fingers. Each of us has been grafted into the true Vine, though in different places. Each of us has some function in the mystical body. We were in Him when He died, and rose, and entered the Father's presence. In Him we have access into this grace wherein we stand. We are in Him, as those twelve loaves stood on that pure table. The gift of Christ, on the other hand, has been made to each one of us, that He might realise Himself through all the experiences of all His members. As of old it required *four* Gospels to reveal to mankind what Jesus Christ was, so all believers are required to set forth and exemplify to the world all the excelling glories of our Emmanuel. It is for this reason that we are told that the Church is His Body, "the fulness of Him that filleth all in all" (Eph. i. 23). It demands a great multitude, which no man can number, to reveal the full beauty of the Second Adam, the Lord from heaven.

—**All One in Him.** Was it not of this that our Lord spoke, when He said: "The glory which Thou gavest Me, I have given them, that they may be one, even as we are one, I in them, and Thou in Me" (John xvii. 22, 23). In such radiance the Church now stands before God. He sees her essential unity. Its denial does not disintegrate it. Its obscuration does not impair it. The very members of the Church that compose the Unity may be unaware of it, and may denounce each other; but, even so, the twelve stones are in the same breastplate and the twelve loaves stand side by side on the same table. The members of a large family of boys and girls may be scattered far and wide over the world, but to the mother, in her daily and nightly prayer, there is but one family, and to her they seem sheltered still under the wings of her brooding love.

When Savonarola was about to be burned, the Papal Legate, dressed in his scarlet robes, stood beside his scaffold, and cried: "I cut thee off from the Church triumphant and the Church militant." But the martyr replied truly: "You may cut me off from the Church militant, but over the Church triumphant thou hast no power." Only two things can cut a man off from the Holy Catholic Church, considered in her loftiest ideals, and these are unforgivingness to the brethren and departure from the living God.

But as surely as the Lord accounts us members of the same mystical Body, He bids us give diligence to *keep* the unity of that Body in the bonds of peace. We are not required to create the unity, but to *manifest* it. We are to recognise as one with us, those who may differ not only in their ritual, and credal expression, but in heart and spirit, giving no sign of recognition or fellowship; but, notwithstanding, we are to think of them as one with us. Without the other neither can be made perfect. Let us, therefore, in this way hasten the time when our Lord shall present the Church to Himself, a glorious Church, without spot, wrinkle, or any such thing.

THE CANDLESTICK OF PURE GOLD

Exodus 25:31-40;27:20,21

31. And thou shalt make a candlestick *of* pure gold: *of* beaten work shall the candlestick be made: his shaft, and his branches, his bowls, his knops, and his flowers, shall be of the same.

32. And six branches shall come out of the sides of it; three branches of the candlestick out of the one side, and three branches of the candlestick out of the other side:

33. Three bowls made like unto almonds, *with* a knop and a flower in one branch; and three bowls made like almonds in the other branch, *with* a knop and a flower: so in the six branches that come out of the candlestick.

34. And in the candlestick *shall be* four bowls made like unto almonds, *with* their knops and their flowers.

35. And *there shall be* a knop under two branches of the same, and a knop under two branches of the same, and a knop under two branches of the same, according to the six branches that proceed out of the candlestick.

36. Their knops and their branches shall be of the same: all it *shall* be one beaten work *of* pure gold.

37. And thou shalt make the seven lamps thereof: and they shall light the lamps thereof, that they may give light over against it.

38. And the tongs thereof, and the snuff dishes thereof, *shall be of* pure gold.

39. *Of* a talent of pure gold shall he make it, with all these vessels.

40. And look that thou make *them* after their pattern, which was showed thee in the mount.

20. And thou shall command the children of Israel, that they bring thee pure oil olive beaten for the light, to cause the lamp to burn always.

21. In the tabernacle of the congregation without the veil, which *is* before the testimony. Aaron and his sons shall order it from evening to morning before the Lord: *it shall be* a statute for ever unto their generations on the behalf of the children of Israel.

(See xxxvii. 17–24 for the realisation of this pattern.)

THE CANDLESTICK OF PURE GOLD

Exodus 25:31-40;27:20,21

The Golden Candlestick. During the day, sufficient light entered through the porch to illumine the Holy Place, but as the night gathered artificial illumination was required. This was provided by the golden candlestick, referred to in the next paragraph of instructions given to Moses. As the closing sentence specifically enjoins the necessity of making all things according to the divine pattern, we are again reminded that all the events of Israel's exodus and pilgrimage, and all the items in the structure of the Tabernacle, were intended to be types and emblems of spiritual realities. We need, therefore, no preface of apology, in our endeavour to unfold those deep thoughts of the Divine Nature, of which we also partake, which underlie this piece of Tabernacle-Furniture. It was constructed on the pattern of eternal reality.

Its Form. Of the exact appearance of the seven-branched Candlestick there is no question, because it is figured in the Arch of Titus, and though the actual article carried off by the Roman Army could hardly have been the original one, there was probably an identity of form. It would be likely that the later artificers would have endeavoured, so far as possible, to repeat the ancient style with the upright central shaft culminating in a lamp, and the three curved branches on either side. It was fashioned by hand—"beaten work." Each branch was ornamented first with an almond flower or cup, above that a representation of the fruit of the pomegranate, and above that again of a lily blossom. The latter supported the lamp. The main shaft was to be similarly ornamented (vers. 34, 35). The gold out of which the candlestick was made is valued at £10,000 of our money, i.e. 40,000 dollars.

Its Place. On entering the Holy Place, as we have seen, in front was hung the veil, with the golden incense altar before it; on the right stood the table of shewbread, the twelve loaves of which, presented weekly, betokened the unity of the people of God, and on the left was the candlestick, equally an emblem of the unity of the Divine race, and its light, therefore, glistened from the altar and the table. "They shall light the lamps thereof, to give light over against it."

Its Import. It is obvious, on the first vision of the candlestick, that it sets forth the ministry of Israel, later of the Church, and always of true religion, in their function of illuminating the world. But the fact that here the candlestick was heavily veiled from human vision, and shone in front of the veil, seems to indicate not primarily the attitude of the Church to the world, but the attitude of the believer toward God. Indeed, everything in the Holy Place bespeaks that attitude, the shewbread table providing the obedience upon which the Spirit of God may be said to feed, the incense altar providing the intercessory prayer which is fragrant to Him, and surely the seven-branched candlestick, glowing there—"a burning and shining light"—is the symbol of the people of God, ever giving back to Him the flame that they have first received from Him, so that the Eternal Spirit beholds His own nature reflected in them, and flashing back with glory to Him who gave it, as the suns and stars of space to some central luminary. First, therefore, we have the nature and function of true religion—it is a lamp that shines and burns; secondly, the nourishment of true religion; thirdly, the ministry of Jesus Christ, as He walks amid the seven golden candlesticks.

I. *The Nature and Function of true Religion.* Whether under the Hebrew or the Christian dispensation, or under any dispensation whatever, the religious life is always the same. It partakes of the nature of the Eternal God. For just as there was an essential oneness between the light of the Shekinah, which shone between the cherubim, and the sparkling light upon the seven-branched candlestick, so there is equal similarity between the eternal nature of God and true religion, wherever you find it. God is often compared to Fire; and though that wonderful glow, that radiance, that fervour, that spiritual energy, which characterise the religious soul, are, of course, infinitely and incomparably small compared to the splendour of the Divine Nature, they are precisely the same in quality with their correspondents in God. God is a Spirit—a Spirit who is represented by fire and flame—and He seeks spirits to be enkindled with fire and flame to worship Him. But whilst there is an essential identity between the nature of God with the fire of its quick energy, its purity and its kindling, that fire dwells essentially and eternally in Him; while with us it needs to be communicated, and therefore the seven-branched candlestick had to be *lit.*

The Spirit of the Man the Candle of the Lord. The spirit of man is, after all, only the candle of the Lord, and if the Church to-day contains many who are exemplifying the religious life with its quick energy and power, its purity and heat, it is only because they have been brought into contact with the glow of the eternal nature and have been kindled by the Divine Spirit (Prov. xx. 27). You may not know the hour or place when you, as a candle, were brought first in contact with Him. It may have been that a mother's hand in your early childhood brought you in contact with the great fire of Love in God's nature, and the tiny taper was ignited and began to burn. Or it may have been in later life, after standing for years as an unlit candle, with all the wealth of knowledge and power latent in you waiting for the spark, that you were suddenly illumined by the touch of God's Spirit, and began to burn and shine—but you never would have been what you are to-day unless there had been the communication of the fire from the altar of the Divine Nature to your heart. The candle had to be lit.

Its Lighting. You will observe that two conditions have to be fulfilled before the candle can be lit. First, there must be susceptibility of ignition; and second, there must be contact. It goes without saying that there is within each of us the susceptibility for God, because we were originally made in His likeness and came forth from His creative hand, but in some cases there has been no contact. Oh, that the hand of the Divine Saviour might be placed against your heart, and so bring you into contact with His heart, that you may catch the spark which leaps forth to kindle you for ever! When that fire is once lit, it burns for evermore. That is what our Lord meant when He said, "Walk while ye have the light, lest darkness come upon you. While ye have light, believe in the light, that ye may be the children of light" (John xii. 35, 36). This is one of the deepest of His utterances. Probably something of the same thought was in the Apostle's heart when he said, "We are transformed into His likeness, from glory to glory, as by the Spirit of God." The wick of the candle becomes absolutely transformed when it touches the central flame. Too many people resemble exquisitely prepared candles, the richest and best materials having been used in their manufacture, and it may be that they stand in golden candelabra, but all is useless because the flame has never been kindled. In some of the pulpits of our Churches, and in positions of influence given to men in our Universities and Schools, we have the unlit candles, dowered with every gift, but waiting until the Divine spark shall illumine them. O soul of man, verily thou art missing thy mark in God's great world, and it is vain to attempt to realise thy great possibilities, until all the wealth of thy nature is ignited and unfolded by that Divine spark which trembles behind the veil, and which God waits to give to thee by a direct contact, such as would make thee glow and burn! One of the greatest things ever said of man was that phrase in which our Lord summed up the influence of John the Baptist—"He was a burning and a shining light." God grant that we may not have the cold light of the moon that shines, but does not burn, but of the sunlight, that fills the world with radiance and from the heat whereof nothing is hid.

Its Light. But if that is our attitude towards God to-day, kindled by Him, burning and shining in His presence, necessarily the world will become illumined. Light is gentle, and the influence of our character may be without voice or language, stealing through the office, the workroom, the social circle, or the home. Light is absolutely humble, falling equally upon the stick and stone, upon the young lambs as they play in the fields as it does upon the golden cross above St. Paul's; and wherever you find the true religion of Jesus Christ, the glow of it will illumine the most obscure corners as well as the more conspicuous platforms of your life. Light is unobtrusive, you do not see *it*; but only the objects on which its wavelets break. You are only conscious of the presence of light because of its revelation of the true nature of all things in heaven and earth. All things, says the Apostle, are made manifest by the light, for that which is made manifest is light. Light in man is twofold: the light of the intellect, which is derived, and the light of the heart, which is direct. Those that open themselves to the influence of God's Spirit have the latter in abundance. "He that is spiritual discerneth all things, and he himself is discerned of no man. . . . We have the mind of Christ."

II. *The Nourishment of True Religion.* Let us pass on to the book of Zechariah, where the candlestick reappears. The people had just come back from Babylon, and were confronted by terrible difficulties, arising first from the opposition of their enemies, and secondly from the incompetence of their leaders. It was then that the vision came to Zechariah. Although the temple was lying in waste, and all around its materials were strewn in débris, and the hands of Zerubbabel were hanging helplessly by his side, the prophet foretold that as his hands had laid the foundation, so they would presently place the pinnacle upon the finished structure; and the vision of the candlestick was given, to assure the people that it would be so, because the power of God was working through them as the oil works through the wick.

The Candlestick. The inner thought of this vision is the wick. It is very insignificant, a piece of soft material which in itself can provide no flame; or at least, if it burns for a little, it soon becomes charred and smokes, but let it be dipped into the bowl of oil, and it will become the ladder by which the golden oil will climb up to illumine and burn. The wick is flexible, soft, and useless as a luminant; but it provides the material through which the oil passes and upon the edge of which it burns. On either side of that golden bowl was an olive tree, indicating, of course, the ministry of Joshua the priest on the one hand, of Zerubbabel the prince on the other— the priestly and the royal function converging to nourish the flame.

The Oil. It was a great comfort, then, that it was not for Israel to accomplish the work, but for God through Israel, and the comfort to us is apparent. There are times in life when the difficulties seem to be insurmountable, "O great mountain!" we cry. The weary length of the years seems to be too great to bear. We question how we shall endure. It is said that Daniel *continued*, but shall we? The night is so dark, and getting darker; the cold is so intense, and getting keener; the difficulties are so many, and becoming more and more perilous—can we last? Will it not be too great a responsibility to continue? Nay, for there is the bowl in which the coil of the wick lies, filled from the olive tree on either side, which for us denote the Priesthood and the Kingship of our Lord. Not the Aaronic Priesthood only, for were it so, it would have closed on Calvary; but the Melchizedek Kingship also, which is eternal. But not Kingship alone, else there would have been no priestly work to put away our sin. We require the work of the Priest as our sacrifice and the work of the King as our supreme Master and Lord. Christ in His twofold office pours into us the oil of the Holy Paraclete, for it is the Holy Spirit Who conveys the virtue of Christ to us. We have contact with Christ through Him. The Spirit of Christ is sent into our hearts, to maintain our living and conscious fellowship with the Infinite and Eternal. All we have to do is to become steeped, and to let the wick of our faith lie deep in the oil of the unction of the Holy Spirit ministered to us from Jesus Christ, who, as mediator, has Himself received the Holy Spirit from the blessed nature of God. The one great necessity is to keep the golden pipe which conveys the oil always clean, and to see that it does not become clogged. Also let us not murmur if the golden snuffers are used. This, not unseldom, is absolutely necessary, because there is an undue preponderance of the wick, which has become charred and uneven, and needs to be removed. A large amount of the discipline of our life is intended to remove the frayed material of pride, selfishness, and depreciation of others, that we may miss none of our possibilities.

The Believer's Light. Abide in Christ, and let Christ abide in you. Draw upon your Lord; let the glory of the hidden Christ steal up into your daily living, so that amid the darkness of the world you may shine as lighthouses along the coast. Remember that the oil which is sold in the shops, or is stored in vast reservoirs, was brought from afar, and is the product of sunlight. It is, so to speak, liquid, sunlight and sun-heat. When you burn oil in your houses, you are actually burning the very light and heat which emanated from the sun. So if you are living as a servant-girl, or a clerk, or as the mother of a family, exhibiting amid the rushing life of our time a sweet, unobtrusive, gentle life, you are revealing the attributes of Deity— the sun-light and sun-heat of the very nature of God.

We must turn aside for a brief consideration of the oil, described by the prophet as "golden," which was specially prepared for burning in the candlestick (xxvii. 20, 21; and Zech. iv. 12). It was to be pure olive oil, made from the unripe fruit obtained by beating and pounding in a mortar, and not by crushing in a mill. It gives a pure, bright light, with little smoke. It seems to have been part of the priestly duty to trim the wicks and light the lamps each night, affording sufficient of this oil for their flame to burn till day-break, when "the lamp of God went out" (1 Sam. iii. 3).

How Provided and Sustained. It was a favourite saying of M'Cheyne when discussing the method of pulpit preparation, that only beaten oil might be used in the sanctuary, intimating that careful preparation was required for all material presented for the consideration of our hearers. It is not a light thing to speak to men for God, and none of us should essay the holy task apart from very careful preparation; but when we have done our utmost in this, we must depend on the kindling of the Divine fire. Ours is the beaten oil at the best, but what is that, unless the High Priest Himself shall cause the lamp to burn?

How often it seems as though God's brightest saints are they which have passed through the greatest pounding and beating. The Almighty Father cannot spare us aught that will promote our furthest and noblest influence. The crushed spice-plant, the broken leaf, the pounded olive, are emblems of hearts which have passed between the rollers of tribulation, and have yielded to God and man a sweet savour of life, which has filled the world. Let us treat all these with reverence. Let our sturdy strength tread with softened footfall in their august presence. Their face may be marred, and their bodily presence unpromising, but they inherit the earth.

III. *Our Lord's Personal Ministry.* The seven candlesticks, in the midst of which John beheld the ever-loving Christ, differed widely from the great seven-branched candlestick. That ancient symbol had all its lamps and branches springing from a single stem. Whereas in his vision, the seer saw seven distinct lamp-stands, with their lamps; representing the little Christian communities which shone amid the dense darkness of Asia Minor during the later decades of the first century. But the vision of the Christ watching, tending, nourishing, and trimming the light is surely necessary to any conception of the religious life, either of the individual or the Church. He is the true Light that lights us all; and He is the eternal necessity of all.

The Full Import. We must not allow this symbol to be watered down, as though it were only an expression for the abiding influence of His teaching and example. All that is true, but it is only a part of the truth. Through all the ages, and in every branch of the true Church, wheresoever two or three are gathered in His Name, He is there in the midst.

He is with us with eyes as a flame of fire, to detect the least infidelity of the heart or inconsistency in the life. He is there with feet like burnished brass, to tread down and destroy all that would set itself in opposition to His holiness or love. He is there to heal with the touch of His right hand, to irradiate with the light of His countenance, to correct, chastise, uplift, strengthen and comfort. To no angel-hand will He entrust either the golden snuffers or the golden oil. The nourishment and perpetuation of His Church is His peculiar office. Because He lives, we live also. As He was the Alpha, so He will be the Omega of our faith. Nothing will be left unattempted that will secure the best of which we are capable. Only let us yield to Him, lest the fate which soon overtook those seven Churches should befall us; for in Asia Minor to-day, instead of the Christian hymn arising on those ancient sites, there is the perpetual cry of the muezzin from the minaret: "There is no God but God, and Mahomet is His Prophet." Such is the mystery of the golden candlestick.

THE SIGNIFICANCE OF THE TABERNACLE

Exodus 26:1-30

1. Moreover thou shalt make the tabernacle *with* ten curtains *of* fine twined linen, and blue, and purple, and scarlet: *with* cherubims of cunning work shalt thou make them.

2. The length of one curtain *shall be* eight and twenty cubits, and the breadth of one curtain four cubits: and every one of the curtains shall have one measure.

3. The five curtains shall be coupled together one to another; and *other* five curtains *shall be* coupled one to another.

4. And thou shalt make loops of blue upon the edge of the one curtain from the selvedge in the coupling; and likewise shalt thou make in the uttermost edge of *another* curtain, in the coupling of the second.

5. Fifty loops shalt thou make in the one curtain, and fifty loops shalt thou make in the edge of the curtain that *is* in the coupling of the second; that the loops may take hold one of another.

6. And thou shalt make fifty taches of gold, and couple the curtains together with the taches: and it shall be one tabernacle.

7. And thou shalt make curtains *of* goats' *hair* to be a covering upon the tabernacle: eleven curtains shalt thou make.

8. The length of one curtain *shall be* thirty cubits, and the breadth of one curtain four cubits: and the eleven curtains *shall be all* of one measure.

9. And thou shalt couple five curtains by themselves, and six curtains by themselves, and shalt double the sixth curtain in the forefront of the tabernacle.

10. And thou shalt make fifty loops on the edge of the one curtain *that is* outmost in the coupling, and fifty loops in the edge of the curtain which coupleth the second.

11. And thou shalt make fifty taches of brass, and put the taches into the loops, and couple the tent together, that it may be one.

12. And the remnant that remaineth of the curtains of the tent, the half-curtain that remaineth, shall hang over the back side of the tabernacle.

13. And a cubit on the one side, and a cubit on the other side of that which remaineth in the length of the curtains of the tent, it shall hang over the sides of the tabernacle on this side and on that side, to cover it.

14. And thou shalt make a covering for the tent *of* rams' skins dyed red, and a covering above *of* badgers' skins.

15. And thou shalt make boards for the tabernacle *of* shittim wood standing up.

16. Ten cubits *shall be* the length of a board, and a cubit and a half *shall be* the breadth of one board.

17. Two tenons *shall there be* in one board, set in order one against another: thus shalt thou make for all the boards of the tabernacle.

18. And thou shalt make the boards for the tabernacle, twenty boards on the south side southward.

19. And thou shalt make forty sockets of silver under the twenty boards; two sockets under one board for his two tenons, and two sockets under another board for his two tenons.

20. And for the second side of the tabernacle on the north side *there shall be* twenty boards:

21. And their forty sockets *of* silver; two sockets under one board, and two sockets under another board.

22. And for the sides of the tabernacle westward thou shalt make six boards.

23. And two boards shalt thou make for the corners of the tabernacle in the two sides.

24. And they shall be coupled together beneath, and they shall be coupled together above the head of it unto one ring: thus shall it be for them both; they shall be for the two corners.

25. And they shall be eight boards, and their sockets *of* silver, sixteen sockets; two sockets under one board, and two sockets under another board.

26. And thou shalt make bars *of* shittim wood; five for the boards of the one side of the tabernacle.

27. And five bars for the boards of the other side of the tabernacle, and five bars for the boards of the side of the tabernacle, for the two sides westward.

28. And the middle bar in the midst of the boards shall reach from end to end.

29. And thou shalt overlay the boards with gold, and make their rings *of* gold *for* places for the bars: and thou shalt overlay the bars with gold.

30. And thou shalt rear up the tabernacle according to the fashion thereof which was showed thee in the mount.

(See xxxvi. 8–38 for the realisation of this pattern.)

THE SIGNIFICANCE OF THE TABERNACLE

Exodus 26:1-30

The Structure of the Tabernacle. It hardly falls within the purpose of this book to enter into an exact consideration of the structure of the Tabernacle. There has been much learned discussion as to the measurements, the question as to whether there was a ridge-pole, and so forth. These points are dealt with exhaustively in various Bible Dictionaries, and in works specially devoted to their elucidation. It is enough for us to know that the Tabernacle was a movable sanctuary, in length twenty-seven feet, and in breadth nine feet, surrounded by a movable courtyard, which enclosed it, the whole consisting of curtains of various fabrics.

—**Externally.** The framework of the structure was formed by boards of acacia wood, each of which was fifteen feet long by two feet three inches broad, twenty of them on either side, and eight at the back. They were threaded together by five horizontal bars; and stood in massive sockets of silver, which were sunk in the ground. Over this framework three sets of curtains were hung, which made the ceiling, and drooped over the boards. The *first* set of curtains consisted of ten widths, which were coupled together by loops of blue and clasps of gold. These composed the immediate covering of the sanctuary, visible to every eye that was permitted to view the sacred interior. They were made of fine twined linen of a soft white hue, something like our best Indian muslin, variegated by cords of blue, purple, and scarlet, with figures of cherubim woven into the fabric while yet upon the loom. Next to these was a similar series of curtains of goats' hair, such as the Arabs still employ as the ordinary covering of their tents. The soft inner wool of the Angora goat yielded itself readily to be made into a fine worsted, and was specially suitable for this purpose. It should be noticed that there were eleven breadths in these curtains, so as to admit of a portion hanging over the front and back of the structure, and also that they were longer than the others, so as more fully to cover them and the wooden boards. Above these two layers of curtains was a third, of very tough and durable texture, which would also protect from rain and storm, being lined within by rams' skins dyed red, affording a kind of morocco leather, and on the outside consisting of seal or porpoise skins.

—**Internally.** Within the Tabernacle, dividing it into one-third the length, and two-thirds, the veil was hung of which we speak in the next chapter. It divided the Most Holy place from the Holy. The former formed a complete cube of nine feet, stood exactly in the centre of the hinder or western half of the court, and contained the sacred Ark. The latter contained the incense-altar, candlestick, and shewbread table.

Its Existence a Fact. The historicity of the Tabernacle has been assailed, but the defence given by Professor James Orr is sufficient to satisfy the candid mind, that the account as given on the pages of Exodus is justified by competent enquiry and adequate reasons. In 1 Sam. iii. 3 we come, incidentally, not only on the old name of the Tabernacle, but on mention of "the lamp of God" burning, as directed, all night; and in 1 Sam. xxi. 4, of the shewbread, the characteristic institution of the Levitical Code. In 2 Sam. vii. 6 it is made abundantly clear that, prior to the temple, Jehovah's dwelling was "a tent and a tabernacle," and that the Ark of God dwelt within curtains. We are not bound to suppose that the Tabernacle continued just as Moses constructed it for 480 years (according to 1 Kings vi. 1) without repair and renewal. Boards will not hold out for ever, curtains will wear out and become faded and torn. It would be impossible for the Tabernacle to retain the fresh and beautiful appearance it had at the first. But loving and skilful hands would carefully repair it from time to time, especially after the fearful outrages perpetrated on Shiloh by the heathen, after the days of Samuel, and described in that most plaintive of the Psalms, the lxxviiith. (See especially vers. 58–67.) The fact that the Ark was preserved with such jealous care until the days of Solomon, would suggest that the Tabernacle in which, with the exception of the brief period of its residence at a private house, it was enshrined, would be worthy of its significance and dignity.

Its Cost No Difficulty. In opposition to the objection that its costliness and skill were more than the Hebrew nation could compass at that time in their history, we must remember the increasing

testimony coming to hand in evidence of the high state of civilisation which the Egyptians had attained at the time of the Exodus.
We may quote the opinion of an expert student of the subject, "that
this description could only have been written by one who had seen
the Tabernacle standing."

Its Import—God in Touch with Human Life. But what was the
signification of this elaborate structure? We may give a fourfold
answer to that question. (1) *It indicated the desire of God to share
our human life.* "Let them make Me a Tabernacle, that I may dwell
among them." The Hebrews were meant to feel that the God of
their fathers was a fellow-pilgrim, that where they pitched He
pitched, that their enemies, difficulties, and long toilsome marches
were His. If His Tent was pitched among theirs, He surely was in
the march. In all their afflictions He was afflicted, and the Angel of
His Presence saved them. He bore and carried them all the days of
old (see specially xxix. 42–46). When David proposed to build a
substantial House, He answered, "Thou shalt not build Me an house
to dwell in, for I have not dwelt in an house since the day that I
brought up the children of Israel out of Egypt, even to this day; but
have walked with all Israel" (1 Chron. xvii. 4, 5). The feeble-minded
and fearful were of good courage, when there was the noise of war,
or an expectation of the onset of the Amalekites, who were constantly skirmishing in the rear of the march. Was not God in the
midst of them? they could not be moved, God would help them, and
that right early. And little children, if they were startled at night by
the howl or cry of the wild beasts of the wilderness, would take
heart again, when their parents reminded them that the light that
shone softly over the sleeping-camp issued from Jehovah's
tent.

A Foreshadowing of the Incarnation. The hearts of men were thus
familiarised with the Humanness of the Divine Nature. God was
willing to dwell with man upon the earth, though the heavens could
not contain Him. Obviously, however, there was a great gulf still
to be bridged, especially for the more spiritual because there was
no real union between the dwelling and its tenant; and godly souls
waited expectantly for that still closer identification of God with
man which was to be given in the Incarnation. Then the Word
became flesh and *tabernacled* among men, and they beheld His glory,
the glory of the Only Begotten of the Father. The fulness of the
Godhead dwells still in a body fashioned after our own, and we

may say, in the words of the seer of Patmos, Behold the Tabernacle of God is with men, and He will dwell with them, they shall hunger no more, neither thirst any more, neither shall the hot sun of the desert smite them, nor any heat, because they shall be led to fountains of water, the emblem and fruition of the Promised Land.

The One God Declared. But (2) the Tabernacle also set forth symbolically certain great truths. It taught, for instance, *a sublime monotheism*. Embodied in every detail was the sacred formula, "Hear, O Israel, the Lord thy God is *one* Lord." The gods of the heathen were many. Crowds of them occupied the niches of the Pantheons; whilst innumerable temples and shrines filled even the most civilised cities. To be quite sure that amid the thronging multitude of their duties they had omitted none, the Athenians erected an altar to any unknown god that might have been unintentionally passed over, and might feel resentment. There was no trace of those divided religious interests. The *Unity* of Jehovah, as the one God of Israel, who was jealous of any rival, and who must be *Only* the object of His people's devotions, is the principal and most impressive affirmation in the Tabernacle, with its single inner throne.

God's Spirituality Attested. There was no image, no likeness. Pompey, with sacrilegious impetuosity, strode into the most holy place, notwithstanding the horrified dissuasions of the priests, and came out expressing his wonder that there was no idol or fetich. The holy Light burned there between the bowing forms of the cherubim, reflected from the Golden Mercy-Seat, and that was all. It seemed as though already the words of our Lord had received anticipatory fulfilment: "God is Spirit, and they who worship Him must worship Him in spirit and in truth."

God's Holiness Emphasised. There was no better way of teaching this to a people, to whom the idea was unaccustomed and obscure, than by placing barriers and impediments in the way of the ordinary crowd, and in selecting an elect representative, of an elect family, of an elect tribe, as alone worthy to approach; especially when even he was not permitted to draw nigh except after special ablutions and with costly sacrifices. Such careful prescriptions enhanced the solemnity of the approach and the awful holiness of the Almighty. That the veil might not be passed, save once in the year, and then by the High Priest only, at whose garment's hem the bells rang with his every movement, assuring the awed hearers that his life was yet preserved, enhanced the sense of the wideness of the gulf which intervened between God and man.

The Dual Aspect of the National Ministries. In the providence of God, the Hebrew nation of old was summoned, like the Church to-day, to perform three ministries for men—to pray for them, to illumine them, and to feed the immortal hunger of the soul. These ministries were represented by the altar of incense, the seven-branched candlestick, and the table of shewbread. Had we met with these three emblems in the outer court, we should not have been surprised; but it is somewhat remarkable to find them in the Holy Place, with only a veil between them and the Shechinah, yet could the lesson be more clearly taught that whatever was done for the great world of men was deemed an acceptable service to the Almighty? True service to mankind is accepted by God as true service to Himself. Inasmuch as we do aught to one of the least, we do it to Him. It is impossible to serve God aright in His secret place, without at the same time ministering to the world; and when we would bless men by our poor efforts, there is the savour of sweet incense in the heart of our Heavenly Father, whether we are rewarded by human praise or not. There is a gauge in Heaven that registers the pressure of our service on Earth.

The Nature of Man. But (3) one of the profoundest aspects of the Tabernacle, as afterwards of the Temple, was its teaching as to *the nature of man*. There is good reason to think that Moses was led to embody in the Tabernacle structure some of those profound thoughts on the essential structure of the soul which have always occupied the noblest of our race. The common people were fed with symbols and parables, but the construction of the Pyramids, and the secrets conveyed to Initiates of the ancient mysteries, are evidence that among the ancients there were schools of spiritual philosophy, which profoundly influenced Egypt, Chaldea, and Greece.

The Interpretation of that Day. There are traces of Divinity schools, where devout students assembled to study the philosophy of God and man thousands of years before our era. It may be that there are more references in the early Hebrew Scriptures to these deep teachings than we ordinarily realise, and that the system of interpretation in vogue among Bible students some fifty years ago has more to warrant it than the materialised thought of Western civilisation is inclined to admit. That allegory of Sarah and Hagar, to which Paul refers, may furnish a truer clue to the reading of Scripture than some moderns might be ready to admit.

The Anticipation of the Future. But even if Moses were not aware of this mystic analogy, he may have been led by the Divine Spirit to construct the Tabernacle on such a method as would set forth to coming generations profound truths; and thus take his position among those who searched what the Spirit of Christ, that was in them, did signify, and to whom it was revealed that not unto themselves, nor to their age, but unto ours, did they minister those things which have been now announced unto us by the Holy Spirit sent forth from Heaven (see Heb. ix. 8: "The Holy Spirit this signifying," obviously in the construction of the Tabernacle).

Man in Relation to God. The Tabernacle, as we have seen, consisted of three parts, of which the middle was the Holy Place, with the Holy of Holies on the one side and the outer court upon the other. The nature of man is also tripartite, the centre being the soul, which is the seat of our personality. There we have as furniture the will, the mind, imagination, reason, the emotions, memory and other indispensable faculties. But on the one side, the forward side, we have the Holy of Holies of the Spirit, while on the other we have the outer court of the body, which brings us into contact with the world around. Holy of Holies, Holy Place, and Outer-Court, yet one structure: Spirit, soul, and body, yet one individual.

Every one has the aptitude and capacity for God, but until regeneration introduces the light of the Shechinah, the shrine of the spirit is dark and empty; and the highest state of man, in that case, is what the Apostle calls *psychic*. The natural or psychic man of 1 Cor. ii. 14, is he whose soul is the supreme governing power of his nature, because as yet his spirit has not awoke to, or been illumined by the Divine Spirit. But when regeneration has supervened, the darkness is past, the true light shines. The light of the Shechinah, representing the presence of God, pours its flood of glorious life into the soul, and through the soul into the outer court of the body, which becomes, in turn, quickened and transfigured by the energy of the indwelling Spirit. "If the Spirit of Him that raised up Jesus from the dead dwelleth in you, He that raised up Christ Jesus from the dead shall quicken also your mortal bodies, through His Spirit that dwelleth in you."

Our Holy of Holies. When our Lord bade each of us enter into his closet and shut the door and pray, there may have been a reference to that closet of our nature which may be described as the Holy of Holies within us. It is there that we may meet God, and that the Holy Spirit will bear witness with our spirit; and it is there that we learn true wisdom. Having therefore, brethren, boldness, in hours of silent meditation, to enter into the Holiest, by a new and living way, which Christ hath consecrated for us, let us draw near.

Old Things Passed Away. (4) *But neither Tabernacle nor Temple are needed now.* Time and change destroyed the one, the armies of Vespasian and Titus destroyed the other. The Moslem holds the sacred site, so that the Jew himself is unable to do more than wail beside the old walls, as he remembers Zion. The Church of the Living God, that according to the foreknowledge of the Father, redeemed by the blood of the Saviour, and sanctified by the Holy Spirit, is God's habitation now; even as it is written: "Ye are no more strangers and sojourners, but ye are fellow-citizens with the saints, and of the household of God, being built upon the foundation of Apostles and Prophets, Christ Jesus Himself being the chief corner stone, in whom each several building, fitly framed together, groweth into a holy temple in the Lord; in whom ye also are builded together for a habitation of God in the Spirit" (Ephes. ii. 19–22, R.V.).

"INTO THE HOLIEST"

Exodus 26:31-37; Hebrews 10:19-22

31. And thou shalt make a veil *of* blue, and purple, and scarlet, and fine twined linen of cunning work: with cherubims shall it be made:

32. And thou shalt hang it upon four pillars of shittim *wood* overlaid with gold: their hooks *shall be of* gold, upon the four sockets of silver.

33. And thou shalt hang up the veil under the taches, that thou mayest bring in thither within the veil the ark of the testimony: and the veil shall divide unto you between the holy *place* and the most holy.

34. And thou shalt put the mercy seat upon the ark of the testimony in the most holy *place*.

35. And thou shalt set the table without the veil, and the candlestick over against the table on the side of the tabernacle toward the south: and thou shalt put the table on the north side.

36. And thou shalt make an hanging for the door of the tent, *of* blue, and purple, and scarlet, and fine twined linen, wrought with needlework.

37. And thou shalt make for the hanging five pillars *of* shittim *wood*, and overlay them with gold, *and* their hooks *shall be of* gold: and thou shalt cast five sockets of brass for them.

19. Having therefore, brethren, boldness to enter into the holiest by the blood of Jesus,

20. By a new and living way, which he hath consecrated for us, through the veil, that is to say, his flesh;

21. And *having* an high priest over the house of God;

22. Let us draw near with a true heart in full assurance of faith, having our hearts sprinkled from an evil conscience, and our bodies washed with pure water.

"INTO THE HOLIEST"

Exodus 26:31-37; Hebrews 10:19-22

The Veil. A richly embroidered Veil, of the same material and workmanship as the inner curtains, which composed the ceiling of the Tabernacle, hung between the Holy and the Most Holy Place. It was glowing all over with figures of cherubim, in blue and purple and scarlet on a white ground. Whether this veil divided the interior in exact halves, as some have supposed, comparing verse 33 with verse 6, or whether it divided it into one-third and two-thirds, as was the case in Solomon's Temple, is not material to the present purpose. It is sufficient for our purpose that there was a division made by this magnificent curtain, draped over four pillars covered with gold. Within was the Ark, with its mercy-seat. Immediately outside was the Altar of Incense; on the right, when approaching the curtain from the Court, was the shewbread table, and on the left the golden candlestick.

The High Priest's Privilege. The High Priest alone might enter that Most Holy Place, once a year, and not without blood, this signifying that the way into the Holiest was not revealed, while the first tabernacle was yet standing. The Christian soul has too often missed the significance of this *parable* (as it is called in Heb. ix. 9) by identifying the Most Holy Place with heaven, but a more careful consideration of the explanatory teaching of the Epistle to the Hebrews proves that this is not the meaning which the Holy Spirit desired to signify. If, as this verse teaches, the way into the Holiest was not made manifest under the Mosaic Dispensation, it stands to reason that it is now made manifest, since Christ has come, a High Priest of the greater and more perfect Tabernacle, not made with hands—that is to say, not of this creation. And if it is not of this material creation, is it not clear that it is immaterial, and therefore spiritual? Besides which, in Heb. x. 19 the writer says, "Having therefore, brethren, boldness to enter into the Holy Place." The Greek word there, rendered "the Holy Place," is the same as is used in ix. 8, ix. 12, ix. 25, where it clearly stands for the Holy of Holies. In addition, the references to the rent veil of the Redeemer's flesh establishes the same position, and when we are bidden to enter into the Holiest, we are in effect asked to take up absolutely and literally that position within the veil which was allotted to the High Priest only once a year.

The Veil and Christian Experience. This division between the two compartments of the Tabernacle suggests the difference that pertains in religious experience, as illustrated in the lives of the saints of Scripture. Moses was a religious man before he beheld the burning bush, but he surely passed within the veil when he stood with God on the mount. David was a religious man in the earlier stages of his life, but he was subject to much failure and one great sin; but the difference between those days and the serene period of his later life, to which Psalm xxiii. is attributable, is manifest. When John asked for fire to fall from heaven on the villages of the Samaritans, he was sojourning beyond the veil, but it was rent for him, and he stood face to face with the Shechinah, when he wrote his Epistles, or beheld the ever-living Christ in his Apocalypse. It may be that up to this moment some reader of these words has been content with the twilight instead of the perfect day, and to that soul rings out the challenge: "Having therefore, boldness to enter into the Holiest by the blood of Jesus, by a new and living way which He has inaugurated for us, let us draw near." This is the argument of Hebrews ix. and x.

Life Within the Veil. I. Let us enumerate the characteristics of the life "within the veil." We must distinguish between the *variants* and the *constants* of that experience.

—Its Variants. *The variants are as follows: Emotion,* which, as its name indicates, is as variable as the surface of the ever-changeful ocean, beneath whose expanse pulsations of power, of greater or less force, are perpetually passing. We cannot command or trust our emotional life, which is affected by so many and conflicting causes. *The Pressure of Temptation,* which is fitful and uncertain, sometimes rushing on us with the force of a tornado, and again like a soft breeze. *Enjoyment in our religious exercises,* which is sometimes keen and ecstatic, and at other times languid and depressed. *Desire for the salvation of others and the coming of the Kingdom.* This also passes from the fire shut up in the bones, so that we are weary of forbearing and cannot stay, to the heavy lethargy of the Enchanted Ground.

It is well for us all to write these down as variants, being affected by physical, psychic, and other causes, that are not directly spiritual; though before we acquiesce in any of them we should carefully examine our hearts, to see whether we are harbouring anything which is disturbing the natural course of religious experience, and either retarding or invalidating it.

—**Its Constants.** Having eliminated the variant, let us turn to the constant. What are the characteristics of life within the veil?

(1) *It is a life of Joyful Assurance.* Too often we are like persons walking through a woodland glade, and our paths are streaked with patches of sunshine; but this experience is one in which the soul knows, and knows that it knows. The First Epistle of John, which is the tableland of love, resounds from end to end with the accent of conviction. The High Priest stood face to face with the Light of Shechinah; but the souls for whom the veil is rent, say with the people of Sychar, "We believe, not because of any word that human lips have spoken, but because we have seen for ourselves, and know that this is the Christ of God." For such there are the riches of the full assurance of understanding, the full assurance of faith, and the full assurance of hope. They for whom the veil is gone are not disturbed by the criticism of documents or the clash of creeds. The darkness is past, the Sun of Righteousness shines clearly and directly upon them, with healing in His beams.

(2) *It is a life which apprehends the near Presence of God.* Of course God is ever equally near. In Him we live, and move, and have our being. There is no far and near, here or there, space or time, in the existence of the Eternal. But to human consciousness there are sensible differences in the proximity or remoteness of the Divine Presence. The Psalmist says, "Thou art near, O God"; and the Patriarch cries, "Oh that I knew where I might find Him!" When, however, the Holy Spirit takes of the things of Christ and reveals them, our Sun no more goes down, neither does the moon withdraw itself, and the Lord becomes our everlasting light, and the days of our mourning are ended. We speak with Christ as a man speaks with his friend. Life is no longer a monologue, but a dialogue. We see one face, hear one voice, detect one presence, and know that He who sent us is with us; our Lord has not left us alone, because we are set on doing the things that please Him. "Whom have I in

heaven but Thee? and there is none on earth that I desire beside Thee."

Even When He Uses Discipline. There may be hours when, in our service for others, we are called to enter the glades of Gethsemane and to cry from our cross that we are forsaken. It may be needful even, sometimes, that God should place us under the shadow of His hand when He passes by. Plants cannot thrive in unbroken light, they require the alternation of sun and shadow. It is necessary that the Divine Face should be slightly veiled, for the same reason that Moses' was; but even then there is a calm assurance of His presence which is almost equivalent to perfect vision. Bunyan places the Land of Beulah immediately before the river, and we hesitate to challenge any statement to which he has affixed his seal, but surely we need not wait for the afterglow, whilst the Heavens are full of sunlight!

(3) *It is a life of Victory.* In physical disease, the atmosphere may be sterilised so as to become aseptic. No microbe of disease can live or breed in it. And when we are filled with the Holy Spirit, the susceptibility of our nature to the appeal of passion is reduced to the smallest possible amount. The explosive material is too wet to catch the spark. When we live and walk in the Spirit we cannot fulfil the lust of the flesh. We know the force of the stream running past us, but our sails are so full of the divine gale, blowing in the contrary direction, that we are able to continue our course undaunted. Ours is no longer the experience of Ishmael, the son of the bondwoman, but of Isaac, the son of the free. For we are conscious that we are to abide in the house for ever; we have received the Spirit of Adoption; we address God, even as Jesus did, as Abba, Father; we hear the Father say, "Son, thou art ever with Me, and all that I have is thine"; and if a son, then an heir. Use your rights, for when you are living in the inner place, and in the power of the Eternal Spirit, the power of the flesh is broken. It has no longer an attraction, it is no more capable of exerting its thrall. If you live in the Spirit, you cannot fulfil the lusts of the flesh. You may sometimes hear its murmurings, as Moses and Aaron had to do, when they went into the camp, but they cannot entice the heart, which is fixed in God.

—Its Strength and Joy. Remember that glorious Psalm cviii. The Psalmist begins by saying, "O God, my heart is fixed; I will sing, yea, I will sing praises." Evidently David was in the Most Holy

Place of religious experience; and he goes on to say, "Gilead is mine; Manasseh is mine; Ephraim also is the defence of mine head; Judah is my sceptre; Moab is my washpot; upon Edom will I cast my shoe; over Philistia will I shout." That is the proud challenge of the life which is hidden with Christ in God. Whilst it abides in the Truth, it is impregnable and all-conquering. No weapon that is formed against it shall prosper, and every tongue that shall rise against it in judgment is condemned.

(4) *It is a life of prevailing Prayer.* We realise that we are allowed as priests to stand beside the Great High Priest in the psychical intercession, and find ourselves caught up and swept along in His intercessions for those whom the Father hath given Him, and for such as are believing through their word. Far and wide our thoughts travel over the world, over the sheep which as yet are not of His fold; and as we pray, there is an accent of conviction and certainty in our prayers. We know that He hears, and we know that we have the petitions that we desire of Him. In the language of that fine portraiture of the results of acquaintance with God, given in Job xxii., we decree things, and they are established. We hear God saying: "Of things concerning My sons, and concerning the work of My hands, command ye Me." We experience the truth of our Lord's words that he who believes shall have "whatsoever he saith."

(5) *It is a life of abounding Love for Others.* Those who know that for them, at least, the veil is gone, that there is no condemnation, that there is a clear sky over them, and the everlasting arms beneath, look with a strange and beautiful love upon their fellows. They seek out their excellences rather than their defects. There is no longer a beam in the eye, making it intolerant of the motes in the eyes of others. "The chord of self has passed trembling out of sight." The soul is baptised into the conditions of all men. It no longer desires things for the sake of possession, but for use and service. It counts itself the servant and debtor of all for the sake of Christ. It travails in birth till Christ is formed in them. So strong is this love that ambition for worldly honour, praise, esteem, position, emolument, is swallowed up in one set purpose, that the Kingdom of God may come, and His will be done, as in heaven so on earth. For them, of whom it is said that no man said that aught of the things he possessed was his own, because they had all things common—it is clear that already the veil had been rent in twain from the top to the bottom.

The Cost of the Way. II. *This new and Living Way was dedicated for us at great Cost.* "Having therefore, brethren, boldness to enter into the holy place by the blood of Jesus, by the way which He dedicated for us . . . through the veil, that is to say, His flesh" (Heb. x. 19, 20, R.V.). It cost our Lord the emptying of His Holy Incarnation, His Cross and Passion, His blood and broken heart. The reason is hid with God, until we are able to receive it, in God's own time and place. In the meanwhile we remember that God sent His own Son in the likeness of sinful flesh, and as an offering for sin, that He might condemn sin in the flesh.

The Calvary Scene. It was towards the late afternoon of the day when Jesus died. The midday darkness had passed, the sun was shining on the earth again, but the air was heavy, and the parching thirst of all men and living things was so acute as even to touch the hearts of the seasoned soldiers, and when the dying Lord said, "I thirst," one of them fetched vinegar on a sponge. Shortly after that He said, "It is finished," "Father, into Thy hands I commend My Spirit," and gave back His soul to God.

The Veil Rent. There were simultaneously an earthquake and other signs in the world of Nature; but the most extraordinary event transpired in the Temple, where the evening sacrifice was being offered. At that hour, being the hour of prayer, one of the officiating priests was within the Holy Place, presenting incense at the altar of incense, which stood immediately before the veil. To his unutterable amazement and horror, it seemed as though two gigantic hands had seized that heavy veil, which was renewed every year, and were rending it from top to bottom, as you might rend tissue-paper. Immediately the whole of the inner sanctuary stood revealed. His eyes beheld the secret which was only unfolded to the High Priest once a year. At first it was absolutely inexplicable, but when afterwards it was discovered that the rending took place at the moment when Jesus of Nazareth was expiring, the connection between the two events was recognised, and the story was mentioned with awe from lip to lip, which probably accounts for the announcement made afterwards, that a great company of the priests became obedient to the faith (Acts vi. 7).

The Way Opened. We know little more than that. The rending of the Temple veil took place, not in our Lord's early prime, when life presented itself in its most rosy hues, or when He sat teaching on the Mount of Beatitudes, or when He was commissioning the

Twelve, but when He was dying—when He was in the act of yielding Himself on the altar to bear away the sin of the world. It was in that supreme moment that the veil was rent, betokening, so far as an outward sign could do, that something had happened, that the veil was no longer needed, that the way to God was open, that the old covenant had passed never to return, and that henceforth the soul of man might enter without hesitancy and fear. Even though, like Aaron, you have failed egregiously and miserably, you are welcome to draw as near spiritually, as he did physically, unto that Presence where Angels bow low with reverence, or hide their faces whilst they cry, "Holy, Holy, Holy is the Lord God of Sabaoth."

The Conditions of Realisation. III. *The Conditions on which this Life may be realised. In general*, it is necessary that we look on this position as the right, through grace, of everyone who is in living union with Christ. We are familiar with the natural rights which belong to us as members of the human family, such as the right to live, to be free, to have a share in the common gifts of the Creator, and to know the privileges and blessings of a home. We have no hesitation in claiming these, and entering upon their enjoyment. But the rights that belong to us as members of the divine family are equally assured. Amongst these may be reckoned justification, sanctification, glorification, a name and a place among the children, and the right to enter on all those privileges which Jesus won by His obedience unto death. "I appoint unto you," He said, "a Kingdom, as My Father hath appointed unto Me."

Possibilities by Faith. Appropriate and enter upon, by faith, this life within the precincts of the Holiest, not because of any merit in yourselves, but because you are one with Jesus Christ. Where He is gone, we may go; where He stands, we may stand; we may enjoy in spiritual fellowship and communion that blessed nearness to God which is the portion of the redeemed. "Having a great Priest over the House of God, let us draw near." *"For we are become partakers with Christ, if we hold fast the beginning of our confidence firm unto the end"* (Heb. iii. 14, R.V.).

Where We have Failed. What wonderful words are these! Do they not show where we have failed? We have not asserted our rights, which He has purchased for us by His blood, by the rending of His flesh, and by the breaking of His heart. *Do not wait to evolve into this experience!* Claim it: appropriate it: take it by faith, and hold it stedfastly by the same. Accept it with boldness, and assert it in fulness of faith, having your heart sprinkled from an evil conscience, and your body washed with pure water. When you look down at your past failures, your unworthiness, your many sins, you may be tempted to renounce your position and return to the miserable experience of the wilderness with its graves of failure. Then look up, and understand what Jesus has done. He has dedicated the new and living way of holiness and consecration—will you not walk in it? He has secured for you this standing in grace and glory, will you not at least step up to it and occupy it? He has fought hard to bring you to this, why will you not accept, humbly and thankfully, what He has secured? You have no hesitation in entering upon houses which you did not build, possessions you have never earned, titles you have never won—if they come to you by inheritance or by will! Why do you hesitate to enter upon your inheritance in Christ? But since His death has occurred, those who are called are entitled to receive the promise of an eternal inheritance! (Heb. ix. 15, R.V.) Why, then, do you hesitate to avail yourself of your Father's gift in Jesus? This is not humility, it is a sinful and ungrateful perversion of God's loving intentions.

The New and Living Way. *In particular*, the steps by which this life may be practically realised are set forth in Heb. x., and are set down below. But, at the outset, it should be remembered that we are told that the entrance into the Holiest is *by a new and living way*. May we not put it thus?—that our Master has inaugurated for us a new way of living, which was fresh to the world of His time, and is as fresh to-day as ever. The dew has distilled on each spring morning since the beginning, but is as fresh still as it was when it lay on the face of unfallen creation. After all, it is not by dreaming, or thinking, or austerities, but by living on the divine plan, that we enter into and enjoy that better life, to which we are invited by the writer when he says, "Having therefore, brethren, boldness to enter into the Holy Place by the blood of Jesus, by the way which He dedicated for us, a new and living way through the veil, that is to say, His flesh . . . *let us draw near*" (Heb. ix. 19–22, R.V.).

Draw Near! 1. *Regard your body as having been prepared for you.* On the earlier pages of Scripture, the Hebrews, like other peoples, presented the bodies of animals to God—the sheep, the ox, the goat. This is an earlier stage of consecration; but surely it is better to present these than the body of the first-born child. "Shall I give my first-born for my transgression, the fruit of my body for the sin of my soul?" But as light grew from more to more, the Psalmist, speaking for the advance-guard of humanity, uttered the memorable sentence quoted here, and which in the first sense was true of the Psalmist himself, but had a deeper and Messianic significance: "Sacrifice and offering Thou wouldest not, but a body didst Thou prepare for Me . . . I am come to do Thy will, O God" (Heb. x. 5-7, R.V.). Here a new conception emerges, and one which may include ourselves. Dare to believe that God Himself has fitted your soul and body, that He gave you the body as the implement of your life-work, and is prepared by His grace to supplement any of its deficiencies. He desires that you may present it to Himself as a living sacrifice holy and acceptable in His sight. The plan or programme of the steps in which you are to walk has also been planned. It is not for you to *carve* your way through the tangled jungle, but to walk in the steps which He has prepared. We were created unto good works, which He has before prepared that we should walk in them (Eph. ii. 10). Only let us see to it that our hearts are sprinkled from an evil conscience, and our bodies washed with pure water; and let it be never forgotten that the pure body is only possible to the pure soul that refuses to give room to anything less than the best and highest.

—**Resolving to do God's Will.** 2. *Determine that you will do the will of God.* There is a sense in which we may repeatedly affirm the words, which have been freshly minted by the Lord: "I am come to do Thy will, O God." If at first you cannot delight to do it, do it, knowing that it is essentially good, perfect, and acceptable. You will never know what marvellous results lie within the compass of very ordinary lives, until you are willing to be the channel and expression of the Eternal Will. The Will of God necessarily provides the rails on which the soul proceeds, when it is propelled by the Divine Spirit, fulfilling the Divine purpose. It may not be always possible to say, at the outset, "I delight to do Thy will, O my God." We begin by the choosing it, advance to obeying it, and end by delighting in it. It is a good and memorable day in a man's life when he is content with this, no longer seeking applause, or craving the smile of man, not endeavouring to please or aggrandise self, but calmly, quietly, and persistently doing it on earth, even as it is done in heaven. How strange that we should so often pray for it to be done, but are so fearful and reluctant to do it ourselves!

—Deeming the Sin-question Settled. 3. *Reckon that the Sin-question has been dealt with, once and for ever.* "By one offering He hath perfected them that are being sanctified." We may often need to wash in the laver, and to be sprinkled from an evil conscience, but we have passed beyond the great brazen altar with its heavy toll of victims appointed for the Day of Atonement. Our great High Priest has offered one sacrifice for sins for ever, and has done it so completely and finally that instead of standing as the ancient priests did, He has sat down on the right hand of God, henceforth expecting till His enemies be made the footstool of His feet (Heb. x. 12, 13, R.V.). And it is on this basis that the covenant is built, in which God says that He will remember our sins and iniquities no more (verse 17). Surely if He forgets our sins, and puts them behind His back, we may have boldness to enter into the Holiest, as though we have never sinned, but had shared from the first the unfallen glory of the first-born sons of light.

—Participating in the Cross of Christ. 4. *Through the power of the Eternal Spirit we must participate in the Cross of Christ.* It was by the Eternal Spirit that He offered Himself without spot to God (Heb. ix. 14); and it was at the moment of that offering, when the body of His flesh was being torn asunder, and His Spirit was passing into the spirit-world, that the veil of the Temple was rent in twain from the top to the bottom. Similarly, when we identify ourselves with His cross, when we take personally and individually that position which He took up as our representative, when we are crucified with Christ, yielding to death our old and selfish nature, without mercy or pity, then the soul experiences that rending of the veil, in virtue of which the way into the Holiest experience becomes plain. After all, the whole question hinges on this! What are we willing to do? "If I live after the flesh, I must die; but if by the Spirit ye mortify the deeds of the body, ye shall live" (Rom. viii. 13, R.V.). Then as we emerge from the tenacious hold of the flesh into the liberty of the sons of God, a great voice will be heard saying, Unfold, Unfold, and the blessed angels will make way for the soul, as it passes beyond their veiled presence to the secret place of the most High, to learn what it is to dwell in the house of the Lord for ever, where there is a new heaven and a new earth, and the former things are passed away.

THE COURT AND ITS CONTENTS

Exodus 27:1-19;30:17-21

1. And thou shalt make an altar *of* shittim wood, five cubits long, and five cubits broad; the altar shall be foursquare: and the height thereof *shall be* three cubits.

2. And thou shalt make the horns of it upon the four corners thereof: his horns shall be of the same: and thou shalt overlay it with brass.

3. And thou shalt make his pans to receive his ashes, and his shovels, and his basons, and his flesh-hooks, and his fire-pans: all the vessels thereof thou shalt make *of* brass.

4. And thou shalt make for it a grate of network *of* brass; and upon the net shalt thou make four brasen rings in the four corners thereof.

5. And thou shalt put it under the compass of the altar beneath, that the net may be even to the midst of the altar.

6. And thou shalt make staves for the altar, staves *of* shittim wood, and overlay them with brass.

7. And the staves shall be put into the rings, and the staves shall be upon the two sides of the altar, to bear it.

8. Hollow with boards shalt thou make it: as it was shewed thee in the mount, so shall they make *it.*

9. And thou shalt make the court of the tabernacle: for the south side southward *there shall be* hangings for the court *of* fine twined linen of an hundred cubits long for one side:

10. And the twenty pillars thereof and their twenty sockets *shall be of* brass; the hooks of the pillars and their fillets *shall be of* silver.

11. And likewise for the north side in length *there shall be* hangings of an hundred *cubits* long, and his twenty pillars and their twenty sockets *of* brass; the hooks of the pillars and their fillets *of* silver.

12. And *for* the breadth of the court on the west side *shall be* hangings of fifty cubits: their pillars ten, and their sockets ten.

13. And the breadth of the court on the east side eastward *shall be* fifty cubits.

14. The hangings of one side *of the gate shall* be fifteen cubits: their pillars three, and their sockets three.

15. And on the other side *shall be* hangings fifteen *cubits*: their pillars three, and their sockets three.

16. And for the gate of the court *shall be* an hanging of twenty cubits, *of* blue, and purple, and scarlet, and fine twined linen, wrought with needlework: *and* their pillars *shall be* four, and their sockets four.

17. All the pillars round about the court *shall be* filleted with silver; their hooks *shall be of* silver, and their sockets *of* brass.

18. The length of the court *shall be* an hundred cubits, and the breadth fifty everywhere, and the height five cubits *of* fine twined linen, and their sockets *of* brass.

19. All the vessels of the tabernacle in all the service thereof, and all the pins thereof, and all the pins of the court, *shall be of* brass.

17. And the Lord spake unto Moses, saying,

18. Thou shalt also make a laver *of* brass, and his foot *also of* brass, to wash *withal*: and thou shalt put it between the tabernacle of the congregation and the altar, and thou shalt put water therein.

19. For Aaron and his sons shall wash their hands and their feet thereat:

20. When they go into the tabernacle of the congregation, they shall wash with water, that they die not; or when they come near to the altar to minister, to burn offering made by fire unto the Lord:

21. So they shall wash their hands and their feet, that they die not: and it shall be a statute for ever to them, *even* to him and to his seed throughout their generations.

(See xxxviii. 1–20 for the realisation of this pattern.)

THE COURT AND ITS CONTENTS
Exodus 27:1-19;30:17-21

The Court. The court which enclosed the Tabernacle was an oblong, three hundred feet in length and seventy-five in breadth. It was enclosed by curtains hung on sixty pillars, placed at intervals of seven feet and a half. Each pillar stood in a bronze socket, inserted in the ground. They were connected by silver rods called fillets, fitted into sockets, sustaining the hangings of fine white linen. There was but one entrance on the East. The Holy of Holies was situated at the opposite end, towards the West, so that those who worshipped would have no temptation to prostrate themselves, after the manner of the heathen, towards the Sunrise. The curtains of the entrance were of the same material as that of the curtains over the entrance to the Tabernacle itself, and were of blue and purple and scarlet and fine twined linen, the work of the embroiderer (compare verse 16 with xxvi. 36).

Its Uses. The court preserved the Tabernacle from accidental or intentional profanation, and gave the priests a certain measure of privacy for the prosecution of their duties. Its presence was a perpetual reminder that man should pause and consider, before he rushes into the presence of the Most High. It seemed to say to every worshipper: "Keep thy foot when thou goest to the house of God. . . . Be not rash with thy mouth, and let not thine heart be hasty to utter anything before God; for God is in heaven, and thou upon earth" (Eccles. v. 2, R.V.). All Israel, from the youngest to the oldest, of all classes, of both sexes, whether princes, priests, or people, were welcome to enter the Temple-court. Those who, like Hannah, were in sore trouble, might stand there and offer their prayers and vows. Those who claimed sanctuary, like Joab, might come to lay hold on the horns of the altar. All who desired to consecrate their offerings to the Lord or to meet with Him were welcomed, and the priests were in attendance to receive their gifts.

Its Furniture: the Altar. Two significant pieces of furniture had their position between the outer opening and the entrance to the Holy Place—the altar and the laver.

I. *The Altar.* Already it had been promised that an altar would be made to God in the place where He should record His name (xx. 24). This pledge was now redeemed. Probably the altar might be described as the altar-case, the bronze exterior being filled with earth, on which the victims were burnt, and which could be renewed from time to time. It was constructed of shittim wood covered with bronze. Brass and iron were almost unknown; but, like the Egyptians, the Hebrews used an amalgam of copper and tin. The shovels and pans were used to remove the ashes, the basins to receive the blood. The firepans, elsewhere translated censers, were probably employed in carrying the burning embers to the altar of incense. It is supposed that the grating and compass were part of the exterior of the altar, in which rings, etc., were inserted for its carriage. The horns were projections at the four top corners, like the horns of bulls. Victims were bound to them, blood was placed on them, and criminals clung to them.

The Altar and the Sacrifices. The position of the Altar just inside the entrance to the court made it as clear as symbology could that the beginning of fellowship between God and man must be in sacrifice. The sacrifice of sin-offerings indicated man's sinnership. He had forfeited his life, which was returned to him because of the forfeiture of the life of the animal he brought. The sacrifice of whole Burnt-offerings suggested and made evident the soul's resolve to yield itself wholly and absolutely to the service of the Almighty. The sacrifice of Peace-offerings, a portion of which was burnt, whilst the worshipper partook of the remainder, indicated that there was a compact of Peace between the Almighty Friend of Israel and the individual or family that desired to enter into union with Him. It was as though that noble summons of Psalm l. 5, was specially applicable to the last-mentioned groups: "Gather My saints together unto Me; those that have made a covenant with Me by sacrifice."

The Better Sacrifice. That same Psalm, however, indicates that after several centuries had elapsed, a loftier conception of the Divine requirements began to prevail: "Hear, O My people, and I will speak; O Israel, and I will testify unto thee. . . . I will take no bullock out of thy house, nor he-goats out of thy folds. For every beast of the forest is Mine, and the cattle upon a thousand hills. . . . If I were hungry, I would not tell thee. . . . *Offer unto God the sacrifice of thanksgiving; and pay thy vows unto the Most High*" (Psalm 1. 7–14, R.V.).

The Shadow and the Substance. But though the spiritual conception of sacrifice became more accentuated, the offerings of the Levitical Code were continued until the overthrow of Jerusalem by Titus, and the Hebrew race has continued, "without sacrifices," ever since. They were but the shadow of good things to come, and, though offered year by year through long centuries, could never take away the sins of which they made remembrance continually. When, therefore, the perfect substance had come, the mere shadow, the imperfect, was done away, presumably by a divine decree. The Temple was no longer God's House. The Divine Tenant had left it. There was a special emphasis, therefore, in our Lord's words: "Behold *your* house is left unto you desolate" (Matt. xxiii. 38). "He taketh away the first, that He may establish the second" (Heb. x. 9). "When that which is perfect is come, that which is in part shall be done away" (1 Cor. xiii. 10).

The Enduring Fact Witnessed to. It should, however, be borne in mind that though the symbol, having fulfilled its purpose, has passed, the things symbolised remain. God is constantly instructing the mind of man by restatements of the old and eternal facts, which are indestructible because fundamental. The Altar represents the great fact of Calvary, when, through the Eternal Spirit, our great High Priest offered Himself without spot to God. The supreme act of Reconciliation, the Burnt-offering, and the Peace-offering were all present in His one oblation of Himself, once offered.

The Conscious Self-Offering of Christ. It should be understood, however, how clear is the distinction between the death of our Lord and the death of these sacrificial victims. They were absolutely unconscious of the religious value attached to their death. They were, so far as they were concerned, quite involuntary, and even refractory. They were offered to ransom the offerer, who made them an offering for his sin. But our Saviour's act was perfectly voluntary. He said: "I lay down My life of Myself. No man taketh it from Me. I have power to lay it down, and power to take it again." We may go further, and say with the Apostle that "God was in Christ reconciling the world unto Himself." The Reconciliation, effected on the cross, was not the act of a third party stepping in to intercept a blow, which must otherwise fall on man from a justly offended God; but of God Himself, who, in the person of Christ, took home to Himself the anguish, the sorrow, the suffering, which are the necessary concomitants of sin. We cannot understand the Philosophy, but we accept the fact, which has given peace to myriads, and we are familiar with many analogies to it in human life. How often, for instance, have parents borne the shame, sorrow, and suffering which their children's wrong-doing have entailed, and how heavily they have paid penalties which have left them bowed, broken, impoverished and disgraced

—An Offering for Us. But, in the death of the Cross, there was not only the spiritual counterpart of the great Day of Atonement in its Sin-offerings, but in its Burnt-offering and Sin-offerings also. There our Lord Jesus yielded Himself absolutely and utterly to the Father's will, and there He set up a Table, that of His Body and Blood, at which, as it has been elongated through the centuries, all the saints have sat. "This is My Body, broken for you": "This is the cup of the new covenant, shed for you. Drink ye all of it."

II. *The Laver.* No particulars are given as to the size or shape of this large bronze vase or basin, which stood between the altar and the holy place. It was evidently kept supplied with water, so as to provide whatever was needed for the various ceremonies. The Priests were also required to wash both their hands and feet on every occasion of their entering the sacred tent, and of their ministering at the altar. The significance of this ordinance was, therefore, extremely clear and simple. The necessity of daily cleansing on the part of those who are engaged even in the most holy service, and of all who would approach God, is so obvious as hardly to require comment. The body washed with pure water has for its counterpart the daily cleansing of the soul, without which no man may minister in the Divine presence.

The Water and the Cleansing Grace of Christ. But a new and tender beauty is given to this holy rite, when we read it in association with John xiii., where before the Feast of the Passover, and therefore before the Institution of the Holy Supper, the Lord rose from the supper, and laid aside His garments, girded Himself with a towel, and began to wash the disciples' feet. It might have been supposed that this was only a beautiful sign of His absolute humility, that though He knew that the Father had given all things into His hands, and that He came forth from God and went to God, yet He was prepared to assume the form and office of a servant, and perform the most menial duties for those He loved. But obviously more than this was implied, as we may gather from the words addressed to Peter, on his expressing his strong remonstrance; and Jesus said, "If I wash thee not, thou hast no part with Me"; and again, "He that is bathed needeth not save to wash his feet, but is clean every whit" (John xiii. 10, R.V.).

Our Need of Cleansing. We can easily understand the spiritual reference of these words. We have, so to speak, bathed our sinful souls in the cleansing grace of Christ. Perhaps this is what He signified when He spoke of the necessity of our being born of water and of the Spirit. It will be remembered, also, that the Apostle spoke of the washing or laver of Regeneration; but who is there of us that is not conscious of the daily soil of life? With us probably the hands amid the grime and dust of modern life demand much the same repeated washing as the sandalled feet of the Oriental. We cannot spend hours, or sometimes even minutes, without requiring soap and water for our hands. They are in constant requisition in the physician's or surgeon's rooms, and in addition the antiseptic carbolic, or its equivalent, is perpetually in evidence. But if this is the case physically, how much more spiritually! We can hardly engage in prolonged social intercourse, or negotiate our business career, or undertake religious duty, without sometimes a vague, and at other times an acute, sense that we have contracted defilement which requires to be confessed and put away. If we have not actually hurt others and injured our own conscience, we may not have been clear and strong enough in our declarations on behalf of the truth. We are told that when the days of festival in which his sons and daughters participated were finished, their father was accustomed to rise early in the morning, and offer burnt-offerings according to the number of them all, for Job said: "It may be that my sons have sinned, and blasphemed God in their hearts." And he had good reason for what he feared, as we all may have.

The Consciousness of Need. We must not have a hyper-sensitive or morbid conscientiousness, as though our Heavenly Father were lying in wait to catch at us at every turn; but we can always discriminate between this and any clear act of wrong, because in the former case there is only a hazy and vague uneasiness, which is often the reaction from nervous over-strain, whereas in the latter there is a clear and positive realisation of some one thing in which we have failed. God is always definite in His dealings with conscience. When the soul is being dealt with by His Spirit, there is no beating around the bush. The sword of the Spirit cuts straight to the infected place. We have no alternative but to go back and pick up the thread of obedience just where we dropped it, in the belief that if we confess our sins, He is faithful and just to forgive us our sins, and to cleanse us from all unrighteousness. There is a wide difference between *sin* and *sins*. The former is the root and trunk of our selfishness or self-ness—the carnal and sensual nature which deflects us, as the metal of the ocean-steamer deflects the needle, whereas the latter are the commissions or omissions of our daily life.

Confession and Pardon. When we confess these failures to our Lord, we must believe in their absolute and immediate forgiveness. We should not wait for the hour of evening prayer, nor even to kneel in our secret place; but wherever we are, and whatever we may be doing, we should lift our hearts to Christ, and ask Him to perform for us the office He did for those men who gathered around Him in the upper chamber. We are told that He *began* to wash the disciples' feet; but I wean that He has never finished this blessed and beneficent office. He has continued through the centuries, and continues, and will not entrust the work to any angel or saint; it is His own prerogative.

The Inexhaustible Love of Christ. It may be asked—how often may we repair to Him with our request for His gracious interposition on our behalf? Will He not tire? How often may His priests wash in the Laver, or invoke His gentle ministry on their behalf? There is no limit to it—absolutely none. We have some hint of this in the introductory paragraph to the incident with which we are dealing: "Knowing that His hour was come that He should depart out of this world unto the Father, *having loved His own which were in the world He loved them unto the end*" (John xiii. 1, R.V.). Those final words do not, of course, mean "to the end of His mortal life," but, as the R.V. margin suggests, "to the uttermost" limit of infinite and Divine love.

—Unto Seventy-times Seven. But there is no limit. There is no horizon. There is no shore. We gather as much from those memorable words the answer to Peter's timid suggestion that it would be sufficient if he forgave his brother seven times. "*Seven times?* said our Lord, nay, Seventy times Seven.*" But this is the strongest combination of perfection that numbers can supply. Here is ten, a perfect number, multiplied by seven, and seven again, the well-known symbol of perfection! What could be more convincing? And if our Saviour demands that man should forgive his brother so often, what may not we expect from Almighty God, who is love? My brother or sister, do not wait for hours to pass till you confess, do not even wait for the embers of your passion to get cold, do not wait till the hot tears of penitence begin to flow, but right there, lift your sorrowful heart to the Redeemer, though it be the millionth time, and He will forgive and restore as at the first. But be sure of this, that long before you reach the millionth time, you will have become so softened and tender, so believing and trustful, so full of the holy love which begets godly fear, that you will not sin as you have done aforetime, but His gentleness will have made you great.

The Priesthood of Aaron and his Sons

Exodus 28:1-43

1. And take thou unto thee Aaron thy brother, and his sons with him, from among the children of Israel, that he may minister unto me in the priest's office, *even* Aaron, Nadab and Abihu, Eleazar and Ithamar, Aaron's sons.

2. And thou shalt make holy garments for Aaron thy brother for glory and for beauty.

3. And thou shalt speak unto all *that are* wise-hearted, whom I have filled with the spirit of wisdom, that they may make Aaron's garments to consecrate him, that he may minister unto me in the priests' office.

4. And these *are* the garments which they shall make; a breastplate, and an ephod, and a robe, and a broidered coat, a mitre, and a girdle: and they shall make holy garments for Aaron thy brother, and his sons, that he may minister unto me in the priest's office.

5. And they shall take gold, and blue, and purple, and scarlet, and fine linen.

6. And they shall make the ephod *of* gold, *of* blue, and *of* purple, *of* scarlet, and fine twined linen, with cunning work.

7. It shall have the two shoulder pieces thereof joined at the two edges thereof; and *so* it shall be joined together.

8. And the curious girdle of the ephod, which *is* upon it, shall be of the same, according to the work thereof; *even of* gold, *of* blue, and purple, and scarlet, and fine twined linen.

9. And thou shalt take two onyx stones, and grave on them the names of the children of Israel:

10. Six of their names on one stone, and *the other* six names of the rest on the other stone, according to their birth.

11. With the work of an engraver in stone, *like* the engravings of a signet, shalt thou engrave the two stones with the names of the children of Israel: thou shalt make them to be set in ouches of gold.

12. And thou shalt put the two stones upon the shoulders of the ephod *for* stones of memorials unto the children of Israel: and Aaron shall bear their names before the Lord upon his two shoulders for a memorial.

13. And thou shalt make ouches *of* gold;

14. And two chains *of* pure gold at the ends; *of* wreathen work shalt thou make them, and fasten the wreathen chains to the ouches.

15. And thou shalt make the breastplate of judgment with cunning work; after the work of the ephod thou shalt make it; *of* gold, *of* blue, and *of* purple, and *of* scarlet, and *of* fine twined linen, shalt thou make it.

16. Foursquare it shall be *being* doubled; a span *shall be* the length thereof, and a span *shall be* the breadth thereof.

17. And thou shalt set in it settings of stones, *even* four rows of stones: *the first* row *shall be* a sardius, a topaz, and a carbuncle: *this shall be* the first row.

18. And the second row *shall be* an emerald, a sapphire, and a diamond.

19. And the third row *shall be* a ligure, an agate, and an amethyst.

20. And the fourth row a beryl, and an onyx, and a jasper: they shall be set in gold in their inclosings.

21. And the stones shall be with the names of the children of Israel, twelve, according to their names, *like* the engravings of a signet; every one with his name shall they be according to the twelve tribes.

22. And thou shalt make upon the breastplate chains at the ends *of* wreathen work *of* pure gold.

23. And thou shalt make upon the breastplate two rings of gold, and shalt put the two rings on the two ends of the breast-plate.

24. And thou shalt put the two wreathen *chains* of gold in the two rings *which are* on the ends of the breastplate.

25. And *the other* two ends of the two wreathen *chains* thou shalt fasten in the two ouches, and put *them* on the shoulder-pieces of the ephod before it.

26. And thou shalt make two rings of gold, and thou shalt put them upon the two ends of the breastplate in the border thereof, which *is* in the side of the ephod inward.

27. And two *other* rings of gold thou shalt make, and shalt put them on the two sides of the ephod underneath, toward the forepart thereof, over against the *other* coupling thereof, above the curious girdle of the ephod.

28. And they shall bind the breastplate by the rings thereof unto the rings of the ephod with a lace of blue, that *it* may be above the curious girdle of the ephod, and that the breastplate be not loosed from the ephod.

29. And Aaron shall bear the names of the children of Israel in the breastplate of judgment upon his heart, when he goeth in unto the holy *place*, for a memorial before the Lord continually.

30. And thou shalt put in the breastplate of judgment the Urim and the Thummim; and they shall be upon Aaron's heart, when he goeth in before the Lord: and Aaron shall bear the judgment of the children of Israel upon his heart before the Lord continually.

31. And thou shalt make the robe of the ephod all *of* blue.

32. And there shall be an hole in the top of it, in the midst thereof: it shall have a binding of woven work round about the hole of it, as it were the hole of an habergeon, that it be not rent.

33. And *beneath* upon the hem of it thou shalt make pomegranates *of* blue, and *of* purple, and *of* scarlet, round about the hem thereof; and bells of gold between them round about:

34. A golden bell and a pomegranate, a golden bell and a pomegranate, upon the hem of the robe round about.

35. And it shall be upon Aaron to minister: and his sound shall be heard when he goeth in unto the holy *place* before the Lord, and when he cometh out, that he die not.

36. And thou shalt make a plate *of* pure gold, and grave upon it, *like* the engravings of a signet, HOLINESS TO THE LORD.

37. And thou shalt put it on a blue lace, that it may be upon the mitre; upon the forefront of the mitre it shall be.

38. And it shall be upon Aaron's forehead, that Aaron may bear the iniquity of the holy things, which the children of Israel shall hallow in all their holy gifts; and it shall be always upon his forehead, that they may be accepted before the Lord.

39. And thou shalt embroider the coat of fine linen, and thou shalt make the mitre *of* fine linen, and thou shalt make the girdle *of* needlework.

40. And for Aaron's sons thou shalt make coats, and thou shalt make for them girdles, and bonnets shalt thou make for them, for glory and for beauty.

41. And thou shalt put them upon Aaron thy brother, and his sons with him; and shalt anoint them, and consecrate them, and sanctify them, that they may minister unto me in the priest's office.

42. And thou shalt make them linen breeches to cover their nakedness; from the loins even unto the thighs they shall reach:

43. And they shall be upon Aaron, and upon his sons, when they come in unto the tabernacle of the congregation, or when they come near unto the altar to minister in the holy *place*; that they bear not iniquity, and die: *it shall be* a statute for ever unto him and his seed after him.

THE PRIESTHOOD OF AARON
AND HIS SONS
Exodus 28:1-43

The Priesthood: The Human Impulse. The idea of a Priesthood is implicated with the consciousness of sin; and this in turn seems to be a necessary consequence of a moral nature that finds itself entangled in selfishness and sin, but carries within it an ideal of perfect goodness. Little children and young natures not yet habituated to the presence and practice of evil; primitive and simple folk who live in contact with Nature; with the brooding thunder-cloud, the snow-clad alp, the infinite solitude of vast spaces; they who from their birth carry with them, more than most, the music of the everlasting chime—these are specially susceptible to the immense chasm and gulf which separates us from the purity of the Eternal Holiness. Others are startled by the irruption of a whirlwind of passion, by repeated falls and failures, or by suddenly encountering the law of God, speaking from Sinai or Calvary.

Every race, therefore, conscious on the one hand of God's majesty and holiness, and on the other, of its own unworthiness, has selected one of its number to stand as mediator between Him and themselves, hearing His voice, and uttering for them things which they dared not say. The consciousness of the gulf between the purity of the highest heaven and the impurity in which men have been shapen has acted as an impelling force, that could devise no better expedient than to seek representation by the fittest of their race.

—Felt by Moses. This universal movement of the human heart was present with Moses when he spent those days of prolonged fellowship with the Divine Mind, during which the conception of the Priesthood, as set down in this chapter, was communicated and elaborated. We shall see that any deficiencies that might pertain to the nature of the selected priest were compensated for by the elaborate dress in which he was habited, the various items of his vestments suggesting characteristics which were demanded by the ideal daysman, but were wanting in its human embodiment. They were holy garments, "for glory and for beauty."

Conditions of the Priesthood: The Office restricted to Hebrews. An Egyptian, Philistine, or Assyrian could not have understood or interpreted the peculiar genius of the Hebrew people. Their representative in the Divine Presence-chamber must be one in whom the Hebrew blood was flowing with no foreign admixture, and by whom the Hebrew ideal would be perfectly realised, with no alien ingredient.

—To Holy Men. It was necessary also that he should be *a holy man*. His purity was therefore set forth in the snowy whiteness of the inner garments (verses 42, 43); but, in order to make more clear and certain the holiness which must characterise him, they placed upon his brow a golden plate, on which the words "Holiness to the Lord" were engraved (verse 36 and following). It was as though they said: "We are conscious that our representative may fail in personal holiness, but on that golden plate of purest metal we have placed our ideal, the high-water mark, which we desire our priest should attain."

—Mindful of God and of Man They needed, also, a man who should *be habituated to the Heavenly Realm*. The High Priest was therefore clothed in a robe of blue (verses 31, etc.). Blue always speaks of depth, whether of the glacier fissure or of the ether above us, of the lake or ocean. Yet in his commerce with heaven they desired that he should not be unmindful of them, or of their concerns, or of the earth, and therefore all round the hem of the skirt were golden bells alternated with pomegranates, that might remind him of the listening ears of the people, and might assure them that he had not fallen into a swoon, or been stricken by the rays of the Shechinah, but was moving to and fro, intent on their service.

—And Acting in a Representative Capacity. But perhaps the most urgent of all needs was *that for direct and personal representation*. This was secured, even against any lapse of memory in himself, by the onyx stones of the ephod, and the precious stones in the breast-plate.

The Ephod. The *Ephod* was a kind of waistcoat, consisting of two pieces, one to cover the chest and the other the back, joined together above the shoulders and united at the waist by a band, called "the curious girdle of the ephod." This band was of one piece with the ephod, being woven on either to the front or the back part. It held the other part in place, and was passed round the body and fastened by a clasp or strings. It should be noted that the materials of the ephod were the same as those used for the veil and curtains of the sanctuary (xxvi. 31 and 36), though the fabric may have been of a more delicate quality. The worshipper was thus kept in harmony with his surroundings. The gold was probably introduced by the needle, as gold-thread, after the fabric had been woven. On each of the shoulderpieces that united the back and front parts of the ephod was a socket of gold holding an onyx or, as most commentators agree, a sardonyx stone, which is an excellent stone for engraving. On these the names of the twelve tribes were cut, in order of their seniority. The presence of these stones on the High Priest's shoulders showed clearly that he entered the sanctuary in a representative capacity, bearing with him the interests, sins, and sorrows of the entire nation. He was there in the name of the whole community.

The Breastplate. This conception was still further emphasised by the *Breastplate*, which was attached to the ephod when it had been put on, and formed its principal ornament. It must have been the most striking and brilliant object in the whole attire of the High Priest. Externally, it repeated the symbolism of the ephod; but internally it fulfilled a still more important function, because it contained the Urim and Thummim, by which the decisions of their Almighty King and Friend were obtained for His suppliant people. Therefore it was called the breastplate of judgment, or decision (verses 29–30).

The breastplate was nine inches square, and was doubled, so as to form a bag in which the Urim and Thummim might be kept. On the exterior were the twelve precious stones in four rows of three each, and on these the names of the tribes were engraved. The breastplate had four rings, two at its two upper corners, and two just behind its two lower corners; a golden cord was to be passed through the upper rings, and attached to the sockets of the shoulder stones; whilst a blue lace or ribbon was passed through the two lower rings, and tied to two other rings set on the front of the ephod a little above the curious girdle (verses 26, 27). By these four fastenings at its four corners the breastplate was securely attached to the ephod.

Thus Aaron not only bore the names of the twelve tribes upon his shoulders but also upon his heart. The former indicated that he sustained them with his strength, the latter that he loved them with a tender compassion.

Office of the Breast-plate. Among the garments of the High Priest the breastplate was what the mercy-seat was amid the furniture of the sanctuary. The two shone with glory: in the case of the Shechinah it was the direct beam, and in the case of the breastplate, reflected. Whenever its wearer stood before the mercy-seat, the whole of the stones of his breastplate flashed with a glory and beauty that never shone on sea or shore.

Is it not probable that for several weeks before the great Day of Atonement, that the High Priest's tent would be besieged by men and women, some of whom might visit it under the shadow of night, each with some special sorrow, temptation, or confession, saying in effect: "You will not forget me, will you, upon that holy day, when you stand before God? I shall be outside offering my heart to Him, but you will be within His secret place. Do not forget me!" How much they needed a *compassionate* nature, that could be touched with the feeling of their infirmities and sorrows, and one who would be *faithful*, not dissipating on himself, or upon lesser concerns, those holy moments when he was face to face with God. In order to secure some certainty that they would be remembered they set their names on his person, so that the very stones would speak for them. "Aaron shall bear the names of the children of Israel in the breastplate of judgment upon his heart . . . for a memorial before the Lord continually" (verse 29).

The Care in Using a Mediator. We have to think ourselves back into their position, for we have never had to deal with God through a human mediator. We have always been able to go directly into His presence with our idiosyncrasies, our sorrows, and our sins. But if we were obliged to approach Him through a daysman or mediator, how nervous we should be lest we should be overlooked or forgotten, or lest some part of our case would be omitted or misrepresented! These Hebrew people did their best to secure the right man as their representative, and endeavoured to supplement any defects in his character and capacity by the costly items of his dress and equipment.

The Failure of the Aaronic Line of Priests. *But, notwithstanding these elaborate efforts to make the priests of Aaronic line efficient, it failed in several particulars, which are enumerated in the Epistle to the Hebrews.* They were compassed with infirmity (Heb. vii. 28). They had to offer sacrifices day by day for their own sins, as well as for the sins of the people (vii. 27).

They *stood* day by day ministering and offering oftentimes the same sacrifices, the which could never take away sins (x. 11).

They were appointed without an oath, and on the basis of a casual commandment (vii. 21).

They were not suffered to continue by reason of death (verse 23).

They were, therefore, necessarily many, and were always transmitting their priesthood to others (verse 23).

They represented a covenant and system which were destined to be superseded (verse 12).

Symptoms of the admitted unsatisfactoriness of the Aaronic priesthood were even on the inspired page. Long centuries after its establishment, they found expression in Psalm cx., where the coming of another Priest, one after the order of Melchizedek, was foretold. Now if perfection had been of the Levitical priesthood, what further need would there have been for another priest to arise, after the order of Melchizedek, and not reckoned after the order of Aaron? (Heb. vii. 11).

Melchidezek. We know little enough of this Canaanitish king, who shines for one brief moment out of the drifting mists of those far-away centuries, recognised by Abraham as God's priest, blessing the patriarch, and receiving tithes from him. He seems to have derived his priesthood from no long line of saintly predecessors. At least their names and genealogy are not recorded. His priesthood did not depend on his pedigree. No definite consecration by the imposition or investiture of human hands signalised his entrance on his office. So far as history records, he had no successors. He stands like a monolith on the sands of the past, the Priest-King of the ancient city of Salem, who blessed Abraham in the name of the Most High God.

Abraham's Attitude to Melchizedek. It was remarkable how absolutely Abraham recognised the sanctity and superiority of this remarkable personage, when he gave him tithes of all, for surely it is the greater who receives tithes and gives the blessing, and the less who receives the blessing and gives the tithes. And the significance of Abraham's act was not confined to himself. As the representative of the house of Israel, of which Levi was part, he recognised the superior claims of the Melchizedek type of priesthood over any line of priests that might spring from himself. In Abraham the Hebrew priesthood itself acknowledged the superiority of the priesthood of Melchizedek. Obviously then we shall make a profound mistake in founding any rules or rites for ourselves, in this Christian age, on the order of Aaron's consecration, investiture, ministry, or mediation, all of which are necessarily inferior to that higher type of priesthood which was foreshadowed in Melchizedek and realised perfectly in Christ.

Christ Our Melchizedek. It is impossible for our religious life to realise its utmost ideal if we confine our view to the Aaronic type of priesthood, whether set forth in a line of earthly priests or as furnishing our sole and only conception of Christ. It is not enough for you to look on Christ as your Aaron. He is that, and more. He is your Melchizedek. It is witnessed of Him that He liveth. He is clothed with glory and honour. He works *in* us as well as *for* us. He communicates the powers of the world to come and of the eternal life. He not only delivers us from Egypt, as the Paschal Lamb, but leads us into Canaan, as the Captain of the Lord's host.

Our Lord's Priesthood All-sufficient. Must the priest be one in nature with those whom he represents? "*Since the children are sharers in flesh and blood, He also Himself in like manner partook of the same*" (Heb. ii. 14, R.V.).

Must the priest be a holy man? "*Jesus was holy, harmless, guileless, undefiled, separated from sinners, who needeth not daily, like those high priests, to offer up sacrifices, first for His own sin*" (Heb. vii. 26, 27, R.V.).

Must the priest be habituated to the heavenly realm? "*We have such a high priest, who sat down on the right hand of the throne of the Majesty in the heavens, a minister of the true Tabernacle, which the Lord pitched, and not man*" (Heb. viii. 1, 2, R.V.).

Must the priest be compassionate for the sins and sorrows of those whom he represents? "*We have not a high priest that cannot be touched with the feeling of our infirmities; but one that hath been in all points tempted like as we are, yet without sin*" (Heb. iv. 15, R.V.).

Must the priest be adjudged as a faithful and trustworthy? "*It behoved Him in all things to be made like unto His brethren, that He might be a merciful and faithful high priest in things pertaining to God*" (Heb. ii. 17, R.V.).

The priests of Aaron's line were compassed by infirmity; but *He* is the Son, perfected for evermore.

They had to offer sacrifices for themselves; but *He*, having been made perfect, became, unto all them that obey Him, the author of eternal salvation.

They stood in daily ministry, because the worshippers, notwith-standing their exact obedience to the Levitical ritual, never lost their consciousness of sins; but *He*, when He had offered one sacrifice for sins, sat down for ever on the right hand of God.

They indeed were made priests without an oath; but *He* with an oath, by Him that saith of Him—

" The Lord sware, and will not repent Himself,
Thou art a Priest for ever."

They indeed were made priests many in number, because that by death they were hindered from continuing; but *He*, because He abideth for ever, hath an indissoluble and unchangeable Priesthood, that doth not pass to another.

Aaron transmitted his priesthood and garments to Eleazar, and Eleazar again to his son, in a long succession; but *He* hath been made Priest, not after the law of a casual commandment, but after the power of an endless life.

The Aaronic priesthood was changed because it belonged to a sanctuary of this world; but Christ having come a High Priest of the good things that were to come, through the greater and more perfect Tabernacle, not made with hands, that is to say, not of this creation, nor yet through the blood of goats and calves, but through His own blood, entered in once for all into the holy place, having obtained eternal redemption.

Christ's Office Possible to Him Alone. No angel could present us perfectly—no seraph with his flaming splendour, no cherub in his tender love, but only He who was born of a woman, who was a child, a boy, a young man, and reached maturity through the natural stages of growth. He was hungry and thirsty, suffered physical weakness and weariness, passed through the experiences of the work-man, the citizen, and the patriot. He knew what popularity and lone-liness were. He knew what it was to be the centre of an enthusiastic crowd, and to be deserted amid the shadows of Gethsemane. There is no shadow of experience cast by events on the human heart of which Jesus was ignorant, though He was absolutely spotless and holy. *We* know evil by yielding to it, *He* by resisting it.

His Infinite Compassion. Christ is infinitely compassionate. He is touched with the feeling of our infirmities. He is the nerve-centre of the Universe; and, as one musical instrument will vibrate to another, so does the heart of Christ vibrate in unison with your heart and mine. He is not only a merciful, but a faithful High Priest. He is true to His troth, true to the pledges He has made, true to the trust we repose in Him, true to the yearnings which He has called into existence. We can be sure that He will perfect that which concerneth us, because His mercy endureth for ever, and He will not forsake the work of His own hands. If we are faithless and unbelieving, He will be found faithful, because "He cannot deny Himself."

His Work for Us. May we not suppose that, when his eldest son was old enough, Aaron took him by the hand and led him through the outer court into the Holy Place, showing him the candlestick, the shewbread, and the incense-altar, whilst the boy listened awe-struck to his explanations? Presently the father would lead him to the magnificent veil, and tell him that behind it the Shechinah shone, and say, "My son, when I am gone, you will stand here, and pull that veil aside, and pass within and see that burning glory." But is not that what our Lord has done for us? He is not only our Mediator, feeling for us, and mingling His prayers with ours, so far as possible; but He leads us into the Father's presence, saying, "I will not pray the Father for you, for the Father Himself loveth you." As the Apostle Peter puts it: "Christ suffered for sins once, the righteous for the unrighteous, *that He might bring us to God.*" It will always be true that our Lord's sacrificial and mediatorial work lies at the base, and underpins all our relations with God, but there is an experience for the believer in Him analogous to that through which John's disciples passed when we pass into a new and deeper knowledge of the Father. We have fellowship with the Father. "None knoweth the Father save the Son, and he to whom the Son willeth to reveal Him."

The Urim and Thummim. Within the breastplate, as we have seen, there was the Urim and Thummim, at which the High Priest inquired on behalf of the people. It has never been absolutely decided what these words represent; but an explanation has been given, which is commended by several considerations. There is some light thrown on the matter by the promise of the risen Saviour to give to eat of the hidden manna, and to give a white stone, and in the stone a new name written, which no man knew but the recipient (Rev. ii. 17).

Seeking Guidance. Probably the folds of the breastplate contained a lustrous and resplendent diamond, on which the name of Jehovah was engraved, but this was only seen by the High-Priest. He only even beheld it when he looked into the crystal depths for the divine answer to his earnest and reverent interrogations. "David knew that Saul devised mischief against him; and he said to Abiathar the priest, Bring hither the ephod. Then said David, O Lord, the God of Israel, Thy servant hath surely heard that Saul seeketh to come to Keilah, to destroy the city for my sake. Will the men of Keilah deliver me up into his hand?" "O Lord, the God of Israel, I beseech Thee, tell Thy servant. And the Lord said, He will come down" (1 Sam. xxiii. 9–11, R.V.). It is not difficult to imagine that in the case of an affirmative, the diamond would flash with *Yes*, or, in the case of a negative, dim with *No*.

A Modern Parallel. Is there not a correlative of this in the experience of the child of God? In union with the Saviour, he also knows the flashing of the divine encouragement, and the dimming of the divine withholdings. There is an inner consciousness of the way and will of God, which is certain and irrevocable. When once the ear is accustomed to it, it is the constant and sure guide of the steps; and they thus become ordered by the Lord.

The Priesthood of Our Lord. Let us make much of the Priesthood of our Lord. When conscious of the least stain on our conscience and heart, let us apply to Him at once for cleansing and purity. When we are oppressed with our ignorance and weakness, let us make Him our confidant. When we are desiring some great gift and blessing, not for ourselves so much as for others, let us believe that He is able to save to the uttermost them that draw near to God through Him, seeing He ever liveth to make intercession for them. When our emotional life is at a low ebb, and we have lost the old glow and passion, let us realise that our acceptance with God depends, not on our frames and feelings, but on Him who stands in the Holiest. Our experience is one thing, our standing quite another. We have access by faith into the grace wherein we stand. We are already presented before God in the Person of our Great High Priest. Our names are already known, and our persons accepted. It is not a question of our appreciation of a fact that makes a fact true. The fact is true, even if we fail to derive much help from it: and the fact is, that "by one offering He hath perfected for ever them that are sanctified."

THE CONSECRATION AND DAILY DUTY OF AARON AND HIS SONS

Exodus 29:1-46;30:22-33

1. And this *is* the thing that thou shalt do unto them to hallow them, to minister unto me in the priest's office: Take one young bullock, and two rams without blemish,

2. And unleavened bread, and cakes unleavened tempered with oil, and wafers unleavened anointed with oil: *of* wheaten flour shalt thou make them.

3. And thou shalt put them into one basket, and bring them in the basket, with the bullock and the two rams.

4. And Aaron and his sons thou shalt bring unto the door of the tabernacle of the congregation, and shalt wash them with water.

5. And thou shalt take the garments, and put upon Aaron the coat, and the robe of the ephod, and the ephod, and the breastplate, and gird him with the curious girdle of the ephod:

6. And thou shalt put the mitre upon his head, and put the holy crown upon the mitre.

7. Then shalt thou take the anointing oil, and pour *it* upon his head, and anoint him.

8. And thou shalt bring his sons, and put coats upon them.

9. And thou shalt gird them with girdles, Aaron and his sons, and put the bonnets on them: and the priest's office shall be theirs for a perpetual statute: and thou shalt consecrate Aaron and his sons.

10. And thou shalt cause a bullock to be brought before the tabernacle of the congregation: and Aaron and his sons shall put their hands upon the head of the bullock.

11. And thou shalt kill the bullock before the Lord, *by* the door of the tabernacle of the congregation.

12. And thou shalt take of the blood of the bullock, and put *it* upon the horns of the altar with thy finger, and pour all the blood beside the bottom of the altar.

13. And thou shalt take all the fat that covereth the inwards, and the caul *that is* above the liver, and the two kidneys, and the fat that *is* upon them, and burn *them* upon the altar.

14. But the flesh of the bullock, and his skin, and his dung, shalt thou burn with fire without the camp: it *is* a sin offering.

15. Thou shalt also take one ram; and Aaron and his sons shall put their hands upon the head of the ram.

16. And thou shalt slay the ram, and thou shalt take his blood, and sprinkle *it* round about upon the altar.

17. And thou shalt cut the ram in pieces, and wash the inwards of him, and his legs, and put *them* unto his pieces, and unto his head.

18. And thou shalt burn the whole ram upon the altar: it *is* a burnt offering unto the Lord: it *is* a sweet savour, an offering made by fire unto the Lord.

19. And thou shalt take the other ram; and Aaron and his sons shall put their hands upon the head of the ram.

20. Then shalt thou kill the ram, and take of his blood, and put *it* upon the tip of the right ear of Aaron, and upon the tip of the right ear of his sons, and upon the thumb of their right hand, and upon the great toe of their right foot, and sprinkle the blood upon the altar round about.

21. And thou shalt take of the blood that *is* upon the altar, and of the anointing oil, and sprinkle *it* upon Aaron, and upon his garments, and upon his sons, and upon the garments of his sons with him: and he shall be hallowed, and his garments, and his sons, and his sons' garments with him.

22. Also thou shalt take of the ram the fat and the rump, and the fat that covereth the inwards, and the caul *above* the liver, and the two kidneys, and the fat that *is* upon them, and the right shoulder; for it *is* a ram of consecration.

23. And one loaf of bread, and one cake of oiled bread, and one wafer out of the basket of the unleavened bread that *is* before the Lord:

24. And thou shalt put all in the hands of Aaron, and in the hands of his sons; and shalt wave them *for* a wave offering before the Lord.

25. And thou shalt receive them of their hands, and burn *them* upon the altar for a burnt offering, for a sweet savour before the Lord: it *is* an offering made by fire unto the Lord.

26. And thou shalt take the breast of the ram of Aaron's consecration, and wave it *for* a wave offering before the Lord: and it shall be thy part.

27. And thou shalt sanctify the breast of the wave offering, and the shoulder of the heave offering, which is waved, and which is heaved up, of the ram of the consecration, *even* of *that* which *is* for Aaron, and of *that* which is for his sons:

28. And it shall be Aaron's and his sons' by a statute for ever from the children of Israel: for it *is* an heave offering: and it shall be an heave offering from the children of Israel of the sacrifice of their peace offerings, *even* their heave offering unto the Lord.

29. And the holy garments of Aaron shall be his sons' after him, to be anointed therein, and to be consecrated in them.

30. *And* that son that is priest in his stead shall put them on seven days, when he cometh into the tabernacle of the congregation to minister in the holy *place*.

31. And thou shalt take the ram of the consecration, and seeth his flesh in the holy place.

32. And Aaron and his sons shall eat the flesh of the ram, and the bread that *is* in the basket, *by* the door of the tabernacle of the congregation.

33. And they shall eat those things wherewith the atonement was made, to consecrate *and* to sanctify them: but a stranger shall not eat *thereof*, because they *are* holy.

34. And if ought of the flesh of the consecrations, or of the bread, remain unto the morning, then thou shalt burn the remainder with fire: it shall not be eaten, because it *is* holy.

35. And thus shalt thou do unto Aaron, and to his sons, according to all *things* which I have commanded thee: seven days shalt thou consecrate them.

36. And thou shalt offer every day a bullock *for* a sin offering for atonement:

and thou shalt cleanse the altar, when thou hast made an atonement for it, and thou shalt anoint it, to sanctify it.

37. Seven days thou shalt make an atonement for the altar, and sanctify it; and it shall be an altar most holy: whatsoever toucheth the altar shall be holy.

38. Now this *is that* which thou shalt offer upon the altar; two lambs of the first year day by day continually.

39. The one lamb thou shalt offer in the morning; and the other lamb thou shalt offer at even:

40. And with the one lamb a tenth deal of flour mingled with the fourth part of an hin of beaten oil; and the fourth part of an hin of wine *for* a drink offering.

41. And the other lamb thou shalt offer at even, and shalt do thereto according to the meat offering of the morning, and according to the drink offering thereof, for a sweet savour, an offering made by fire unto the Lord.

42. *This shall be* a continual burnt offering throughout your generations *at* the door of the tabernacle of the congregation before the Lord: where I will meet you, to speak there unto thee.

43. And there I will meet with the children of Israel, and *the tabernacle* shall be sanctified by my glory.

44. And I will sanctify the tabernacle of the congregation, and the altar: I will sanctify also both Aaron and his sons, to minister to me in the priest's office.

45. And I will dwell among the children of Israel, and will be their God.

46. And they shall know that I *am* the Lord their God, that brought them forth out of the land of Egypt, that I may dwell among them: I *am* the Lord their God.

22. Moreover the Lord spake unto Moses, saying,

23. Take thou also unto thee principal spices, of pure myrrh five hundred *shekels*, and of sweet cinnamon half so much, *even* two hundred and fifty *shekels*, and of sweet calamus two hundred and fifty *shekels*,

24. And of cassia five hundred *shekels*, after the shekel of the sanctuary, and of oil olive an hin:

25. And thou shalt make it an oil of holy ointment, an ointment compound after the art of the apothecary: it shall be an holy anointing oil.

26. And thou shalt anoint the tabernacle of the congregation therewith, and the ark of the testimony,

27. And the table and all his vessels, and the candlestick and his vessels, and the altar of incense,

28. And the altar of burnt offering with all his vessels, and the laver and his foot.

29. And thou shalt sanctify them, that they may be most holy: whatsoever toucheth them shall be holy.

30. And thou shalt anoint Aaron and his sons, and consecrate them, that *they* may minister unto me in the priest's office.

31. And thou shalt speak unto the children of Israel, saying, This shall be an holy anointing oil unto me throughout your generations.

32. Upon man's flesh shall it not be poured; neither shall ye make *any other* like it, after the composition of it: it *is* holy, *and* it shall be holy unto you.

33. Whosoever compoundeth *any* like it, or whosoever putteth *any* of it upon a stranger, shall even be cut off from his people.

(See xxxix. 1–31 for the realisation of this pattern.)

THE CONSECRATION AND DAILY DUTY OF AARON AND HIS SONS

Exodus 29:1-46;30:22-33

The Aaronic Priesthood. Aaron's investiture for the High Priestly office presents many points of interest, because principles are foreshadowed which received their profoundest recognition when our Lord on Calvary yielded His Spirit to the Father. But as a whole his priesthood assumes a secondary position in our regard, because though it came later in the development of the Hebrew people, it did not typify the essential work of our Lord, as Melchizedek's did. Aaron's priesthood was symbolical of Christ's, when on the cross He became the Propitiation for the sins of the whole world, but Melchizedek's is the symbol of that which He exercises for ever. Indeed, when we learn that Melchizedek was made like the Son of God, we begin to think that the elements of the Melchizedek-priesthood have ever resided in our Lord, and that He has always been a Priest after the order of Melchizedek (Heb. vii. 17).

The Melchizedek Priesthood. The Melchizedek order is superior to the Aaronic in several respects: and Abraham is quoted as having practically acknowledged this, when he gave him tithes of all, and received his blessing: "without any dispute the less is blessed of the better" (Heb. vii. 4–9, R.V.).

—**Contrasts.** 1. The Aaronic priesthood was made after the law of a casual commandment, whereas Melchizedek was priest after the power of an indissoluble life. It is witnessed of him, "Thou art a priest *for ever*" (vii. 11–19).

2. The Aaronic priesthood was constituted and continued without an oath; but in the case of Melchizedek, the Psalmist said (Ps. cx. 4) that the Lord *sware* and would not repent Himself, "Thou art a priest for ever" (vii. 20, 21).

3. In the Aaronic priesthood there was a constant succession of priests, because they were not permitted to continue by reason of

death; whereas Jesus, because He abideth for ever, hath His Priesthood unchangeable. It is inviolable by Time or Change, and partakes of the Timelessness of eternity (vii. 22, 25).

4. The priests of Aaron's line were obliged to offer sacrifices, first for their own sins, before they offered for those of the people; but the Priest who is after the order of Melchizedek had no need for this, for He had no infirmity, being the Son, who is perfected for evermore (vii. 26–28).

5. The Aaronic priests were perpetually engaged with death, with sacrificial offerings of blood, with a system of reconciliation and atonement, that was interminable, because the blood of bulls and goats could never take away sins or perfect the conscience of the worshippers; but our Lord has once and for ever finished His work of reconciliation. "He offered one sacrifice for sins for ever, and sat down on the right hand of the throne of God." Aaron's Priesthood typified our Lord's Priesthood up to His Death on the cross; but the Melchizedek priesthood passes far beyond into the glorious Life and Ministry, the prayer and intercession of Him who liveth, and was dead, who is alive for evermore, and has the keys of Hades and of Death.

The Consecration Ceremony. For these reasons, the High Priesthood of Aaron, as we have said, assumes a secondary importance, because, typically, it has been superseded by Melchizedek's. But still, that which was given in pattern on the Mount must contain thoughts from God which we do well to ponder; the more so, because we are taught that there is a sacred oneness between our Lord and ourselves. "Both He that sanctifieth and they that are sanctified are all of One." We can never forget that all believers have been summoned to be a royal priesthood and a holy nation. Of us it has been said, on the highest authority, that we were loosed from our sins, that we might become priests unto God. Therefore let us draw nigh, and take this Scripture to our comfort and edification.

There were four distinct stages in the solemn ceremonial.

(1) *Ablution.* "Aaron and his sons thou shalt bring to the door of the Tabernacle, and thou shalt wash them with water." Those who are approaching God on the behalf of a man, or man on the part of God, must be pure in heart and life! "Be ye clean, that bear the vessels of the Lord." We recall those sublime words addressed originally to Levi, and expressive of the highest type of priestly service: "My Covenant with him was of life and peace; and I gave

them to him that he might fear, and he feared Me, and stood in awe of My name. The law of truth was in his mouth, and unrighteousness was not found in his lips; he walked with Me in peace and uprightness, and did turn many away from iniquity" (Mal. ii. 5, 6, R.V.). Such was the divine ideal, and Malachi remonstrated with the priests of his time for their disastrous decline from this high standard, and summoned them once more to approximate to its measure.

(2) *Investiture.* "Thou shalt take the garments, and put upon Aaron and his sons," etc. (verses 5-9). Leviticus viii. 7-9 gives a fuller enumeration. The holy crown indicated the royal rank of the High Priest, who combined the royal and sacerdotal functions, and was therefore a complete type of our Lord. "Behold," said Zechariah, "the man whose name is the Branch; . . . and He shall build the Temple of the Lord; and He shall bear the glory, and shall sit and rule upon His throne; . . . and the counsel of peace shall be between them both" (Zech. vi. 12, 13, R.V.). There should be a royalty about our personal priesthood also. No assumption of sanctity, and yet a sense like that which Nehemiah evidently entertained when he said, so finely, "I am doing a great work, I can not come down!" We are called to be a *royal* priesthood; and we are to be *kings*, as well as priests, unto God. Let us put away therefore all that is unseemly and frivolous, and walk worthy of our high calling of God in Christ Jesus. Let us bear ourselves, as Zebah and Zalmunna confessed that Gideon's brethren bore themselves. "Each one of them was as thou art, the children of a King."

When we are informed that Moses was bidden to *consecrate* Aaron and his sons, the literal rendering of the words would be: "Thou shalt fill the hand of Aaron and the hands of his sons." Some sign of the office to be fulfilled was generally placed on the open palm of the official being installed; and, in the present instance, we learn from verse 24, that certain portions of the offerings were placed there. The Church of Christ must approach the world with her hands filled. When the world sees us eager to participate in its pleasures, it forms its own conclusions: or when it sees us sad and morose, it is led to the same conclusions—that the love and joy of Christ do not content or fill the heart. We must teach them that we do not want to run with them to the same excess of riot, because our hearts are enriched to all satisfaction and to all generosity. Men must see evidence in us that Christ can fill the poorest lot so full with His presence, that having all sufficiency in all things, all His people may abound unto every good work.

(3) *The Anointing.* "Then shalt thou take the anointing oil, and pour it upon his head, and anoint him" (verse 7). This oil was extremely rich and costly, and particular directions were given for its preparation. Pure myrrh, sweet cinnamon, which was probably imported by the commerce of that day from Sumatra or China; sweet calamus, the product of Mesopotamia or India; cassia, of which the native habitat was Java or the Malay Peninsula—were the principal ingredients. These required to be prepared with a considerable amount of scientific knowledge, which was possessed in an eminent degree by Bezaleel (xxxi. 3; xxxvii. 29). But the combination of so many sweetly scented spices must have produced a delightful fragrance. The Orientals take an especial pleasure in delicious scents poured on the sultry air, or wafted on the gentle breeze. "All thy garments smell of myrrh, and aloes, and cassia." "Who is this that cometh up from the wilderness, perfumed with myrrh and frankincense?" This sacred oil was restricted in its use to the anointing of the priests and for service within the holy precincts. It might not be manufactured and employed generally. It was, therefore, with a peculiar unction of special significance that, first, the Tabernacle, and then the High Priest, was dedicated to God's service (see Lev. viii. 10–12).

Our Unction. We, also, as the holy Apostle reminds us, have had and may have "the Unction of the Holy One," who, in this connection, can be no other than our Lord. He is the Christ—the Anointed; and He sheds the sacred chrism. His anointing took place specially at the commencement of His public ministry. He sheds the same oil of joy and grace on our heads, as one by one we yield ourselves absolutely to His service. We recall His ascent on high, and how He led captivity captive and received gifts for men, even for the rebellious; and of these gifts the most conspicuous was that of the Holy Spirit. "Having received of the Father the promise of the Holy Spirit, He hath shed forth *this*." He had His Pentecost at the waters of the Jordan, and we have our Baptism in Fire. Of Him it is said, that in Him dwelleth all the fulness of the Godhead bodily, and of that fulness all we have received, or may receive; for He giveth the Spirit without measure to all penitent and believing souls. It must be remembered, however, that "on the flesh" of the ordinary man that holy unction cannot be poured. We must crucify the flesh with its affections and lusts, must give it no quarter, must treat it with absolute ignominy and contempt; and then on plans that God has made, with words that He has taught, and in strength which He has imparted, we shall go forth with the world of men as they who have a mission from the Eternal. "Let them place a holy mitre on his head," said one, when interceding for a strangely dishevelled priest; and what could we wish better for each other than that each child of God, called to any ministry whatever, might be anointed with the sevenfold gift and grace of the Holy Spirit?

(4) *The Sacrifice.* "And thou shalt bring the bullock," etc. (vers. 10, etc.). Aaron and his sons stood together with their hands upon *the bullock's* head, as though to transfer their sins. Its blood was smeared on the horns of the altar, and poured at its base. Part of the entrails were burnt on the altar, and the remainder of the carcase burnt outside the camp, since it was a sin-offering, and therefore unclean (Lev. iv. 11, 12). Next, they identified themselves with *the ram,* which was designated as a burnt-offering, and therefore typical of their desire to be entirely surrendered to the service of God. It was burnt whole upon the altar; and as they stood there, they would have desired nothing so much as that they might be living sacrifices unto God consumed by the fire of a divine love; but, alas, two of them were destined to be destroyed suddenly and awfully. *The other ram* was known as "the ram of consecration" (verse 22).

The Blood. Its blood, when it had been killed, was used after a unique fashion, being placed on the right ears and thumbs and toes of Aaron and his sons. It was as though, says one, the life of the victim they had offered was given back to reward them for the discharge of their sacred duties. Whatever we give to God, He returns to us with interest. But there is more than this thought here. The blood was the ransom-price, the purchase-money; and its application to ear, and thumb, and toe meant that these had been redeemed from common and unworthy purposes to be used only in the service of God. Oh that each of us would regard the several members and senses of our mortal body as being redeemed from all evil, and purified by our Lord for His peculiar use!

The Blood Sprinkled. The garments of Aaron and his sons were next sprinkled with blood and oil. Portions of the offerings, which, though now burnt in the fire, were afterwards to be reserved for their use, were placed by Moses on their hands, and afterwards waved by him towards the four corners of the heavens, to indicate that though reserved for the servants, they were essentially God's own. A sacrificial feast followed, and crowned the proceedings of the day (verse 32).

A brief digression ensues at this point (verses 29, 30), enacting that the whole garments made for Aaron were to be preserved after his death, and used at the consecration of successive priests, who were to wear them for seven days after their investiture.

A Protracted Ceremony. The ceremony which we have thus briefly described was repeated on seven succeeding days, and must have produced a profound impression. To our refined taste, there may seem a large amount of what is inconsistent with the worship of the Father of our Lord; but may we not rather magnify the patience which was willing through such carnal ordinances to educate the Hebrew race to be the teachers of the sublimest spiritual religion that the world has ever seen! Of course it became ultimately a lifeless and spiritless ritual, against which Isaiah and the Prophets fulminated their strongest denunciations; but it was needful to begin where the people stood, and to lead them out gradually from the abominable sacrifices of the nations around them. These often included children—"the first-born of the body for the sin of the soul." When we were children we thought and acted as children do, but having become mature, we have put away childish things. Let us then not depreciate God's training of the childraces. "When Israel was a child."

Habits of Devotion. No religious life can long exist, or at least thrive, without regular hours and habits of devotion, which these diurnal offerings suggest. Morning and evening prayers have been the habit of all ages. With the one we go forth to our labour till the evening, asking that our Father will give us His God-speed and guidance and protection. With the other we entreat forgiveness and mercy. "Let my prayer be set forth before Thee as incense, and the lifting up of my hands as the evening sacrifice." Pious Jews added a third opportunity, and prayed at noon (see Ps. lv. 17; Daniel vi. 10). Without doubt it is good to follow their example here, where possible; but for most it is not possible. Yet we all may repeat the holy strain of which Keble sings, while, with busy feet, we tread the world's highways.

Peter and John went up to the Temple at the hour of prayer, and we must never forget the frequency and constancy with which our

Lord maintained His attendance on the sacred rites of His people, though conscious of their liability to pass away. A great example surely to us all to maintain the sacred institutions of religion, both in our own households and in the outward ordinances of God's worship.

Precious Promises. The chapter ends with many great and precious promises. Jehovah promised to meet His people at the door of the Tabernacle, and speak with them; that He would sanctify both it and the priesthood with the glory of the Shechinah; that He would dwell among His people and be their God. How happy they would have been, had they but remained faithful to the Covenant: then had their peace been as a river and their righteousness as the waves of the sea, and their enemies would have submitted themselves unto them!

THE GOLDEN ALTAR OF PERPETUAL INCENSE

Exodus 30:1-10;34-38

1. And thou shalt make an altar to burn incense upon: *of* shittim wood shalt thou make it.

2. A cubit *shall be* the length thereof, and a cubit the breadth thereof; foursquare shall it be: and two cubits *shall be* the height thereof: the horns thereof *shall be* of the same.

3. And thou shalt overlay it with pure gold, the top thereof, and the sides thereof round about, and the horns thereof; and thou shalt make unto it a crown of gold round about.

4. And two golden rings shalt thou make to it under the crown of it, by the two corners thereof, upon the two sides of it shalt thou make *it*; and they shall be for places for the staves to bear it withal.

5. And thou shalt make the staves *of* shittim wood, and overlay them with gold.

6. And thou shalt put it before the veil that *is* by the ark of the testimony, before the mercy seat that *is* over the testimony, where I will meet with thee.

7. And Aaron shall burn thereon sweet incense every morning: when he dresseth the lamps, he shall burn incense upon it.

8. And when Aaron lighteth the lamps at even, he shall burn incense upon it, a perpetual incense before the Lord throughout your generations.

9. Ye shall offer no strange incense thereon, nor burnt sacrifice, nor meat offering; neither shall ye pour drink offering thereon.

10. And Aaron shall make an atonement upon the horns of it once in a year with the blood of the sin offering of atonements: once in the year shall he make atonement upon it throughout your generations: it *is* most holy unto the Lord.

34. And the Lord said unto Moses, Take unto thee sweet spices, stacte, and onycha, and galbanum; *these* sweet spices with pure frankincense: of each shall there be a like *weight*:

35. And thou shalt make it a perfume, a confection after the art of the apothecary, tempered together, pure *and* holy.

36. And thou shalt beat *some* of it very small, and put of it before the testimony in the tabernacle of the congregation, where I will meet with thee: it shall be unto you most holy.

37. And *as for* the perfume which thou shalt make, ye shall not make to yourselves according to the composition thereof: it shall be unto thee holy for the Lord.

38. Whosoever shall make like unto that, to smell thereto, shall even be cut off from his people.

(See also xxxvii. 25–29 for the realisation of this pattern.)

THE GOLDEN ALTAR OF PERPETUAL INCENSE
Exodus 30:1-10;34-38

The Altar of Incense. The natural place for a description of the Altar of Incense would seem to have been in ch. xxv., where we have the description of the Ark, the Mercy-Seat, the Table of Shewbread, and the Candlestick. And no sufficient reason has been given for its insertion here. There can be little doubt, however, that in its intrinsic importance, as well as in its proximity to the veil, it was one of the most sacred pieces of the furniture of the Holy Place. Though there is some ambiguity here as to whether it stood within or without the veil, there is none in xl. 21–29, where it is distinctly classed with the golden candlestick and the table of shewbread, as belonging to the Holy Place.

Its Structure. The golden altar was of small dimensions, being a cubit in length, a cubit in breadth, and two cubits high. It was therefore 21 inches in length and breadth, and 3 feet 6 inches high. A crown or raised moulding of gold ran round the top; and, like the Altar of Burnt-offering, it had four horns, one at each corner. Below the golden crown were the golden rings, through which the staves of shittim wood, overlaid with gold, were placed for carriage when the camp moved to another site. On the march, like the other pieces of furniture, the Incense Altar was covered with a blue cloth, and then with a covering of badger-skin (Num. iv. 11).

Its Offering: Incense. Unlike the brazen altar, no burnt-offerings, meal-offerings, or drink-offerings were presented at this golden altar, only incense, which not in the Tabernacle and Temple only, but in all religions, has been offered as the symbol of prayer. "Let my prayer be set forth as incense before Thee; the lifting up of my hands as the evening sacrifice" (Ps. cxli. 2, R.V.). Most minute and special were the instructions given to Moses, and issued to the priests, concerning the composition of the incense to be offered.

The ingredients, as we learn from the closing paragraph of this chapter, were of a rare and precious quality, were beaten very small, and mixed in equal proportions and it was strictly prohibited that it should be used for any other purpose, or by any private individual.

Two Ceremonial Uses of Incense. There were two services in the Jewish ritual when incense was specially employed. On the great Day of Atonement, the High Priest, divested of his splendid robes, and clothed in simple linen, filled his censer with coals from the brazen altar, and passed into the inner sanctuary. Taking a handful of fragrant incense, he cast it on the living embers, and the Most Holy Place was at once filled with a dense cloud of aromatic fragrance. Such an emblem found its fulfilment in Christ's appearance for us in the Father's presence, where, clad in the simple attire of our Humanity, He ever liveth to make intercession. "For Christ entered not into a holy place made with hands, like in pattern to the true; but into heaven itself, now to appear before the face of God for us" (Heb. ix. 24, R.V.).

The second service in which incense was employed was in the ordinary daily service of the sanctuary. We are told that it fell by lot to Zacharias, according to the customs of the priest's office, to burn incense, while the people stood without, at the hour of prayer—"the whole multitude of the people were praying without" (Luke i. 10). The cloud of incense arose each morning when the priest extinguished the lamps of the seven-branched candlestick, and again in the late afternoon when he kindled them.

The Prayers of the Saints. In Rev. viii. 3, 4, R.V., the veil is lifted by the hand of the Beloved Seer, and we are allowed to behold the Angel—who surely can be no other than Christ, the Angel of the Covenant—standing beside the golden altar in heaven, and adding much incense to the prayers of *all* the saints: "And the smoke of the incense, *with* the prayers of the saints, went up before God out of the angel's hand." There is, therefore, not one saint, however sinful, so unworthy, so weak and feeble, who may not claim, that, as the spiral column of his prayer rises towards the Eternal Majesty of God, there shall not be added to it the much incense, merit, and power of the Saviour's intercessions. It is that addition to our prayers which makes them acceptable and prevalent, so that we may obtain the petitions that we have desired of God.

The Catholicity of Prayer. *One* golden altar for the prayers of *all* the saints. Open any book of private devotion containing specimens culled from all ages and sections of the Church, and they all breathe the same spirit, and are adapted for private use amid the altered conditions of our modern life. The saints of the Greek, the Roman Catholic, and the Anglican Churches, the saints of every sect and denomination and of no Church at all, have contributed to the great book of common prayer, whose pages are being turned by all the world. However divided in all beside, we are one when we come to praise, adoration, and intercession. "The Holy Church throughout all the world doth acknowledge Thee"; and lifts up holy hands to Thee, breathing forth similar petitions in similar phraseology.

Its Volume. But what a wealth of prayer has passed through the Mediator, as comprehended in that phrase "the prayers of all the saints." Students have often lamented the loss of the great libraries of the world. They have regretted the stupidity of the monks in respect to their palimpsests, involving the destruction of so many precious manuscripts. We have often wondered what treasures might not have been ours had the Alexandrian library never been consumed. What a wastage there has been of records and remains committed to various kinds of writing! But the loss to mankind through the destruction of ancient literature is small, compared with the loss suffered through our inability to preserve the prayers of the Church.[1] If only prayers could assume visible shape and form and be embodied in the celestial clothing of angels, what troops of bright and glorious messengers would have thronged the shining rungs of the ladder that Jacob saw connecting earth and heaven! The steps of the Temple of Prayer would have become worn and hollowed by their tread, although each should leave an almost imperceptible impression!

The Apostles' Prayers. We think of *the prayers of the glorious company of the Apostles*—of the prayers of Peter in his prison before he fell asleep, of the prayers of John as he poured forth his heart for the seven Churches of Asia from the lone isle of Patmos, of the prayers of Paul to which he makes so many allusions, and of which we have a handful of glorious specimens, and of the prayers of the other obscurer Apostles, of whom such slender records have come to us.

The Prayers of Prophets in all Time. We add to these *the intercessions and petitions of the goodly fellowship of the Prophets*, dating

[1] Suggested by some words of Henry Ward Beecher.

back through the Old Testament dispensation, of Moses on the Mount, of Samuel for the Ark, of Elijah for Israel, of Elisha for the recurring human needs that gathered around his daily path, of Isaiah and Ezekiel, of Daniel and Nehemiah, of John the Baptist, of Savonarola, of Luther, of Huss, of Knox, of Baxter, of John Howe, and of thousands more, through whom the Spirit of Prayer found vent as from deep abysses. One of the greatest pieces of prayer on record is that, for instance, in which Martin Luther poured forth his mighty soul in prayer on the eve of his appearance before the Papal Legate.

The Prayers of Martyrs. We add to these, the pleadings of the Noble Army of Martyrs, of Latimer and Cranmer, of Rutherford and Alleine, of the tortured boys of Uganda, and the mangled victims of the Boxer riots. From dens and caves of the earth, from the moor of the Covenanters and the Alpine Valley of the Piedmontese, from galleys under the lash, from the dark dungeons of the Inquisition, from the invaded homes of the Huguenots, from block, scaffold, and stake, prayers have ascended from lips in mortal agony, which must have been extraordinarily precious to Him for whom they were to be prematurely sealed in death.

The Prayers of the Church. To these we add the liturgies and litanies, the supplications and intercessions of *the Holy Church throughout all the world.* What a wealth of prayer arises as mòrning —and especially the morning light of the Lord's Day—moves noiselessly over the face of the globe! From one continent after another arises the voice of praise and prayer, led by priest and presbyter, uttered from the printed page or the exuberance of free speech, mingled with the tears of penitence or glistening with the glow of assured hope. "And when He had taken the book, the four living creatures and the four and twenty elders fell down before the Lamb, having each one a harp and golden bowls full of incense which are the prayers of the saints" (Rev. v. 8, R.V.). It is as though the prayers of saints, like the perfume of a continent of flowers, mingling with the holy perfume of the much merit of the Redeemer, fills heaven itself with ambrosial fragrance.

The Prayers of All Saints. What a phrase this is—the prayers of *all* saints! The prayers of men like Dr. Johnson, who thought that his prayers were never answered. The strong prayers of men who take the Kingdom of Heaven by violence, the tremulous prayers of frail women, and the lispings of little children! Prayers offered amid the damask splendour of royal palaces, and in poor houses, asylums, and hospitals, amid symptoms of poverty and want! Prayers offered amid worshipping throngs, where the telepathy of kindred hearts makes it easy, the prayers of lonely persons, who keep vigil in sick chambers, or sail amid the godless crews on ocean steamers, or live on the edge of civilisation, the advanced outposts of the great human army moving slowly forward to occupation. Then think of your prayers and mine, though indeed we are not worthy to be called saints, as mingling their tiny contribution, a flower to the parterres of spring, a drop in the tidal river, an atom in the pervasive perfume of the far spaces of the many mansions. Can it be that God counts them fragrant! In any case Christ mingles with them His intercessions. It is this that makes them permanent and prevalent. Only let us see to it that they are such that He can accept, that they are offered in His name, *i.e.* are consonant with His character, baptised with His Spirit, and steeped in His love!

The Hour of Prayer. In the morning, when Aaron extinguished, and again in the evening when he lit the lamps, he cast incense upon the glowing coals. The pious Jews prayed three times in the twenty-four hours. "Evening and morning, and at noonday, will I complain and moan; and He shall hear my voice" (Ps. lv. 17, R.V.). "And when Daniel knew that the writing [which prohibited prayer for thirty days, save to the king] was signed, he went into his house (now his windows were open in his chamber towards Jerusalem); and he kneeled upon his knees three times a day, and prayed, and gave thanks before his God, as he did aforetime" (Dan. vi. 10, R.V.). But modern saints have done the like. Speaking of the home in which the Apostle of the New Hebrides was born, Dr. Paton says of his father: "The closet was a very small apartment, between 'the but' and 'the ben,' having room only for a bed, a little table, and a chair. This was the sanctuary of that cottage home. Thither daily, and oftentimes a day, generally after each meal, we saw our father retire, and shut-to the door; and we children got to understand by a sort of spiritual instinct (for the thing was too sacred to be talked about) that prayers were being poured out there for us, as of old by the High Priest, within the veil of the Holy Place. We occasionally heard the pathetic echoes of a trembling voice pleading as if for life, and we learned to slip out and in past that door on tiptoe, not to disturb the holy colloquy. The outside world might not know, but we knew, whence came that happy light as of a new-born smile that was always dawning on my father's face: it was a reflection from the Divine Presence, in the consciousness of which he lived."

Regular Seasons of Prayer. We should pray in the morning. When the beasts of the forest are retreating to their lairs, man goes forth to his labour until the evening; but he should not go forth from a prayerless closet or an altarless home. He should commit himself and those he loves to the Father's care; he should put on his armour, and specially the panoply of all—prayer; he should remember all who travel by land and water, all who have to die before sundown, all to whom that day is to stand out in after-memories as the saddest or the gladdest of their experience. Yes, and when the evening falls, and the flowers close their petals, and the birds wheel in great circles to their nests, when the sounds of toil are hushed, and a great silence falls upon the earth, when the black dust has gathered on the soiled feet and the heavy burden has chafed the shoulders raw, we should kindle the embers in the prayer-censer and cast in much incense.

Prayer Without Ceasing. But we must not limit our prayers to these times. It is right and necessary to have set times. Most important is it that young people especially should be trained in holy habits, which—like the coral islands built from the depths of infinitesimal accretions—are the result of an innumerable series of prayers, offered without break at specified hours. Such habits help us in all our after-life, and form a strong barrier, which we are foolish to tamper with. But we must be careful not to crystallise all our devotion to one or two points in the day's experience. We must pray without ceasing, and in everything give thanks. Men ought always to pray, and not to faint. We are to pray at all seasons and in all circumstances, often talking aloud to our Lord, as to one whom we might see, if only our eyes were not holden. The children do not confine their loving embraces to the formal greeting of dawn or eve, but seize every opportunity of flinging themselves into our embrace. Whenever a wave is rolling past you towards God, launch a prayer on it. Whenever a puff of wind rises, spread your sail, and take advantage of it. When you hear the goings in the tops of the trees, as though angels were hastening across their rustling leaves on their way home to God, strike your tent and follow, though it is high noon.

Opportunities of Prayer. As the Jew brought the first-fruits of field and garden, let us bring the first notes of each glad hour, the first yield of each new harvest. There are times when joy is at its full and demands expression in thankfulness. And in those hours when thoughts are high and imaginations radiant and affections vibrating with joy, what is more natural and beautiful than to turn to God with the soul's glad laughter and song! There are other times when we catch something of the beauty of the Divine life, and are filled with longing and yearning, as though our soul were pleading for its birthright or smitten with home-sickness. And at such times why should we not let ourselves mount up to the very heavens, and stand before the eternal glory of Love, and join in the happy processions of the radiant spirits in the highest! At other times we bear the burden of God's cause on earth. The glory of Christ in the salvation of souls and the upbuilding of His Church appears infinitely desirable. In the expressive language of Scripture, we travail until Christ be formed in the hearts of those we love. It is as though we were honoured to keep vigil with Christ for one brief hour in the garden. But at such times who shall deny us the right to pour out our souls with strong cryings and tears!

The Manner of Prayer. If you cannot fix your minds for long, let your words be few and concise and to the point. It is not the *length*, but the *strength* of prayer that appeals to heaven. The cry of the drowning Peter was short, but it brought the immediate response of the Saviour. If you cannot pray in thought, pray in speech. If you cannot pray kneeling, remember that David *sat* before the Lord. Pray as you find it easiest and best, only come *boldly* to the throne of grace to obtain mercy and find grace to help in time of need.

The Fragrance of Prayer. So far as our poor prayers have any fragrance, it is in their intercessory character. Unselfishness is the perfume of the disciples' prayer, as of the Master's. Our Lord prayed for Simon, when He knew that he was about to be sifted as wheat, and for those thoughtless hands that had nailed Him to the cross. In the model prayer which He taught His disciples, He made it impossible for them to do otherwise than pray for others when they prayed for themselves. We cannot ask for daily bread without including all who need not bread only, but love, and truth, and faith. We cannot ask for forgiveness without including our enemies as well as our friends, the ignorant and careless, the prodigal and rebel, the prisoner in the cell, and the criminal on the scaffold. We cannot ask for deliverance from temptation and evil, without including all who are vain in their self-confidence as well as those who are weak and simple. Whenever we use the Lord's Prayer, as it is called, if we use it intelligently, we scatter the incense on the coals, and join in the ceaseless intercessions of our Lord. He takes up our poor weak petitions and joins them with His own, so that they accumulate volume and cogency in their passage. Watch the breaking of the big billows on the coast, and remember that each pulse of motion began in a tiny ripple caused by the touch of a catspaw of wind; and understand how a tiny prayer of yours may result in a billow that will break in thunder at the foot of the prayer throne.

Our Lord's Example in John xvii. It is in John xvii. that we can best study the true norm and type of Prayer. It is the incense Altar of the Gospels. There blend in these transcendent sentences the most extraordinary self-consciousness and the most absolute self-obliteration. He was conscious that the Father had loved Him before the foundation of the world; conscious of His absolute unity with the Father, so that there was a reciprocal *inness*; conscious that He had come to bless mankind. But He obliterates Himself. Sixteen times He mentions this world. It was as though, as He stood at the golden altar of Intercession, He forgot all the anguish of the morrow's tragedy, and thought only of His own, of those whom the Father had given Him, of those who should believe through their words, and of the great world of men, utterly thoughtless and care-less, and going down into destruction, unwarned and unsaved. These are His petitions: That My joy may be fulfilled in them: that they may see and share My glory: that they may be with Me where I am: that they may be one, even as We are.

Intercessory Prayer. With such examples before us, who dares pray selfishly! Let us make intercession for the saints according to the will of God. If we will only yield ourselves up to the Divine Spirit, He will instil in our hearts the desires and petitions which Christ is uttering before the throne, and there is no prayer compar-able to that. Before you begin to pray, keep silent for a space until you are conscious that the Spirit of Prayer is moving within you, and rising up towards God, and almost certainly the prayer which He suggests will have very little of *I*, *me*, or *my*, and will be replete with *we*, *us*, and *our*. There is no such clue to liberty in prayer as prayer for others. Our captivity, like Job's, is always turned, when we pray for our friends. Often when we have been pleading for others, our Father hearing us turns and says: "What you have asked for others shall be granted, not to them only, but to you." It is well to have the egotism and selfishness of prayer strained off, by the necessity of asking for them in the same breath as for ourselves; and unselfish prayers will speed happily, as ships with fair winds, and come quickly to the desired haven.

Some Other Suggestions. The rubric of the golden altar is exceedingly suggestive, and almost every particular is replete with instruction.

(1) *We are taught by its close proximity to the Holy of Holies that prayer is the supreme act of the religious life.* The altar and the incense offered thereon are declared to be most holy (verse 36). The silent tear, the unchecked sigh, the unutterable groan, compose a language which is as sweet to God as the first articulate syllables of a little child to the parent. The kindling of the spirit's love, and the aspiration of its desire, which He Himself has kindled, are instantly recognised and responded to. Our Father who is in secret *seeketh* those who will worship Him in spirit and in truth; and when He finds them, He will much more give good things to them than the fondest of earthly parents will give good things to their children. "Fear not, little flock, it is your Father's good pleasure to give." But why are we so slow to engage in the noblest function of which we are capable; and one which, whilst it elicits and strengthens the loftiest faculties of the soul, gives supreme pleasure to God! Let no day begin or close without a visit to the incense-altar:

> " For what are men better than sheep or goats,
> That nourish a blind life within the brain,
> If, knowing God, they lift not hands of prayer,
> Both for themselves and those who call them friend?
> For so the whole round earth is every way
> Bound by gold chains about the feet of God."

(2) *Prayer is offered at an altar, therefore it involves sacrifice.* It is not natural or easy to our carnal nature. Indeed, it is only as we do violence to ourselves, as we deny our lower inclinations, as we are prepared to give up time and strength and deny ourselves society and pleasure, that we can really pray. A man has, like the Apostles, to give himself to prayer. He must stir himself up, who would take hold on God. "In prayer," says one, "the profoundest act of conscience and obedience is inwardly accomplished, for prayer is only

so far a laying hold and appropriation of God, as it is likewise *a sacrifice*; and we can only receive God unto us, when we likewise give ourselves unto Him. He who offers no sacrifice in his prayer, who does not sacrifice his self-will, does not really pray."

(3) *There is a close connection between the Altars of Brass and of Gold.* The one stands for Calvary whereon our Saviour died, the other for the throne, where He ever lives. The coals for the altar of incense were brought from the altar of burnt-offering (Lev. xvi. 12, 13). The relationship of the two Altars was further indicated by the correspondence between the times of their special use, for at the same hour, day by day, as the smoke of the burnt sacrifice ascended to God, the fragrant cloud of incense arose from the incense-altar. The *continual* burnt-offering, the morning and evening lamb, answered to the *perpetual* incense offered also morning and evening. Is not the lesson patent that we cannot pray aright unless we enter into the meaning of the Death of the Cross? And if we truly apprehend *that* we shall naturally and easily enter on a life of prayer. It has been truly said: "The incense-offering was not only a spiritualising and transfiguring of the burnt-offering, but a completion of it also." The consecration of the burnt-offering, i.e. the coming and delighting to do the will of God, finds its loftiest expression in the diffusion of the incense into the air, which is the symbol of the going forth of the soul to unite itself with the great origin and goal of its existence.

(4) *The application of the blood of sin-offerings reminds us that our best prayers are imperfect.* Once in the year, on the great day of Atonement, the High Priest, after burning incense within the veil, and sprinkling the blood of bullock and ram before the mercy-seat, took of the blood and put it on the horns of the altar of incense, "to make an atonement for it, to cleanse it and hallow it from the uncleanness of the children of Israel" (Lev. xvi. 18, 19). The lesson is obvious—even our prayers, the fruit of our holiest moments, need the cleansing efficacy of our Lord's work of Reconciliation. This was still further accentuated by the prescribed action of the High Priest when either he or the people had committed an offence through inadvertence. He was to put of the blood of the sacrifice on the horns of the altar of incense, for the expiation of his own sin and the sin of the people (Lev. iv. 3–21).

(5) *By the horns of the altar, which were symbols of power, we are reminded of the might of prayer.* Believing prayer moves mountains;

unties the hardest knots, unlocks prison-doors; is more effective, as Queen Mary confessed, than regiments of soldiers; opens and shuts heaven; brings showers upon the parched ground; claims and wins heathen lands for the Gospel; moves the Arm that moves the world; obtains whatsoever it saith; and puts in motion those divine and irresistible forces which we call revival, and which are due to the uplifting of the sluice-gates of divine energy for the salvation and uplifting of men. *Brethren, let us pray!*

THE RANSOM MONEY

Exodus 30:11-16;38:24-31

11. And the Lord spake unto Moses, saying,

12. When thou takest the sum of the children of Israel after their number, then shall they give every man a ransom for his soul unto the Lord, when thou numberest them; that there be no plague among them, when *thou* numberest them.

13. This they shall give, every one that passeth among them that are numbered, half a shekel after the shekel of the sanctuary: (a shekel *is* twenty gerahs:) an half shekel *shall be* the offering of the Lord.

14. Every one that passeth among them that are numbered, from twenty years old and above, shall give an offering unto the Lord.

15. The rich shall not give more, and the poor shall not give less than half a shekel, when *they* give an offering unto the Lord, to make an atonement for your souls.

16. And thou shalt take the atonement money of the children of Israel, and shalt appoint it for the service of the tabernacle of the congregation; that it may be a memorial unto the children of Israel before the Lord, to make an atonement for your souls.

24. All the gold that was occupied for the work in all the work of the holy *place*, even the gold of the offering, was twenty and nine talents, and seven hundred and thirty shekels, after the shekel of the sanctuary.

25. And the silver of them that were numbered of the congregation *was* an hundred talents, and a thousand seven hundred and threescore and fifteen shekels, after the shekel of the sanctuary:

26. A bekah for every man, *that is*, half a shekel, after the shekel of the sanctuary, for every one that went to be numbered, from twenty years old and upward, for six hundred thousand and three thousand and five hundred and fifty *men*.

27. And of the hundred talents of silver were cast the sockets of the sanctuary, and the sockets of the veil; an hundred sockets of the hundred talents, a talent for a socket.

28. And of the thousand seven hundred seventy and five *shekels* he made hooks for the pillars, and overlaid their chapiters, and filleted them.

29. And the brass of the offering *was* seventy talents, and two thousand and four hundred shekels.

30. And therewith he made the sockets to the door of the tabernacle of the congregation, and the brasen altar, and the brasen grate for it, and all the vessels of the altar.

31. And the sockets of the court round about, and the sockets of the court gate, and all the pins of the tabernacle, and all the pins of the court round about.

THE RANSOM MONEY

Exodus 30:11-16;38:24-31

The Ransom Money: Its Origin. The Tabernacle structure was, for the most part, reared by the voluntary offerings of the people, but an additional sum was required for the provision of silver and brazen sockets in which the boards of the Tabernacle and the pillars of the court were fixed. This amount, together with the metal for the completion of the fastenings and the provision of the vessels of the altar, was raised by a compulsory levy of half a shekel (amounting to about two shillings and fourpence of our money) from each person over twenty years of age. The rich might not give more, nor the poor less, and every one, from Moses himself downwards, was called upon to contribute. This money was viewed as a ransom-price for the soul.

Its Continuation. Afterwards the annual contribution of this sum for the upkeep of the Temple became a permanent arrangement. "They that received the half-shekel came to Peter, and said, Doth not your Master pay the half-shekel?" (Matt. xvii. 24, R.V.).

A Thanksgiving for Mercy Shown. The precise significance of the phrase, "and atonement for your souls," is not perfectly easy to explain; but there seems to have been a nervous fear of the effect of a census in inducing pride, and so incurring the Divine displeasure. There is a trace of this in the present passage, "that there be no plague among them, when thou numberest them" (verse 12). In David's time, also, Joab was extremely afraid of the prejudicial effect of the royal intention to number the nation. "And Joab said unto the king, Now the Lord thy God add unto the people, how many soever they be, an hundredfold, and may the eyes of my lord the king see it; but why doth my lord the king delight in this thing? . . . And David's heart smote him after he had numbered the people. And David said unto the Lord, I have sinned greatly in that I have done. . . . I have done very foolishly" (2 Sam. xxiv. 3–10, R.V.).

"These sheep, what have they done? let thine hand be against me and my father's house" (1 Chron. xxi. 17, R.V.). In another account, the suggestion to number the people is attributed to Satan; and the plague which ensued was believed to be the direct infliction of deserved penalty. It appears, therefore, that this money was intended to avert the evil results that might accrue to any who failed to pay it; and it was also the thankful acknowledgment, on the part of each individual, in allowing him to be one of a great redeemed race.

" Who is like unto Thee, O Lord, among the gods?
  Who is like Thee, glorious in holiness, fearful in praises, doing wonders? . . .
  Thou in Thy mercy led the people *which Thou hast redeemed* " (Exod. xv.
  11–13, R.V.).

Ourselves Our Redemption. The question may be addressed to each reader: Do you recognise that you belong to a redeemed world? Even if all do not avail themselves of the Redemption which has been achieved, yet it is available for all; and more benefits than we can ever estimate are always accruing since God so loved the world that He gave His only begotten Son. As Israel was entangled in the land of Egypt, so entangled that it seemed impossible to break the meshes, until God delivered by His right hand, so our nature, which was meant to have dominion over the fish of the sea, and over the fowl of the air, and over the cattle, and over all the earth, has been brought under the power of the senses and appetite. We are entangled and shut in by the tyrannical demands and craving. All may not be conscious of this, but it is a blessed consciousness. It is better to know yourself to have been entrapped and seduced, than never to have realised your high descent and your royal possibilities.

The Worth of Experience. Browning describes a sculptor creating a statue of Laocoön without the snakes entwining about his limbs, and it is placed in the market-place, to test the opinion of the passers-by. Some think that it is the statue of one who is yawning, or awakening and stretching himself. But the man who had been conscious of the wrestle of his soul with serpents knew that the artist had left out the reason for the tremendous contortions of the father and his sons. We, at least, know by inner experience what entanglement means. Every plunge for spiritual freedom only made our case more desperate, until the Redeemer stepped out of the infinite glory to undertake our case. The Lamb was slain from before the foundation of the world, the blood has been sprinkled on the threshold of our world, the Red Sea has been passed, the Land of Promise is in view. He who might have taken advantage, Himself provided the remedy. How can we be thankful enough for the grace of our Lord Jesus!

The Indebtedness of all Men. There was no favouritism in His saving act. The best and greatest of men, as well as the lowest and worst, had come short of the glory of God. There was no difference in our absolute need of redemption from the guilt and power of evil. Wealth, rank, education, intellectual power made no difference to our infinite moral and spiritual deficiency and delinquency. And as there was no difference in the need, there was no difference in the remedy. "The Righteousness of God through faith in Jesus Christ is unto all them that believe; *for there is no distinction*; for all have sinned and fall short of the glory of God" (Rom. iii. 22–24, R.V.). *And there is no difference, either, between Jew and Greek,* "for the same Lord is Lord of all, and is rich unto all that call upon Him, for, whosoever shall call upon the name of the Lord shall be saved" (x. 12, 13, R.V.). "The rich shall not give more, and the poor shall not give less." The rich might not give more, lest he be made proud, and the poor must give as much, that he might not be excluded from the benefits of the great deeds of the Lord.

A Personal Question. The question, therefore, is, Are you numbered among those who have availed themselves to the full of the riches of that grace and the exceeding riches of that glory which are yours through Christ? Have you thankfully paid your ransom-money, the token of your thankful recognition and believing appropriation?

A Heavy Tax. The total amount of this poll-tax was about £35,207 of our money. It may seem difficult to imagine how the Israelites should be possessed of so much wealth in the desert; but they had been enriched first by the spoils of the Egyptians and after-wards of the Amalekites, and this in addition to their ancestral wealth. As a matter of fact, this numbering or census was not until the second year of the Exodus had commenced. The erection of the Tabernacle took place on the first day of the first month of the second year, whereas the general census was taken on the first day of the second month (Exod. xl. 17; Num. i. 1). It is probable that the tax therefore was paid before the actual lists were made out. The names were given in when the contributions were paid, though the actual counting only took place afterwards. Or it may be that when the census was made the people had become so depleted of their ready money, that it was resolved to consider the silver offered shortly before as being the prescribed poll-tax, so that they were not exposed to the pressure of a second demand.

The Conditions of the Census. Israel was still encamped before the mount; and the numbering was the first step towards the ordering of the camp, preparatory to the march, which began on the twentieth day of the second month of the second year. The two conditions of the census were, that each man should declare his pedigree, and be able to go forth to war (Num. i. 2, 3, 18). These conditions still obtain in the ranks of the redeemed. It is necessary, before any of us can fight against the rulers of the darkness of this world, that there should be no doubt about our pedigree. The mixed multitude that came out of Egypt failed in this. But among the children of Abraham the genealogical trees were kept with careful precision. Our first pedigree was in the dust, but Blessed be the God and Father of our Lord Jesus Christ, who hath begotten us again unto a living hope by His Resurrection from the dead. They who believe in Christ have been born from above, and have been translated out of the bondage of corruption into the glorious liberty of the sons of God. "As many as received Him, gave He the right to become children of God, . . . which were born, not of blood, nor of the will of the flesh, nor of the will of man, but of God" (John i. 12, 13, R.V.).

The New Birth. Nothing is more important than this. As we were born into the world of sense and matter, so we need to be born into the world of the spirit, which is the real and eternal world. As we have learned to use the body, with its senses and aptitudes, so we must learn to use the spirit, with its affinity towards God. We may not be able to indicate the day or the hour, but we must know ourselves to be children of God, first, because old things are passed away, and all things have become new; and secondly, because God hath sent the Spirit of His Son into our hearts. "Ye received not the Spirit of bondage again unto fear; but ye received the Spirit of Adoption, whereby we cry, Abba, Father. The Spirit Himself beareth witness with our spirit, that we are children of God: and if children, then heirs" (Rom. viii. 15–17, R.V.).

Our Place in the Church of Christ. We should also pitch under our own standard; which, in our case, may be interpreted to signify some branch of the visible Church to which we may be attracted by choice or birth, or both. None is perfect, but we must choose the one that best suits our characteristics and helps us. Belong to one of these, the one nearest your ideal. Be true to it, though retaining a catholic sympathy for all who love the Lord Jesus Christ. Do not be content with looking on. Do something! If you cannot march in the van with the stalwarts, help to carry the Tabernacle, if nothing better. The vessels are to be given in charge to faithful souls, that they may guard, through the Holy Ghost, what has been committed unto them. "Ye are holy unto the Lord, and the vessels are holy. . . . Watch ye and keep them, until ye weigh them at Jerusalem, in the chambers of the House of the Lord" (Ezra viii. 28, 29, R.V.).

THE DESIGNATED ARTISTS

Exodus 31:1-11

1. And the Lord spake unto Moses, saying,

2. See, I have called by name Bezaleel the son of Uri, the son of Hur, of the tribe of Judah:

3. And I have filled him with the spirit of God, in wisdom, and in understanding, and in knowledge, and in all manner of workmanship.

4. To devise cunning works, to work in gold, and in silver, and in brass,

5. And in cutting of stones, to set *them*, and in carving of timber, to work in all manner of workmanship.

6. And I, behold, I have given with him Aholiab the son of Ahisamach, of the tribe of Dan: and in the hearts of all that are wise hearted I have put wisdom, that they may make all that I have commanded thee;

7. The tabernacle of the congregation, and the ark of the testimony, and the mercy-seat that *is* thereon, and all the furniture of the tabernacle.

8. And the table and his furniture, and the pure candlestick with all his furniture, and the altar of incense,

9. And the altar of burnt offering with all his furniture, and the laver and his foot,

10. And the cloths of service, and the holy garments for Aaron the priest, and the garments of his sons, to minister in the priest's office,

11. And the anointing oil, and sweet incense for the holy *place*: according to all that I have commanded thee shall they do.

(See xxxv. 30—xxxvi. 1 for realisation of this pattern.)

THE DESIGNATED ARTISTS
Exodus 31:1-11

The 'Artificers of the Tabernacle. The Almighty not only gave the pattern of the Tabernacle, but designated the men under whose direction and through whose genius and skill it was to be realised. "See, I have called by name Bezaleel" . . . "and I, behold, I have appointed with him Aholiab." Whilst their names were being thus mentioned in the secret place of the Most High, the two men were, in all probability, absolutely ignorant of what was awaiting them. The last thing that occurred to them was that they were to be summoned to this high task. As boys in Egypt they have often, no doubt, lingered to watch skilled artists at their work, and had stood intently watching deft fingers executing fair and beautiful designs, like those which modern discovery is retrieving from the debris of the past.

Their Position in Egypt. Presently, we may well believe, they developed precocious talent in first imitating and then originating fair and curious designs in various arts, as far removed as stone-engraving from wood-carving. They could devise cunning works, and could themselves work in all manner of workmanship. Perhaps they had become so proficient that they were employed by the priesthood and even by royalty to adorn the temples or palaces of Egypt, and might have secured their liberty from the toil of the brick-kiln and the lash of the taskmaster.

Their Choice at the Exodus. But, when the trumpets rang out their summons to depart, there was no hesitation as to their duty, and as their compatriots were mustering in the open spaces or marching through the midnight streets they joined them, with their wives and children, accounting the hope of the Messiah greater riches than all the treasures of Egypt. They, too, like their great leader, had respect unto the recompense of reward: and it came to them, as it always does come to the loyal-hearted and true. To them it happened, as so often, that, having surrendered all things for Christ, they found that they were restored and multiplied in their experience.

Their Work by the Way. During the earlier part of the march, they perhaps busied themselves in helping their fellow-pilgrims in the location, adaptation, and even the beautifying of their tents. What a lesson is suggested here to young men and others who are conscious of powers which as yet have obtained no adequate recognition or occasion! Go on doing what lies to your hand! Be faithful in the very little! Help those whose lives and homes are immediately adjacent to yours! As you are faithful in a very few things, the hour will strike when you will be summoned to rule over many things. He who shepherds his father's sheep in the pastures will be presently called to guide Israel like a flock. Even now God may be speaking your name to those who have loved you and have passed over into His Presence, saying, "Your prayers are heard; lo, I have called your son to be a Missionary or Minister of My Gospel. Your daughter is even now preparing to carry the blessing of salvation to those who sit in darkness and the shadow of death." In the meanwhile, yield yourselves to His moulding hand. The diamond of rare size and brilliance may require months of careful handling ere all its facets are cut.

Bezaleel's Office. *Bezaleel*[1] was clearly designated as the supreme director of the construction of the Tabernacle; and for this end he was specially filled with the Spirit of God (verse 3). Naturally this was not without his personal acquiescence. But probably Bezaleel hardly realised what it meant when, in his wanderings through the camp, or beyond its precincts, either at night, when the stars blazed as we have never seen them in these Northern climes, or by day, when those cylindered peaks shone with resplendent colour, he felt his nature specially absorbed into the Being of God. He only knew that he opened his entire being to the gracious infilling of the Divine Nature, and that he surrendered all personal claim and ambition, if only God would occupy spirit, soul, and body with His divine and awful Presence. It was in answer to these devout and eager aspirations, that out of His fulness he received, and grace upon grace, like successive billows following one upon another from the ocean.

[1] In the R.V. his name is Bezalel, but it also appears in English Literature under his A.V. name.

Natural Gifts the Entrusted Talents. Natural gifts form the mould into which the divine fulness is poured to constitute them talents. The king gave to each of his servants according to their several ability—the ability standing for the natural faculty, which the royal recognition and bestowment enlarged, ennobled, and transfigured. See that by the reception of God's Spirit, your natural faculties become heavenly deposits. "That good thing which was committed unto thee guard through the Holy Spirit which dwelleth in us" (2 Tim. i. 14, R.V.).

How the Spirit Wrought in Bezaleel. The Spirit of God wrought in Bezaleel in three directions—in Wisdom, in Understanding, and in Knowledge. These three words indicate distinct phases of the soul-life. *Wisdom* denotes the original genius which creates. It is that inventive faculty of conception which no amount of painstaking toil can emulate, the superb endowment of a Beethoven, a Michael Angelo, or a Dante. *Understanding* denotes the aptness to appreciate and reproduce the suggestions and conceptions of the mind—the way in which they can be realised, the machinery to be created, the material to be employed, the instruments to be selected. *Knowledge* is the information which is acquired by experience— the facility obtained by use, the colours to be mixed on the palette and how to mix them, the dye necessary to produce a certain colour in the fabric, the blending of colours to produce a given effect, the handling of metals in the furnace or by the hammer.

The Awakening Power. These three faculties were doubtless present in embryo in the heart of the great artist; but when the Holy Spirit came on him, it was as though some Arctic island were floated into the midst of a tropical ocean, and all the seeds which had been lying dormant, beneath the strong hand of the Frost-King, suddenly became relaxed in the genial heat, and broke into luxuriant verdure. It was so with Gray, when he wrote his masterpiece on the Village Churchyard; and with Tennyson, who probably will be remembered in coming time rather by the *In Memoriam* than the Arthurian epic. Directly men and women yield themselves to the Spirit of God, the whole nature awakes, as in the fairy story the sleeping palace awoke at the winding of the bugle-call.

The Office of Aholiab. With Bezaleel was Aholiab. The words of his designation are carefully selected: "And I, behold, I have appointed *with* him Aholiab." Clearly the supreme direction of the entire structure was with Bezaleel, but Aholiab was his faithful second and helper. A further reference informs us that he had entire charge of the textile fabrics, both woven and embroidered. He was "a craftsman, and a cunning workman, and an embroiderer in blue, and in purple, and in scarlet, and fine linen" (xxxviii. 23, R.V.). Probably he was especially alive to the beauty of colour, and had a peculiar gift in reproducing in various forms the glorious lines of mountain, sky, and valley, of the golden sand of the wilderness and the purple of the sea.

The Value of Co-operation. It was good for Bezaleel to have such a fellow-workman, and specially good to feel that *all* the good gifts of God had not been entrusted to his ample soul. It is always good for great souls to feel that they are not perfectly self-contained and self-sufficient. It is good for them to learn humility and interdependence. There is no record of rivalry or jealousy between the two. There were no rival parties in the camp. No one said, "I am of Bezaleel," or, "I am of Aholiab." Probably all were so intent on the great object in view, and so eager to contribute as much help and encouragement to its accomplishment, that there was no opportunity for the intrusion of rival claims. "None were for the party, and all were for the State." Oh, when shall so great a zeal for the glory of Christ and of His Church fall on Christians of all sects and denominations, that Ephraim shall not envy Judah, nor Judah vex Ephraim but when with absolutely pure motives and unbiased hearts we shall strive together for the truth of the Gospel!

Other Helpers. It is interesting to learn that, in addition to these two, others were called in, concerning whom this remarkable statement is made: "In the hearts of all who are wise-hearted I have put wisdom, that they may make all that I have commanded thee." Wisdom is put into the hearts of the wise-hearted. To those who have shall more be given, and they shall have abundantly. Give of what you have, and it shall be given you, full measure, pressed down, and running over. It is as you use your little gift, whatever it may be, and constantly part with what you have, that you will find the sphere of your usefulness, and rise to a higher influence for good in the Kingdom of God. The young preacher feels on each succeeding Sunday evening that he has preached his last thoughts, and wonders how he will hold out, but into the heart of the wise-hearted God puts wisdom.

The Link Between Religion and the Beautiful. In the remainder of this paragraph we are constantly reminded of the connection between Religion and the Beautiful. The garments are finely wrought, and we remember that they were "for glory and *for beauty*" (xxviii. 2). The beautiful is not necessarily religious, but religion is likely to assume the form of beauty; therefore the Psalmist speaks of the beauty of holiness. Wherever beauty is associated with purity and rightness you are catching a glimpse of that primal creation which underlies all the phantasies and illusions of the present. Do not account it a waste that so much time and strength were expended on the Tabernacle, that genius and art were enlisted, that good men and women sought to embody their ideals in rich and lovely forms, that the rarest stones enhanced its wealth and flashed in the light of the Shechinah and the candlestick. All was intended, like Mary's alabaster box, to express a supreme love and realise a sublime plan. Our best is not good enough to say all our hearts want to say in the hours when tidal waves of holy emotion are rolling over our souls. Then the sweetest music is not sweet enough, and the highest art is not high enough, and jewels are not rare enough. One pearl of great price is altogether inadequate: we want a tray full of such. "Praise Him with the sound of the trumpet: praise Him with the psaltery and harp. Praise Him upon the loud cymbals: praise Him with the high-sounding cymbals. Let everything that hath breath praise the Lord. Praise ye the Lord" (Ps. cl. 3–6, R.V.).

The Master and His Servants. Bezaleel could not build the Tabernacle alone, and Jesus Christ needs the co-operation of every soul whom He has redeemed. And "to each one is given the manifestation of the Spirit to profit withal. For to one is given through the Spirit the word of wisdom, and to another the word of knowledge, according to the same Spirit; to another faith, in the same Spirit," etc. (1 Cor. xii. 7, etc., R.V.). But each is called to fulfil some tiny piece of work in the great fabric which is rising through the ages for a habitation of God through the Spirit. If you do not know what your part is, ask the Master Architect to show you. Jesus said, "I will build My Church"—it is for Him, therefore, to select His workmen, and show them to what section of the growing fabric they are to address themselves. You may have to spin or weave, to design or execute, to dig the foundation or carve the pinnacle, to see to the comfort of the workers or carry them refreshment. Probably your sphere will be indicated by your natural aptitudes, by what you enjoy doing, and by what you can do best. Only do something!

The Office of Teacher. It is said of Bezaleel and Aholiab that they were specially qualified to teach (xxxv. 34). This is one of the most priceless gifts of all. They are many who know, but cannot make others know; who see, but are unable to impart their visions. Seek this great gift. For nothing will men be more thankful. Do not be niggard or stinting in your endeavour to pass on to others what God has taught you, or to communicate from the house-top what He has spoken to your ear in the closet. It is much to be an evangelist or herald of the truth, but perhaps it is an even greater work to remove misconceptions, to instruct the ignorant, and lead the saints into the deep things of God. It is written, "And they shall be all taught of God." It is necessary to be disciples before we can become Apostles, to sit at the feet of Jesus before we go everywhere publishing the good news. It takes time and patience. Line has to be upon line, and precept upon precept. But what a pleasure it is when the great teacher, like a Columba or a Bede, is able to civilise vast tracts of country through the young and ardent souls whom they have trained in the knowledge of God.

The Great Qualification. But, after all, the crying need of us all is to be filled, as Bezaleel was, with the Spirit of God. It is not enough to have the Spirit, the Spirit must have us. It is good that the shallowest waves of Pentecost have come up the sands to our feet, but we need the full tide. The dawn may have struck up into your heart, but has it grown into the perfect daylight that fills the whole arch of heaven? It is the privilege of every believer to live in the Spirit, to walk in the Spirit, to be filled by the Spirit. The poor sempstress puts her penny in the slot of the gasmeter, and works as hard as the needle will fly, becaues she has no other, and her children's bread depends on her finishing her task. But God giveth not the Spirit *by meter* (this is the actual Greek word in John iii. 34). Will you not expand the lungs of your heart, and take a long, deep inspiration, and believe that, according to your capacity, so it is unto you? It is not necessary to *feel* that you have received. Dare to believe it, and that your Father has given you what you asked, though the Spirit is so gentle and ethereal that He eludes our coarse tests, and enters like the summer zephyr, which hardly rustles the leaf of the sensitive plant, and fails to shake the over-blown petal to the grass beneath.

GOD'S SABBATH-REST AND OURS

Exodus 31:12-17

12. And the Lord spake unto Moses, saying,

13. Speak thou also unto the children of Israel, saying, Verily my sabbaths ye shall keep: for it *is* a sign between me and you throughout your generations; that *ye* may know that I *am* the Lord that doth sanctify you.

14. Ye shall keep the sabbath therefore; for it *is* holy unto you: every one that defileth it shall surely be put to death: for whosoever doeth *any* work therein, that soul shall be cut off from among his people.

15. Six days may work be done; but in the seventh *is* the sabbath of rest, holy to the Lord: whosoever doeth *any* work in the sabbath day, he shall surely be put to death.

16. Wherefore the children of Israel shall keep the sabbath, to observe the sabbath throughout their generations, *for* a perpetual covenant.

17. It *is* a sign between me and the children of Israel for ever: for *in* six days the Lord made heaven and earth, and on the seventh day he rested, and was refreshed.

GOD'S SABBATH-REST AND OURS

Exodus 31:12-17

A Reminder. It is somewhat strange to have this recurrence to the great law of the Sabbath, which, it might be supposed, had already been adequately dealt with. But here, and again in xxv. 1–3, fresh emphasis is laid upon its observance. It has been thought that the intention was lest the people's zeal in Tabernacle construction might induce a laxity in the maintenance of Sabbath-observance. Be that as it may, we may at least be reminded that our zeal for God's service must never interfere with that deep restfulness of heart, and that careful use of the Lord's Day, out of which the highest and best service must emanate.

The Sabbath a Sign. Two new particulars are introduced by this paragraph. First, that the Sabbath was to be a sign—it has been called "a distinguishing badge," and "a sacramental bond"— between God and Israel; and, secondly, that its desecration was to be punished with death.

Before that time, the rite of circumcision had been the only visible sign of the Covenant into which Jehovah had entered with the seed of Abraham (Gen. xvii. 9–14; Acts vii. 8). But something else was required to differentiate the *entire* nation from the rest of mankind; and this was afforded by the absolute cessation of servile toil on the seventh day of the week. Juvenal mentions this as the distinguishing mark of the Jew in the days of the Empire; and, as all the world knows, it is equally distinct and distinguishing to-day. It was also a sign that God was sanctifying His people. The word means to set apart, and to set apart, not only outwardly but inwardly, by an all-pervasive indwelling. When God said that He would sanctify the people of Israel these two thoughts were involved, first, that He would set a distinguishing and characteristic mark upon them, and secondly, that He would dwell among them, filling them with the sense of His Presence, journeying with them in their march, resting when they rested, elevating and purifying their standards, aspirations, and communal life. Each of these objects was realised through the institution of the Sabbath, by which the Hebrews were differentiated from all other nations, and in which time was given for the spiritual to pervade and master the material. On the Sabbath the din of worldly toil ceased, and gave opportunity for the still small voice, the dust of the march subsided, so that the pure and heavenly horizons might come in view. The setting a part of one day in seven for religious worship reminded Israel, and made clear to all mankind, that they were a religious people, and that they were prepared to make sacrifices of a very distinct nature for their religious duties. No nation can allow a permanent invasion of the Rest-Day without invalidating its claim to be a religious and God-honouring people, and breaking those sacred covenant-bonds by which the divine help and deliverance are secured. Disregard of God is evidenced in nothing more certainly than by a disposition to break in upon the day of rest; and no such infringement can take place without the gravest injury being perpetrated on religion and morals. By the institution of the Sabbath, God made it clear that He regarded man as a religious being, that He claims his thought and time, and that for man's own sake, physical, moral, and religious, it is necessary that there should be the weekly pause.

The Punishment of the Sabbath-Breaker. The infliction of death on the Sabbath-breaker seems at first sight severe. But it must be remembered, on the other hand, that this repeated insistence on the keeping of the Sabbath rendered the breach of its observance a premeditated and presumptuous violation of the Divine Reign. The Hebrew nation was not an *oligarchy*, ruled by a few, nor a *democracy*, ruled by the crowd, nor an *aristocracy*, ruled by the best, but a *theocracy*, i.e. ruled by God. And the offender who deliberately set God at defiance was guilty of an act of high treason. He destroyed, so far as in him lay, the entire convenant between God and His people. If all did as he did, the whole nation would have been thrown out of the covenant, and the alliance which had been established in the days of Abraham, and had been the basis of the Exodus, would have been shattered into a thousand fragments. Hence it was that, all through the history of the chosen people, the maintenance or violation of the Sabbath was deemed an infallible sign of health or decline, of consecration or apostasy.

The Power of the Sabbath Law. It is an interesting fact that through all the centuries of Jewish history, whatever other offences they may have been guilty of, the nation, as a whole, has been true to the Sabbath law, as we have said. To employ the words of Exod. xxxi. 16, R.V., "They shall keep the Sabbath, to observe the Sabbath throughout their generations, for a perpetual convenant." Can it, therefore, be doubted that the Almighty also will respect that Covenant? Sooner shall His covenant of day and night cease, than that He should fail to perform His side of that sacred pledge which He has made with the children of Abraham; and probably all the agitation and ferment of modern Europe will eventuate in the sweeping away of the last obstacle to the return of the chosen people to the chosen land. "Thus saith the Lord: If My covenant of day and night stand not, if I have not appointed the ordinances of heaven and earth; then will I also cast away the seed of Jacob . . . for I will cause their captivity to return, and will have mercy on them" (Jer. xxxiii. 25, 26, R.V.).

Grounds of the Sabbath Law. *But the ground on which the command for Sabbath Observance rests is very remarkable.* "For in six days the Lord made heaven and earth, and on the seventh day He rested and was refreshed" (ver. 17).

Its Necessity. There are many grounds on which we might argue for the preservation of the rest day. (1) *It is a physical necessity.* Man is a seven-day clock which requires the weekly rest to recuperate exhausted energies, and impart a new zest to his daily occupation. (2) *It is a family necessity.* The parents and children are too busily engaged in the pursuit of education and business during the six working-days to cultivate each other's companionship, and the seventh-day rest is urgently needed to afford opportunities for the maintenance and cultivation of the common home-life. (3) *It is a national necessity.* The heated machine of our political and social activity requires the cooling pause of the rest-day, when men of all shades of politics kneel under the same roof in the presence of the Almighty Ruler of us all.

The Work of Creation. (4) *The ground mentioned here is very remarkable.* "For in six days the Lord made heaven and earth, and on the seventh day He rested, and was refreshed." The days of the first chapter of Genesis, by general consent, may be reckoned as *æons,* and represent in Apocalyptic vision the majestic steps up which creation advanced from the formlessness of its earlier stages to the order and beauty of the later, of which God said, "They are very good."

That the heaven and earth owe their existence to God is the statement not only of Scripture, but of science. "Science," said Lord Kelvin, when speaking at London University College, "positively affirmed creative power. Was there anything so absurd as to believe that a number of atoms, by falling together of their own accord, could make a sprig of moss, a microbe, or a living animal? Biologists only knew God in His works, but they were absolutely forced by science to admit, and to believe with absolute confidence in a directive power—in an influence other than physical, dynamical, or electrical forces." In a letter which appeared in the *Times* shortly afterwards he said: "Scientific thought is compelled to accept the idea of creative power"; and further: "Forty years ago I asked Liebig, when we were walking together in the country, if he believed that the grass and flowers which we saw around us grew of mere chemical forces. 'No,' he answered; 'no more than I could believe that a book of botany describing them could grow of chemical force.'"

The Rest of God. But what are we to infer from the words *He rested, and was refreshed*? Clearly this was not the result of weariness. "The everlasting God, the Lord, the Creator of the ends of the earth, fainteth not, neither is weary." Though engaged for untold ages in creating out of nothing, and in shaping what He had created, there was no exhaustion in His design, no slackening of His interest, no over-strain of His power.

Clearly, also, it was not the rest of inaction. When the Jews sought to slay Jesus because He had done this work on the Sabbath day He answered them, "My Father worketh hitherto, and I work." It was as though He said: "Go back to your ancient record, the Book of Genesis, and you will find there that of each of the days of Creation it was said, the evening and the morning was the first, second, third, fourth, fifth, and sixth day. But there was no evening and morning to the seventh day; and My Father, though He rests, works ceaselessly. He maintains the universe, controls and guides the course of human history, unlocks the gates of day, and draws the dusky curtains of the night; opens His hand to satisfy the desire of every living thing. He has been at work up to this very moment, and it was His direction and impulse that wrought through Me to the healing of this man."

The Rest after Finished Work. The rest of God was that of completion and satisfaction. "The heavens and the earth were finished, and all the host of them." All the work of building the house for human life and rearing a platform for the mighty drama of redemption was concluded. There were other and greater works waiting to be done, but, so far as the material universe was concerned, there was nothing to be altered or added.

The Lord's Day Memorial. It is into this rest that we are summoned to enter. And of its blessed peace and joy the weekly rest-day returns as a gracious reminder. As each Sabbath came to the Jew, so does each Lord's Day come to the Christian. We are reminded by its frequent recurrence of the possibility of entering upon our inheritance; nay, more, we are incited and urged to enter it. "There remaineth, therefore, a Sabbath-keeping for the people of God." "Let us therefore give diligence to enter into that rest, that no man fall after the same example of disobedience" (Heb. iv. 11, R.V.). As each rest-day breaks upon the earth, ask yourself seriously, "Do I know anything of that peace which is the reality of which this day is the type? Have I entered into the rest of God? Has my life attained its divine ideal and purpose, in harmony with the Spirit of the Creator Himself?"

Six Days of Training the Religious Experience. The work of the six days may be taken as indicating the successive stages in the education of the soul into this divine experience. There is, without doubt, a supreme moment in the life of the regenerate soul, when God creates His own nature within it. "If any man is in Christ, he is a new creation." It is not the reshaping of old materials, but the positive calling into being a new and wonderful life, which is to attain to the excellency of the stature of Christ. A love of God, that was never experienced in that cold heart; a hatred of sin; a taste for things that were once irksome; a loathing of things once loved—all are indications of the Creator's workmanship. But the work is far from done. Large regions of the hinterland are still given up to the trackless waste and the wild beast. But from the first moment of the new birth the Holy Spirit broods over the formless void, to mould and form, to conduct the soul, with infinite patience, to its perfecting.

How great a comfort it is to realise that this is God's method! Sometimes it seems as though the fabric on which He has been expending care and time is suddenly overthrown, as the vegetation of the carboniferous age were plunged into the dark cellars of the ground. But in such hours we must joyfully acknowledge that all is not gone, but that God is still at work, and on the base of what He has already done is about to build up more. He never grows faint nor discouraged, because only through successive stages can character advance towards the Second Adam of the sixth day and the Sabbath-Keeping of the Seventh. "We know not what we shall be."

God's Work in You. What is Its Stage? How far has the Almighty Craftsman got in His work on your soul? Has he reached the *first* day, when Light begins to penetrate the dark recesses of the soul, revealing it to itself, and leading to an agony of conviction and penitential grief? Have you reached the *second* stage, the stage of separation, where you are conscious that a great division is at work separating the below from the above, the earthly and the heavenly, the carnal and the spiritual, as by a far expanse of firmament? Or is your present experience that of the *third* day, when as the silt dropping from the laden waters causes the land to appear, so in you also, firm habits of character are beginning slowly to reveal themselves? Or, perhaps, you are living in the *fourth* day, when the envelope of the environing mist is beginning to break away, and you are beholding, for the first time, clearly the face of Christ? Or yours may be the activity of the *fifth* day, with its various forms of life. But what are all these compared to the wonders of the *sixth* day, when God makes you into the image of His Son, when, as you have borne the image of the earthly, you begin to bear the image of the heavenly, when old things have passed absolutely and for ever away, and behold all things are become new!

God's Patient Working. Ah, soul! upon whom God's creative and formative processes have commenced, He may yet take years and æons of years, until Christ is perfectly formed in thee, and thou shalt be manifested as His Son; but He will perfect that which concerneth thee, because His mercy endureth for ever, and He will not forsake the work of His own hands. The nature of Christ cannot be deduced from our sinful nature, it must be imparted. It must grow as the child Jesus grew, because it can only be ours in proportion as we apprehend and appropriate the fulness of Christ. Objectively we stand fully accepted and complete in Jesus; but experimentally we only receive as much as we see our need of and accept.

The Rest for Us. Thus we come to the Rest of which the Sabbath spoke. We enter into the Rest of God, and the Rest of God enters and pervades our soul. We know that we have passed from death into life; that we are justified from all things; that we are accepted in the Beloved; that we are sons of God and joint heirs with Christ; that all things work together for good; that the grace of God will always be sufficient for our need; and that grace will one day flower into glory; and out of these convictions comes the Peace of God that passeth understanding and the inward calm out of which the noblest service emanates.

TABLES OF THE TESTIMONY

Exodus 31:18;32:15-20;34:1,28,29

18. And he gave unto Moses, when he had made an end of communing with him upon mount Sinai, two tables of testimony, tables of stone, written with the finger of God.

15. And Moses turned, and went down from the mount, and the two tables of the testimony *were* in his hand: the tables *were* written on both their sides: on the one side and on the other *were* they written.
16. And the tables *were* the work of God, and the writing *was* the writing of God, graven upon the tables.
17. And when Joshua heard the noise of the people as they shouted, he said unto Moses, *There is* a noise of war in the camp.
18. And he said, *It is* not the voice of *them that* shout for mastery, neither *is it* the voice of *them that* cry for being overcome; *but* the noise of *them that* sing do I hear.
19. And it came to pass, as soon as he came nigh unto the camp, that he saw the calf, and the dancing; and Moses' anger waxed hot, and he cast the tables out of his hands, and brake them beneath the mount.
20. And he took the calf which they had made, and burnt *it* in the fire, and ground *it* to powder, and strawed *it* upon the water, and made the children of Israel drink *of it*.

1. And the Lord said unto Moses, Hew thee two tables of stone like unto the first; and I will write upon *these* tables the words that were in the first tables, which thou brakest.

28. And he was there with the Lord forty days and forty nights; he did neither eat bread, nor drink water. And he wrote upon the tables the words of the covenant, the ten commandments.
29. And it came to pass, when Moses came down from mount Sinai with the two tables of testimony in Moses' hand, when he came down from the mount, that Moses wist not that the skin of his face shone while he talked with him.

TABLES OF THE TESTIMONY

Exodus 31:18;32:15-20;34:1,28,29

Tabernacle and the Tables. When Moses received the first invitation to come up into the Mount and be there, the Almighty told him that He was about to give him the tables of stone, on which He had written (xxiv. 12); and when directions were communicated for the construction of the ark, it was assumed that some embodiment of the law would be forthcoming, which would be placed in that sacred receptacle (xxv. 16). It was therefore befitting that, when God had made an end of communing with Moses upon Mount Sinai, He should give him the two tables of the Testimony, tables of stone, written with the finger of God. We might almost go so far as to say that the entire Tabernacle was designed with the view of the safe-keeping of the law, written upon these stone tablets, in the very heart of the national life.

An Appeal to the Nation. We use these words "national life" advisedly, because we are not unmindful of the language uttered by one of the greatest of modern statesmen. "May I ask you," said John Bright to the citizens of Birmingham in 1858, "to believe, as do myself devoutly believe, that the moral law was not written for men alone in their individual character, but that it was written as well for nations, and for nations as great as this of which we are citizens. If nations reject and deride that moral law, there is a penalty which will inevitably follow. It may not be at once; it may not come in our life-time; but rely upon it that while the sword of Heaven is not in haste to smite, yet it will not linger. We are not left without a guide. It is true that we have not, as an ancient people had, the Urim and Thummim—those oracular gems on Aaron's breast, from which he took counsel—but we have the unchangeable and eternal principles of the moral law to guide us; and, only so far as we walk by that guidance, can we be permanently a great nation, or our people a happy people."

The Permanence of the Law Signified. *The use of stone bore witness to the imperishableness of the Divine Law.* Stone is more enduring as a custodian of engraving than metal. Gold and silver are comparatively soft, iron corrodes, steel was unknown at that period. The material selected to receive the moral law was the most indestructible that the world contained. Even now those tablets may exist, and one day may be discovered amid the remains of the great past. We are reminded, therefore, that no jot or tittle shall pass away from the law until all be fulfilled. The Apostle brings out a strong contrast to the stone tablets of Sinai when he says that the Spirit of the living God writes not now on tables of stone, but on tables which are hearts of flesh (2 Cor. iii. 3); and yet perhaps memory is just as indestructible, and retains the impression of the Divine law with equal tenacity as granite.

The Writing—God's. *The law was written by the finger of God.* We cannot understand precisely what is intended, but realise that the Eternal would not transmit to the loftiest of the sons of light the duty of making clear that holy law, which was commanded to Israel "for their good always." Everything was done to invest the the law with majesty and authority; to no inferior being could be delegated the promulgation of law which from all eternity had been shaped and compacted in the Divine mind; before ever God's thought had clothed itself in creation, or filled the morning stars with singing.

The Writing—On Both Sides. *We are told also that the tables were written on both their sides* (xxxii. 15). Does not this teach that the moral law is written both within and without the human heart, pressing externally upon us as a rule of righteousness which we are constrained to obey, and approved from within by the voice of conscience? There is no room for the insertion of any other law. Human accretions are forbidden, because there is no space for them; and may it not be that the additions which man has made to the Divine law have led, not only to most of the divisions of the Church, but to much of the atheism and infidelity, which resent obligations that are not witnessed to by the moral consciousness?

The reason for the proclamation of the law, and its engraving upon these tables is clear. Paul explains it exactly when he says, "I was alive without the law once, but when the commandment came, sin revived, and I died."

The Necessity for the Law. It is necessary that God should set before men the norm or type of the life that He Himself is living, and of which we are capable, in order that He may reveal the true nature of sin, and lead men to abhor it. Adam in Paradise lived an easy, contented life, of which probably his own gratification was the law. He looked upon the tree, and saw that it was good for food, and pleasant to the eyes. What was good and pleasant was his supreme law; and so he might have continued to live in innocent self-indulgence, using the world around for animal gratification, with no knowledge of the injury that he was doing to himself and of the blessing that he was forfeiting. It was necessary therefore that the command should come, "Thou shalt not eat." He was told that he must refrain from gratifying his desire for his own pleasure, and begin to acknowledge a higher ideal. Then it was for the first time he knew himself to be a sinner. The law came to show him that the life he was living was a violation of the principles of his moral nature, obedience to which could alone secure blessedness for him.

How the Law Works. It is as though in a certain village, a lad endowed with the elements of a beautiful voice were to use it after his own fancy, in such a way as to injure the vocal organs and undermine his health. The villagers may gather around him in the evening, full of admiration; his fame may spread throughout the countryside, but all the while, though he is unconscious, he is approximating to an absolute silence that will put an untimely end to his career. Finally he goes to the great city, consults a professor of music, sings in his presence, and is examined by a specialist. The laws of voice production are explained to him, and it comes on him as a thunderclap to understand the mistake that he has made, the injury that he has inflicted upon himself, the inevitable failure of all his ambitions. A new and higher law has suddenly broken in upon the lad, and there is no option but to accept its absolute condemnation for his own efforts, and to submit to its rule. He was alive without the law in his own estimation until he caught sight of its majestic beauty and irrevocable demands, then he died to his own way, renounced it, and yielded himself to the influence of the higher and better method.

The Case of St. Paul. The same process took place in the history of St. Paul. Through long years he had lived according to the highest order of Pharisee. He had no conception of anything better than to fast twice in the week, to give tithes of all he possessed, and to refrain from extortion and injustice. Indeed, he verily thought that he ought to do many things contrary to the name of Jesus.

When he thrust men and women into prison, broke up the Christian meetings, and even imbrued his hands in Stephen's blood, he thought that he was doing God service. Then in the person of Jesus of Nazareth the law of infinite love, mercy and forgiveness broke into his soul, and he was overwhelmed with remorse. The commandment which was unto life he found to be unto death. He saw that the commandment demanded not simply an outward obedience, but searched the inward motive. It was as though a new light pervaded the recesses of his soul, and revealed the hideous things which were nestling there. He learned that what he had thought to be good would not pass muster amid the holy radiance that shone from the face of Jesus, reflected there from the heart of God.

The Case of the Israelites. The same law wrought here at Sinai, and when God uttered His law from the mount, and afterwards entrusted it to the hands of Moses in this written form, the intention was to show the people who had become steeped in the sensuality of Egypt, and whose notions of morality had become impoverished and corrupted, that the true blessedness of man could be attained, not by his following the impulses and passions of his evil heart, but by self-discipline, self-control, the refusal of the lower, the forsaking of the things that were behind, and the pressing up and on to those that were before.

The Purpose of the Law. Let it never be forgotten, therefore, that law is the expression in a preceptive form of a life which God is living, and for which man was created; it comes to change the sin of ignorance into the sin of presumption; it comes to teach that the law for human life is not self-indulgence, but self-sacrifice; it comes to reveal man to himself, that he may be shut up to the mercy and help of God. The law entered that sin (i.e. knowledge of sin) might abound, and that where sin abounded grace might abound more exceedingly; that as sin reigned unto death, even so might grace reign, through righteousness, unto eternal life through Jesus Christ (Rom. v. 20, 21).

Law and Sin. The course of human life has been compared to a river, flowing through a level plain slowly but steadily towards the sea. So smooth is its surface that a traveller approaching could not tell in what direction it was flowing, or whether it was flowing at all. A rock in mid-channel, protruding above the surface, reveals the current by the rippling circle of water at its base. The obstruction makes known both the direction and velocity of the river's flow.

It detects the movement, though it does not produce it. Such is the relation between sin in the soul and the law which reveals it. Our life, before the law of God enters, rolls downward like a river—one great volume of enmity against God. Because all is sin, the self-deceived man does not notice that there is any. But when the law of God enters, collision between it and the direction of our life makes it known that hitherto we have been living without God in the world.

The People's Fall. When Moses drew near the scenes which were being enacted at the foot of the mount, he fell in with Joshua, who must have been waiting for his descent. The sounds of unholy revelry reached their ears, which Joshua mistook for the shouts of combatants. Moses, however, having been instructed as to the actual nature of the proceedings, declared that it was not the voice of them that shouted for mastery, nor the voice of them that cried for being overcome, but the noise of them that sang. Then, as the two came suddenly round the corner of the gorge through which they were descending, and the whole terrible spectacle burst on their view, Moses' anger waxed hot, and he cast the tables out of his hand, and they were broken beneath the mount. For this act he was never rebuked. It partook of the nature of that anger described by the Apostle when he says, "Be ye angry, and sin not." Indeed, probably it would have been impossible for anyone to have been in contact with the holiness of God for six weeks without the reaction of hot indignation and horror, when brought suddenly face to face with such a revelation of the evil of man's heart. But as those tables leapt from crag to crag, and lay presently splintered and broken at the foot of the mount, were they not an emblem of the way in which man's sin breaks the Divine law and cancels the covenant of works?

The Law and the World of Sin. The descent of Moses into that scene is an emblem of the law's entrance into a world of sin. The law comes not to a people waiting to receive the knowledge of God's will, but busy with their own plans of self-indulgence. Its advent, therefore, can only be in wrath. It falls upon the idolatrous crowd, and grinds them to powder; it casts a spell of silence over the voice of those that sing, and the shadow of death upon the idolater.

The New Tables Laid Up. But the story does not end here. The Lord bade His servant hew two tables of stone, like unto the first, and on these He wrote the words which were on the first tables, i.e. the **Ten Commandments.** These Moses brought down the mount and placed reverently in the ark, laying the golden slab of the mercy-seat above them. Upon that slab of gold the Shechinah of God's purity shone; beneath it were the tables of the law; but the mercy-seat, being covered with the blood of Atonement, told that sacrifice had been offered and accepted, and that the penitent need fear no longer the penalty that followed on the violation of law.

Law and the Great Propitiation. The mercy-seat, as we have seen, was the propitiatory, a place where God and the sinner were made at one. All that was meant, however, can only be understood by those who have seen the Lamb of God bearing away the sin of the world. Sinai can only be fully understood when the truth it signified appeared. It was when Jesus said, "It is finished," that the truth broke upon the world that the true Atonement cannot be a life which God can claim—a creature life—but the life which God Himself offers—Himself. Some dim glimpse of this thought may have been caught by the more earnest worshippers under the law, but to many it must have remained veiled, as is the depth of Gospel truth to many believers now. The Israelite was specially taught to connect his acceptance, not with a work which he had invented, but with one which God had appointed. It was by God's way, and not by his own, that he was brought nigh, and this substitution of God's way for man's involved an act of obedient faith, which ultimately led into the Holy of Holies, laid open by the death of Jesus.

The Cross Explained by Sinai. Never was the mercy-seat so precious to the worshipper under the old dispensation as when he realised the demands of God's holy law; and men are never likely to apprehend the meaning of the Cross unless they too have shivered under the thunders of Sinai. Then we understand for the first time the words, "Christ hath redeemed us from the curse of the law, having been made a curse for us"; then we open our hearts to the blessed Spirit, that He may reproduce Christ within us. He who gave the law, and conformed to it during His human career, becomes within us the fountain of obedience. When the love of Christ is shed abroad in our hearts by the Holy Spirit, our love becomes the congenial atmosphere through which He secures a recognition of and loyalty to the law, such as could never have been secured by the *must* of Sinai, but is easy beneath the spell of the wooing note of Calvary.

THE GOLDEN CALF

Exodus 32:1-6,21-29

1. And when the people saw that Moses delayed to come down out of the mount, the people gathered themselves together unto Aaron, and said unto him, Up, make us gods, which shall go before us; for *as for* this Moses, the man that brought us up out of the land of Egypt, we wot not what is become of him.

2. And Aaron said unto them, Break off the golden earrings, which *are* in the ears of your wives, of your sons, and of your daughters, and bring *them* unto me.

3. And all the people brake off the golden earrings which *were* in their ears, and brought *them* unto Aaron.

4. And he received *them* at their hand, and fashioned it with a graving tool, after he had made it a molten calf: and they said, These *be* thy gods, O Israel, which brought thee up out of the land of Egypt.

5. And when Aaron saw *it*, he built an altar before it; and Aaron made proclamation, and said, To-morrow *is* a feast to the Lord.

6. And they rose up early on the morrow, and offered burnt offerings, and brought peace offerings; and the people sat down to eat and to drink, and rose up to play.

21. And Moses said unto Aaron, What did this people unto thee, that thou hast brought so great a sin upon them?

22. And Aaron said, Let not the anger of my lord wax hot: thou knowest the people, that they *are set* on mischief.

23. For they said unto me, Make us gods, which shall go before us: for *as for* this Moses, the man that brought us up out of the land of Egypt, we wot not what is become of him.

24. And I said unto them, Whosoever hath any gold, let them break *it* off. So they gave *it* me: then I cast it into the fire, and there came out this calf.

25. And when Moses saw that the people *were* naked; (for Aaron had made them naked unto *their* shame among their enemies:)

26. Then Moses stood in the gate of the camp, and said, Who *is* on the Lord's side? *let him come* unto me. And all the sons of Levi gathered themselves together unto him.

27. And he said unto them, Thus saith the Lord God of Israel, Put every man his sword by his side, *and* go in and out from gate to gate throughout the camp, and slay every man his brother, and every man his companion, and every man his neighbour.

28. And the children of Levi did according to the word of Moses: and there fell of the people that day about three thousand men.

29. For Moses had said, Consecrate yourselves today to the Lord, even every man upon his son, and upon his brother; that he may bestow upon you a blessing this day.

THE GOLDEN CALF

Exodus 32:1-6,21-29

The People, and the Absence of Moses on the Mount. Terrified by
the loud thunderings and lightnings, the thrilling trumpeting of Sinai,
with which the Almighty inaugurated His Law, the people of Israel
entreated Moses that he would henceforth act as a daysman and
mediator between God and them. "Go," said they, "into the immediate pavilion of the Almighty, and stand there and receive His Word,
and then return and impart it to us in modulated tones." Acting
upon their suggestion, Moses therefore betook himself up the steep
mountain-side of Sinai, and being lost presently to view in the
mists, stepped into the pavilion of God's presence, and remained
there for some six weeks. The seventy elders that accompanied
him part of the way, content with having seen the Sapphire Throne
beneath His feet, and having ate and drank in His presence, returned,
and for a little time Israel was pacified. But as week succeeded week,
they became restless, and began to wonder what might have become
of their great leader. They felt on the one hand that the embodiment
of Deity had been withdrawn from them, that the moral restraint of a
holy life had also ceased to operate, and in the recoil the licentious
passions that had been surging in the hearts of the people since they
lived in the land of Egypt began to crave for gratification. The moral
restraint having been withdrawn, and the difficulty of realising the
spirituality of God being so great, the people began to relapse into
idolatry. They said, "Something has happened to our great leader,
he must have met with an accident in his long and perilous ascent,
or he may have been consumed with the burning fire whose glory
dazzled our sight, or he may have been absorbed into the Deity.
In any case, we know not what has become of him, and it seems as
if he may never return. Therefore, Up! make us something that we
can see, some embodiment of Deity that shall go before us, and

bring us to the land to which we travel." This is an amazing scene, but full of the most impressive lessons.

Moses the "Man of God." (1) *The uplifting and restraining character of a holy life.* Moses is perpetually referred to as the "man of God." We notice that even Caleb, who had known him intimately for many years, so describes him (Josh. xiv. 6). It is interesting when our bosom companions and the servants of our household speak of us as men of God, for they know our every action and see us as we are. Hundreds of years after, in the Book of Ezra (iii. 2), Moses is still described as the "man of God." This description was also applied to Elisha, who was a softer and gentler character than Elijah. Elijah stood on the rocky pinnacle, and rebuked kings amid the thunders and lightnings, but Elisha was one who went in and out amongst the people, healing and blessing them, so much so that the wife of one of the great landowners, who lived in the neighbouring mansion, said to her husband, "I perceive that this is a holy man of God that passes by us continually." It is evident to the most casual eye, when a man is of a really holy and consistent character. It is a great designation, the "man of God." We all know what it is to be "a man of the world." There are many men who are perfectly cognisant of the world around, of its habits and customs, of its good form or bad, not knowing that they are standing upon a bubble that may break at any moment; that they are swimming with a life-buoy which is beginning to leak and will be unable always to sustain them amidst the storms. We know "the man of letters." It is much to be able to charm the imagination and guide the thought of people. We honour the statesman, who, like Pitt, guides the country with eagle eye, and stands supreme amongst his fellows; and the commercial man, who prefers his good name to any profit that may come by chicanery; but the "man of God" is the supreme title of all. We feel that there is a flame burning in his heart, and that his life is like some broad river, spreading fertility and beauty everywhere.

The Power of the Holy Life. The people had seen Moses under many difficult circumstances. They had beheld him face to face with Pharaoh, daring to hurl back a retort on the greatest tyrant the world had seen; they had wondered at him amid the awful terror of the night of the passage through the Red Sea; and when Moses had spoken from Sinai God had answered him with a voice. They felt that so long as Moses was there they had an incarnation of

Deity, and that God was with them and near them. They realised the moral restraint and uplifting influence of his soul. One man, by the nobility and purity and simplicity of his character, kept two and a half millions of people on the high uplands of monotheism and spirituality. After such a fashion all of us are called to live in the home, in the business house, and amongst men, with so much of God in us that to see us will make men think of God; and to have us with them is to experience a moral restraint arresting them in the gratifying of their passions. Thus we shall be as an antiseptic in the midst of pollution, our influence proceeding not so much from what we say as from what we are. When Moses' presence was withdrawn the people said to Aaron, "Make us gods."

—**A Power in all Ages.** We are called not only to be Christians, but Christs, to reduplicate and repeat the life of Jesus to men. It is in the strength of your character, in the flash of the eye, the blush of purity on the face, the instinctive shrinking of the soul from contact with pollution, the uplifting of the heart toward God which people experience who live in your proximity and listen to your talk. It must be a living and evident fact that you have no complicity with the evil influences around you and that your nature aspires God-ward. The Christian soul resembles the flower that has no speech nor language, and whose voice is not heard. We cannot see the lily growing out of the filthy pond without instinctively being led to desire to be clean. We cannot see the long line of snow-clad Alps, rising from the valleys where mists and miasma lurk, without desiring to climb up and stand amidst those eternal snows. What a tribute to the magnificence of this man's character who thus presented God to the people! As long as they had Moses they had been clean, he restrained them, and was a barrier against a tide of filth.

Aaron's Weakness. (2) *The injury done to society by the weakness of moral character.* We should have thought that when Moses was gone, the most natural thing would be for the people to go to Aaron and say, "Moses has gone, be to us in his stead." But they never thought of it, because, although probably Aaron had never been betrayed into any moral evil, by that instinctive knowledge which we all have as to the quality of another's soul, they knew that Aaron was a weak man. It is a remarkable thing in life that men will sooner or later betray themselves, and others will estimate them by a moral diagnosis which is absolutely certain in its action. You may be a priest; you may pose a mediator, to guide people in their intercourse with God; you may parade the religious ceremonial with which you are associated, but the world looks beneath the dress of the priest to the character of the man. You may dress Aaron as you like, put the breastplate upon his heart and the golden mitre upon his brow, but public opinion will read Aaron, and know that he at least is not the incarnation of Deity. We always attribute strength to true goodness, and doubt a goodness which is not pervaded with virility.

Aaron Temporises. In this diagnosis the people did not mistake, for there were two signs of moral weakness in Aaron's behaviour. *First*, when they demanded that he should prepare a calf as a visible deity, instead of meeting them, as he should have done, with a direct negative, he set himself to place difficulties in the way of carrying out their desire. He reasoned with himself, "It is a mere passing whim. I will not therefore contradict them, lest they stone me, but I will throw back the difficulty upon them, and let them obtain from their wives and children their earrings and ornaments." It is a custom in the Orient, where banks are few and untrustworthy, for the people to carry as much wealth as possible in ornaments upon their persons. He said to himself, "They will never deny themselves their rich jewels, and thus I shall be delivered from doing what I know to be wrong." We are often tempted to reason after a similar fashion. We know that a thing is wrong, but instead of saying so, we endeavour to evade the fact, and try to get the credit of virtue by raising a side issue. But the event does not justify our expectations. So far from Aaron's hopes being realised, they were falsified, and the people began to pour in with their golden ornaments, stripping their persons in their enthusiasm, and Aaron, to his mortification, found himself compelled to carry out their purpose. In this there was an exact counterpart in Pilate's paltering with the demand of the High Priest that Jesus should be crucified. In each case the result was the same.

Aaron's Defence of Himself. *Secondly*, when Moses came down from the mount, full of burning indignation, Aaron replied to his hot remonstrances by saying, "Brother, you understand this people, that they are stiff-necked. They gave me the gold, I put it into the furnace, and *there came out this calf.* I did not do it; it was the furnace that did it. Pity me, I am the unlucky creature of circumstances." There is a type of man that lays the whole stress of his failure on circumstances, and unjustly accentuates these. "It was not I, but the furnace." You are called to deal with a sensualist—

a profane, evil-living man. You ask him how he came to this, and he will answer—"I was thrown into a bad set at college; I was swept into a wild circle when I came to London. In my business they flattered me, and in my poverty they trampled on me. I am no saint; but then you cannot blame me. Look at my circumstances; it is the furnace that did it." A woman of society and fashion will say, "I admit that I am not what I might be, but then look at my set; it is the furnace that did it." A man will doubt God, question the Bible and truth, and excuse himself by saying, "It is not I, it is the drift of modern tendency; it is the furnace that did it." "There came out this calf."

The Influence of the Infirm Character. Yes, streams are always flowing, the streams of impurity, of worldly materialistic living, of atheism—but are you going to launch forth on the stream? That is the point. Of course, if you yield, you will soon be swept into the current. There are scores of young people who might be gripped and held back if you were strong, but your weak compliance with the habits and traditions around will relax the one saving influence of their lives. At this very moment God in His high heaven was talking with Moses about Aaron's garments, and sketching out for him the great programme of his priesthood, which certainly would have been carried out, whatever the people determined to the contrary, because God would have protected him. Whilst this mighty future was being planned for him yonder, see how he was demeaning himself in the plain beneath!

Religion a Failure Unless Spiritual. (3) *Nothing but spiritual religion can overcome the power of the flesh.* What is idolatry? It is not a rudimentary knowledge of God, but the recoil from spiritual religion. You might think that the idolater had never known God, and therefore made a piece of wood or stone to represent Him; but that is a wrong conception, and contrary to experience. The whole testimony of the Bible is that the idolater may be one who has known God, as St. Paul clearly shows in Rom. i. 21, R.V.—"Knowing God, they glorified Him not as God, neither gave thanks; but became vain in their reasonings, and their senseless heart was darkened." It is clear also from this story that the people knew God. They had seen His blazing glory and heard His voice on Sinai, yet they made this calf. In fact, the conception of the Deity set before them by Moses had been so spiritual that the effort had been too great for these sensuous people to realise his high ideals. Had they only lived up to them, sin would have been impossible, because their spiritual life would have been kept open to the Spirit of God, and through that union the power of God would have rendered them impervious to temptation. But when Moses was gone, with his restraining presence, there came an almost inevitable rebound. They said, "This spiritual religion is too high, we cannot attain to it. We must have religion, of course; we have no desire to forsake the God of our fathers, but let us lower this high standard set before us by Moses to something we can see and touch, and which appeals to the sense." It is very interesting and remarkable to observe that directly they lowered their religious standard from the spiritual to the sensual, and so intercepted the gracious resisting power of God's Spirit, passion at once asserted itself, and they gave themselves up to the licentious dance, referred to by Herodotus, but which it is impossible to describe in the present day.

The Opportunity of Passion. The reason why so many are overcome by passion is because they refuse to live on the spiritual level with God, and decline to the lower level of sense. The connection between themselves and the Divine Spirit thus becomes choked or cut. None of us need be overcome with inordinate desire, if we would live in the Spirit, walk in the Spirit, and be occupied by the Spirit. If only we would absorb, in living fellowship with the heart of Christ, the spiritual power which is there, no passion, however mighty its fascination, would be able to master the soul. "Walk by the Spirit, and ye shall not fulfil the lust of the flesh. For the flesh lusteth against the Spirit, and the Spirit against the flesh; for these are contrary the one to the other; that ye may not do the things that ye would" (Gal. v. 16, 17, R.V.).

What Idolatry Is. This study of the proclivity of the human heart towards idolatry, i.e. towards something that can be apprehended by the senses as the object of religious worship, is very illuminating. Idolatry is the endeavour to realise by the senses and intellect, that which only reveals itself to the spiritual faculties of the soul. The essence of idolatry is not expressed in the words, "I have no care for God in heaven, these idols therefore shall be my gods," but in the confession, "I know that there is a God in heaven, but the knowledge of Him is too wonderful for me; it is high, and I cannot attain to it; my spiritual sight is dim, and I will make these living embodiments of His being." Had any one suggested that Israel should apostatise from the God of Abraham, they would have stoned him to death.

They had no desire to break the first commandment and to have other gods than Jehovah; but they found the demand of the second commandment too vigorous. They must have an image, a visible representation, an idol (from the Greek *eidōlon*, i.e. something to be seen).

What it is Followed. This explains the idolatry of Judaism and of Romanism, and the tendency among us all to set up certain habits and forms, certain views and creeds, the affirmation of schools of thought and the fashion of a church-set, as the *fetich* of the religious life. We do not presume to live without God, but we are glad to substitute any intellectual or physical alternative for the worship of God in spirit and in truth. It is easy to reduce our spiritual life from the high spiritual level of Jesus to a mere habit of thought or action, which costs no effort, soothes our consciences, and has the appearance of godliness whilst denying the power. The faith that sees God demands a pure and holy soul, but where this is too heavy a toll to pay, we invent a method of our own, which gives us a religion after a fashion, and winks at practices which the Eternal Light could not tolerate. The advantage of an idol is, that we can take it with us, as Rachel hid her father's teraphim. But God will not go our way: if we want Him, we must go His.

The Prophet and the Priest. In the distinction between Moses and Aaron, we have an illustration of the contrast between the prophet and the priest. The prophet brings the human conscience into the presence of God: the priest negotiates between God and man. The prophet denounces idolatry and tramples its effigies beneath his feet: the priest condones it, in compassion for weak human nature. The prophet is more or less of a revolutionary: the priest, fearful of losing his own position, endeavours to maintain the established course of society. The prophet bears the burdens of the Lord, and is very zealous for His honour: the priest is eager to get in his dues. The prophet ennobles the human spirit by arousing it to hold fellowship with the Father of spirits, whilst the priest is indifferent to its enervation, so long as it turns to himself. Therefore the priesthood, speaking generally, has always stood in the way of freedom, independence, and the liberty wherewith Christ makes His people free.

The Senses and the Soul. How remarkable was the act of Moses in forcing the people to drink of the dust of the golden calf (verse 20)! It has been finely said that the world is drinking still of the dust of its idolatries. The penalty of making an image of God to the sense, instead of seeking God with the spirit, is the destruction of all the nobler attributes of the soul. "They that make them are like unto them, so is every one that‚trusteth in them," was a true witness that the prophet made concerning idols and idol-makers. The connection between idolatry and the grossest sensuality is proverbial; and the reason is apparent. Directly you allow the senses to take possession of the soul, they paralyse its resistance, they make havoc of its will.

The Divine Answer to Human Need. From the idol which man's fancy has imagined and his hands fashioned, let us turn thankfully to the divine answer to the human heart, in its appeal for some visible, tangible form, which human eyes have seen and hands have handled. The passionate cry of the ages was uttered through the lips of Philip when he said, "Lord, show us the Father, and it sufficeth us"; and Jesus answered, "He that hath seen Me hath seen the Father." The manufactories that turn out images of the Virgin and of the saints would soon be deserted of their workpeople, if men would realise that the glory of God shines in the face of Jesus. Men have thought that the Eternal God has mocked their yearnings and despised their cries, and have invented for themselves images and ikons, which have borne a tender, sympathising, and pitiful aspect. These, they have said, are our gods. But are they not guilty of the very sin which disgraced the lower slopes of Sinai? As Israel turned from the splendours of Sinai to fashion the calf, and found that the end of those things was death, so of still sorer judgment are those worthy who turn away from God in Christ, imagining that a woman would have more tenderness than He has, and that to touch the hem of His garment is to be preferred to the radiant bliss of the fellowship which John enjoyed on His breast.

"Who is on the Lord's Side?" On Moses reaching the camp, he did three things: (1) He destroyed the calf; (2) He remonstrated with Aaron; (3) He took his station at the main gate of the camp and cried: "Who is on Jehovah's side? Here to me." He could not endure that the Amalekite tribes, that probably were peering down from the cliffs on the naked orgies of the people, should not also behold the condign justice and judgment with which the Almighty would avenge them. At all costs the unseemly revel must be stopped. He gave orders therefore to the faithful band that gathered to his call to go in and out throughout the camp, visiting the whole of it, and slaying, if necessary, every man, even his son or his brother.

He told them that their zeal in this matter would secure consecration: "Consecrate yourselves this day unto the Lord, that He may bestow a blessing upon you." This act on the part of the Levites secured for them the priesthood; and long after it was said of the tribe: "My covenant was with them of life and peace. The law of truth was in his mouth, and he did turn many away from iniquity."

A Call Even Now. But is not this clarion call still ringing: "Who is on the Lord's side?" Was there ever a time when stalwarts like these were in greater demand? We have to hold God's truth against many idols which are placed in competition with it. Idols of the tribe, of the forum, and of the heart. But before we can hope to cope with the heresies and superstitions of our age, we must turn the sword in against ourselves. "Little children, keep *yourselves* from idols," is very pertinent advice. Whilst condemning others, let us see to it that no mote or beam is in our own eyes. Do we know what it is to worship God in the Spirit, to glory in Christ Jesus, and to have no confidence in the flesh? Have we, with Jacob, put away the strange gods of our souls, i.e. all that detracts from our face-to-face fellowship with God? Have we purified ourselves from all filthiness of the spirit as well as of the flesh? Have we put off the garment of the old man, and put on the new man, which is created in the image of God? Then will be fulfilled for us the magnificent blessing wherewith Moses, the man of God, blessed Levi before his death:

> " Thy Thummim and Thy Urim are
> with Thy godly one, . . .
> Who said of his father, and of his mother,
> I have not seen him;
> Neither did he acknowledge his brethren.
> Nor knew he his own children: . . .
> They shall teach Jacob Thy judgments,
> And Israel Thy law:
> They shall put incense before Thee,
> And whole burnt offering upon
> Thine altar."
>
> (Deut. xxxiii. 8–10, R.V.)

THE FOURFOLD INTERCESSION OF MOSES

Exodus 32:7-14,30-35

7. And the Lord said unto Moses, Go, get thee down; for thy people, which thou broughtest out of the land of Egypt, have corrupted *themselves*:

8. They have turned aside quickly out of the way which I commanded them: they have made them a molten calf, and have worshipped it, and have sacrificed thereunto, and said, These *be* thy gods, O Israel, which have brought thee up out of the land of Egypt.

9. And the Lord said unto Moses, I have seen this people, and, behold, it *is* a stiff-necked people:

10. Now therefore let me alone, that my wrath may wax hot against them, and that I may consume them: and I will make of thee a great nation.

11. And Moses besought the Lord his God, and said, Lord, why doth thy wrath wax hot against thy people, which thou hast brought forth out of the land of Egypt with great power, and with a mighty hand?

12. Wherefore should the Egyptians speak, and say, For mischief did he bring them out, to slay them in the mountains, and to consume them from the face of the earth? Turn from thy fierce wrath, and repent of this evil against thy people.

13. Remember Abraham, Isaac, and Israel, thy servants, to whom thou swarest by thine own self, and saidst unto them, I will multiply your seed as the stars of heaven, and all this land that I have spoken of will I give unto your seed, and they shall inherit *it* for ever.

14. And the Lord repented of the evil which he thought to do unto his people.

30. And it came to pass on the morrow, that Moses said unto the people, Ye have sinned a great sin: and now I will go up unto the Lord; peradventure I shall make an atonement for your sin.

31. And Moses returned unto the Lord, and said, Oh, this people have sinned a great sin, and have made them gods of gold.

32. Yet now, if thou wilt forgive their sin—; and if not, blot me, I pray thee, out of thy book which thou hast written.

33. And the Lord said unto Moses, Whosoever hath sinned against me, him will I blot out of my book.

34. Therefore now go, lead the people unto *the place* of which I have spoken unto thee: behold, mine Angel shall go before thee: nevertheless in the day when I visit I will visit their sin upon them.

35. And the Lord plagued the people, because they made the calf, which Aaron made.

THE FOURFOLD INTERCESSION OF MOSES
Exodus 32:7-14,30-35

The Divine Care. Barely three months had passed since the people had made the transit through the Red Sea, and every hour of that period had been marked by evidences of the Divine care. For them the table in the wilderness had been spread; for them the waters had gushed out pellucid and crystal from the rocks; for them the fleecy cloud, the cumulus cloud, slowly advanced across the sky, and spread its fleecy folds over them; shading them from the heat by day, whilst at night its lambent flame shone over the camp. Even now, where rose the sheer cliff of Sinai, the Presence-Cloud was brooding filled with light and glory.

The People's Folly. But notwithstanding this, and their protestations that they would serve God only and keep His law, they demanded the outward semblance of Deity, violating not the first commandment—for they never intended to renounce Jehovah— but the second; and demanding to worship the Almighty under the form of some creation of their hand. Not only had they made this image, probably after the fashion of Assyria, where their forefathers had dwelt, but had worshipped and circled around it in dances too terrible to describe. Moses felt keenly the sin and shame of their action, of which he first heard from the lips of the Almighty Himself, and realised that nothing could prevent, so far as human thought went, the infliction of a dire penalty upon the people whom he loved. He expected that penalty to fall inevitably, *first*, because of the righteousness of the Divine Nature, *secondly*, because of the inviolability of God's Word, and *thirdly*, because of the transcendence and sublime significance of the ten commandments, which had just been committed to his charge.

The Fear of Moses. Moses feared that the penalty might befall in either or all of these ways. Their sin might lead to their absolute destruction, so that their very existence would be obliterated: or it would certainly exclude them from that protection, which seemed absolutely necessary as they descended into the valleys of the wilderness: or even, if they were divinely protected, they must forfeit the unique privilege and honour of the Divine Presence: or the covenant, which had been broken by their sin, would never be renewed.

It was as though Israel had bound themselves by four strong knotted cords; from which they could not free themselves; and it remained for him, therefore, to untie them by his personal efforts.

—**His Position.** Our Lord said on one occasion, that what His people loosed on earth should be loosed in heaven; and here is an instance in which a man of God succeeded in unpicking the hard and difficult circumstances around which a nation lay gasping, like the monarch of the forest in the hunter's net. He appears, in the first instance, to have feared that he would have difficulty in bringing God to look at the matter as he did. On the one hand, if eternal justice did not punish this sin, surely the giving of the Law would have been absolutely useless. If the penalties were not insisted on, perhaps the promises would not be kept. Besides, God might appear to wink at sin. On the other hand, if the heavy hand of judgment fell, and the dust of the people mingled with the sands of the desert, the Egyptians would laugh derisively and say that Jehovah had now discovered, what they had learnt long before, that the people were absolutely worthless, good for nothing but to be treated as slaves. This faithful soul, therefore, stood between two cross-currents that met at his feet. But how greatly he misconceived of God!

The Entreaty of Moses. As we read the narrative, it would almost appear as though Moses were pressing God to retreat step by step, and yield to his importunity; but, in point of fact, God was only drawing him on to comprehend the love and grace of His character. It is as though the mother, when teaching her nursling to walk, were to retire backward, as though pushed by his tiny hands, whereas, in point of fact, she is teaching him, unconsciously to himself, to walk. Our Father is so intent on leading us to advance, that He appears to yield to our importunity. "The Kingdom of Heaven suffereth violence, and the violent take it by force." There are two instances of this in Scripture. The one, where the God of Abraham appeared to retreat before His servant's fervour for Sodom; the other, where Jesus appeared to yield to the woman of Syrophenicia. In each case the suppliant was led to assume a position of appropriating faith that had never before been reached, like the furthest wave of an advancing tide, flung far forward up the shore, This is the secret of delayed prayer. Prayer is educative. A man who prays grows; and the muscles of the soul swell from thin whipcord to iron bands.

Four Agonies of Moses. It is to be noticed that before each of the four following agonies (in the strict sense of that term), Moses passed through a deep spiritual experience, which served as a prelude to what followed. He refused the suggestion to be made the father of a great nation (verse 10); he came to the conclusion that he would offer himself as a sacrifice (verse 30); he told His Almighty Friend that he positively dared not adventure the journey alone (xxxiii. 15); and finally he beheld His glory, or at least the rear-guard of that glory, as the procession swept down the mountain gorge (xxxiv. 6). Whenever you are summoned to pass through some profound experience, you may be absolutely assured that you will become endued with additional spiritual power, so that this transcendent experience acts in two ways. Before we can take a new advance in the school of prayer and intercession for others, there has to be a fresh and deeper work experienced in ourselves; and, vice versa, such work, wherever experienced, will be followed by a new power in our dealings with God. Moses' *first* effort was to secure that the people should not be destroyed. His *second* effort was to secure that their sin, which seemed unpardonable, should be forgiven. His *third* effort was to secure that not the angel, but God Himself, should continue to go with them. His *fourth* effort was that God would restore the Covenant which bound Him to His recreant and rebellious nation. In each of these efforts he was abundantly successful.

(1) *Would their sin compel God to destroy and blot them out?* Whilst Moses was considering that possibility, the thought was suggested to his mind, whether it would not, after all, be better, that the people, who were a stiff-necked people, rebellious and blind, should be destroyed, and that out of his own family and beneath his own tutelage, a new young, fresh, God-fearing nation might originate. "The Lord said unto Moses, I have seen these people, and, behold, it is a stiff-necked people: now therefore let Me alone, that My wrath may wax hot against them, and that I may consume them: and I will make of thee a great nation" (verses 9, 10, R.V.). This suggestion must be classed with a similar statement in the Book of Genesis: "It came to pass after these things, that God did prove Abraham, and said unto him, Abraham; and he said, Here am I.

And He said unto him, Take now thy son . . . whom thou lovest, even Isaac, and get thee into the land of Moriah; and offer him there for a burnt-offering" (Gen. xxii. 1, 2, R.V.). It was never intended by the Almighty that Isaac should be offered, but Abraham had the opportunity of proving that he loved his God as much as any of the surrounding peoples did theirs, and was ready to make all sacrifices on His behalf. There was no intention to destroy Israel, but the suggestion was allowed to come, to reveal him to himself. So, after fasting for forty days, our Lord was tempted to use His divine power to make stones into bread, to stay the cravings of His hunger.

The Offer to Moses Put Aside. But Moses would have none of it. He had left the home of Pharaoh's daughter to identify himself with this people; and now, though they had turned from him, he would not abandon them, but wove the bond of affinity between them and him tighter than ever. He desired no independent existence, he wanted no glory for himself; their lot should be his lot, their destiny his destiny, and he would stand or fall with the people of his birth. That was a supreme and necessary decision. Before ever we can pray for people and deliver them, we must identify ourselves with them. We must feel our oneness with them, afflicted with their afflictions, and touched with their infirmities. We must share their sorrows, and even bear their sin. When Moses had put aside all thought of his own ambition, and had definitely associated himself with the fortunes of his people, he was able to look God in the face and say: "Father, Thou canst not destroy them; and there are three reasons why Thou canst not. First, Thou hast done so much for them with Thy mighty power and outstretched arm that Thou canst not contradict all Thy previous attitude. Second, if Thou shalt destroy them, the Egyptians will deride Thee, and Thou canst not do it for Thy own honour's sake. Third, if Thou should destroy them, where is Thy covenant with their fathers, to whom Thou hast pledged Thyself to bring their children into the land of promise?

The Pleading of Humble Souls. Such is the manner in which, in all humility, great souls plead with God; they take their stand upon His promises, and, so to speak, argue the case with Him. It is a wonderful thing when a man dares to say, "Father, Thou canst not help blessing us; we hold Thee to thy Word. Thou canst not fail us, because Thou canst not deny Thyself." When a man can speak to God like that, it seems as though he cannot be gainsayed. It is as though God answers him saying: "Ask me of things to come, and concerning My sons, and concerning the work of My hands, command ye Me." We are also reminded of those words of our Lord: "He shall have whatsoever he saith." The Lord repented of the evil which He said He would do unto His people. In the seventh verse, God says to Moses, *Thy* people: in the eleventh verse Moses says to God, *Thy* people: and there they are left. They are His people and the sheep of His pasture. God acted as though He repented; but, really, Moses had obtained a new and deeper vision of His nature.

(2) *Could their sin be forgiven?* We have seen the wrath with which Moses entered the camp. The broken tables of the law; the dust of the idol mingled with the water that descended from the Mount; and the corpses that strewed the passages of the encampment, all proved the heat of his hot indignation. But if he felt like that, what might not God be feeling in His high heaven! Had they not committed the unpardonable sin, for which there is no forgiveness in this world, or the next? Would the blood of bulls and goats ever suffice to take away their sin?

The Plea and Offer of Moses. The next morning there came the awful reaction. The thunder-storm had broken in a shower of rain. Moses said: "My people, you have sinned a great sin; peradventure I will make an atonement for it." During the forty days which had preceded he had been talking with God a good deal about atonement, for all these chapters are filled with the Divine prescriptions regarding atonement; and whilst he lay sleepless all night in his tent, the first and only consideration with him was, whether he could not prevail with God to accept him as a sacrifice on behalf of the guilty nation. It was a noble resolve. We recall those great words of one who seemed to be the Lawgiver of the Church, as Moses was Lawgiver to the nation: "I say the truth in Christ, I lie not, my conscience bearing witness with me in the Holy Ghost, that I have great sorrow and unceasing pain in my heart. For I could wish that I myself were anathema from Christ for my brethren's sake" (Rom. ix. 1-3, R.V.). Yes, and a greater than either said, "This is My blood, shed for many, for the remission of sins." So he climbed the well-worn mountain path, and stood again before the Lord, and said: "My people have sinned a great sin. Yet, if Thou wilt forgive their sin——" and then came a pause. It was an unfinished sentence, broken by the extremity of the emotion that boiled within. Can we finish the sentence? "If Thou wilt forgive, then Thou wilt reveal

Thy noblest attribute; if Thou wilt forgive, my tongue shall sing Thy praise as long as I live; if Thou wilt forgive, Thou wilt bind the people to Thine heart for ever. But, if not without blood, and if that of beasts does not avail, may I not be their atonement,—blot me, I pray Thee, out of Thy book which Thou hast written, out of the Book of Life, out of the book of eternal blessedness; blot it out. Take *me*, if only Thou wilt spare them."

A Greater Propitiation Prepared. The Almighty did not fully answer that challenge, because He saw across the plains of time the upreared cross on which, in the person of His Lord, He would make reconciliation for the sins of the people. Him would God set forth to be a propitiation, to show His righteousness, in the passing over of sins done aforetime. Every man, was the reply, must stand for his own sin. Moses could not make an atonement, because he was himself a sinner, and no sinful mortal can make an atonement for his brother. "Whosoever hath sinned against Me, him will I blot out of My book." But, in virtue of the true mercy-seat, and the love that was to give Christ to the cross, forgiveness was granted, and Moses was bidden to lead the people to the land of promise, with the promise that God's Angel should go before them. Thus Moses knew that his second prayer was answered.

(3) *There was the further question of the escort.* He knew that the people were forgiven, but it hurt him to hear that an Angel was to be deputed to accompany them. The burden of two-and-a-half million of people was too heavy for him to carry, even with Angel-help. What though the desert gorges were glowing with the flame-cloud, and an angel-escort accompanied the march, he could never rest until he had secured the Divine presence. He must secure somehow the withdrawal of that sentence, "I will not go up in the midst of thee, for thou art a stiff-necked people." He spoke of it to the people, who awoke to realise what they were forfeiting, and to show their penitence, divested themselves of their adornments. It is supposed, indeed, that from this time and onward they discontinued the use of adornments, as evidence of their contrition for their apostasy. Moses, however, felt that nothing but prayer would obtain the reversal of the sentence. He could not be always ascending Sinai. The camp needed his superintending care, and as there was as yet no dedicated shrine, he probably took his own tent, and erected it outside the camp, as a temporary meeting-place between God and all faithful souls. Thither he went himself, and

we are told that when Moses went out unto the tent, every man stood at his tent-door, and looked after his retreating person. They said, "He is going in to pray for us;" and when the curtain fell behind him, the pillar of cloud descended and stood at the door of the tent, and God talked with Moses face to face, as a man talks to his friend. So soon as he found himself alone with God, he said, "Let Thy Presence go with me, I beseech Thee. If Thou dost not go with me, I cannot go. Angels are not enough; they are fair and sweet and strong, but I want Thee. I cannot go unless Thou shalt go. Wilt Thou leave me, a lone man, to thread this desert with this people? Thou hast put the burden upon me, and am I to stand by myself and bear it all? I cannot go without Thy pledged Presence." Ah, it is good when a man gets to close grips with God. "And the Lord said unto Moses, I will do this thing also that thou hast spoken: for thou hast found grace in My sight, and I know thee by name. . . . My Presence shall go with thee, and I will give thee rest" (xxx. 17).

(4) *There was the Question of the Broken Covenant.* Ah! Those broken pieces of the tables of stone, splintered yonder at the mountain foot, which he had cast down in his hot anger! They were emblems of the broken covenant, could he get it reknit? He said, "Show me, I pray Thee, Thy glory. Grant to me to see Thy face." And God said, "Prepare two tables of stone." What did that mean? With what a beating heart did Moses hew those tables from the rock with his own hands! Never before had he engaged in such sacred toil as the fellow-worker of God. Bearing them carefully in his hands, he ascended once again the mountain, and the Lord descended, and stood with him there, and proclaimed his name. "Abide here in this place!" So it seemed to him that God arranged it. Then the shadow of God's hand fell on him. He saw nothing, but heard the measured beat of the wings of the seraphim, as they passed in harnessed bands down the mountain gorge. He heard also the harpers harping upon their harps. He heard also the voice of the Eternal proclaiming the attributes of His character, the first of which quieted for ever his forebodings. Then, as the cortège was passing away, he could have gazed and gazed, but, forgetting his eager desire to see God's glory, he made haste and bowed his head, and worshipped, and gave himself to intercession. Let my Lord go in the midst of us, and pardon our iniquity and sin, and take us for Thine own inheritance. And this was the divine reply "Behold, I will make a covenant, before all thy people I will do

marvels, such as have not been wrought in all the earth, nor in any nation" (xxxiv. 10). To this was added the return of the Tables of Stone, not now blank, but.covered, as the others had been, with the divine script. Then Moses knew that the sin of his people was put away for ever, and that they were taken back into their olden place.

"ALONE, YET NOT ALONE"

Exodus 33:12-17

12. And Moses said unto the Lord, See, thou sayest unto me, Bring up this people: and thou hast not let me know whom thou wilt send with me. Yet thou hast said, I know thee by name, and thou hast also found grace in my sight.

13. Now therefore, I pray thee, if I have found grace in thy sight, show me now thy way, that I may know thee, that I may find grace in thy sight: and consider that this nation *is* thy people.

14. And he said, My presence shall go *with thee*, and I will give thee rest.

15. And he said unto him, If thy presence go not *with me*, carry us not up hence.

16. For wherein shall it be known here that I and thy people have found grace in thy sight? *is it* not in that thou goest with us? so shall we be separated, I and thy people, from all the people that *are* upon the face of the earth.

17. And the Lord said unto Moses, I will do this thing also that thou hast spoken: for thou hast found grace in my sight, and I know thee by name.

"ALONE, YET NOT ALONE"

Exodus 33:12-17

The Leader and His Helper. After Israel had sinned in making the golden calf, there was evidently an alteration in the Divine purpose and promise; for God said, "Now lead *thou* the people to the land that I have promised; nevertheless, I will send an angel with thee"—meaning that Moses was to assume the responsibility of leadership, and that there would be a convoy of angels, but that the Divine presence of the Jehovah-Angel would be withdrawn.

As we can well understand, this withdrawal filled the heart of Moses with extreme dismay, and in this, the third of his intercessions —for we remember that there were four—in which he thought that he was pressing God back, though in fact God was drawing him on, he entreats that God would graciously return to His earlier promise, and that He would accompany His people's pilgrimage in person. In answer to this prayer, he obtained the promise—"My Presence shall go with thee, and I will give thee rest."

The Solitariness of Moses. *The urgency of his request. There was the sense of absolute aloneness.* The loneliness of the crowd is more terrible than of perfect solitude, and though Moses was within reach of Aaron, Miriam, Zipporah, Caleb, Joshua, and the seventy elders, who were prepared to share the burden of government, yet he was absolutely lonely, because his spiritual life and ideals were so much loftier than theirs. Who was there that could understand him when he spoke of secrets into which angels cannot pry? Had he not entered within the veil, and talked with the King of kings? It has been suggested that he was the loneliest of men—more lonely than Elijah, when he thought himself the survivor of the prophets; than Paul, when all men forsook him in his old age, standing at Nero's bar; than Luther in conflict with the Papacy; than Columbus breaking into unknown seas. Only our Lord has trodden a lonelier path, because He was led out as a scapegoat into the wilderness.

The Untrodden Way Ahead. *Before him lay an unknown path.* Thus far the ground they had trodden was perfectly familiar to him. He had often visited those mountain solitudes with his flock. It was there that the burning bush had flamed before his gaze. All the wild ravines, and all the green pastures were as familiar to him as the survivors of our homes. But from the moment they left Sinai for Kadesh-barnea their path would lie through unknown deserts, and be beset by daring and experienced foes. It was a prospect before which the stoutest might quake. If God were with him, not merely in His chariot of cloud, but as Companion and Friend, he would have no fear; but otherwise "carry us not up hence."

The Responsibility of Leadership. They were always turning back to Egypt. Can you not understand them in this, finding the clue to their behaviour in your own soul? You may have been brought out of the slavish tasks and heavy tyranny of the taskmaster, into a free and bracing air. You have caught the gleam of a fairer day, and heard the challenge of a nobler age. You have gained power from Christ to master the world, the flesh, and the devil. It has seemed in your brief hours of triumph, that Egypt will never again fascinate or allure; and then, without the least provocation or warning, so far as you know, you feel the old longings arise and the old appetites pulling you back. You cannot forsake your companions, you cannot face Gethsemane, you cannot endure the Cross and despise the shame. It was a people who experienced these backward-drawings of the tide more keenly than any other, and who were always erring in their heart, that the great lawgiver had to carry, as a nursing father carries a sick child, to the Land of Promise.

The Yearning for Rest. We all know this. Few are the hands that do not tug at oars too long in their sweep! Few are the eyes that do not watch eagerly for the westering sun! Few are the hearts that do not repeat to themselves the old refrain, of the place where the wicked cease from troubling and the weary are at rest. Every-one cherishes the hope of a rest-time before he goes hence, where love shall wait on him, and soft breezes shall fan him, and the sounds of Nature shall be his lullaby. Offer a man the choice between vast wealth, supreme glory and accomplished ambitions, on the one hand, and on the other rest, in which his nature shall be anchored in perfect safety, shelter, and equilibrium; the choice will be for *rest,* or for those other conditions, if they will only guarantee a calm alcove or haven, where the wild winds shall cease to blow, and the waves shall only break in ripples on the sand. Such was the cry of this strong and noble nature.

And So the Need of God. For all these reasons the servant felt that he must have the Master with him. So great was their pressure, that he felt more than ever impelled to plead with God, and to say, "My God, we have come to this, Thou and I: if Thou dost require this work of me, Thou must Thyself accompany me. Be my Presence-Chamber, allow me to live in Thy secret place; I must have that comradeship, that companionship, that intimacy which one who is called to do work like mine requires, or he will die. If Thy presence go not with me, not the presence of an angel, however fair and glorious his face; not the presence of even a squadron of angels, however carefully they might keep watch and ward around the host by day and night; not even the cloud by day or the pillar of fire by night will suffice—I must have *Thee*."

O pilgrim of the night! O child, stepping out into the waste of untrodden ways that lie before thee, canst thou not appreciate this, and hast thou not often cried aloud after the same fashion?

The Response of God. *The graciousness of the Response.* "My Presence shall go with thee." "Lo, I am with you all the days, even unto the end." We are full of presentiments. There is the presentiment of some sudden catastrophe, that may overtake our homes or ourselves. We say to ourselves, as we look into dear faces, "We must take care, whilst we have time, to keep their eyes from tears, and dimple their cheeks with laughter." There is the presentiment of change, when we may be wrested from what we love and cling to, and have to go out into an unknown land. There is the dread of growing old, with its loss of the quick interests of youth and middle age. But we must not linger in this chamber of our soul, "living with pain and dreams." Let us go forth to stand in His Presence, where there is fulness of joy. God kept His word with Moses. His pavilion was the cloud; but nearer than cloud or light was the enwrapping sense of His nearness. Never an anxiety which was not poured into His ear and lovingly shared: never an emergency, which He did not meet: never an appeal, that before it was uttered was not anticipated. If you have had a kind and wealthy friend, whose one thought is to make life easier and happier for you, and will multiply that Friend a million times, you will then have some poor scintillation, of how the soul fares who travels in the Divine Convoy.

God, "Exceeding Abundantly." When our Lord spoke of yielding to the importunity of our friends, He said, that if a man asked for a coat, we were to give him our cloak also; and that if we were compelled to go one mile, we were to travel two. Would the Master lay down that law, and not fulfil its obligations? If, then, we ask Him to go with us on our journey to Heaven, carrying our burdens and providing for our needs, will He do this, and only this? He will assuredly see us home, but He will do exceeding abundantly. Listen: He added to His answer to Moses' request, a clause which met his unuttered desire,—"I will give you rest." Moses only asked God to go with him, but He said, "I will do exceeding abundantly, I will secure you from all wearing anxiety, I will take the lines from your forehead, I will give you rest."

There are some presences which you would like to have beside you when you come to die. The step is so soft, the touch so gentle, the heart so warm. But, O Lord Jesus, if Thou shalt be with us when we leave the valley for the stream, there shall breathe through our chamber and heart the Rest of a summer sunset, when the distant bells ring in the mellow air, and the glory lies on the hills.

The Cleft of the Rock

Exodus 33:18-34:27

18. And he said, I beseech thee, shew me thy glory.

19. And he said, I will make all my goodness pass before thee, and I will proclaim the name of the Lord before thee; and will be gracious to whom I will be gracious, and will show mercy on whom I will shew mercy.

20. And he said, Thou canst not see my face: for there shall no man see me, and live.

21. And the Lord said, Behold *there is* a place by me, and thou shalt stand upon a rock:

22. And it shall come to pass, while my glory passeth by, that I will put thee in a clift of the rock, and will cover thee with my hand while I pass by:

23. And I will take away mine hand, and thou shalt see my back parts: but my face shall not be seen.

1. And the Lord said unto Moses, Hew thee two tables of stone like unto the first: and I will write upon *these* tables the words that were in the first tables, which thou brakest.

2. And be ready in the morning, and come up in the morning unto mount Sinai, and present thyself there to me in the top of the mount.

3. And no man shall come up with thee, neither let any man be seen throughout all the mount; neither let the flocks nor herds feed before that mount.

4. And he hewed two tables of stone like unto the first; and Moses rose up early in the morning, and went up into mount Sinai, as the Lord had commanded him, and took in his hand the two tables of stone.

5. And the Lord descended in the cloud, and stood with him there, and proclaimed the name of the Lord.

6. And the Lord passed by before him, and proclaimed, The Lord, The Lord God, merciful and gracious, longsuffering, and abundant in goodness and truth,

7. Keeping mercy for thousands, forgiving iniquity and transgression and sin, and that will by no means clear *the guilty*; visiting the iniquity of the fathers upon the children, and upon the children's children, unto the third and to the fourth *generation*.

8. And Moses made haste, and bowed his head toward the earth, and worshipped.

9. And he said, If now I have found grace in thy sight, O Lord, let my Lord, I pray thee, go among us; for it *is* a stiff-necked people; and pardon our iniquity and our sin, and take us for thine inheritance.

10. And he said, Behold, I make a covenant: before all thy people I will do marvels, such as have not been done in all the earth, nor in any nation: and all the people among which thou *art* shall see the work of the Lord: for it *is* a terrible thing that I will do with thee.

11. Observe thou that which I command thee this day: behold, I drive out before thee the Amorite, and the Canaanite, and the Hittite, and the Perizzite, and the Hivite, and the Jebusite.

12. Take heed to thyself, lest thou make a covenant with the inhabitants of the land whither thou goest, lest it be for a snare in the midst of thee:

13. But ye shall destroy their altars, break their images, and cut down their groves:

14. For thou shalt worship no other god: for the Lord, whose name *is* Jealous, *is* a jealous God:

15. Lest thou make a covenant with the inhabitants of the land, and they go to a whoring after their gods, and do sacrifice unto their gods, and *one* call thee, and thou eat of his sacrifice;

16. And thou take of their daughters unto thy sons, and their daughters go a whoring after their gods, and make thy sons go a whoring after their gods.

17. Thou shalt make thee no molten gods.

18. The feast of unleavened bread shalt thou keep. Seven days thou shalt eat unleavened bread, as I commanded thee, in the time of the month Abib: for in the month Abib thou camest out from Egypt.

19. All that openeth the matrix *is* mine; and every firstling among thy cattle, *whether* ox or sheep, *that is male.*

20. But the firstling of an ass thou shalt redeem with a lamb: and if thou redeem *him* not, then shalt thou break his neck. All the first born of thy sons thou shalt redeem. And none shall appear before me empty.

21. Six days thou shalt work, but on the seventh day thou shalt rest: in earing time and in harvest thou shalt rest.

22. And thou shalt observe the feast of weeks, of the first fruits of wheat harvest, and the feast of ingathering at the year's end.

23. Thrice in the year shall all your men children appear before the Lord God, the God of Israel.

24. For I will cast out the nations before thee, and enlarge thy borders: neither shall any man desire thy land, when thou shalt go up to appear before the Lord thy God thrice in the year.

25. Thou shalt not offer the blood of my sacrifice with leaven; neither shall the sacrifice of the feast of the passover be left unto the morning.

26. The first of the first fruits of thy land thou shalt bring unto the house of the Lord thy God. Thou shalt not seethe a kid in his mother's milk.

27. And the Lord said unto Moses, Write thou these words: for after the tenor of these words I have made a covenant with thee and with Israel.

THE CLEFT OF THE ROCK

Exodus 33:18-34:27

The Desire for Deeper Intimacy with God. Moses was the spokes-man of humanity when he said, in the rapture of fellowship with God, "Show me, I pray Thee, Thy glory." For twice forty days he had been within the cloud, the earthliness of his nature had been refined, and his whole being was imbued with the light and love of God. But much will have more! The holiest of God's saints are those who press nearer and ever nearer into His secret fellowship, in order that they may be satisfied with the vision of His face. We hardly know all that Moses meant when he uttered this prayer, but he must have been under the influence of a similar impulse to that which led Philip to cry—"Shew us the Father, and it sufficeth us." What a contrast is wrought in the heart of man through fellowship with God! When first the vision of infinite purity breaks upon us, we cry with Peter, "Depart, for I am a sinful man, O Lord"; but when once we have been brought into union and fellowship with the Eternal, our thirst for God becomes insatiable, and with the patriarch at the close of his night wrestle, we cry, "Tell me Thy name."

God's Answer. There was infinite tenderness in the Lord's pro-posal that Moses should stand in the cleft of the rock, lest the burning splendour should overpower him. Does not God draw nigh the soul still, and speak in similar words? When bereavement befalls us, and the light of our eyes is removed, and a shadow falls over all the world, may we not hear Him saying, "Behold, there is a place by Me. I have put thee in this cleft of the rock, and am cover-ing thee with My hand." When our heart is disappointed in human affection, and it appears as though all faith in our fellows is shattered; when we find that the deposit that we placed in the bank of human love is forfeited, and when our soul prefers death to life, again we hear that strong and tender voice saying, "Behold, there is a place by Me. I have put thee in this cloven rock, and will cover thee with My hand." When we are threatened with the loss of our early faith, and no longer believe with the unquestioning simplicity of our childhood; when imperious questions arise and demand answer, again the Father draws nigh His child, and says, "My child, thou canst not understand, but come nearer to Me; there is a place by Me, the full splendour of My Glory cannot be beheld by mortal vision, but I will put thee in the cleft of the rock, and will cover thee with My hand." The hand covers only for so long as we are unable to bear the revelation, but it is removed so soon as the tempered glory will not be too strong for us.

The Cleft in the Rock. The mention of the *cleft* in the rock reminds us of the tempest, earthquake, and glacier action which have torn the mountains and cleft great gashes in their sides, and we turn from these to Christ, the Rock of Ages who was cleft for us. We understand that if we hide in His riven side, where the spear rent Him, we are sheltered for ever, at infinite cost to Him. We look out upon God from the place which is called Calvary; we stand upon the Rock of the finished work of the Redeemer; we are hidden beneath the pierced hand, and from that vantage-point are able to see things that prophets and kings desired to see in vain.

The Mercy of God Discovered. When God made known His name to Moses, it became clear how close the affinity had become between the mortal and Eternal. There must have been a previous understanding of the tender love of God on the part of Moses, though it surpasses our knowledge as to whence he derived it. He had beheld the terrors of the Exodus, the ten plagues, the overthrow of Pharaoh in the Red Sea, and the penalty paid by Israel for the fashioning of the golden calf; and yet he was prepared to understand, as few even since Pentecost have understood, the Divine grace and compassion. We do not wonder that David, amid the pastoral scenes of Bethlehem, with its flowing brooks and green verdure, and the soft breath of summer air around him, should have sung of the shepherd-care of God, and of the goodness and mercy which followed him all the days. The surroundings in which he spent those happy years of his boyhood predisposed him to gentle thoughts of the Almighty; but for Moses there were only the splintered peaks, the burning sand, and cloudless expanse of sky. There was nothing in the brooding cloud, or flashing lightning, or trembling earth to stimulate the sense of loving kindness and tender mercy. Yet Moses seems to have come to the very same discovery of God as John did, after being trained in the inner secret of Christ's love, and they reached hands across the centuries—Moses the shepherd of Israel and John the disciple whom Jesus loved—saying, "God is Love."

The Scene of the Discovery. It must have been a very memorable one. Perhaps Israel gathered to see the great Lawgiver, as he rose up early in the morning and again ascended the mountain, as the Lord had commanded him. On this occasion not even Joshua was permitted to accompany him. No man might come up with him, neither might any man be seen on any part of the mount; even the flocks and herds were driven down into the valley. Before the sun had risen far above the horizon, and when the shadows fell far across the valley from the mighty shapes of the mountains, that figure was seen ascending slowly, reverently; and as we think of Moses and the mountain, it seems as though the mountain itself were dwarfed to insignificance, and had become but as a pedestal upon which the feet of this mighty man of God rested. Of the two Moses was greater than the mountain, and through all after-time even Sinai is chiefly memorable because of its association with his glorious character. Years before, as a lonely man, he had stood before the burning bush, where the Shechinah of God gleamed out and shone with a supernatural brilliance, but now there was to be an even greater theophany.

God's Children in the Mountains with Him. God is always calling us into His mountains. Ruskin says that the mountains serve three great offices, in order to preserve the health and increase the happiness of mankind. Their first use is to give motion to water. Every fountain and river, from the streamlet that crosses the village lane to the silent march of the multitudes of waters in the rivers, owe their existence to the mountain ranges. Next to this there is the important function of the mountains in constantly changing the currents of the air, moistening it with the spray of waterfalls, aerating it as the mountain peaks catch and reflect it, and ultimately sending it forth, cool, fraught with ozone, refreshed and quickened, to replace the exhausted air of mighty cities. The third great use of these immense natural altars is to cause perpetual change in the soil of the earth—the highest summits being crumbled into fragments and pulverised, broken by frosts and ground by torrents, so that materials are produced which are distributed by the streams further and further from the mountain's base. The turbid, foaming water bears some appointed burden of soil to enrich the valleys. Thus the desolate and threatening ranges of mountain, which have often filled men's hearts with terror, are found to be replete with beneficence for the wealth of human life. We all need to tread these great mountains. It is only as we climb them that we can see the glory of God in Nature.

The Messages of the Mountains. If you have never climbed the mountains and stood amid the snows, and watched the sunset or sunrise, or been awed by the awful silence, or felt yourself an infinitesimal atom amid the old wrinkled hills, you can hardly realise how deeply they speak to the heart of man, and dwarf to insignificance the objects which he pursues with so much fever, and even the sorrows that threaten his heart. And yet for all of us there are mountains of vision, of fellowship with God, whose pinnacles lift us into union, whose snows rebuke our uncleanness, whose everlasting strength gives us stability. There is Horeb, with its still small voice; and Carmel, crowned with its altar; and Pisgah, with its far-reaching view; and Hermon, with the memory of the Transfigured Christ. Ascend these in thought and prayer! See the mighty rivers rising from their slopes, breathe the fresh air baptized and quickened, adore the Hand which is constantly shedding the grit of the mountains to recruit the exhausted energies of the soil, and transform those lessons into the bread of your spirit. But if these conceptions of the magnificence and might of the Creator are too great for the soul's naked vision, then ask that you may be placed in the cleft of the rock, so that only the tempered after-glow of the Divine Nature may be seen.

The Revelation of the Name of God. "Merciful." The Hebrew word means "tenderly pitiful." With man there are crimes that need to be punished, there is justice that must be administered, there is conviction that must be wrought deep, and harrowed in by the Spirit of God. But men and women need not only judgment and justice, penalty and conviction, but tender pity, for so much of wrong is due to ignorance, to inherited passion, to mistake, to blindness and darkness, to waywardness, fickleness, and changeableness. Humanity, like a half-grown idiot, stumbles on, blind and dull and stupid, crying out for help, weeping in the dark night, groping its way; and it needs something more than the strong hand of justice—not punishment only, but pity; not correction only, but sympathy—a High Priest who is touched with the feeling of our infirmities. It is a very sweet and beautiful thing that, amid all the sins of Moses' life, he spoke of God in the first place, and God spoke to him of His tender pitifulness. It is like the mist with which God waters the early grass. The torrent of rain would oppress vegetation, but Shakespeare speaks of "the gentle rain that droppeth from heaven upon that which is beneath." We place the globe of glass upon the delicate plant, that the mist which gathers upon it may sufficiently moisten it, so the distilling dew of God's gentleness upon the tender herbage is here manifested. In this very paragraph we have the command that no kid shall be seethed in its mother's milk, probably because the accumulation of milk when the kid had been taken away would be harmful to the mother, therefore there is the provision, three times revealed in the Pentateuch that the kid should remain with its mother until it was weaned and able to feed itself. Oh, the tenderness of God, that does not break the bruised reed, nor quench the tiny spark, the smouldering flax! That is the first thought given by God amid the granite of Sinai. Do not be afraid of Him. He is merciful—as a father pitieth his little dwarfed or crippled child, "so the Lord pitieth them that fear Him."

—**Gracious.** But we are told in addition that He is "*Gracious.*" That word has gone out of fashion. Our fathers petrified it; they made it the foundation-stone of a structure of granite, in which the souls of men could find no rest, and therefore we rather dread that word—Grace. And yet there is no greater word in language than the word that stands for the undeserved, free gift of the Love of God. "Nothing in my hand I bring"—that must be the plea of each one of us; we are saved by grace, not our tears, not our prayers, not our feelings. Nothing of good in us has attracted God to us; He loves us because He will love us, and when once He has set His love upon us because He would, He will not withdraw it; but, in spite of our sin, our wandering, our waywardness, He who loved us because He would, will continue to love us because He will. He causes His sun to shine upon the evil as well as upon the good; He sends His rain upon the unjust as well as the just—upon the man or woman who like a barren patch has yielded only thorns to the hand which has nurtured and loved, and yearns to save it, in spite of all.

—**Long-suffering.** God is not only merciful and gracious, He is "*Longsuffering.*" We read in 1 Corinthians xiii. that "Love suffereth long, and is kind; is not easily provoked." You have thought that your sin has cut off the mercy of God—but He is not easily provoked;

you have thought that your waywardness has shut up for evermore
His tender mercy—but He waits to be gracious. Just as the husbandman waits for long months until the result of his patient culture shall
appear, so does God wait, and will not weary. Moses thought that
his prayer had averted God's wrath, but God desired to undeceive
him, and to show that his pleading had been anticipated, and was
only the reflection of the longsuffering that had waited through the
ages to be manifested to the sons of men. You think you have worn
out God's patience, but it would take a greater sinner than you to do
that. Indeed, it is impossible to exhaust the patience of God. He
beareth all things, believeth all things, endureth all things, His
love never faileth. The Lord God, tenderly pitiful, gracious, and
longsuffering.

—**Plenteous in Goodness and Truth.** That word truth is not
veracity, but *troth*,—the word used by the man to the woman and
the woman to the man in the marriage ceremony—"I plight thee
my troth." "O soul, thou canst not reckon upon thyself, but reckon
upon God, for He is plenteous in troth; He will not run back;
He will not fail, who hast led thee to trust Him; He will not let His
faithfulness fail. Reckon upon God's faithfulness to thyself and to
His promises. Plenteous in goodness! We can never see its horizon.
When He makes stars, He strews them in plentitude upon the Milky
Way; He scatters spring flowers with both hands. When He makes
beauty, He does it so profusely that there is loveliness everywhere,
from the tiniest insect to the glowing seraphim. It reminds us of
what Isaiah said—"He will *abundantly* pardon"; and of Paul, who
says, "Where sin abounded *grace did much more abound*." The alps
of sin are overtopped by these other words—"Forgiveness according
to the *riches of His grace*." Oh, that unforgiven and doubting
souls might take these words to themselves—"Plenteous in Goodness and Truth."

"Forgiving Iniquity, Transgression, and Sin." The prefix "for"
is really the intensive—it means much giving. God does not wink
at sin, or turn His face from sin, or refuse to notice sin, or gloss
over sin; but every time we sin, and come back to Him in true
penitence, He comes Himself to undo the result and extract the
poison. Giving is forgiving; forgiving is absolute giving. It is as
if God gave Himself to us for every sin we commit with a new impress,
a new plenitude, with a new purpose of deliverance from the love
and power of it. There is nothing more terrible than the way in

which sin clings to a man and dogs his footsteps. Let a man once steal, and he is never trusted again, even though he has made reparation for it. Men look at their fallen brothers through their sin; but God looks at man through the idealised life, with a love that imputes to him every virtue for Christ's sake. A woman sometimes does that with her boy or girl. As long as she can, she will impute to them something wonderful that no one else can see in the child. So God always reckons to us what we are capable of being, and He gives Himself to us in order that we may become that. You shall not be simply forgiven and saved from the results of your sin, but you shall be treated from this very hour as if you had never committed it. You need not be a bird with a broken wing, a woman with a broken heart, whose voice can never again reach its old ringing note. Because God forgives you, He restores you; He puts you back where you were before you fell; He treats you as though you had never fallen; it will never be mentioned or thrown up at you at the judgment seat. No angel in the distant vista of eternity will come across an account book with that debt of yours recorded in it. God has destroyed the account book, there is no record kept, "He remembers it no more." The three words used—"Forgiving iniquity, transgression and sin"—cover every possibility of sin, so that whatever your sin may be denominated, it comes under that category.

—**Just.** But here there comes a dark line—"*He will by no means clear the guilty.*" That, of course, is spoken in mercy both to the individual and to society. He will not clear the individual, He cannot, because unless the guilty man repents, it would not be right to forgive him. You could not be happy if you were not holy; you could not have peace if the wound had not been probed and cleansed to the very heart. David forgave Absalom without his confessing or being penitent for his sin, and he became a rebel, and had to pay the penalty of death on the battlefield. God wants to do sure work, and He cannot clear the guilty unless there is repentance; He cannot clear you except on the basis of the atonement that He Himself has made on the cross.

—**Punishing Sin.** "*He visits the sins of the fathers upon the children,*" in their misshapen bodies and darkened minds. You say, "Is that right?" Ah, but remember that He keeps mercy for thousands—not thousands of individuals, though that is true, but thousands of generations. He mercifully curtails the result of sin to the fourth generation. It is said that, in London, the fifth generation ceases to propagate itself; that men and women cease to bear children. Surely that is good, for if a family is rotten to the core, and will not repent and turn to God, it is better to let that family die out. The result of sin stops at the fourth generation in mercy. But supposing the child of a drunkard is afflicted with epilepsy—and they often are—that affliction may be the means of saving the child from becoming a drunkard, and, as is the case in homes for these stricken waifs, it may be trained and brought up to know and love Christ. He will by no means clear—we must get right with God, we must become a penitent, we must forsake our sin and seek forgiveness—and it is ours instantly.

The Need of God Perceived. Directly Moses heard this, he fell on his face and worshipped, and said, "I beseech Thee, go with this people, for they are a stiff-necked people." You would have thought that the very fact that they were a stiff-necked people would have been a reason why God should not go with them; but Moses said—"If Thou art a God like that, Thou art the God that stiff-necked people want." We are reminded of those words, "Good and upright is the Lord, *therefore* will He teach sinners in the way." Are you stiff-necked? Here is the God you want—tender, forgiving, strong. Moses said, "Pardon our iniquity and our sin, and take *us*"—that is the climax, "Take us, a stiff-necked people, take us for Thine inheritance." He said in effect, "No one else can get aught from people such as we are; but a God like Thou art can. Take us for Thine inheritance." There is not a man or a woman that may not get comfort from this, for God will take a stiff-necked man, an obstinate, self-willed woman—He is equal to every emergency—and though up till now the soul has borne nothing but thorns and thistles, He will get golden harvest out of the barren plot of land. He takes the old tumble-down shanty and remodels it into a palace. He comes and lives in it to transfigure and sanctify. "The Lord's portion is His people, Jacob is the lot of His inheritance. He found him in a desert land, and in a waste howling wilderness; He compassed him about; He cared for him; He kept him as the apple of His eye" (Deut. xxxii. 9, 10, R.V.). "Blessed is the people whose God is the Lord, and the nation that He hath taken for His inheritance."

The Covenant Renewed. "Behold," said Jehovah, "I make a covenant: before all thy people I will do marvels, such as have not been wrought in all the earth." He promised to drive out the

Amorite, the Canaanite, the Hittite, the Perizzite, the Hivvite and the Jebusite; but there were conditions which the people must fulfil; and a brief summary is given of the chief points of positive observance which He required, in addition to their obedience to the moral law.

These points may be reduced to twelve: 1. That no treaty of peace should be made with the Canaanites (12). 2. That all their images, altars and groves should be destroyed (13). 3. That there should be no intermarriage between their sons and daughters and those of the heathen (15, 16). 4. That no molten image should be made to represent God (17). 5. That the passover feast should be observed (18). 6. That the firstborn should be dedicated or redeemed (19, 20). 7. That the Sabbath rest should be observed at all times of the year (21). 8. That the feasts of Pentecost and Tabernacles should be maintained regularly (22). 9. That at all the three great festivals all the males should appear before God (23). 10. That no leaven should be used with any sacrifice (25). 11. That the first fruits of all things should be offered to God (26). 12. That no kid should be seethed in its mother's milk (26).

From this we gather generally that whilst God binds Himself by His covenant on the one hand, He expects that we will conform to the highest ideals of Christian faith, and of obedience, in heart and life. It is the obedient, loving soul with whom God dwells in perfect union and for whom He fulfils the abundance of His promises.

"HE WIST NOT"

Exodus 34:29-35; 2 Corinthians 3:18 R.V.

29. And it came to pass, when Moses came down from mount Sinai with the two tables of testimony in Moses' hand, when he came down from the mount, that Moses wist not that the skin of his face shone while he talked with him.

30. And when Aaron and all the children of Israel saw Moses, behold, the skin of his face shone; and they were afraid to come nigh him.

31. And Moses called unto them; and Aaron and all the rulers of the congregation returned unto him: and Moses talked with them.

32. And afterwards all the children of Israel came nigh: and he gave them in commandment all that the Lord had spoken with him in mount Sinai.

33. And *till* Moses had done speaking with them, he put a veil on his face.

34. But when Moses went in before the Lord to speak with him, he took the veil off, until he came out. And he came out, and spake unto the children of Israel *that* which he was commanded.

35. And the children of Israel saw the face of Moses, that the skin of Moses' face shone: and Moses put the veil upon his face again, until he went in to speak with him.

18. But we all, with unveiled face reflecting as a mirror the glory of the Lord, are transformed into the same image from glory to glory, even as from the Lord the Spirit.

"HE WIST NOT"

Exodus 34:29-35; 2 Corinthians 3:18 R.V.

The Transfigured Face. For forty days, with no sustenance from bread or water, Moses followed hard after the vision of God, absorbed with an eternal passion, not counting the hours, which passed like a dream. He talked with God as a man talks face to face with his friend; all unaware of the marvellous change his fellowship was effecting. At God's dictation, he wrote the Covenant, as we have it in this Book, and finally God gave him the two tables of stone on which He had imprinted His autograph. With these in his hand, Moses, unconscious of what had befallen him, descended to the plain, where the tents of Israel were lying at the foot of the mount. "And when Aaron and all the rulers of Israel saw Moses, behold, the skin of his face shone; and they were afraid to come nigh him" (ver. 30).

The Apostle Paul, naturally enough, has laid hold of this thought, for there was a marvellous affinity between Paul and Moses. Their dispensations were different, but the fire that burned within was the same. Paul would have been the Moses of the Decalogue, as Moses would have been the Paul of the Gospel. And laying hold upon this, his ardent spirit delighted in it, and said: "We all have our Sinai, our mount of vision; we, too, stand under the shadow of the hand of God within the niche of the rock, where we behold with unveiled face the glory of the Lord in the face of Jesus Christ; and we also are changed into the same image; our faces also should shine, though we wist it not."

(1) *The Glory of the Human Face Divine.* In this case we use the word *Divine* in the unique sense in which it belongs to Christ. There are many beauties and glories upon the human face. There is the glory of intellectual expression; there is the glory shed forth from the soul of the musician or painter; there is the glory of human love, which every great artist has striven to set forth in the smile

of the Madonna towards the Babe at her breast. There is the glory, too, upon the face of true piety, for indeed in country districts where neither form nor physiognomy were specially cultured or refined, we have seen on very commonplace faces a light which never shone on sea or shore. The face sometimes seems like a rare vase, in which the light shines through the transparent porcelain. But none of these conceptions of the human face and its glory can indicate to us what that glory must have been that shone upon the face of Christ—the glory of God in the face of Jesus Christ, for the face of Christ was as a mirror in which we see God. In St. Peter's at Rome, one of the rarest paintings is placed so high above the heads of the people, that it is quite impossible to view it, but in the aisle a mirror is placed, in which you can see the picture reflected. So the glory of God shone upon the face that Mary kissed, beaming from His features, as well as from the moral and miraculous radiance of His life.

—**Reflecting Glory of God.** In considering the various ways in which Jesus Christ reflected the glory of God, we must be guided by the vision that Moses had of that glory. It appealed to his moral and spiritual perceptions. Though God is the Maker of all the glory of the universe, we have no picture or painting of His glory as it passed down the ravine. Even inspired lips are dumb when they attempt to describe the lustre of the sapphire throne. The whole stress of the narrative is laid upon the moral attributes of God—"The Lord God, merciful and gracious, longsuffering, and abundant in goodness and truth,"—the threefold attributes—mercy, truth and justice. So in the face of Christ there shone a revelation of the moral glory of God, and of the supreme dignity of the human soul, when living in union with God.

The Light of Christ on Human Problems. From the face of Jesus has been reflected light upon five great problems. (1) *He shed light upon the problem of the Being of God.* Before that, man had only faintly guessed at God as a Father—"Like as a father pitieth his children"—but Christ taught us that the essential nature of God is Fatherhood; and by the impartation of the spirit of sonship. He established an everlasting relationship between the Father and the human soul that was begotten in His likeness. (2) *Light fell from the face of Christ upon the great problem of sin.* He showed how sin may be discovered, confessed, forgiven, obliterated, and the soul justified and sanctified. He insisted that this was possible for the most vicious and degraded of mankind. Out of the mud He could

make priceless jewels; out of black coal He could extract diamonds.
(3) *Light fell upon the problem of human suffering and pain.* Christ
showed that when it was borne in submission to the will of God,
it became part of His own great atonement, remedial in its operation
upon mankind, not to be resented, but borne in patient faith and
meekness. (4) *Light also fell upon the problem of the passive virtues.*
Beneath His touch humility and meekness, simplicity and forbear-
ance, were proved to be transcendent in their strength and worth,
and became eagerly sought after by those who were on the outlook
for goodly pearls. (5) *Light fell upon the problem of the future.* Men
had guessed that there was a life beyond, but were not sure. Even
Moses himself was not certain, but Jesus Christ brought "life and
immortality to light." Just as before the sun rises the landscape
contains mountains and hills, rivers and fields, but all are concealed,
and the sunrise does not create them, but reveals them; so all truth
lay as a panorama before the minds of men, and could not be discerned by the purest and wisest until Christ came as the Sun of
Righteousness to reveal it. The glory of God in the face of Jesus
Christ lit up the firmament. "Let there be light, and there was light."
That is what Paul found in Christ, and that is what we may find in
Him. God grant that the veil of our passion, of our obtuseness, of
our selfishness may be rent, so that we may see the glory of God in
the face of our Saviour!

(2) *The Transference of Glory, from the Face of Christ to our
Faces.* "We all, with unveiled face beholding [or reflecting] as a
mirror the glory of the Lord, are transformed into the same image,
even as from the Lord the Spirit" (2 Cor. iii, 18, R.V.). Let us look
into the deep and exquisite meaning of this verse, which is the pivot,
and gives the point of view for the whole paragraph. You need not
wait to understand the Greek language before passing an opinion
as to whether to adopt the one version or the other. If you quietly
read the entire paragraph, you will be convinced, however scant
your knowledge of the Greek, that the rendering of the Revised
Version is the true one, and for this reason—the Apostle had been
showing that the old covenant had a glory all its own; and this, by a
quick transition of thought, had led him to remember the veiled
face of Moses, behind the veil of which a glory shone of such
brilliance that the children of Israel could not behold it. His aim,
therefore, was to bring out the contrast between the veiled glory of
Moses and the unveiled glory of the Christian Church, and it would

be an altogether unusual and unnatural deviation from his line of thought to say that we, as part of the Church, were beholding "as in a mirror." Moses did not behold in a mirror, Moses saw God *face to face*; and if we beheld God's glory in a mirror, we should be occupying an inferior position to Moses, whereas, the whole gist of the Apostle's argument is that the Christian Church occupies a better.

Christians Reflect the Glory of Christ. Obviously, therefore, in the first place, following the line of argument that the Christian Church is in a superior position to that occupied by Moses, we must surely have as direct a vision as he had, and better. Moses beheld directly; surely, therefore, we do not see in a mirror, but we, too, see face to face.

Then to turn to another point, Moses, so far as he was allowed, reflected the glory of God, and it shone from his face. It would be illogical to turn from the idea of Moses shedding the glory from his face, and to speak of the Church as beholding, bending towards the mirror in which the glory of God shines. To carry out the true conception, surely the Church must equally shed forth the glory of God, as Moses did; the additional point being emphasised, that in the case of Moses the glory was veiled, while in the case of the believer that glory is unveiled; and, with unveiled face, without reserve, we all transmit and shed forth the glory of God. On either of those two lines of argument, we are obliged to adopt the reading of the Revised Version, and to believe that the Apostle urges that Christian people are to make a point of reflecting Jesus; they are to be the mirrors for the purpose of shedding amongst men His glory; and in the effort to do this they become transfigured into His own glorious beauty, from glory to glory.

But whilst that is the obvious line of the Apostle's teaching, it does not altogether do away with the thought suggested by the Authorised Version; because, if we are to reflect, we must first behold, only we do not behold as in a mirror, we behold by direct vision. There must be a vision in our case, as in the case of Moses, if, like him, we are to reflect; we must gaze directly upon the glory of God in the face of Jesus Christ without a veil between, if we are to pass on to others that glory which we behold, and, as we do so, become transfigured into His likeness.

All May Do This. *This privilege is open to us all.* "But we *all*." That word denotes the universality of this duty—we *all* have to reflect, we *all* have to shine. No doubt the contrast is suggested from the case of Moses, who, alone of all Israel, was called up to Sinai's peaks, and allowed to gaze upon God. He went so far as to put fences around the lower parts of the mountain, so that the people were absolutely deterred from advancing. Granted that he took a few of the elders of Israel to one of the lower slopes, and that his servant Joshua accompanied him some way higher, yet none of these saw the glory of God face to face, and none of them reflected it. Moses alone passed up into the very presence of God, and spake with Him as a friend speaketh to his friend.

In this most happy age there is no aristocracy of blessing, there are no fences to serve as a line of demarcation between the mass of people and the elect few. There is no arbitrary selection of this or the other to scale the mountain steeps to catch the rays of the Divine glory: we *all* have the right to direct fellowship with God; we *all* may shed abroad, in the home, in the counting-house, upon the wan and weary faces we meet day by day, something of the glow, the lustre, the splendour of that light that never shone on sea or shore. There is no believer that may not have to-day all the privileges that Moses had. For you the inner secret; for you the face-to-face communion; for you the vision of God. No fences, no barrier, no reserve.

Our Vision and Reflection must be Unveiled. It is important to remember that there are no esoteric doctrines in Christianity. The old teachers in the Greek academies were accustomed to hold back certain mysteries, which they unfolded to their disciples, but not to the uninitiated. There should be nothing of that sort with ourselves, whether in our daily life or as workers for God. Our faces should always be unveiled. By act and word we should explain, elucidate, unravel the deepest mysteries of God.

In our daily life, especially, it is imperative that there be nothing to intercept or hinder our testimony. Too often a veil is cast upon our face by quick temper; by the expression which is caught from some unholy passion and emotion; by the shyness and reserve of a false shame; by the simper of frivolity, insanity and stupidity. How many people's faces are veiled, so that their sweet, noble selves are hardly discernible? You may object: "I am naturally shy and reserved, I do not like to reveal myself, I always hide my real feelings." Yes, but you must distinguish between hiding your emotions *about* Christ and hiding Christ. It is not a good thing to be always airing your secret experiences and prayers. Nothing hardens the soul so much as, when kneeling before God in fellowship, to allow the devil to whisper: "Here is a subject about which you may speak, and which will bring you credit." You have no right to tell secret passages between you and your Lord. But there is all the difference between veiling your personal emotions and veiling Christ's face by some covering that ought never to be there.

The Power of Reflected Light. One summer day, when walking on the slope of a Surrey hill, the sun setting behind me, right away across the valley I espied a remarkable light. It was more brilliant than electric light, and seemed to rise from the ground. At first I supposed that someone had lit a fire with resinous wood that sparkled and flashed, but there was evidently no smoke. It seemed as though some angel had dropped a brilliant star down there upon the ploughed field, and that it was burning itself out. Finally, on reaching the spot, I discovered that an old piece of broken glass had caught the light of the setting sun, and was bathed in a supernatural glow. An old piece of bottle-glass—yet so brilliant—the bottle-glass not being visible, because of the light that shone on it! We are to reflect Jesus, as a mirror reflects and flashes in the light that falls upon it. If there be a veil between the mirror and the sun, there is no possibility of its reflecting the radiant beams; and if there is any sin upon your heart which hinders your fellowship with Jesus, there is no possibility of your passing on His beauty. Only remember that the mirror is unseen, whilst the light is seen. So shall it be with us—"We preach not ourselves, but Christ Jesus as Lord, and ourselves your servants for Jesus' sake." (2 Cor. iv. 5, R.V.).

The Transformation that Ensues. One used to say, "Behold Christ, you will become Christ-like." But it is better to say: "Reflect Christ, and you will be changed into His likeness." Give yourself to this, put your will into it. Constantly look up and watch what Jesus may be saying or doing at the precise moment; then think or speak in close conformity to what He would have done and is doing, repeat Him to men, and in doing so you will be transfigured, because a series of acts like this will form habit, and habit will become character, and character will shape destiny. The mere quiet contemplation of Jesus is not enough. Arouse yourselves to be like Him, to imitate Him, to step out in simple faith and obedience. Do not wait for some gradual change to pass over you as the result of meditation and beholding. Reflect Jesus Christ in every thought, act, and speech. This is the quickest way to become transformed. After all, the mirror does not quite meet the case, because it may reflect without becoming transfigured. It is better therefore to think of a bar of iron, whose dull, dark heart is placed in the furnace until it is saturated with light and heat. Or think of some cloud near sunset, which not only reflects the sunlight, but in the reflecting is bathed through and through with radiance, so that every part becomes illumined and translucent.

The Glory of Christ and the Glory of Moses. The difference between Moses and Christ lies here. When Moses saw the glory, and reflected it, it was only skin-deep, and it died away upon his face. In the case of Jesus the glory did not come from without, but from within; it welled up in fountains and cascades, and issued forth from every pore of the body of His humiliation. You may look upon Jesus from the outside, and only get a transient likeness; whilst if you have fellowship with Him, and He is formed in your heart by the power of the Holy Spirit, you will be transfigured, beginning from the spirit, and passing thence to soul and body. This is perhaps the deepest thought.

Growth in Christ. You may imitate the Redeemer, and even then be greatly disappointed; but if the Holy Spirit shall beget the living Christ in your soul, and form Him there, you will no longer be like a man who beholds his face in the glass, and goes away to forget what manner of man he was, but you will grow up in all things into Christ, who is our Head, and men will see Him in you.

—A Gradual Process. The process is gradual. "From glory to glory." We go into the sculptor's room, and find the process of transforming the block of marble into the angel figure a very slow one. And so with us. It is quite absurd to say that we are going to overcome all our difficulties and temptations and become like Jesus Christ in a single bound. It is "from glory to glory." Such is the process of this world and of the next; and probably all the eternity that lies before us will see our dull natures approximating towards the perfect glory of our Lord. Do not lose hope for yourselves and for one another, even if there are still so many traces of the un-Christlike nature. Do not be harsh in your judgment of others: the work is advancing from glory to glory; one degree is leading to another; the little of yesterday has grown into a closer resemblance of the infinite Christ, and nearer to the same image.

Let us not fail to honour the Holy Spirit. Ponder the title given to Him—"The Lord the Spirit." Worship Him for His Deity. Reverence His condescension. And let Him work an unhindered miracle of grace in the growing Christliness of your being.

THE GIFTS OF THE WILLING-HEARTED

Exodus 35:1-29;36:2-7

1. And Moses gathered all the congregation of the children of Israel together, and said unto them, These *are* the words which the Lord hath commanded, that *ye* should do them.

2. Six days shall work be done, but on the seventh day there shall be to you an holy day, a sabbath of rest to the Lord: whosoever doeth work therein shall be put to death.

3. Ye shall kindle no fire throughout your habitation upon the sabbath day.

4. And Moses spake unto all the congregation of the children of Israel, saying, This *is* the thing which the Lord commanded, saying,

5. Take ye from among you an offering unto the Lord: whosoever *is* of a willing heart, let him bring it, an offering of the Lord; gold, and silver, and brass,

6. And blue, and purple, and scarlet, and fine linen, and goats' *hair*.

7. And rams' skins dyed red, and badgers' skins, and shittim wood,

8. And oil for the light, and spices for anointing oil, and for the sweet incense,

9. And onyx stones, and stones to be set for the ephod, and for the breastplate.

10. And every wise-hearted among you shall come, and make all that the Lord hath commanded;

11. The tabernacle, his tent, and his covering, his taches, and his boards, his bars, his pillars, and his sockets,

12. The ark, and the staves thereof, *with* the mercy seat, and the veil of the covering,

13. The table, and his staves, and all his vessels, and the shewbread,

14. The candlestick also for the light, and his furniture, and his lamps, with the oil for the light,

15. And the incense altar, and his staves, and the anointing oil, and the sweet incense, and the hanging for the door at the entering in of the tabernacle,

16. The altar of burnt offering, with his brasen grate, his staves, and all his vessels, the laver and his foot,

17. The hangings of the court, his pillars, and their sockets, and the hanging for the door of the court,

18. The pins of the tabernacle, and the pins of the court, and their cords,

19. The cloths of service, to do service in the holy *place*, the holy garments for Aaron the priest, and the garments of his sons, to minister in the priest's office.

20. And all the congregation of the children of Israel departed from the presence of Moses.

21. And they came, everyone whose heart stirred him up, and every one whom his spirit made willing, *and* they brought the Lord's offering to the work of the tabernacle of the congregation, and for all his service, and for the holy garments.

22. And they came, both men and women, as many as were willing hearted, *and* brought bracelets, and earrings, and rings, and tablets, all jewels of gold: and every man that offered *offered* an offering of gold unto the Lord.

23. And every man with whom was found blue, and purple, and scarlet, and fine linen, and goats' *hair*, and red skins of rams, and badgers' skins, brought *them*.

24. Every one that did offer an offering of silver and brass brought the Lord's offering: and every man, with whom was found shittim wood, for any work of the service, brought *it*.

25. And all the women that were wise-hearted did spin with their hands, and brought that which they had spun, *both* of blue, and of purple, *and* of scarlet, and of fine linen.

26. And all the women whose heart stirred them up in wisdom spun *goats'* hair.

27. And the rulers brought onyx stones, and stones to be set, for the ephod, and for the breastplate;

28. And spice, and oil for the light, and for the anointing oil, and for the sweet incense.

29. The children of Israel brought a willing offering unto the Lord, every man and woman, whose heart made them willing to bring for all manner of work which the Lord had commanded to be made by the hand of Moses.

2. And Moses called Bezaleel and Aholiab, and every wise-hearted man, in whose heart the Lord had put wisdom, *even* every one whose heart stirred him up to come unto the work to do it:

3. And they received of Moses all the offering, which the children of Israel had brought for the work of the service of the sanctuary, to make it *withal*. And they brought yet unto him free offerings every morning.

4. And all the wise men, that wrought all the work of the sanctuary, came every man from his work which they made;

5. And they spake unto Moses, saying, The people bring much more than enough for the service of the work, which the Lord commanded to make.

6. And Moses gave commandment, and they caused it to be proclaimed throughout the camp, saying, Let neither man nor woman make any more work for the offering for the sanctuary. So the people were restrained from bringing.

7. For the stuff they had was sufficient for all the work to make it, and too much.

THE GIFTS OF THE WILLING-HEARTED

Exodus 35:1-29;36:2-7

A Needed Reminder. Very significantly this chapter commences with the reiteration of the necessity of keeping the Sabbath-day rest. It may have been necessary to remind the people that, amid all the din of their preparation for the new Tabernacle, they were not to allow work, even though connected with a religious object, needlessly to break the repose of the camp during one day in seven. For us, probably, the lesson, which we must never forget, is, that our activity must always spring out of rest, and that the most profuse and generous giving of the Christian soul is effected after hours of repose and contact with the unseen and the eternal. If we always live in a hurry, we shall never conceive our highest projects, and shall never reach the furthest reaches of Christian giving. Mary sat at the feet of Jesus before she arose to anoint Him from the alabaster box; and, throughout the history of the Church, the greatest acts of munificence have been wrought by people who have come out of seclusion, or from the retirement of the village, or from those blessed homes where the young life is being nurtured in seclusion, fenced around from the turmoil of the world, until the boys and girls are able to go forth, as from the Sabbath of their childhood, to perform the strenuous work of manhood and womanhood.

—On a Great Occasion. The people had now gathered again around Moses, and Moses reiterated, item by item, the charge that he had received some time before; indeed, before the golden calf had been erected or the people had circled it in their delirium of idolatry. It might have been supposed that this failure on the part of Israel would have abrogated God's injunction, but it was not so. The failure of Peter on the night of our Lord's betrayal did not affect his commission or the fact that our Lord had designated him as the rock-man; and, however great your sin and failure may have been, it cannot abrogate or cancel or obliterate those words that

God has spoken of you in time past, the power of which may yet live through your life, albeit there has been an interspace of failure. "If thou wilt take forth the precious from the vile, thou shalt be as my mouth." The golden calf could not alter God's purpose to dwell among the people, and all your sin cannot alter God's purpose to dwell in your heart, His tabernacle, by the Holy Ghost.

The Charge to Israel. Notice, first, the charge that Moses gave to the people. Second, their retirement from his presence. Third, their almost immediate return—the flow, the ebb, and the returning tide.

—God's Presence Promised. I. *The charge which Israel received.* Standing probably upon a pinnacle of rock, Moses disclosed to them four things. (1) That God Almighty was prepared to dwell amongst them. When presently they broke up their camp and started across the desert sands, they were not to suppose that they had left Him behind them amid those inaccessible peaks and rocks; but that if they camped He would camp; if they advanced, He would advance; if they met the foe, He was in the midst of them, and Israel could not be moved, because "God would help her, and that right early." "I will dwell in the midst of thee"; it was a premonition of the incarnation of Christ, who has joined the cavalcade of humanity, never again to desert it. It was a foretaste of His eternal Presence—"Lo I am with you alway, to the end of the age."

—God's Tabernacle to be Built. (2) Moses said also that they might enjoy the ineffable delight and honour of building a tabernacle for God. God must give the plan, or their purpose would be incoherent; but when He had given the plan, it was for them to execute it, because its successive accomplishment depended solely upon their compliance. God could, had He chosen, by the will of His creative fiat, have reared upon the desert sands a tabernacle more fair than human fabric could ever constitute, but He desired to educate them, to give them a share in His eternal purpose, to let them feel that they were co-operating with Him in carrying out His great design. That purpose runs through the whole Bible, and through all life. Our Father courts and demands our co-operation in all the work which He is doing upon this earth. He originates the plan, but He calls for skilful hands and wise hearts to co-operate with Him. We are co-workers with God in building and tillage.

—By Spontaneous Offerings. (3) Moses made clear that the gifts were to be spontaneous. Again and again he used those words "willing-hearted," and the Hebrew phrase signifies a heart driven by a holy purpose. Tennyson somewhere uses the phrase—"Whose heart drove him on like a goad"—*that* is the precise thought here. The God-prompted purpose was to drive them forward, to impel them irresistibly. What a contrast that was to their previous experience in Egypt! Those cities were built by forced labour under the lash of the taskmaster, just as all the vast monuments of antiquity were produced by slave labour. There is not a wall, or a canal, or an aqueduct belonging to the great past which was not constructed and cemented by the blood and tears and agony of vast gangs of men and women. But God said, There shall be no crack of the whip, no constraint, no pressure, save of love, brought to bear upon Israel's generosity. The people shall be told what is wanted, and then it shall be left for the impulse of the Divine Spirit to drive them, as the wind bears the yachts and fishing-smacks to their havens.

The Abundant Opportunity. (4) It was clearly indicated also, that there would be a great wealth of opportunity. Those who had costly heirlooms were to give of their treasure, onyx stones, and stones to be set in the breastplace; those who could only collect the acacia wood of the desert were to bring that; the people who had nothing at all to bring—the very poor people—might work with their skilful hands. Women who were specially clever with their hands could spin the flax, or weave the soft white wool of the Angora-goat, into hangings and curtains for the growing glory of the House. Thus a great and wide variety of work was offered to them. And when Moses had spread all this out before the people and told them what was needed he still refrained from telling them the exact pattern, because the offers were to be unconditional. Men were not to say, "I am not going to give until I have been consulted." They were not to say, "I claim to have a hand in the designation of the plan and the destination of my gift." They were to give and they were to make; but when the material was collected God Himself would see to it that it was built into a properly co-ordinated structure. The unconditional giving of this people was admirable.

It is improbable that Moses spoke at any length; he certainly did not hasten to strike while the iron was hot; he did not conclude his statement by a moving and pathetic appeal. He did what would have appeared to the collectors of modern times a most unwise thing, in letting the people go. "They will grow cool. There is no enthusiasm in those tents to stir them to mighty deeds. Surely it would have been wiser to place them in competition, one against another. Let this man call out his amount, and that man his. Work them up and extract from them their utmost by the excitement of rivalry." No! Moses simply said, "Go; that is all I have to say to you; go, and think it over!" It is very remarkable that there is nothing said about the immediate reception with which the people greeted his words. They seemed as though they were amazed, awed, dumbfoundered, and had not a single word to say. Quietly, gradually, orderly, they departed! And if Moses had not been a man of faith and prayer he might have said, "I wonder if anything will come of that!"

II. *The People's Retirement to consider.* We are not told exactly what took place when they got to their tents. It seems as though a sort of sob went right through the camp. They remembered what God Almighty had done for them in bringing them out of Egypt, in destroying their foes, and in liberating them by His mighty and out-stretched hand. Again they heard the rattle of Pharaoh's chariots behind them; again they looked out upon the teeming waters of the Red Sea at their feet; again they saw that Cloud of Light become a barrier between them and pursuit; again they felt themselves treading the ooze at the bottom of the Red Sea, whilst the heaving waters fenced them in on every hand; again they heard the voice of Miriam ringing out—"Sing ye to the Lord, for He hath triumphed gloriously; the horse and his rider hath He thrown into the sea." As they thought of all this, they felt as we do sometimes at the close of the Lord's Supper when we sing:

> " Were the whole realm of nature mine,
> That were a present far too small.
> Love so amazing, so divine,
> Demands my life, my soul, my all."

With full hearts, burning towards God, they said, "The best we have is Thine." Upon the heels of that thought came the further thought, of God's constant provision for their need; they remembered how the manna had fallen with the utmost regularity through the year; they remembered how the water had flowed for their thirst; they remembered how Amalek had fled before the face of God; they remembered how the desert march had been strewn with goodness and mercy, and as they looked up to Him, again they said, "For all these daily common mercies, how can we thank Thee?"

And then the third thought came, as they looked around their tents and saw the accumulation of much which they had received, and acquired, and could give. It is calculated that the Tabernacle cost about a quarter of a million of our money; and as they looked upon their wealth, of which some had come down from Abraham and Jacob, and some had been accumulated during those prosperous years in Goshen before the slavery intervened, and some had been taken from the dead Egyptians and from the fleeing hosts of Amalek —they realised that there was nothing which had not been given to them by God. As they looked around they said, "The best is His. From Thee have all things come, and of Thine own will we give Thee."

III. *The Return of the People.* "All the congregation of the children of Israel departed from the presence of Moses," and the next verse begins "And they came!" Can you not see them? How long, think you, had elapsed? Did Moses speak in the morning, before the sun was hot, and did they come back to him in the evening, when the stars were beginning to shine? We know not, but they came! Words fail us in attempting to depict the eagerness, the impetuosity, the gladness of their return. It is not likely that they came in any order. Here was a prince, one of the leaders of the tribes, bringing a price-less jewel to be set; here were crowds of those whom we should term middle-class people, coming with their precious amulets, ear-rings, nose-rings, and all the jewellery in which Eastern women indulge. The men also abounded in jewels, as the Egyptian monu-ments indicate, and they came bringing these. It is also said that large numbers of women brought their mirrors of burnished copper, and out of these was made the laver. An Egyptian woman would always carry a mirror when she worshipped, as the monuments indicate, and the Israelites had probably copied the example; and either for their personal embellishment or for purposes which we cannot discover of worship, the mirror was a constant appendage of an Oriental woman's attire. Some brought beams of acacia wood, the endurable wood of which the Tabernacle was made; and others brought what they had spun—the blue speaking of peace, the purple of royalty, the scarlet of blood and atonement—"Grace, mercy, and peace from God our Father." They brought also morocco, rams' skins dyed red, and sealskins, which supplied the waterproof and weather-proof coverings which were placed over the other wrappings, so as to preserve them in damp and heat.

The Offerings. These things were all laid out in heaps, and we are told that they did it willingly. The Spirit drove them; they did it gladly, and so profusely that at last Bezaleel and the others said, "Stop them; we have more than enough." There was actually a strike among the workmen, because they could not get through all the material! Can you not see the desert sand covered with the gifts of the people? How glad they were! and everyone went back lighter, not only in pocket, but also in heart. The whole camp felt that God had forgiven them; that God had really taken them back again into union with Himself; that from henceforth they were to be a people for His own possession; and that the Lord God would dwell among them.

God and Ourselves. It is a great story, when we think of the material out of which God made these willing workers. And if He can appropriate material like that, and transform vast numbers of men and women who yesterday were engaged in idolatry and lascivious dances into devout worshippers, what could He not do with us, if only we would let Him have the right of way through our lives! It is not probable that they had any regrets. We remember that the woman, when she found that Jesus was prepared to open within her soul the fountain of living water, left her water-pot. So these people would not have surrendered their mirrors unless they had become permanently possessed of a new love; and would not have surrendered their ornaments and treasures unless they had acquired gold and silver, and precious stones of heavenly treasure! What shall we do to awaken a similar spirit amongst ourselves?

Our Stewardship. First, we shall never get right until we look at the money we possess as a sacred stewardship. Is it not too true that the idea of ownership of money, as if it were our own to use as we like, is constantly hindering and restraining our generosity? What a noble example was set by Abraham's servant, that faithful and wise steward, who never considered himself; who never dreamt of using his master's money to line his own nest; who was content to administer it, saying to himself, "My master will care for me when I am old!" A good deal of our unwillingness to give arises from our mistrust of God. We say, "I must take care of myself, for I do not know what may happen presently." Of course it is not wrong to exercise forethought, and to make legitimate provision by life insurance and in other ways for the future, but that surely is not inconsistent with a very generous treatment of all we possess as a stewardship, to be used for God with absolute accuracy and good faith.

The Willing Offering. Second, the Apostle Paul teaches a great lesson, for he introduces his words "Now concerning the collection" by that sublime chapter on the Resurrection, with its defiance of death and the grave. Probably there is no passage of his writings in which he more easily and boldly touches the infinite, except it be the twin chapter, Romans viii. It is when he has lifted us into the presence of the Risen Christ, seated at the right hand of God, with all things put under His feet; and has told us how this mortal is to put on immortality, and this corruptible to put on incorruption, and that the time will come when death shall be swallowed up in victory—it is just at this climax that he says "Now for the collection!" There is no doubt that it is when the soul is acclimatized in the atmosphere of these great and eternal truths, that it gives with a free heart.

—Its Impulse. Third, we shall never give aright until we are constrained by the love of Christ. It is not until the love of Jesus comes to these chilled hearts of ours that they will ever be really right. When we get the summer air breathing through our characters; when we get the tropical love of God shed abroad in our hearts; then we shall be constrained to hold everything as for Him.

But though it is good to give under the impulse of a moving appeal, or the rushing torrent of a divine love, it is still better to give systematically and on a plan. The Apostle knew well the importance of periodic storing of the Lord's portion, and urged it on the Corinthian believers (1 Cor. xvi. 1, 2). It seems almost impossible to induce persons to adopt this habit in mature life. Their habits are soon stereotyped, and remain rigid. But it is not difficult to imbue the young with the ideal of systematically setting apart either actually in a bag, or by opening a private ledger-account with the Lord, a definite proportion of all moneys received. A child cannot begin too young. In this, also, it is true, that if he is trained in the way he should go, when he is old he will not depart from it. If any should say, "I reckon that all is the Lord's"—let such be very careful to see by actual figuring-out, that they do not give less than a tenth, and as much more as they choose.

THE GLORY OF CONSUMMATED WORK

Exodus 39:32-43;40:1-38

32. Thus was all the work of the tabernacle of the tent of the congregation finished: and the children of Israel did according to all that the Lord commanded Moses, so did they.

33. And they brought the tabernacle unto Moses, the tent, and all his furniture, his taches, his boards, his bars, and his pillars, and his sockets,

34. And the covering of rams' skins dyed red, and the covering of badgers' skins, and the vail of the covering,

35. The ark of the testimony, and the staves thereof, and the mercy seat,

36. The table, *and* all the vessels thereof, and the shewbread,

37. The pure candlestick, *with* the lamps thereof, *even with* the lamps to be set in order, and all the vessels thereof, and the oil for light,

38. And the golden altar, and the anointing oil, and the sweet incense, and the hanging for the tabernacle door,

39. The brasen altar, and his grate of brass, his staves, and all his vessels, the laver and his foot,

40. The hangings of the court, his pillars, and his sockets, and the hanging for the court gate, his cords, and his pins, and all the vessels of the service of the tabernacle, for the tent of the congregation.

41. The cloths of service to do service in the holy *place*, and the holy garments for Aaron the priest, and his sons' garments, to minister in the priests' office.

42. According to all that the Lord commanded Moses, so the children of Israel made all the work.

43. And Moses did look upon all the work, and, behold, they had done it as the Lord had commanded, even so had they done it: and Moses blessed them.

1. And the Lord spake unto Moses, saying,

2. On the first day of the first month shalt thou set up the tabernacle of the tent of the congregation.

3. And thou shalt put therein the ark of the testimony, and cover the ark with the vail.

4. And thou shalt bring in the table, and set in order the things that are to be set in order upon it; and thou shalt bring in the candlestick, and light the lamps thereof.

5. And thou shalt set the altar of gold for the incense before the ark of the testimony, and put the hanging of the door to the tabernacle.

6. And thou shalt set the altar of the burnt offering before the door of the tabernacle of the tent of the congregation.

7. And thou shalt set the laver between the tent of the congregation and the altar, and shalt put water therein.

8. And thou shalt set up the court round about, and hang up the hanging at the court gate.

9. And thou shalt take the anointing oil, and anoint the tabernacle, and all that *is* therein, and shalt hallow it, and all the vessels thereof: and it shall be holy.

10. And thou shalt anoint the altar of the burnt offering, and all his vessels, and sanctify the altar: and it shall be an altar most holy.

11. And thou shalt anoint the laver and his foot, and sanctify it.

12. And thou shalt bring Aaron and his sons unto the door of the tabernacle of the congregation, and wash them with water.

13. And thou shalt put upon Aaron the holy garments, and anoint him, and sanctify him; that he may minister unto me in the priest's office.

14. And thou shalt bring his sons, and clothe them with coats:

15. And thou shalt anoint them, as thou didst anoint their father, that they may minister unto me in the priest's office: for their anointing shall surely be an everlasting priesthood throughout their generations.

16. Thus did Moses: according to all that the Lord commanded him, so did he.

17. And it came to pass in the first month in the second year, on the first *day* of the month, *that* the tabernacle was reared up.

18. And Moses reared up the tabernacle, and fastened his sockets, and set up the boards thereof, and put in the bars thereof, and reared up his pillars.

19. And he spread abroad the tent over the tabernacle, and put the covering of the tent above upon it; as the Lord commanded Moses.

20. And he took and put the testimony into the ark, and set the staves on the ark, and put the mercy seat above upon the ark:

21. And he brought the ark into the tabernacle, and set up the vail of the covering, and covered the ark of the testimony, as the Lord commanded Moses.

22. And he put the table in the tent of the congregation, upon the side of the tabernacle northward, without the vail.

23. And he set the bread in order upon it before the Lord; as the Lord had commanded Moses.

24. And he put the candlestick in the tent of the congregation, over against the table, on the side of the tabernacle southward.

25. And he lighted the lamps before the Lord; as the Lord commanded Moses.

26. And he put the golden altar in the tent of the congregation before the vail:

27. And he burned sweet incense thereon; as the Lord commanded Moses.

28. And he set up the hanging *at* the door of the tabernacle.

29. And he put the altar of burnt offering *by* the door of the tabernacle of the tent of the congregation, and offered upon it the burnt offering and the meat offering; as the Lord commanded Moses.

30. And he set the laver between the tent of the congregation and the altar, and put water there, to wash *withal*.

31. And Moses and Aaron and his sons washed their hands and their feet thereat:

32. When they went into the tent of the congregation, and when they came near unto the altar, they washed; as the Lord commanded Moses.

33. And he reared up the court round about the tabernacle and the altar, and set up the hanging of the court gate. So Moses finished the work.

34. Then a cloud covered the tent of the congregation, and the glory of the Lord filled the tabernacle.

35. And Moses was not able to enter into the tent of the congregation, because the cloud abode thereon, and the glory of the Lord filled the tabernacle.

36. And when the cloud was taken up from over the tabernacle, the children of Israel went onward in all their journeys:

37. But if the cloud were not taken up, then they journeyed not till the day that it was taken up.

38. For the cloud of the Lord *was* upon the tabernacle by day, and fire was on it by night, in the sight of all the house of Israel, throughout all their journeys.

THE GLORY OF CONSUMMATED WORK

Exodus 39:32-43;40:1-38

A Great Day for Israel. At last the construction of the various pieces of furniture, the weaving and spinning, were done, and on the New Year's day of the second year of the Exodus, God bade Moses rear up the tabernacle, and with his own hand place each article in its own position. The command was given directly to Moses, and by him immediately and precisely obeyed.

It must have been a wonderful and memorable day for Israel. They brought the tabernacle to Moses in its various pieces, and they seem to have been so laid out, perhaps on the sand, perhaps on the lower slopes of Sinai, that he was able to see them. "And Moses saw all the work, and, behold, they had done it; as the Lord had commanded, even so had they done it; and Moses blessed them" (ver. 43). Then on the first day of the first month of the year, he proceeded to rear up the tabernacle, and insert its furniture. By the time of the evening-sacrifice, all was done. He had placed the shew-bread table with its loaves on the right, and the candlestick on the left-hand of the Holy Place, lighting its lamps; had set the Altar of Incense near the vail, and burnt sweet spices and incense on it; had washed in the water of the laver, anointing it, and the great altar, and all its vessels. He had also offered there the burnt-offering and the meat-offering; had reverently placed the Ark in the Most Holy Place, hiding it with the curtain. Aaron and his sons also had been invested with their robes, and inducted into their office; and the Priesthood, which was to last till the fall of Jerusalem, had been inaugurated with due solemnity.

Retirement. When all was completed, the congregation, deeply moved and solemnised, retired to their tents, and night began to settle on the mountains. Moses, also, with one last loving look at the structure, standing in complete and beautiful symmetry, also retired from the scene, full of thankfulness. Was it then that he composed the ninetieth Psalm? surely nothing could have been more exactly in keeping with the spirit and purpose of that day:

> " Let Thy work appear unto Thy servants,
> And Thy glory upon their children.
> And let the beauty of the Lord our God be upon us:
> And establish Thou the work of our hands upon us;
> Yea, the work of our hands establish Thou it."
>
> (Vers. 16, 17, R.V.)

The Presence Manifested. They had hardly reached their tents, and the darkness had only just fallen, when there was a wonderful seal given of the Divine satisfaction and acceptance of the people's gifts. The cloud which had guided their march from Succoth, and was brooding over the temporary Tent of Meeting, seems to have moved thence, and to have cast its fleecy enfolding glory upon the new structure. Simultaneously, a brilliant light, of surpassing glory, here spoken of as "the glory of the Lord," which was undoubtedly the Divine Shechinah, shone from within the Tabernacle itself, so much so that the very curtains were transfigured by its glow and the whole place was transfigured and rendered resplendent with glory. When Moses, seeing what was taking place, hastened back from his tent, that he might see that great sight, which recalled the bush that had burned with fire, he found himself debarred from entrance. The Presence of God was so manifestly in possession, that no mortal could behold it and live. The words of the Apocalypse were indeed anticipated, "Behold, the Tabernacle of God is with men, and He shall dwell with them, and they shall be His people, and God Himself shall be with them and be their God." If only Israel had been true to the suggestion of that Divine Presence, there would have been no more sorrow, nor crying, nor pain, and their march to Canaan would have been a triumphal progress. The forty years would never have been spent in the desert; *that* generation would have possessed the land; and the settlement would have been effected without loss or carnage. But, in any case, from that moment Israel realised that the God of their fathers was their fellowpilgrim, and that Immanuel was their portion.

A Presence for our Bodies. *The reference of this to our mortal body.* In John i. 14 we are told that the Eternal Word was made flesh, and dwelt among men. The word translated *dwelt* is *tabernacled.* He dwelt in a tent or tabernacle; and the Evangelist, speaking for himself and his fellow-apostles, said: "We beheld His glory, the glory as of the Only-Begotten of the Father"—a glory that specially shone through His mortal flesh on the Mount of Transfiguration. There was an exact parallel between the irradiation of the Shechinah through the completed tabernacle, and the transfiguring light that made our Lord's vesture seem white as snow.

—**The Body as a Tabernacle.** We learn also from 2 Cor. v. 1, that "if the earthly house of *this tabernacle* be dissolved, we have a building." With this we compare the words of Peter, in his Second Epistle, when he speaks of putting off his tabernacle shortly, as the Lord had showed him. All these passages support the conception that the body is but a tabernacle, the tent of the soul, as slight, frail, and transitory as a tent, and that there is as clear a distinction between the soul and the body as between the occupant of a tent and the slight curtains beneath which for a time he dwells. If, then, the body is the tent or tabernacle, with its aspect towards the outer world, must not the Holy Place, with its candlestick, incense-altar, and shewbread represent the soul, with its various faculties? And must not the Holy of Holies, tenanted by God's sacred Presence, represent the spirit?

A Wonder and a Warning. The very elaboration with which all the details of Tabernacle-construction are given, indicate that some profound teaching underlies them, and we are reminded of the Psalmist's words,—"I will praise Thee; for I am fearfully and wonderfully made. . . . My substance was not hid from Thee, when I was made in secret, and curiously wrought in the lowest parts of the earth. Thine eyes did see my substance, yet being unperfect; and in Thy book all my members were written, which in continuance were fashioned" (Ps. cxxxix. 14-16, R.V.). We speak the literal truth, then, in affirming that the elaborate treatment of these items in the construction of the tabernacle has a secondary reference to the way in which this wonderful nature of spirit, soul, and body has been built up. God is always making our bodies out of the dust of the ground, and breathing into us the living soul, and bringing us in contact with the Second Adam, to receive His quickening Spirit. It is thus that in us, too, the fire begins to burn, which irradiates the faculties of the mind, whilst ennobling and invigorating the body. Let us freely open our nature to the life of Jesus, that we may bear the image of the Heavenly, and realise His invigorating health. "To you that fear My name shall the Sun of Righteousness arise with healing in His wings, and ye shall go forth and gambol as calves of the stall."

The Tabernacle and the Church. *The further reference of this to the Church.* The Tabernacle in the old dispensation is in many respects the counterpart of the Church in the new. (1) As the Tabernacle was built on the plan revealed in the Mount, so there must be a Divine plan of the Church for we are told, that long before our Saviour laid her foundations in His death and resurrection, He loved the Church. Evidently there must have been an ideal Church, which so attracted Him that He was gladly willing to give Himself to win her.

(2) As the Tabernacle was made in different portions, which were made independently of each other and by different hands, so the Church is being constructed, each age, each country, each denomination contributing something. None have seen more than their own small bit of the glorious Church, as she has been revealed to the eye of her Lord; and we do not all understand how our work will fit in with the rest; it is enough to accomplish our share as perfectly as we can, leaving the ultimate fitting-together and erection to the great Architect Himself.

As Moses finished the work—"Thus was all the work of the Tabernacle finished"—so the last member will be added to the Body of Christ and the last name will be appended to the long list in the Book of Life.

The Great Day of Completion. Ah, happy day, when angel voices shall be heard proclaiming, "It is done, and the mystery of God is finished!" Then will the Church be manifested. "When Christ shall appear, we shall appear with Him in glory." And as she stands forth in her completed loveliness, the Divine light will be seen in her, as in the Tabernacle of old. "Arise, shine, for thy light is come, and the glory of the Lord is risen upon thee. For, behold, darkness shall cover the earth, and gross darkness the peoples; but the Lord shall arise upon thee, and His glory shall be seen upon thee. And nations shall come to thy light, and kings to the brightness of thy rising" (Isa. lx. 1–4, R.V.). When all is done that must be done, and all the scaffolding is removed, the beauty, symmetry, and completeness of the Divine Ideal will be revealed, and will constitute a sanctuary for Jehovah.

The Tabernacle and Our Life work. *This is also a reference to our life work.* Repeatedly we are reminded of the absolute and untiring obedience of Moses. Throughout this chapter the sentence is repeated like a bell—"as the Lord commanded Moses." He was the recognised constructor of the whole system of the Hebrew constitution, religious ritual, and Tent of Meeting. But he might have said with our Lord: "The Son can do nothing from Himself; but what things soever the Father doeth, these also He doeth likewise." But notice that when a man builds on God's plan, and submits himself to the Divine Will, God will set His seal of approval on the result of his labours. He placed the crown on Moses' obedience, when He entered the Tabernacle, saying: "This is My resting-place for ever; here will I dwell; for I have desired it. I will abundantly bless her provision; I will satisfy her poor with bread. I will also clothe her priests with salvation; and her saints shall shout aloud for joy" (Ps. cxxxii. 14–16, R.V.). In some such manner God will attest His acceptance and approval of our poor efforts. His people, who wait for Him, shall never be ashamed; though we sow in tears, we shall reap in joy. Our materials may be scanty and cheap, but the Lord will be a wall of fire round about them, and the glory in the midst.

The Indwelling Lord our Guide. *Where the Lord dwells, He guides.* When the cloud was taken up, the Lord moved forward; when it rested, they rested. So God is our guide, and the guide of His people. They that rest under His protection or march under His convoy shall not want any good thing. The manna always falls, and the waters flow, where the cloud broods. Keep with the cloud and you shall not want any good thing: but be as careful not to lag behind, as not to anticipate and go before. Guard against indolence on the one side, and impetuous haste on the other.

Sometimes when riding or walking at night through a wood, one cannot see the road or path, because of the darkness that covers the ground, but on looking up we can always discover the track marked out, by the path of light between the trees overhead. So when the way is hard to find, and human intelligence fails, look up! Yonder is the Presence-cloud! It will be over you by day for a shield, and by night for a sun. When it moves, your enemies shall flee before you: and when it settles, you may sleep securely beneath the un-slumbering keeping care of Jehovah. "Happy are the people who are in such a case: yea, happy is the people whose God is the Lord!"